Families in Transition

STUDIES ON THE HISTORY OF QUEBEC/
ÉTUDES D'HISTOIRE DU QUEBEC

John Dickinson and Brian Young
Series Editors/Directeurs de la collection

Habitants and Merchants in Seventeenth-Century Montreal
Louise Dechêne

Crofters and Habitants
Settler Society, Economy, and Culture in a Quebec Township,
1848–1881
J.I. Little

The Christie Seigneuries
Estate Management and Settlement in the Upper Richelieu Valley,
1760–1859
Françoise Noël

La Prairie en Nouvelle-France, 1647–1760
Louis Lavallée

The Politics of Codification
The Lower Canadian Civil Code of 1866
Brian Young

Arvida au Saguenay
Naissance d'une ville industrielle
José E. Igartua

State and Society in Transition
The Politics of Institutional Reform in the Eastern Townships,
1838–1852
J.I. Little

Vingt ans après *Habitants et marchands,*
Lectures de l'histoire des XVIIᵉ et XVIIIᵉ siècles canadiens
Habitants et marchands, Twenty Years Later
Reading the History of Seventeenth- and Eighteenth-Century Canada
Edited by *Sylvie Dépatie, Catherine Desbarats, Danielle Gauvreau,
Mario Lalancette, Thomas Wien*

Families in Transition
Industry and Population in Nineteenth-Century Saint-Hyacinthe
Peter Gossage

Families in Transition

*Industry and Population in
Nineteenth-Century Saint-Hyacinthe*

PETER GOSSAGE

McGill-Queen's University Press
Montreal & Kingston · London · Ithaca

© McGill-Queen's University Press 1999
ISBN 0-7735-1847-9

Legal deposit third quarter 1999
Bibliothèque nationale du Québec

Printed in Canada on acid-free paper

This book has been published with the help of a
grant from the Humanities and Social Sciences
Federation of Canada, using funds provided by the
Social Sciences and Humanities Research Council of
Canada. Financial support has also been received
from the Université de Sherbrooke via the Fonds
d'appui aux activités de création et d'édition savante.

McGill-Queen's University Press acknowledges the
financial support of the Government of Canada
through the Book Publishing Industry Development
Program (BPIDP) for its activities. We also acknowl-
edge the support of the Canada Council for the Arts
for our publishing program.

Canadian Cataloguing in Publication Data

Gossage, Peter, 1956–
    Families in transition : industry and population in
    nineteenth-century Saint-Hyacinthe
    (Studies on the history of Quebec - études d'histoire
    du Québec)
    Includes bibliographical references and index.
    ISBN 0-7735-1847-9
    1. Saint-Hyacinthe (Quebec) – Population – History –
    19th century. I. Title. II. Series: Studies on the
    history of Quebec
    HN110.S32G68 1999 304.6'09714'523 C99-900497-2

Typeset in 10/12 Baskerville by Acappella

For Annmarie

Contents

Tables

Figures

Preface

This book began life in the late 1980s as an idea for a doctoral dissertation about the linkages between two major historical transitions. Teachers such as Brian Young and Richard Rice had taught me to place the transition to industrial capitalism at the centre of any project designed to advance an understanding of social change in the nineteenth century. That lesson was not forgotten. But I was also drawn to the "demographic transition," a dramatic shift in population patterns which saw traditional, high-fertility regimes yield to others, usually referred to as "modern." Teachers such as Jean-Claude Robert, José Igartua, and Louise Dechêne helped me to learn the careful, plodding methods of historical demography and to ask good questions about past populations. I have not forgotten those lessons either.

These two transitions have much in common. For one thing, they are among the most sweeping changes to have affected Western societies since the eighteenth century. For another, they seem often to have gone hand in hand. Take France, Britain, and the United States – countries in which industrial capitalism profoundly reshaped social relations in the nineteenth century and in which very significant demographic changes have occurred. In fact, the Whiggish generalizations seem to write themselves: "Industrialization, urbanization, and modern values led to declines in birth rates, while medical progress increased infant survival and life expectancy," and so on. But such simple versions of this complex story fail to explain *why* or *how* industrial capitalism created the necessary conditions for the demographic transition, and vice versa. Indeed, whereas these two transitions are undoubtedly part of the same story, attempts to explain their interconnectedness have often fallen short of the mark.

Families in Transition may, or may not, go some way toward clarifying this extremely complex relationship. Its readers must judge. Along the way, however, they will be asked to think about whether or not industrial capitalism affected other aspects of family life in the nineteenth century: when and with whom people married, for example; and whether they lived on their own, in "nuclear" families, or with large groups of kin, boarders, and domestic servants.

The industrial and demographic transitions are also similar in that they were both vast structural shifts which took place in the *longue durée*. Nevertheless, if we are to make any sense of the past the behaviour of individual men and women must be related to these transitions as well. They are processes, moreover, which occurred in Quebec on a timetable broadly similar to that of other Western societies. While that position may mark this study as a work of unreconstructed "revisionism," to use the vocabulary set out in Ronald Rudin's important and controversial analysis of recent Quebec historiography,[1] it is a label I can live with. That is, as long as it refers to a kind of history that assumes that people in Quebec experienced the same structural changes as those reshaping other Western societies, and that they responded to those changes in particular, sometimes original, and at times conventional, ways.

Families in Transition will probably not please those who champion an essentially political history, designed to instill national sentiment by celebrating the public accomplishments of our forefathers, whether Canadian or *québécois*.[2] This is as it must be. I have always found the greatest pleasure and stimulation in the kind of history that teaches us about those whom we usually call "ordinary" women and men, their challenges and struggles, their victories and defeats. If this book accomplishes anything, I hope it will make its readers think about what was really important to people in the past. They were, after all, just like us. In effect, most were more concerned with their communities, their jobs, and especially, I would argue, their children, than with long dead politicians and national identity.

There is also an unfashionable emphasis in this book on quantitative analysis which, to be frank, might not be as strong were I to begin this study anew in today's postmodern era. But numbers are a necessary part of any study of past populations. Moreover, quantitative history does not have to be boring. My hope is that readers of this book will look beyond the tables and graphs to the people whose lives they represent. I have tried to encourage this by presenting individual examples to further illustrate the patterns revealed by the rates, proportions, and central tendencies. After all, population history, is, and must be understood to be, about people.

I could not have written this book without the help and support of many individuals. When it was still a dissertation, this study benefited from the financial support of the Social Sciences and Humanities Research Council of Canada and La Fondation de l'Université du Québec à Montréal, both of which provided doctoral fellowships. This assistance was, and is, greatly appreciated. I have already mentioned my Ph.D. supervisors, Jean-Claude Robert, Louise Dechêne, and José Igartua, all of whom helped me through many decisions and many drafts. Once again they have my thanks.

Many people discussed various aspects of the project with me, and at various stages. Annmarie Adams, Gérard Bouchard, Danielle Gauvreau, Yves Landry, Yolande Lavoie, Marvin McInnis, Francine Mayer, Sherry Olson, Joy Parr, and Marc St-Hilaire all generously shared of their time and insights. I have also had the good fortune to work with Hélène Langlois of the Université du Québec à Montréal (UQAM) computing centre, as well as with Yves Otis, upon whom, like so many Quebec historians, I have come to rely for his impeccable work with computer graphics. As well, in recent months, Chantal Goyette has helped me to prepare the tests of statistical significance that were absent from earlier drafts. All these people helped to make this a better book than it might otherwise have been. I thank them sincerely.

It would be impossible to name all the librarians and archivists who helped me along the way. But I must express my gratitude to the pastor of Saint-Hyacinthe-le-Confesseur parish, Mgr André Beaulé, who gave me virtually unlimited access to his parish registers, although I am afraid I may have overstayed my welcome in his *parloir*. My thanks also go to Jean-Noël Dion, archivist for both the Séminaire de Saint-Hyacinthe and the Société d'histoire régionale de Saint-Hyacinthe (and an accomplished regional historian in his own right); without his help, I am convinced that nobody could write anything sensible about the history of the town. I know I could not.

The work of Ann Gossage, who had the difficult task of typing all the tables for the dissertation, was, and is, much appreciated. Although the tables have been greatly revised and reformatted since then, her initial work has served me well. As well, I thank, Julien Bréard, who provided research assistance for a recent revision, establishing record links from my family reconstitution files to nominative lists from the 1901 manuscript census. Although the work was done in aid of this book, it also serves as part of a wider investigation of fertility decline in Quebec now underway under the direction of Danielle Gauvreau and myself. I thank Danielle for her openness to this sharing of data, for her good counsel as a research collaborator, and for her understanding of the regular absences from our joint venture that constituted my pattern in recent months as I attempted to finish this book. I would also like to thank my colleagues and friends in the Département d'histoire et de sciences politiques at the Université de Sherbrooke for providing the atmosphere of collegiality, support, and respect that has helped make it possible to bring this project to fruition.

Bettina Bradbury and Brian Young both read the penultimate draft in its entirety. I thank them for their generosity, their insights, and their comments. I also appreciate the contributions of the three anonymous reviewers who volunteered their services to McGill-Queen's University Press and to the Humanities and Social Sciences Federation of Canada. Along with Bettina and Brian, these readers challenged me to improve the study in numerous ways; I only hope they will find that their efforts have been rewarded. The people at McGill-Queen's also deserve my sincere thanks. Peter Blaney, Philip Cercone, and Aurèle Parisien have all lent strong support to the project, providing the right advice at the right time and helping me over various hurdles in the publication process. The efforts of editors Wendy Dayton and Joan McGilvray to help me write a readable book of population history are also sincerely appreciated. Except where otherwise indicated, translations in this book were prepared by the author, with the able assistance of Natahsa Dagenais. She has my thanks

Although the members of my extended family have grown in number during this project's long gestation period, they have remained constant in their love and support. Thanks for everything go to Audrey, Bill, Dave, Linda, Hannah, Henry, Mary, Steve, Joe, Lewis, Thom, Isabelle, Ann, Mike, Michael, Luke, Bill Sr, Barb, Kaye, Jack, Peter, Mary Helen, Burke, Allison, Paul, Mary Ann, Colin, Jamie, and Hayden. Thanks, too, go to Brenda Lockwood, who is more like family than anything else, and whose help in recent months has been truly indispensable.

Finally, I owe my deepest debt of gratitude to Annmarie Adams and Charles David Adams-Gossage. The best thing I ever did was to marry Annmarie, whose love and encouragement sustain me and who has given me joy, serenity, and the marvel that is Charlie. This book, paper clips and all, is for her.

Knowlton, Quebec
July 1998

Abbreviations

Families in Transition

Introduction

In the second half of the nineteenth century, Quebec society experienced an unprecedented set of transitions. Industrial capitalism
reshaped the workplace, transformed social relations, and fuelled
urban growth and institutional change. Factories drew thousands of
families from rural areas, contributing to the growth of one major
city, Montreal, and of such smaller ones as Quebec, Hull, Sherbrooke, Valleyfield, and Saint-Hyacinthe. A new railway network
provided the steel framework for the industrial economy, carving
out new patterns of regional economic differentiation in the process.
The state became larger, more complex, and more powerful, even as
the Roman Catholic Church expanded its influence. Church and
state struggled for hegemony over a vast network of new social and
educational institutions, designed both to impose order on the
popular classes and to fill an ever-growing range of urgent social
needs. Sharpening class differences found expression in industrial
disputes, as labouring men and women organized to defend their
interests against those of capital. And social distinctions were etched
into the new urban geography, as the wealthy moved into distinct and
exclusive bourgeois areas such as Montreal's "Golden Square Mile,"
and the working class built equally distinct if less opulent neighbourhoods of their own.[1]

The impact of industrial capitalism on one of the most basic
human activities, work, is well documented in the Quebec context. By
the turn of the twentieth century, much more work was being done in
large units organized and controlled by capital than had been the

case 50 years earlier. Factory work was fundamentally different from farm and craft production for a number of reasons, besides the scale of operations and the level of mechanization. Perhaps most significant was the unprecedented degree of separation between home and workplace, or between "family time" and "industrial time," to use Tamara Hareven's phrase. Structuring these new dichotomies was the wage relationship, as an increasingly large proportion of Quebecers either exchanged their labour power for a wage, or depended on wages earned by family members. Wage dependence created a new kind of household, characterized, on the one hand, by the fragility of its economic foundations and, on the other, by its resourcefulness and ability to adapt to the new industrial setting.[2]

Other major consequences of the industrial capitalist transition for Quebec society have only been hinted at or assumed. Surprisingly little is known, for instance, about the impact of industry on family formation and reproduction. Other periods of Quebec's demographic history – the French regime, for example – are much better documented.[3] Historical demographers and others working on population patterns in the later nineteenth century have mainly focused on rural regions and on the important question of migration.[4] Relatively little attention has been paid to Quebec communities where industrial development did occur, or to whether that development affected patterns of family formation and reproduction in a significant way.[5] But if urban Quebec in the late nineteenth century has received relatively little attention from those interested in family and population, it is fair to say that urban places other than Montreal have received virtually none at all.[6]

Interest in these issues, however, is real and substantial. It has been stimulated by the vast international literature on family life and, more particularly, on the relationship between economic and demographic regimes. Researchers have focused on the changes and continuities in the role of family in periods of economic transition, both in historic Europe and in the developing world today.[7] This focus highlights the role of family at the intersection of economic and demographic regimes, articulating systems of production and reproduction to each other.[8] Certain studies have emphasized the important continuities that linked rural, pre-industrial settings with the urban, industrial ones.[9] But the suggestion that individuals and families often adopted new marital, residential, and reproductive strategies in response to dramatically altered economic situations persists. Indeed, this kind of argument is made strongly in many of the best studies in family history.[10] An interest in the dynamic relationships between economic structure and demographic behaviour has informed the research for this book since its inception. How can we characterize the familial and demographic behaviour of families who lived through Quebec's industrial capitalist transition in the second half of the nineteenth century? How, if at all, did the new economic realities affect patterns of family formation and reproduction? Did people develop new approaches to marriage, household composition, and fertility – the three broadly demographic aspects of family life that will be examined in detail here – as industrial capitalism transformed other aspects of their lives? And in the urban places, where factory work and wage labour took hold, were the new patterns of privilege and dispossession, which can be read so clearly in the labour history and the urban geography of this period, reflected as well in its historical demography?

In the case-study traditions of both historical demography and social history, I explore these themes for a single community, one which experienced considerable industrial development in the second half of the nineteenth century. The town of Saint-Hyacinthe is located on the Yamaska River some 50 kilometres east of Montreal, in the heart of Quebec's *Montérégie* area (see Figure 1-1). Beginning in the 1860s, Saint-Hyacinthe developed a significant manufacturing sector, with industrial capitalist production concentrated in the leather goods and textile sectors. These highly mechanized industries, many of which received municipal aid in the form of bonuses and tax relief, drew on large local reserves of relatively unskilled labourers who could be induced into factory work for very low wages indeed. The town, in short, developed on a "light industry" model often considered to be typical of the Quebec manufacturing sector in this period. This book asks whether the presence of boot-and-shoe and knit-goods factories in this modest industrial town, the availability of wage labour for men, women, and children in those factories, and the concomitant emergence of a "family wage economy" made a difference to young people – particularly as they decided if, when, and with whom to marry; where and how to establish their households; and how many children to bring into the world. We might assume at the outset that they did. But detailed demographic analysis is necessary in order to determine exactly what that difference was.

For this study I have chosen to apply, in a modified version, one of the most powerful techniques of historical demography. Known to specialists as "family reconstitution," the method – akin to a kind of community genealogy – involves the piecing together of individual family histories from local records of births, marriages, and deaths. It was developed for use in French rural parishes where population sizes and geographic mobility were relatively low and where parish registers were the only, or almost the only, population records of any value.[11] Thanks in large part to collective research initiatives that have led to the creation of two major population databases, the technique has been widely applied in Quebec, mainly for the pre-Conquest era and for the population of the Saguenay region in the period since 1840.[12] But it has only rarely been applied to urban settings in nineteenth- and twentieth-century Quebec.[13] The main reason for this gap in usage is methodological. High levels of geographic mobility – particularly the mobility of working families who moved from place to place in search of a job, a better wage, or more suitable lodgings – make it very difficult to reconstruct family histories in urban, industrial contexts.

This study represents an attempt to help fill this gap, by applying the family reconstitution technique to the population of Saint-Hyacinthe in the second half of the nineteenth century. It relies, therefore, on a set of methods that will, in their broad outlines, be familiar to historical demographers and to family historians acquainted with quantitative approaches, but that will, for more general readers, require some explanation.[14]

The family reconstitution method involves the careful reconstruction of the reproductive behaviour of large groups of individual families. When enough family files, or *fiches de famille*, have been compiled, statistics can be generated about marriage age, fertility, birth spacing, infant mortality, widowhood and remarriage, and a range of related issues. When the *fiches* are completed with information from manuscript-census returns, as is possible and desirable for Quebec populations in the later nineteenth century, further information, especially about household structure and geographic and social mobility, can be added.[15]

In urban settings, however, the labour-intensive character of family reconstitution means that certain limits on data collection must be imposed. It is especially necessary to work within well-defined geographic limits, even though, in the case of nineteenth-century Quebec, this raises such issues as the lack of uniformity between parish and municipal boundaries, the tendency of both to evolve over time, and the inclination of individuals to move back and forth across them.[16]

The issue of religious diversity must also be dealt with, since Quebec's records of birth, marriage, and death were kept by religious, rather than civil, officials. One option is to simplify matters by restricting attention to the *Catholic* population of a given territory. For Saint-Hyacinthe, this is a viable strategy, since at most census dates in the later nineteenth century, French-speaking Roman

Catholics made up about 98% of the local population.[17] Clearly, different approaches would have to be adopted for a study of Montreal or Sherbrooke, cities with substantial non-Catholic and English-speaking populations.

Restricting attention to the Catholic population of a clearly and consistently defined territory was the first set of limits on the family-reconstitution study reported in this book. A second set involved the adoption of a selective, rather than an exhaustive, approach to the creation of *fiches de famille*. In this study, then, attention is focused on a single Saint-Hyacinthe parish, the one that contained the bulk of the urban population throughout the period under review. And rather than all the information being collected from its registers of baptisms, marriages, and burials, only those acts pertaining to three cohorts of married couples were identified, assembled into *fiches de famille*, cross-referenced with census information, and analyzed.

The parish selected for study was Saint-Hyacinthe-le-Confesseur, also known as *la paroisse de la Cathédrale* because it was created, in 1852, as the episcopal see for the new diocese of Saint-Hyacinthe. Although it always contained a rural minority, the parish was established to serve the town of Saint-Hyacinthe. Its boundaries were drawn in the 1850s to include the town in its entirety, as well as some more thinly settled tracts of land on either bank of the Yamaska, downstream from Saint-Hyacinthe.[18] Studying the parishioners of the cathedral, then, provides a rather good approximation of the demography of the town of Saint-Hyacinthe. It also offers the advantage of incorporating a small agricultural population, which can be referred to as a point of comparison.

The Catholic population of Saint-Hyacinthe-le-Confesseur parish increased from just under 4,500 in 1861 to almost 7,000 30 years later (see Table 1-1). An exhaustive family-reconstitution study for a population of this size would have been impossible to complete within any reasonable time frame. I therefore chose to narrow the focus still further, by concentrating on couples who married at three different stages of the town's development. The reproductive lives of the 289 couples married from 1854 to 1861, the 277 couples married from 1864 to 1871, and 340 of the 450 couples married from 1884 to 1891 were thus reconstituted.[19] This method yielded *fiches* for 912 couples, whose married lives are the focus of this book.

An important nuance needs to be added here, however; namely, that the method adopted did not involve tracing families *outside* the study region. It focused instead on these three sets of couples to the extent that their familial and reproductive lives could be observed *within Saint-Hyacinthe*. As shown in chapter 3, some couples never established residences in the town or its immediate vicinity. Daughters of Saint-Hyacinthe families who married young men from the surrounding region and settled outside the parish provide the most obvious example. Others who married at the cathedral spent only limited parts of their married lives in the area.[20] Such couples nonetheless fall within the scope of some of the analyses presented here.

One implication of this methodological choice is that, for the most part, this book is about the family lives of couples who married in Saint-Hyacinthe, established households there, and remained in town long enough to be picked up in at least one census enumeration. This means, for example, that out of 675 previously unmarried men in the three cohorts, 399 – or 59% – were included in the analysis of men's age at first marriage (compare Tables 3-6 and 3-8). It means that of the 912 couples, 386 (42%) were included in the analysis of household structure (Table 4-1). It also means that of the 912 brides in the three marriage cohorts, 386 could be included in the fertility analysis (Table A-3).

Are these numbers large enough? And do these variously constituted subsets of the three marriage cohorts serve as a "representative sample" of the population of Saint-Hyacinthe in the later nineteenth century? These are fair questions, and ones given serious thought. The answer to the first, I believe, is yes. The answer to the second is that without reconstituting the entire population of Saint-Hyacinthe – including people who lived there for only a year or two, or who grew up there but moved away as young adults – it is impossible to know. Perhaps couples who married in town and remained there for significant portions of their adult lives were exceptional in some way. Did they marry earlier? Were they likelier, as newlyweds, to live with parents or other kin? Did they have larger families? Any number of systematic biases may have been introduced by the exclusion of the most geographically mobile elements of the local population from the analysis.

On the other hand, the deliberate selection of three sedentary fragments of the local population can yield certain interpretive benefits. Since the intention of this study was to explore the various ways in which families responded to local economic conditions and to a particular type of capitalist industrialization, it is not an unreasonable strategy to focus squarely on several hundred couples who lived under those local conditions for relatively substantial periods of time. And whereas a pure cliometrician might argue that the sampling errors introduced by matrimonial exchange, geographic mobility, and other sources of lost information are serious, I prefer to think of this particular cup as half-full rather than half-empty. Indeed, it is an arguable point whether the four hundred or so couples for whom it has been possible to assemble relatively complete *fiches de famille* constitute a sample at all. It is at least possible to argue that they do not: that their lives are worth examining in their own right rather than as a formal statistical sample – representative or otherwise – of a larger population.[21]

Such, then, are the methodological principles that underlie this study and that define its possibilities and limitations. As we have seen, the general idea is to use the methods of historical demography to study the impact of a particular kind of industrial capitalist development on patterns of family formation and reproduction in Saint-Hyacinthe. The heart of this book can thus be found in the results of the family-reconstitution study, which are reported in chapters 3, 4, and 5. But before turning to that analysis, it is necessary to lay some groundwork, by examining the economic and social setting in which these relationships are to be examined. Accordingly, chapter 1 describes Saint-Hyacinthe's physical setting and early settlement history, sketches in the broad contours of its population history in the later nineteenth century, and attempts to situate the town within the wider context of Quebec's urban and industrial development after 1850. This discussion serves as a platform for the more detailed analysis of local economic change which is to be found in chapter 2. Saint-Hyacinthe underwent an important series of transformations in the nineteenth century, driven first by the arrival of the railway in 1848 and, second, from the 1860s, by the emergence of an industrial-capitalist manufacturing sector, dominated by labour-intensive light industries. These changes constituted the shifting ground on which Saint-Hyacinthe's men and women built their material and familial lives. Hence they are deserving of sustained attention.

The story of industrial development in this community serves as the essential context for the demographic analyses contained in the subsequent chapters. Chapter 3 contains a detailed portrait of the three cohorts of couples who married in Saint-Hyacinthe between 1854 and 1891, and whose reproductive lives are studied throughout the rest of the book. Most importantly, this chapter documents the emergence of a socially differentiated pattern in the timing of family formation. The age at which young men and women married, in particular, was sensitive to the changing structure of economic opportunity associated with the transition to industrial capitalism.

From marriage, the discussion turns, in chapter 4, to household and residential strategies, particularly those used by newly formed families. In this chapter, however, the emphasis is on continuity rather than change. In Saint-Hyacinthe, most young couples established independent, nuclear households soon after their weddings – a pattern that remained intact as the local economy became more industrial in character. Young married couples only very rarely shared accommodations with non-kin; moreover, only a very few lived as dependents in households headed by their parents or other relatives.

Finally, chapter 5 focuses on reproduction and on patterns of marital fertility in industrializing Saint-Hyacinthe. The analysis here is inspired by current debates over the nature of the long-term fertility transition that has transformed family life in most Western societies over the past two centuries. It paints a picture of a socially differentiated fertility decline among Saint-Hyacinthe's francophone, Catholic women, even at this relatively early date.

Marriage patterns, household composition, and fertility: these are the components of family life that will receive detailed attention in the ensuing pages, once the broad framework of significant social and economic change has been established. As we shall see, new demographic patterns emerged as the town became larger and more fully industrialized. These patterns echoed the increasing social distance between a privileged bourgeoisie and a struggling industrial working class. The emergence of socially differentiated models of marriage and reproduction in Saint-Hyacinthe demonstrates the importance of industrial capitalist development in the reorganization of family life in the later nineteenth century. It also illustrates the importance of these new forces within a French-speaking, Catholic population whose demographic and familial behaviour has most often been portrayed as monolithic and resistant to change. At the same time, the stories of transition lived by these Saint-Hyacinthe families underline the complexity of what some have called the "demo-economic system," the dangers of mechanistic interpretations, and the need to integrate a wide range of factors – personal, social, ideological, and cultural as well as economic – into a balanced account of demographic and familial change during industrialization.

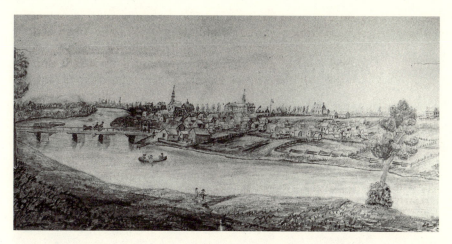

1   Saint-Hyacinthe in 1837, as sketched from the opposite bank of the Yamaska River by the surveyor L.P. Renault-Blanchard. (ASSH, section A, series 17, dossier 18)

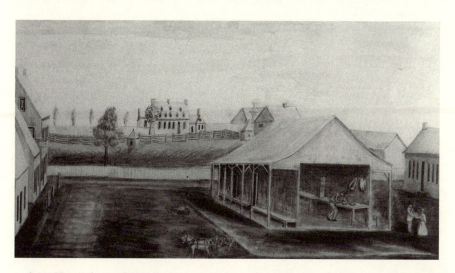

2   Saint-Hyacinthe market and seigneurial manor, as sketched by Blanchard in 1837. (ASSH, section A, series 17, dossier 18)

3   Saint-Hyacinthe owed much of its nineteenth-century economic development to its favourable position with respect to railways. This turn-of-the-century photograph shows the Saint-Hyacinthe station of the Grand Trunk Railway. (ASHRSH, Collection Hélène Nichols (BFG 44); E.H. Richer et fils, Saint-Hyacinthe, ca. 1908)

4   Saint-Hyacinthe continued to serve as the market town for an important agricultural region, even as its manufacturing sector developed. The central market was an important local institution, as this turn-of-the-century photograph suggests. (ASHRSH, Collection Hélène Nichols (BFG 44); Pinsonneault, édit., Trois-Rivières)

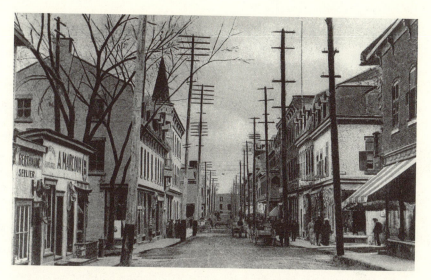

5 Cascades Street was the town's principal commercial artery, with its concentration of small and large retail shops. This photograph, taken about 1900, looks northwestward from the corner of Cascades and Mondor streets. (ASHRSH, Collection Hélène Nichols (BFG 44); Émile Solis, Libraire-Importateur, Saint-Hyacinthe, ca. 1900)

6 Saint-Hyacinthe in 1874. This winter scene shows the area around the Barsalou Bridge, the town's main manufacturing site, and institutional development on the ridge. The church on the left is Notre-Dame-du-Saint-Rosaire. The large factory on the right is the McMartin-Hamel shoe factory, a business which would fail the next year. (ASHRSH, section B, series 14, album 4)

7 The Côté brothers' boot-and-shoe factory, the descendant of Saint-Hyacinthe's first industrial concern, was still in operation at the turn of the century. It had moved to new premises on the river front, at the foot of Saint-Simon Street. This building is still standing. (ASHRSH, Collection Hélène Nichols (BFG 44); U. Fournier, Saint-Hyacinthe, ca. 1906)

8 Louis Côté: Inventor, municipal politician, industrial capitalist. His boot-and-shoe factory, founded in 1865, was a fixture of the local economy for the rest of the century. (ASHRSH, section B, series 14, album 2)

9 A member of the seigneurial family, Georges-Casimir Desssaules was a prominent local manufacturer and financier. As mayor in his prime and as a senator later in life – he lived to be 102 years old – Dessaulles was a major player in the social and political life of Saint-Hyacinthe. He was also the father of journalist Henriette Dessaulles, whose youthful diaries provide a precious glimpse into bourgeois life in the 1870s. The house where they lived is pictured in Illustration 25. (ASSH, section A, series 17, dossier 5)

10 Founded in 1864, the Ouvroir Sainte-Geneviève provided employment to destitute women in the production of woollen cloth and soap. Inmates were paid little: only 40 cents per week in the 1870s. The *ouvroir* also seems to have had a daycare function similar to that documented by Micheline Dumont for the *salles d'asile* of Montreal. (*Saint-Hyacinthe Illustré. Edifices publics, religieux et industriels* [1909], 28)

11   The Duclos-Payan tannery was an important industrial concern in Saint-Hyacinthe during the period covered by this book. It was established in 1874, with the help of a 10-year exemption from municipal taxes. The engraving shown here appeared in an elaborate 1886 album promoting the town as an industrial site. (*St. Hyacinthe Illustré/Illustrated* [1886], 13)

12   Saint-Hyacinthe was ravaged by fire in 1876 and 1903. By one account, the fire of 3 September 1876, the aftermath of which is depicted here, destroyed as many as 600 houses in the lower town. (*Canadian Illustrated News*, 16 September 1876)

1 Saint-Hyacinthe in Context

What kind of a place was nineteenth-century Saint-Hyacinthe? In the early part of the century, it was a small village at the heart of a thriving agricultural region in one of the more recently settled parts of Quebec's seigneurial heartland. At mid-century, the railway transformed this community as much as any other in Quebec, giving it a role it had not known before – that of regional *entrepôt* and service centre – and fuelling rapid, but ultimately limited, demographic growth. In the final decades of the century, industrial capitalist enterprise reshaped the town again. With the aid of a sympathetic municipal council and, after 1879, of a protected domestic market, industrial capitalists such as Louis Côté, Georges-Casimir Dessaulles, and others established a series of labour-intensive manufacturing establishments in the city. In so doing, they encouraged further population growth by employing hundreds of men, women, and children in the mass, mechanized production of consumer articles such as socks, underwear, and shoes.

Above all, then, nineteenth-century Saint-Hyacinthe was a place that underwent a series of profound transitions. To understand the full scope of these transitions is to place this community and its families in several contexts. Chapter 2 will document in some detail the restructuring of the local economy in the second half of the nineteenth century, with special attention given to the emergence of capitalist industry and its consequences for the local labour market. Before examining these crucial shifts, however, it is useful to provide certain notions of local geography; of early settlement patterns; of local demographic trends in the later nineteenth century; and, in particular, of the place of Saint-Hyacinthe within Quebec's expanding urban network in the decades after 1850.

A BEND IN THE RIVER

The Yamaska is a sinuous river whose several branches have their headwaters in the Eastern Townships. Flowing first east and then north, these streams converge to follow a course that runs parallel to the Richelieu, before draining into Lake St. Pierre about 12 kilometres east of Sorel. At a sharp bend in the river, about 50 kilometres upstream from Lake St. Pierre, is Saint-Hyacinthe (see Figure 1-1).

The townsite has three main geographic features, the first of which is the Yamaska itself. The river turns nearly due east a few kilometres above Saint-Hyacinthe, only to resume its northward course at the point early settlers named *la cascade*. Into this elbow in the river juts a low-lying plain, which flooded frequently before the rapids that gave the site its name were dammed in 1822. This alluvial plain is bounded by a ridge that runs first toward the northeast and then almost due north, veering away and then converging with the course of the river, and delineating the zones of low and high ground that became the upper and lower parts of the town of Saint-Hyacinthe.[1]

The course of the Yamaska is not only sinuous but turbulent. Frequent falls and rapids mark its northward course from the lakes of the Townships to the St. Lawrence. Unlike the more easily navigated Richelieu, the Yamaska was a poor avenue into the interior for eighteenth-century colonists. As a result, settlement came relatively late. In 1765, when Chambly on the Richelieu was already a community of 544, the village of Saint-Hyacinthe did not yet exist.[2]

But the potential for agricultural development in the lower Yamaska region was great. Saint-Hyacinthe, after all, is situated in the heart of the *Montérégie*: that unique region named for the rocky outcroppings – Mont Saint-Hilaire, Mont Saint-Bruno, Rougemont, and others – that here punctuate the broad, flat expanse of the Montreal plain. These hills, however, are exceptional. Most of the bedrock in the area remains buried beneath anywhere from six to 55 metres of clay soils, left behind after the retreat of the postglacial Champlain Sea. A rich legacy to Quebec farmers, these soils were especially well suited to agriculture, once cleared of their dense forest cover.[3]

EARLY SETTLEMENT AND VILLAGE DEVELOPMENT

The seigneurie of Saint-Hyacinthe was granted by the French Crown in 1748 to François Pierre de Rigaud de Vaudreuil. Christian

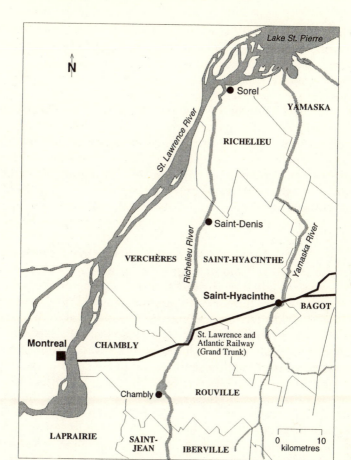

Figure 1-1 Saint-Hyacinthe in the Montreal plain. Sources: Courville et al., *Paroisses et municipalités de la région de Montréal, Canada: Atlas toponymique*

Dessureault has identified several stages in its early settlement history.[4] An initial phase, from 1748 to 1755, saw minimal development; Rigaud de Vaudreuil took no steps to encourage settlement and in 1753 sold the seigneurie – then known as *'Maska* – to Jacques-Hyacinthe Simon Delorme *dit* Lapointe for 4,000 livres. Delorme was a military entrepreneur, based in Quebec City, who was attracted by the region's forest resources, and particularly by its rich pine and oak stands, so coveted by the Royal Marine.

Settlement got under way in earnest in the years from 1756 to 1779. By 1758, Delorme had established his residence and initiated timber-cutting and saw-milling activities at *rapide-plat*, some six kilometres downstream from *la cascade*, on the right bank of the river.

These operations required an on-site labour force, and the first land concessions in the seigneurie were made in the early 1760s to the *défricheurs-bûcherons* working at this location. Settlement of the rest of the seigneurie proceeded very slowly; a total of only 87 concession deeds were signed in the period prior to 1778.

The population of the seigneurie expanded significantly between 1780 and 1794, and particularly in the early 1780s. In the four years from 1780 to 1784, the area of conceded land quadrupled, with the total number of concessions increasing to at least 415. These years also saw the spatial redistribution of the regional population. As settlement proceeded along the Yamaska toward the southeast, *rapide-plat* lost its central position. *La cascade* – well located between the river concessions and others situated to the west – became the focal point of the seigneurie.

The years around the turn of the nineteenth century saw a second wave of territorial and demographic expansion. Over 150 new land deeds were signed in the last five years of the eighteenth century. Meanwhile, the number of communicants in the parish of Saint-Hyacinthe – its territory at this time was identical to that of the seigneurie – grew from 930 in 1793 to 1,500 in 1798. Expansion accelerated further after 1800. Almost 400 new deeds were signed in the first five years of the new century, and the number of communicants doubled between 1798 and 1806. With a steady stream of colonists arriving each year and high rates of natural increase, the seigneurial population increased from 1,360 in 1791 to 10,051 in 1821, and 14,098 in 1831.

Most of these settlers, as in other parts of the St. Lawrence Valley, were grain farmers; indeed, about two-thirds of the household heads enumerated in 1831 declared themselves to be *cultivateurs*. As Dessu-realt points out, Saint-Hyacinthe farmers were better positioned than most to face the challenges of Lower Canadian agriculture in the mid-nineteenth century:

Cette seigneurie ... est l'un des terroirs les plus fertiles du Québec. Les terres sablo-argileuses des pourtours de la rivière Yamaska sont particulièrement favorables aux cultures céréalières qui dominent le paysage agraire durant le premier tiers du XIXe siècle. Certes, la qualité des sols n'est pas totalement uniforme. Ainsi, à La Présentation, les paysans de la rivière Salvail et des Étangs disposent de terres plutôt humides, parsemées de petits marécages qui conviennent davantage à l'exploitation de prairies naturelles qu'aux cultures céréalières. Néanmoins, le type de sols de la plaine maskoutaine, commun aux cinq paroisses de la seigneurie, devrait plutôt favoriser l'essor économique de la paysannerie.[5]

The village of Saint-Hyacinthe emerged in this context of agricultural settlement and seigneurial development. By the 1770s, authorities had already indicated their belief in the future of *la cascade* as a village site. In 1771, a cemetery was established on the ridge overlooking the alluvial plain. The next year, the seigneur built a new mill at the foot of the rapids, a location with clear advantages in water power over *rapide-plat.* Delorme's decision to locate the seigneurial gristmill at the *cascade* site was crucial. From this point on, Catholic authorities were clear in their intention of building a parish church and presbytery there, a project that was completed in 1780.

Decisions made by seigneurs and clerics in the 1770s certainly influenced the early development of the village of Saint-Hyacinthe. But only the demographic expansion of the late 1790s and early 1800s could ensure any degree of sustained development. In 1778, in anticipation of this type of growth, Delorme created a second seigneurial domain, measuring about 62 hectares and encompassing most of the alluvial plain. In the later 1790s, the seigneur began to concede lots measuring 669 square metres each on the territory. The nucleus of the village of Saint-Hyacinthe was formed between 1794 and 1805, during which time the first 68 concession deeds, covering some 134 lots, were signed. By the latter date, the village of Saint-Hyacinthe had some 89 houses, mostly strung along the road leading to Saint-Denis (later Bourdages Street) and the Chemin du Roi (later Girouard Street). It was home to 72 families, 56 unmarried men, 60 widows and single women, and 111 children.[6] It was also the site of a new manor (1798), a new stone church (1797), and an extensive new seigneurial mill (1800).[7]

By about 1805, then, the village of Saint-Hyacinthe was well established. With its population of several hundred, many of whom were professionals, merchants, and artisans who served the agricultural population of the surrounding region, it was not unlike scores of other Lower Canadian villages and *bourgs*, the expansion of which in this period has been so well documented by Serge Courville.[8] Demographically, it was comparable to Saint-Denis on the Richelieu. But because of its peripheral position in the Lower Canadian communications network, it had nowhere near the same economic importance.

In this particular village, growth in the early nineteenth century was modest; it was also two-tiered. A grid of streets emerged from southwest to northeast in the lower town, as the plain filled up with residences, a public market, several inns, and various artisans' shops. Institutional development, on the other hand, occurred almost exclusively on the ridge, as convents, schools, a courthouse, and a hospital took up positions on high ground, near the parish church and the seigneurial manor.[9]

As just suggested, commercial development in the early part of the century was hindered by poor communications. Because the Yamaska River below Saint-Hyacinthe is shallow and unnavigable, grain intended for the urban and export markets had to be transported over land to Saint-Denis on the Richelieu and then loaded onto river vessels bound for Montreal. For this reason, Saint-Denis more than Saint-Hyacinthe profited from the agricultural development of the Yamaska region during this period. As late as 1840, as Rudin points out, Saint-Hyacinthe was an unincorporated village that functioned, in commercial terms, "exclusively as a collection point for grain merchants operating out of ... Saint-Denis."[10]

Despite its unfavourable position with respect to navigation, the ascendancy of Saint-Hyacinthe in the lower Yamaska region was assured in the 1840s. Part of the reason may have been that some Saint-Denis merchants moved their operations to Saint-Hyacinthe in the wake of the rebellions.[11] But surely the arrival of the St. Lawrence and Atlantic Railway in 1848 was the crucial factor. This rail link allowed Saint-Hyacinthe merchants to ship grain directly to Montreal, just as it improved their access to merchandise for retail and wholesale distribution in the region. Demographic growth followed. In 1845, the village already had some 2,500 inhabitants; three years after the arrival of the railway, in 1851, the population had increased to almost 3,200. By mid-century, Saint-Hyacinthe had emerged as the principal commercial centre for an agricultural region that encompassed most of Bagot, Rouville, and Saint-Hyacinthe counties.[12]

Cereal-based agriculture was thriving in this region of Lower Canada in the mid-nineteenth century. In 1861, farms in Saint-Hyacinthe county were prosperous. Slightly larger than the provincial average (36.8 hectares, compared to 35.6), they were also more extensively cultivated: 71% of the occupied land in the county was improved, compared to 46% for Lower Canada as a whole.[13] Although the shift from the wheat "staple" to other cereals was well underway, wheat had not entirely fallen by the wayside, as it had in older areas. Saint-Hyacinthe county's farmers (about 2,000 in number) produced almost 75,000 *minots* of wheat in 1861. On average, they devoted 1.7 hectares of land to wheat production – not very much, perhaps, but more than twice the provincial level. Other grains, however, such as rye, barley, and particularly oats, had become even more important to the rural economy. The county produced over 360,000 *minots* of oats in 1861, for example, and the average farmer devoted 5.7 hectares of

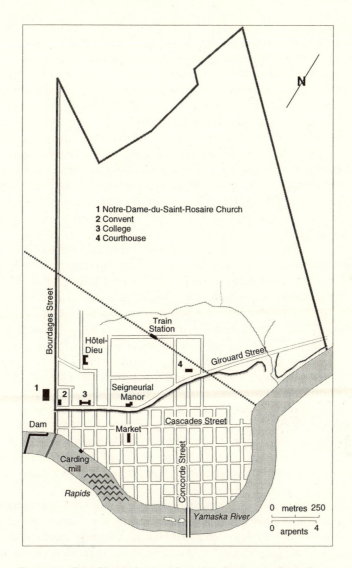

Figure 1-2 Saint-Hyacinthe at mid-century. Source: NA, Renault-Blanchard, "Plan des limites du village de Saint-Hyacinthe"

land to its cultivation. As with wheat, this was more than the provincial average of 2.4 hectares.[14]

With its new economic importance and size and its strong position at the heart of a thriving agricultural region, the village of Saint-Hyacinthe took on a new municipal structure and a new set of administrative and service functions at mid-century. Although the parish of Saint-Hyacinthe was recognized as a municipality in 1835,[15] the village itself was not incorporated until August of 1850.[16] The municipality, divided into four numbered wards or *quartiers*, had its status upgraded from village to town in 1853 and from town to city in 1857.[17]

This, it seems, was a community with ambitions. At no time during this period did the population of the village approach its northwestern limits.[18] However, municipal authorities saw fit to include in the town charter of 1853 a proviso for the annexation of land located directly upstream from the southwestern boundary at Bourdages Street. This proviso was repeated in the city charter of 1857, but not acted upon until 1888, when *Quartier 5* was annexed to the original four (Figure 1-3).[19]

In addition to its new municipal status, Saint-Hyacinthe took on new religious and judicial functions in the 1850s. In 1852, it was chosen as the episcopal see for a vast new Catholic diocese covering some 21 seigneuries in the Richelieu-Yamaska area and, until the creation of the Sherbrooke diocese in 1874, most of the Eastern Townships.[20] This confirmed the religious vocation of Saint-Hyacinthe, already the site of several important Catholic institutions, including a classical college (founded in 1811), the convent of the Soeurs de la Congrégation de Notre-Dame (1816), and the Hôtel-Dieu hospital (established by the Grey Nuns in 1840). The judicial role of the village, which had had a courthouse since 1835, was also confirmed and expanded in the 1850s. The judicial district of Saint-Hyacinthe was created in 1858, with the newly chartered city as its *chef-lieu*.[21]

DEMOGRAPHIC TRENDS, 1851–1901

The growth of an important commercial and service centre at the heart of this prosperous agricultural area accelerated as the century progressed. The town of Saint-Hyacinthe grew substantially in the second half of the nineteenth century, and particularly after 1871. Positive migratory balances were fostered by industrial development and by the inability of rural areas in the region to absorb further demographic growth, particularly as a new, more specialized, market-oriented agriculture emerged.[22] In effect, Saint-Hyacinthe's population tripled in the 50 years after 1851, exceeding 9,000 by 1901. In the same interval, the general population of the province of Quebec barely doubled.[23]

More detailed demographic analysis will help convey the contours of Saint-Hyacinthe's urban growth in the later nineteenth century.

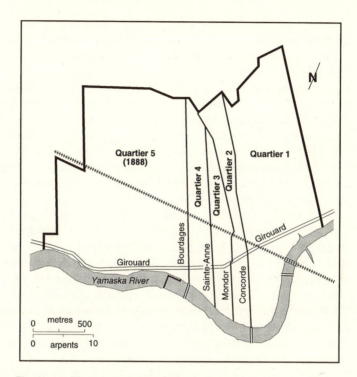

Figure 1-3 The *quartiers* of Saint-Hyacinthe.
Source: ASRSH, "Plan de la Cité de Saint-Hyacinthe"

But the institutional developments of the 1850s, which had an impact on local geographic boundaries, must be assessed before the population trends can be understood. Two events were particularly important: the incorporation of the Village of Saint-Hyacinthe in 1850; and the subdivision, or *démembrement,* of the Catholic parish in 1853.

One consequence of the municipal incorporation in 1850 is that the town's population could now be clearly distinguished from that of the parish in published census returns. Prior to this date, the village population had been subsumed within that of the parish in these records, making comparisons between the earlier and later periods tricky.[24] Comparing population figures for Saint-Hyacinthe before and after the annexation of *Quartier 5* in 1888 presents a similar problem.[25]

The creation of the diocese of Saint-Hyacinthe also affected local territorial boundaries, resulting as it did in the formation of two new parishes where there had been only one. The circumstances surrounding the splitting of the parish require some explanation. Although its registers had been open since 1777, Saint-Hyacinthe was only recognized as a parish in 1832, when it was erected canonically as Saint-Hyacinthe-le-Confesseur. Its territory, about nine by 13 kilometres, included the village and a portion of the surrounding countryside. The municipality of the Parish of Saint-Hyacinthe, established in 1835, had identical boundaries to those of the Catholic parish.[26]

When the diocese was created in 1852, however, new parish boundaries were needed. The first bishop, Mgr Jean-Charles Prince, intended to establish his episcopal palace in the local presbytery and to take over the parish church as his cathedral. But his application to the Legislative Council of the Province of Canada for the ratification of this arrangement was refused. Mgr Prince therefore used his episcopal authority to divide the parish in two. Accordingly, the brand new parish of Saint-Hyacinthe-le-Confesseur was detached from the original parish of the same name in October of 1853, becoming the episcopal see of the new diocese. Its cathedral – its registers opened in January 1854 – was intended to serve the devotional needs of the village of Saint-Hyacinthe, of three *rangs* located downstream from Saint-Hyacinthe, and of the tiny village of Saint-Joseph, directly across the river. The territory that remained of the old parish – renamed Notre-Dame-du-Saint-Rosaire – was located directly to the east, on both sides of the river. Easily twice the area of Saint-Hyacinthe-le-Confesseur, it had about the same number of inhabitants (See Figure 1-4 and Table 1-1).[27]

As a result of these gymnastics, the territory of Saint-Hyacinthe seigneurie, which since 1835 had been a single municipality and a single parish, was divided into two municipalities in 1850 and into two parishes in 1853. Such a situation would be simple enough if the religious and civil boundaries coincided exactly. But, as we have seen, part of the new parish of Saint-Hyacinthe-le-Confesseur lay outside the limits of the village. The municipal status of this territory, which had a population of about 800 in the 1850s, was still unresolved. In 1855, it was annexed for civil purposes to the municipality of Notre-Dame-du-Rosaire.[28] In May of 1861, however, the pertinent section of the 1855 Act was repealed and the territory that lay "without the present limits of the city of Saint-Hyacinthe" but "within the present limits of the parish of Saint-Hyacinthe-le-Confesseur" received its own separate civil status as the municipality of the Parish of Saint-Hyacinthe-le-Confesseur.[29]

This type of institutional and territorial change is custom-made to confound students of historical demography, who must rely on consistent definitions of geographic boundaries. This book simplifies the situation somewhat by focusing primarily on the demographic behaviour of the cathedral parish (Saint-Hyacinthe-le-Confesseur) in the

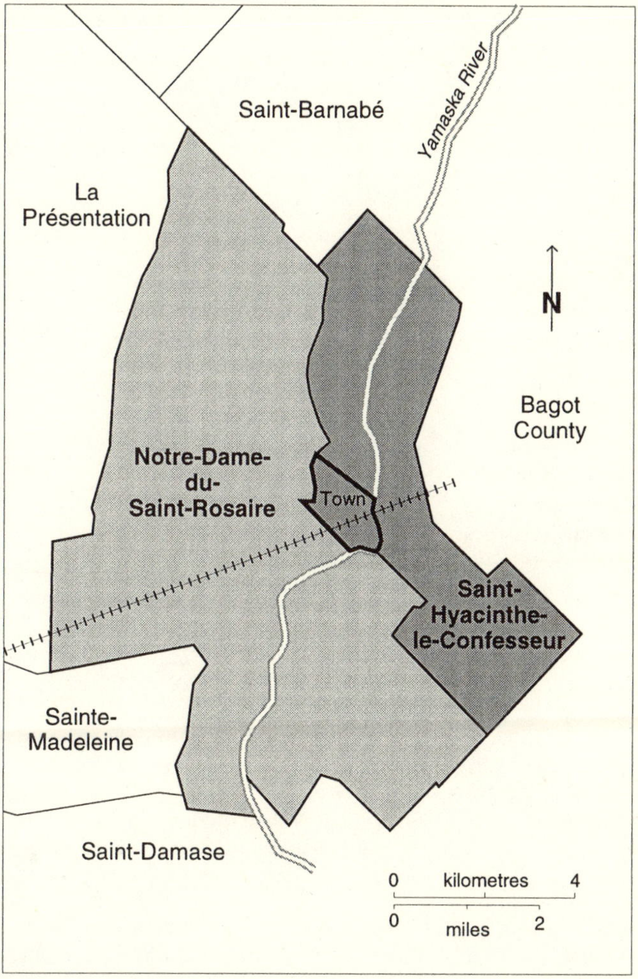

Figure 1-4 The parishes of Saint-Hyacinthe-le-Confesseur and Notre-Dame-du-Saint-Rosaire. Sources: Hopkins, *Atlas of the City and County of St. Hyacinthe*, ASHRSH, Décret canonique de la Paroisse de Saint-Hyacinthe-le-Confesseur; AESH, *Registre des Requêtes*, series 1, vol. 1, 21–3

period after 1850. This Catholic parish encompassed the town of Saint-Hyacinthe in its entirety until 1888, when the new *Quartier 5* was annexed (to the municipality, but not to the parish).[30] It also included the rural municipality of Saint-Hyacinthe-le-Confesseur, whose agricultural families will provide a recurrent point of comparison to the urban population that is of primary interest here.

Table 1-1
Population, Catholic Population, and Number of Households in Municipalities in
the Saint-Hyacinthe Area: 1851–1901

Year	Population	Catholics	Households
A. VILLAGE — TOWN — CITY OF SAINT-HYACINTHE			
1851	3,195	–	–
1861	3,695	3,621	–
1871	3,746	3,689	–
1881	5,321	5,156	1,068
1891	7,016	6,901	1,274
1901	9,210	9,040	1,714
B. MUNICIPALITY OF SAINT-HYACINTHE-LE-CONFESSEUR			
1861	790[a]	–	–
1871	788	785	–
1881	935	928	201
1891	940	939	132
1901	673	671	132
C. MUNICIPALITY OF NOTRE-DAME-DE-SAINT-HYACINTHE			
1851	3,313[b]	–	–
1861	2,846[c]	–	–
1871	2,581	2,560	–
1881	3,240	3,211	647
1891	2,799[d]	2,776	545
1901	521[e]	514	96

Sources: Except as otherwise noted, population figures come from the published returns of the
Canadian census in the six census years between 1851 and 1901 inclusive.

Notes

[a]   ASSH, "Notes historiques sur la paroisse de Saint-Hyacinthe," vol. 1.

[b]   This apparently includes the future municipality of Saint-Hyacinthe-le-Confesseur, even
though the temporary annexation of that territory by the municipality of Notre-Dame did
not occur until 1855.

[c]   ASSH, "Notes historiques." In the published census tables, this population is combined with
that of Saint-Hyacinthe-le-Confesseur, to give a total of 3,636 for "Saint-Hyacinthe, parish."

[d]   *Quartier* 5 of the City of Saint-Hyacinthe was created in 1888 through an annexation
involving the most urbanized part of the Parish of Notre-Dame-de-Saint-Hyacinthe. This
explains the drop in population between 1881 and 1891.

[e]   There must have been important dismemberments of this municipality in the 1890s. One
such case involved the incorporation of the Village of La Providence in 1899. There may
have been others.

Having explained these territorial changes, it is now possible to
conduct a preliminary analysis of demographic trends in Saint-
Hyacinthe in the second half of the nineteenth century. Table 1-1
gives the total population, the Catholic population, and the number
of households in the three municipalities in the immediate Saint-
Hyacinthe area for the census years between 1851 and 1901. As Part A

of the table shows, population growth in the town of Saint-Hyacinthe was far from regular. Between 1851 and 1871, the town barely grew at all; indeed, its population increased by 16% in the 1850s and by a mere 1% in the 1860s. Over the next thirty years, however, the population grew by at least 30% each decade, stimulated by industrial development and by the annexation of *Quartier 5*.[31]

Rudin offers a convincing explanation of these trends. Industrial development in Saint-Hyacinthe was weak between 1851 and 1871. During this interval, only one manufactory of any importance was established in the town. Moreover, the local bourgeoisie – many of them economic liberals and municipal boosters – complained of industrial stagnation. As a result, migratory balances were negative; the town, like so many other parts of Quebec during this period, failed to retain its natural increase.[32]

The situation changed after 1871, however. As we shall see in chapter 3, local industrial development was encouraged by a municipal council that lavished cash bonuses and long-term tax exemptions on prospective industrialists. Rudin shows how these policies and the factories they attracted succeeded in reversing migratory balances by creating opportunities in wage labour: industrial jobs that not only encouraged local people to stay but also attracted migrants from outside the town. As well, urban growth was fostered by the very real economic pressures in the surrounding countryside, where the limits of agricultural growth – at least in terms of the number of working farms – seem to have been reached by the 1860s.

In-migration, encouraged by local industrial development, was, therefore, the crucial factor in the demographic expansion of Saint-Hyacinthe after 1850. Because municipal and parish boundaries did not coincide in the second half of the nineteenth century, the calculation of precise migratory balances for the town of Saint-Hyacinthe during this period is impossible. It is possible, however, to calculate net migration among Catholics in the parish of Saint-Hyacinthe-le-Confesseur between 1861 and 1891.[33] As Table 1-2 shows, the parish experienced a net out-migration of approximately 500 individuals in the interval between 1861 and 1871. This trend, though, was dramatically reversed in the 1870s, a decade of industrial expansion in which net in-migration was 1,144. A pattern of in-migration (and, perhaps as importantly, attenuated out-migration) continued in the 1880s, although the positive balance was less than half what it had been in the previous decade. After 1891, given the rapid industrial expansion of the first half of the decade,[34] one would expect in-migration to have once again stimulated demographic growth. Although generating the figures for the interval 1891–1901

Table 1-2
Catholic Population, Baptisms, Burials, Natural Increase, Total Increase, and
Net Migration for Parish of Saint-Hyacinthe-le-Confesseur: 1861–1901

Year	Catholic Population	Interval	Baptisms	Burials	Increase Natural	Total	Net Migration
1861	4,411[a]						
1871	4,474[c]	1861–1870	1,923[b]	1,363	560	63	–497
1881	6,084[d]	1871–1880	2,294	1,828	466	1,610	1,144
1891	6,879[e]	1881–1890	2,629	2,295	334	795	461
1901	8,463[f]	1891–1900	3,042	2,500	542	1,584	1,042

Notes

[a] *Census of the Canadas, 1860-61* and ASSH, "Notes historiques." This figure assumes the entire rural population of the parish was Catholic.

[b] All data on baptisms and burials are from APSHC, Parish registers (*Registres des baptêmes, mariages et sépultures*), 1861-1900.

[c] *Census of Canada, 1870-71.*

[d] *Census of Canada, 1880-81.*

[e] Total population of *Quartiers* 1 to 4 = 6,084 (from manuscript census). Town as a whole is 98.4% Catholic. Assuming the same proportion in *Quartiers* 1 to 4, Catholic population of those sectors = 5,940. Plus 939 from Saint-Hyacinthe-le-Confesseur = 6,879.

[f] Total population of the town = 9,210. Assume that, as in 1891, *Quartiers* 1 to 4 contained 86.1% of the total. Population estimate for *Quartiers* 1 to 4 = 7,927. Assume that, as for the town as a whole, *Quartiers* 1 to 4 are 98.3% Catholic. Catholic population of these sectors = 7,792. Plus 671 in Saint-Hyacinthe-le-Confesseur = 8,463.

required some brave assumptions, the results certainly bear out this view.[35] Migratory balances in the 1890s were almost as strongly positive as the levels of the 1870s.

As students of population history know well, migration is only one influence on rates of demographic growth or decline. Natural increase – the difference, whether positive or negative, between locally occurring births and deaths – can be just as important. Marriage rates must be considered too, given their impact on the number of children born in a community, particularly in contexts such as this where relatively few were born out of wedlock.

Figure 1-5 and Table 1-3 give the annual number of baptisms, marriages, and burials in the parish of Saint-Hyacinthe between 1854 and 1924, as well as the crude rates of birth, marriage, and death from 1854 to 1901. A striking feature of Figure 1-5 is the high ratio of baptisms to burials in the years prior to 1865, and the much closer fit between the two curves in the ensuing years. The large number of baptisms early in the period may be the result of a high proportion of recent migrants – many of whom would have been young couples – in Saint-Hyacinthe during the period immediately after the arrival of the railway. In 1861, as Table 1-3 shows, the birth rate in this new urban

Table 1-3
Birth, Marriage, and Death Rates for Catholic Population of the Parish of
Saint-Hyacinthe-le-Confesseur: 1861–1901

Year	Baptisms	Annual Number[a] of Marriages	Burials	Rates per 1,000 Inhabitants		
				Birth	Marriage	Death
1861	233	38	130	52.9	8.7	29.4
1871	189	42	152	42.3	8.9	34.0
1881	215	65	200	35.3	8.9	32.8
1891	292	54	219	42.5	7.8	31.9
1901	283	59	219	33.4	7.0	25.9

Source: APSHC, Parish registers, 1859–1903; published census, 1861–1901; manuscript cenus,
1891
Note
[a] Averages for five years around census dates.

parish was about 53 per thousand, slightly above the rate for Quebec
as a whole (50 per thousand) and only slightly lower than the rate for
the rural Saguenay region (56 per thousand).[36]

The baptism and burial figures are easier to interpret for the
period after 1865. Generally speaking, the surplus of births over
deaths in this period was not large. A fluctuating birth rate and a
relatively high level of mortality created the rather slow pace of
natural increase that can be read in Table 1-2. The birth rate in the
parish decreased between 1861 and 1871 to a level (42 per thousand) slightly below the provincial figure.[37] It then declined appreciably in the second half of the 1870s, a period of economic crisis and
urban reconstruction, in the wake of a devastating fire in 1876.[38]
Birth rates were higher toward the end of the eighties, when a boom-
ing economy brought many young couples into the population. The
late 1890s, a period of economic recession, saw yet another drop in
natality; the rate of 33.4 per thousand recorded for 1901 was some
16% below the level for the province as a whole in that year.

Between 1861 and 1871, the mortality rate in the parish of Saint-
Hyacinthe increased from 29 per thousand to 34 per thousand. Both
of these values were over 30% higher than the provincial mortality
levels, and the 1871 rate was over double the figure for the Saguenay
region.[39] These were characteristically urban mortality levels, entirely
comparable to those found in larger Quebec cities, and reflective of a
dangerous water supply and of the high rates of infant and child mortality that will be discussed in chapter 5. Mortality rates did decline
steadily after 1871. But they remained significantly above provincial
values, which were themselves moving downward. Over time, the burial curve followed the baptism curve fairly closely, reflecting the fact

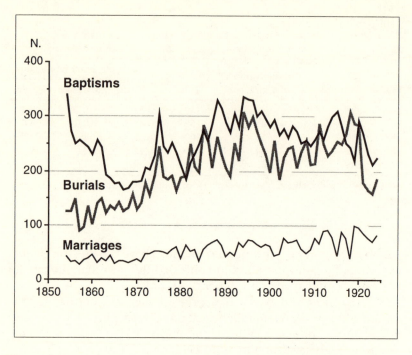

Figure 1-5 Baptisms, marriages, and burials, parish of Saint-Hyacinthe-le-Confesseur, 1854–1924. Sources: APSHC, Parish Registers, 1854–1924; "Répertoire des registres de la nouvelle paroisse"

that infant deaths represented the majority of all burials. Occasional crisis mortality was not unknown in this industrializing town, however. For two years during the 1880s (1882 and 1885), the number of burials in the parish exceeded the number of baptisms. The 1885 mortality crisis was the result of a smallpox epidemic that killed at least 49 individuals in Saint-Hyacinthe between early October of 1885 and the end of April, 1886. The cause of the 1882 mortality peak may also have been smallpox, but this is less clear.[40] Other years of crisis mortality were 1911 and 1917–18, when Spanish flu ravaged this community as it did the rest of Canada.[41]

With respect to marriage, the upward trend in the absolute numbers of local marriages clearly reflects the growth of the parish population. Marriage rates were high – almost nine per thousand – until 1881. Their subsequent decline – to under eight per thousand in 1891 and to seven per thousand in 1901 – took place in the context of changes in patterns of family formation, which will be examined in chapter 3.

SAINT-HYACINTHE IN URBAN QUEBEC

These comparisons between local demographic patterns and province-wide trends help situate Saint-Hyacinthe within the context of Quebec's nineteenth-century urban development. Breaking with an earlier tradition, Quebec historians since the mid 1970s have paid increasing attention to urban life, particularly to its evolution during the nineteenth-century transition to industrial capitalism.[42] Montreal, the emerging metropolis, has received the lion's share of the attention, with historians focusing on such important topics as industrial work, social class, private and public space, family, gender, health, and housing.[43] Montreal – with its dominant position in the transportation, commercial, and financial networks, its rapid population growth (from just under sixty thousand in 1851 to over a quarter of a million in 1901), and its clear position on the leading edge of Quebec's industrial-capitalist transition – certainly deserves the attention it has received from historians of the nineteenth century.

Particularly after 1870, however, a number of smaller Quebec communities were also growing at substantial rates. Saint-Hyacinthe was one of several towns in which industrial development drew hundreds of migrants from surrounding rural areas to settle in burgeoning working-class neighbourhoods. None of these centres, of course, attracted industrial capital and wage workers the way Montreal did. Indeed, by the turn of the century, two-fifths of the province's urban population lived in Montreal, which represents a high level of concentration in a single city. But, as this figure implies, three-fifths of Quebec's urban dwellers thus lived in less imposing towns and cities such as Quebec City, Sherbrooke, Hull, Trois-Rivières, Valleyfield, Saint-Jean, Chicoutimi, Magog, and Saint-Hyacinthe.[44] In an era in which industrial capital and railway construction were changing the rules of the game, each place had its own particular pattern of development, based on a specific combination of industries, geographic advantages, and other attributes. By looking briefly at several of these towns and cities, we can get a better picture of the general context of secondary urban development – another fundamental context in which the Saint-Hyacinthe story must be situated.

Quebec City

Quebec City, to begin with, had been comparable in size and importance to Montreal in the early part of the nineteenth century. But its prominence was based on its strategic position at the head of maritime navigation on the St. Lawrence – an advantage that was lost when the channel was deepened in the 1840s – and on traditional industries such as the timber trade and wooden shipbuilding. The fact that Quebec failed to keep pace with Montreal's rapid industrial and demographic growth after 1850 is well known.[45] Still, with a population of almost 70,000, Quebec was easily the province's second city in 1901, five times larger than third-place Hull.

At the turn of the century, Quebec City's manufacturing sector was dominated by leather-related industries, a concentration that had emerged more clearly in the years following the imposition of the National Policy tariff. As Jacques Ferland has shown, Quebec in 1891 accounted for 30% of the value of boots and shoes produced in Canada – a close second to Montreal in this, but in no other, manufacturing sector. In fact, the city had become Canada's leading centre for the production of inexpensive shoes, to the point where certain producers in other centres "trouvaient plus profitable de se procurer une partie de leur stock chez les fabricants de Québec et d'en défrayer les coûts de transport, au lieu de produire ce type de chaussures dans leur usine ou chez un concurrent de leur région."[46] In 1900, Quebec's 30 shoe factories employed some 4,000 workers and produced some $4 million worth of merchandise. As Ferland points out, this was an extremely labour-intensive sector, one in which productivity did not improve substantially between the 1870s and the end of the century, and one in which the lion's share of the invested capital went into wages.[47] Other industries located in the old capital were similarly labour intensive. A good example is the Dominion Corset Manufacturing Company, founded in 1886 by Georges-Élie Amyot; by the turn of the century, it was employing hundreds of workers, most of them women, in the production of women's undergarments.[48]

In economic terms, Quebec City's early prominence had been tied to its monopoly over maritime navigation and to its dominant position in the forest products trade: from squared timber through fully rigged sailing ships. Some of the larger towns that emerged in Quebec during the second half of the nineteenth century also owed their growth to the trade in wood products. Every village and small town, of course, had its carpenters and cabinetmakers. There might be a small sawmill as well, producing boards for local construction needs; a cooperage; or even a specialized woodworking shop, producing such items as door and window frames or axe and scythe handles.[49] But this was a period during which vast forests were being cleared for agriculture in the new "colonization" regions beyond the St. Lawrence valley; a period that saw the rapid expansion of domestic, and especially American, markets for sawn lumber and, later, pulp and paper. In this context, larger communities such as Hull and

Trois-Rivières – whose manufacturing activity was concentrated in these industries and which had managed to control their regional, forest-based economies – also rose to prominence.

Hull

Hull, for example, grew rapidly in the final decades of the nineteenth century, from a population of under 4,000 in 1871 to almost 14,000 in 1901.[50] Odette Vincent has demonstrated the extent to which this demographic growth depended on expansion in a single economic sector: forest products. In fact, a single entrepreneur, Ezra Butler Eddy, can be considered – as he is in Vincent's account – the father of "modern industry" in the *Outaouais* region of western Quebec.[51] Eddy was a New Englander who arrived in Hull Township in the 1850s and who, over the next 20 years, accumulated substantial capital in the production of sawn lumber and related items such as matches, buckets, and washboards. His fortunes improved dramatically in the 1870s when he was able to acquire two valuable properties from the Wright family: timber concessions along the tributaries of the Ottawa River and the major water-power site in the region, located on Hull island at the base of the Chaudière Falls.[52]

With these advantages, and despite a devastating fire in 1882 – a common thread in Quebec urban history during this period – Eddy was able to consolidate his dominion over the Hull economy during the 1880s and 1890s. He was one of the first Canadian lumber barons to recognize the potential profits to be gained from the production of wood pulp and paper products. Allied with local investors, he founded the E.B. Eddy Manufacturing Company in 1886; the plant began the production of wood pulp that same year and of paper in 1890. Using a range of modern technologies, Eddy expanded his product lines considerably in the subsequent decade to include brown paper, tissue paper, and newsprint.[53] In 1891, his various enterprises already provided some 1,000 jobs – most of them difficult, insecure, and low-paying – to local men, women, and children. By 1902, that number had doubled; about 2,000 local residents were employed in the production of everything from wooden matches – many girls and young women worked in the industry's extremely dangerous conditions – to newsprint.[54]

Trois-Rivières

Trois-Rivières is another Quebec community which, like Hull, can trace its nineteenth-century development to its close relationship with the forest. In their study of the Mauricie region, René Hardy and Normand Séguin make these links very clearly. A much older community than Hull, Trois-Rivières had a population of just under 5,000 in 1851. By the turn of the twentieth century, the city had doubled in size and, like Saint-Hyacinthe, had acquired significant new service and administrative functions along the way.[55] The town's demographic growth followed the rhythms of the region's forestry sector, particularly the sawn lumber industry. Sawmills were not new to the Saint-Maurice River valley in the decades after 1850s. What was new was the scale of production in mills such as those operated by Norcross and Philips, George Baptist, James Dean, and Joseph A. Gagnon; together, these mills turned out millions of board feet of lumber each year, to be sold in markets located in the United States, Great Britain, continental Europe, and Latin America.[56] Expansion in this industry largely accounts for the substantial growth of the local population in the 1860s and 1870s. By 1881, 648 people worked in the local sawmills and in other wood-products industries; this was over one-half of all manufacturing workers in the city.[57]

The boom in the lumber industry, however, came to an abrupt end in the 1880s. By 1891, only 151 jobs remained in the wood products sector in Trois-Rivières, thus accounting for less than one-fifth of manufacturing employment. Moreover, the town's population had actually declined from its 1881 level.[58] It was heavy industries, in the form of pulp-and-paper mills and hydroelectric projects, that were emerging in the Mauricie region during the 1880s and 1890s. But the new industrial sites were located upstream from Trois-Rivières, at places such as Grand-Mère and Shawinigan, rather than in the regional capital. Still, Trois-Rivières benefited from its position as an ocean port located at the confluence of the Saint-Maurice and St. Lawrence rivers and, in the 1890s, entered a new phase of demographic growth. The increase (from 8,334 in 1891 to 9,981 in 1901) was stimulated by the town's busy harbour, by its position at the hub of the regional exchange network, and by a more diversified manufacturing sector in which leather and metallurgical production had overtaken forest products as the major source of employment.[59]

Valleyfield

Outside Montreal, then, Quebec's industrial and urban development in the second half of the nineteenth century was not insignificant. It did, however, tend to be fairly specialized. Take Quebec City, for example. Although a unique case, it is also interesting, with its local manufacturing sector focusing not merely on leather goods but more specifically on inexpensive, mass-produced boots and shoes. Hull and Trois-Rivières also provide good examples of regional economic specialization. Both were commercial *entrepôts* serving expanding agroforest regions, and able, therefore, to attract sawmills and other wood-processing industries. Even more notable for its level of economic specialization, however, was Valleyfield, a town that owed its considerable growth in the last three decades of the nineteenth century to the emergence of a single industry: cotton textiles.

Cotton textile production in Quebec prior to the 1870s, according to Hamelin and Roby, "est le lot de quelques audacieux qui ne craignent pas la concurrence anglaise ou américaine."[60] The real beginnings of the Quebec cotton industry date from the early 1870s, with the establishment of the Dominion Cotton Mills in Hochelaga, near Montreal in 1873 and of the Montreal Cotton Company in Valleyfield in 1874.[61] Montreal Cotton began production in 1877 in its new factory located on the Beauharnois Canal, from which it obtained the hydraulic power to run some 27,000 spindles and 520 weaving machines.[62] Owned by a consortium of Montreal and British businessmen that included Hugh Allan, Andrew F. Gault, and Samuel Barlow (a Lancashire producer of textile machinery), the Valleyfield operation was the second largest in Canada in the 1870s. Between 1882 and 1905, the factory was expanded no less than five times, making it the largest operation of its kind in the country, with 5,000 looms (400 of them electrically powered) and a workforce of up to 2,500 men, women, and children.[63]

There is no mystery, then, to the rather extraordinary demographic growth of Valleyfield in the last three decades of the nineteenth century. The town grew as a direct result of the expanding demand for wage labourers in the local textile mill. In 1871, Valleyfield's population of 1,800 made it the eleventh largest community in the province. By 1901, with its 11,055 people, it was Quebec's fifth largest city, behind only Montreal, Quebec, Hull, and Sherbrooke.[64] With respect to relations between labour and capital, it was also one of the province's more fractious communities. Workers at the Valleyfield textile mill, many of them young women, experienced the same difficulties – including low wages, long hours, harsh work discipline, and the grinding monotony of the work – as textile workers all over the world. Despite the company's attempts at welfare capitalism (including company housing, recreational equipment, and a pure milk dispensary), there were at least 11 strikes, some of them violent, in this cotton mill between 1880 and 1908.[65]

Sherbrooke

As in Valleyfield, cotton textile production witnessed significant expansion elsewhere in Quebec in the wake of the 1879 National Policy tariff, which raised duties on imported cotton from 17.5% to 30%. In fact, the value of all categories of textiles produced in Quebec quintupled between 1881 and the end of the century.[66] New cotton mills were established in Coaticook, Lachute, Chambly, Saint-Henri, Magog, and Montmorency in the first half of the 1880s,[67] with important consequences for regional labour markets and urban development in all of these areas. Many of these small communities resembled Valleyfield in that the local cotton mill was virtually, if not literally, the only industrial employer in town. In Sherbrooke, however, where cotton textile production in Canada had begun in the 1840s, the situation was somewhat different.

In fact, Sherbrooke's experiment with cotton textiles, though precocious, was short lived. The first of its kind in Canada, the Sherbrooke Cotton Factory was founded in the summer of 1844, with $25,000 of subscribed capital, in a four-storey building erected not far from the junction of the Magog and the St. Francis rivers.[68] It was one of a number of industrial and transportation projects promoted by the British American Land Company – or BALCO – during this period. With Alexander Galt as commissioner, the land company broke with previous policy and began to try to bring manufacturers to Sherbrooke, its headquarters, in order to make use of the impressive water-power sites along the Magog, sites which BALCO just happened to own. In 1848, the land company was the largest shareholder in the cotton factory, which was running 1,000 spindles and turning out 300,000 yards of rough, grey calico each year. Two of its officials, Galt and Edward Hale, were also among the major shareholders.[69] In 1851, however, after injecting new capital into the operation, BALCO officials ceded it to Adam Lomas, who was also active locally in woollens production. Then, in 1854, a fire in the factory brought an abrupt end to cotton production in the city. When the cotton industry revived in the Townships under the National Policy tariff, it was the smaller centres, namely Coaticook and Magog, that entered the fray, rather than the regional capital.[70]

Under Galt's stewardship, BALCO continued to invest in local industries. The company was especially active in Sherbrooke in the late 1840s and early 1850s, "establishing factories, complete with equipment, and then leasing them to interested parties."[71] By 1853, these included a tannery, a cotton factory, a paper mill, a pail factory, a joiner's shop, a machine shop, an iron foundry, a grist mill, and a sawmill. Despite Galt's enthusiasm, his superiors in Britain continued to worry that these investments were unjustified. They had some reason, for, in 1866, only 223 workers were employed in Sherbrooke industries, with no one firm employing more than 50.[72]

However, despite the early demise of its cotton mill, Sherbrooke's development in this period was nonetheless linked to the fortunes of the textile industry. It was woollen textiles, though, which held pride of place in the local economy, particularly after the establishment of the Andrew Paton woollens mill in 1866.[73] Initially, Andrew Paton was the sole owner of the mill which, when built in 1866 at a cost of $400,000, was the largest of its kind in Canada – a distinction it would retain throughout this period.[74] But in 1868, financial difficulties forced the reorganization of the firm as Andrew Paton and Company, with Paton as manager and the backing of a group of blue-chip investors that included Galt and Heneker, from Sherbrooke, and Montreal railway baron George Stephen.[75] By 1871, the new woollens mill was employing 194 workers, producing tweeds with wool imported from Australia, New England, and South America and using Quebec wool – reputedly coarser – in the production of flannels.[76] It expanded regularly in the 1870s and 1880s, taking on new product lines and steadily increasing its work force: a combination of a handful of skilled workers imported from Great Britain and hundreds of inexperienced, low-wage workers from the surrounding countryside.[77] By the most conservative estimate, the size of the workforce had reached 438 by 1877, 540 by 1882, and 725 by 1892.[78]

Although woollen textiles production played a key role in the development of Sherbrooke after 1866, this was not a one-industry town. Rudin suggests that in the early years of its existence, the presence of almost 200 workers in the Paton mill stimulated local consumer demand sufficiently to cause a 135% increase in employment in other local manufacturing industries between 1866 and 1871.[79] Demographic expansion certainly accelerated in the decades corresponding to the Paton mill's expansion. Virtually nil in the 1850s, population growth was in the order of 50% in the 1860s, 60% in the 1870s, and 40% in the 1880s.[80] The availability of jobs in woollen textiles was certainly part of the reason for that growth. But the city took on many other manufacturing functions in this period as well, as it staked out a strong position within the growing railway network of southern Quebec and asserted its control over a regional hinterland with important agricultural, forest, and mining resources.

Because of its railway links and its connections to an emerging mining district, for example, Sherbrooke developed a thriving metallurgical sector, particularly toward the end of the nineteenth century. The history of the foundry business in this community dates back to the 1830s. Certainly local founders such as William Arms received a boost in the late 1840s, when many contracts related to the construction of the St. Lawrence and Atlantic Railway were tendered locally.[81] But it is useful to pick up this story in 1870, when two brothers Richard Smith (a founder) and Andrew Smith (an accountant) opened a firm specializing in tools and in machinery for sawmills and paper mills. Richard's many patented inventions, especially for paper-making machinery, attracted investors and enabled the firm to re-organize in 1872 as Smith-Elkins Manufacturing. In the 1880s, the company began production of industrial boilers and steam engines for the Quebec market. But financial difficulties and a fire brought a halt to the firm's activities in 1887. Its assets were acquired by Sylvester B. Jenckes, a local machinist who had been in business since 1850, producing mechanical saws and other sawmill equipment, boilers for pulp mills, and mining machinery. The business of the Jenckes Machine Company was stimulated by mining and industrial development in the region and, particularly, by the discovery of asbestos in nearby Thetford and Coleraine townships in 1877.[82] With expanding product lines, markets that now extended across Canada, and new factory buildings located near the railway tracks rather than the rivers, Jenckes increased its workforce from 150 in 1892 to 250 in 1898.[83] Sherbrooke was also home to the repair shops of the Quebec Central Railway, which was built in the 1870s to link Sherbrooke with Quebec City and which ran directly through the asbestos region to the east.[84] Moreover, the city's concentration in mining machinery was accentuated in 1890, when Jenckes and several American partners established the Rand Drill Company. By the turn of the century, the company, specialized in the production of drills, compressors, and mining machinery, was employing some 75 workers.[85]

Common threads

Quebec City, Hull, Trois-Rivières, Valleyfield, and Sherbrooke: each of these communities had its own experience of the transition to industrial capitalism during the nineteenth century. And every major industry that emerged in these places – boots and shoes in Quebec, wood and paper products in Hull and Trois-Rivières, cotton textiles in Valleyfield, woollen textiles and industrial machinery in Sherbrooke – placed its own specific set of demands on the men, women, and children who made them run. But there are common threads running through many of these stories. Factories producing inexpensive shoes, wooden matches, paper bags, printed cotton fabric, and heavy tweeds all relied on a combination of machinery, turned at first by water power, and later by steam and electricity. They also relied on large pools of wage workers who could be induced to sell their labour power for very low wages indeed, particularly if they were women and children, as many were. Many of these workers were members of poor, French-Canadian families, displaced by demographic growth and structural change in the countryside, and looking for options other than the backbreaking work of clearing new land for agricultural "colonization" in remote regions or emigration to the mill towns of New England. And although the description does not necessarily fit the sawmills and paper mills of Hull and Trois-Rivières, much less Sherbrooke's machine shops of the 1890s, it is fair to say that a certain type of industrialization, which we can refer to as being based on a light-industry model, was extremely widespread in the towns of Quebec in the second half of the nineteenth century.

Saint-Hyacinthe, therefore, can offer an example of what families living in urban Quebec during the second half of the nineteenth century may have been experiencing. This is a town with an expanding manufacturing sector based on the kinds of labour-intensive industries that emerged in many other Quebec communities during this period: large-scale factories using a relatively unskilled (and inexpensive) workforce to mass produce such consumer goods as cloth, boots, shoes, socks, and underwear. As we have seen, Saint-Hyacinthe is a town that experienced demographic growth comparable to that of industrial centres such as Hull, Valleyfield, and Sherbrooke, as it drew hundreds of families to its tanneries, shoe factories, knit-goods mill, and other manufacturing establishments. But while Saint-Hyacinthe had much in common with other parts of urban Quebec, we must turn to its particular combination of capital, resources, technology, and social relations, if we are to understand the conditions in which its people struggled to reinvent their familial and reproductive lives in the latter part of the nineteenth century.

2 Genesis of an Industrial Town

The rise of industrial capitalism in the nineteenth century was accompanied by changes in all sectors of the Quebec economy. As industrial towns and cities grew, agriculture became more specialized, market oriented, and capital intensive. At the same time, modern networks of exchange and transportation emerged, and the range of services provided in such regional centres as Saint-Hyacinthe became wider and more complex. Shoe and textile factories, crowded working-class neighbourhoods, and wage dependency emerged in the context of the ever-evolving regional and local economies. It is useful, therefore, to spend some time thinking about agriculture, exchange, and services in Saint-Hyacinthe in the years after the arrival of steam locomotives in 1848. We then turn our attention to the manufacturing industries established in this community; to the ensuing reconfiguration of the local labour market; and to the particular pattern of constraints and opportunities experienced by the men, women, and children working in two key local industries: the production of leather footwear and of knit goods such as woollen socks and underwear.

AGRICULTURE, EXCHANGE, AND SERVICES

In the later nineteenth century, Saint-Hyacinthe stood at the centre of an agricultural region, one experiencing the important transformations of the day. During this period, trends in Saint-Hyacinthe county, in fact, mirrored developments in rural Quebec as a whole.

Although the total area under cultivation did not increase between 1861 and 1901 – perhaps it had reached its limits by 1861 – the size of the average farm increased perceptibly (from 36.8 to 40.1 hectares), while the total number of farms in the county decreased by some 16%.[1] The shift away from wheat toward other crops, especially animal feeds such as oats and hay, was dramatic. At the turn of the twentieth century, farmers in the county were devoting about 70% less land to wheat production than they had in 1861. Moreover, levels of hay and oats production, measured on this basis, were 24% and 45%, respectively, above provincial averages.[2]

The increased presence of hay and oats in local fields was linked to another trend in both Quebec and Saint-Hyacinthe agriculture during this period: the new importance of livestock and, particularly, of dairy cattle. The rise of dairy production signals the specialization and commercialization of Quebec agriculture in this period, as farmers increasingly produced for sale rather than subsistence and geared their production to specific markets.[3] In Saint-Hyacinthe county, the average number of milk cows increased from 3.6 per farm in 1861 to 7.0 in 1901 (the provincial average was 5.0), while the emergence of the two commercial creameries and 14 cheese factories in operation in the county by the turn of the century dated from the 1870s. By 1901, the county's cheese factories, creameries, and domestic producers were turning out over one million pounds of butter and almost three million pounds of cheese per year – spectacular increases over the four hundred thousand pounds of domestic butter and the mere two thousand pounds of domestic cheese produced in 1861.[4]

As the urban population of Saint-Hyacinthe increased, moreover, so did local demand for the agricultural produce of the region. Farmers in surrounding parishes responded to the needs of thousands of city dwellers for meat, poultry, eggs, vegetables, fruit, and dairy products, as well as hay, firewood, and lumber. Much of this trade was channelled through an important local institution: the public market. As we shall see shortly, the history of Saint-Hyacinthe's public markets in the nineteenth century – two were in place for most of the period under study – was one of constant renovation and expansion, as municipal authorities attempted to keep up with the growing volume of local trade in the agricultural produce of the region.

Further evidence of concentration and specialization in the agricultural sector is provided by a Saint-Hyacinthe business directory, published in 1902.[5] In recent years, Saint-Hyacinthe has acquired a reputation as a centre for agri-business; it is, according to modern-day municipal boosters, le capital agro-alimentaire of Quebec. But already in 1902, Saint-Hyacinthe had begun to witness the emergence of large-scale, highly capitalized, specialized farming operations, and not only in the dairy sector. In the 1902 directory, an advertisement for the "St. Hyacinthe Poultry Farm" touted it as "the most extensive poultry farm in the province [with] six incubators and brooding house, having a capacity of 1,750 chickens; or a total of 6,000 a year." It went on to say that this operation, which also included "a piggery of thoroughbred stock, a dairy, and a catsup manufactory," covered an area of 29.1 acres.[6] This is less than the county average and therefore unremarkable, except for the fact that the farm was situated in an urban location, at the corner of Sainte-Héloise and Desprès streets in Saint-Hyacinthe's *Quartier* 5.

As we have already seen, Saint-Hyacinthe asserted its role as regional *entrepôt* in the later nineteenth century, channelling local goods – including eggs, poultry, and catsup – out to Montreal and other markets, and funnelling imported goods and other manufactures in, to town dwellers and farm families in the lower Yamaska region. As in every other North American region during this period, railway development was the key to the town's assumption of this role. In 1871, the town was served by one railway line, the Grand Trunk, which had absorbed the St. Lawrence and Atlantic in 1853. In the 1870s, as Ronald Rudin has shown, a group of municipal leaders managed to have Saint-Hyacinthe included in plans for a north-south line, running from the head of navigation on the Yamaska to Lake Champlain.[7] Two decades later, this time without any support from civic authorities, a third line was built through the town: the United Counties Railway, connecting Iberville to Sorel via Saint-Hyacinthe.[8] By 1902, the community was well linked by rail to the region, the province, and continent. It boasted three railway stations: the Grand Trunk station on Laframboise Street (Illustration 3), a short distance from the heart of the town; the Quebec Southern Railway, on Desaulniers Street in the newly developed *Quartier* 5; and the Canadian Pacific Railway station across the river in Saint-Joseph village.[9] More and more industrial producers counted on these rail lines for fast, reliable access to markets and raw materials. Local agents, moreover, peddled tickets for at least five railways – the CPR, the Grand Trunk, the Intercolonial, the Quebec Southern, and the Vermont Central – giving residents of Saint-Hyacinthe and its region who could afford to travel – or, as with migratory wage-labourers, who could not afford not to travel – access to destinations all across Canada and the United States.[10]

If railways provided the most important link between the lower Yamaska region and the wider world, Saint-Hyacinthe's public markets represented crucial links within the regional exchange network. First established in the 1820s, the town's central market moved to its permanent site – in the block bounded by Cascades, Saint-Simon, Saint-Antoine, and Saint-François streets – in 1830.[11] In order to cope with the growing volume of trade, the wooden building underwent an important expansion in 1836 and two further renovations in 1843 and 1852.[12] With the rapid demographic and institutional growth that followed the arrival of the railway, however, city authorities decided to move the original market building to a new site and to replace it in the centre of town with a larger, more impressive brick building. In 1856, the wooden market building was moved to a site in *Quartier* 1 that had been designated as a new market for hay, wood, and live animals. In the original market square, work was completed on the new *marché central* in October, 1856.[13]

In the 1850s, 1860s, and 1870s, business flourished at both the central market and the "haymarket," to the great satisfaction of the city council, which regulated and drew substantial revenues from these commercial institutions. The haymarket was, for a time, as busy as the central market, with trade focusing on hay; livestock; fuel, including coal, oil, cordwood, and peat; and construction materials, from sawn boards to brick, plaster, and lime. Expanding trade justified the construction of a new building in 1868. But as the century drew to a close, activity at the haymarket declined, and local residents began to regard it as a noisy, smelly nuisance and to exert pressure to have it shut down.[14]

For its part, the brick central market of 1856 thrived for two decades, until it was destroyed in the disastrous fire of 3 September 1876. The importance of this institution to local affairs is reflected in the alacrity with which it was rebuilt. Architects were hired four days after the fire; construction contracts were tendered two months later; and the new, two-storey brick building was occupied seven months later, in June 1877. Activity in the new, larger building soon picked up where it had left off, and the structure had to be expanded again in 1889.[15] By 1898, the building housed 42 butchers' stalls, two stalls for the sale of leather, one restaurant, and two other commercial spaces, in addition to the public hall and offices located on the second floor.[16] Most of the many market gardeners who came to town to sell fruit and vegetables, and the other traders who had no need for a butcher's bench, sold their wares directly from their wagons, arranged in a more or less orderly fashion by the market clerk on the streets surrounding the building (Illustration 4). A March 1897 list of prices reveals the range of products that could be obtained at the Saint-Hyacinthe market from dawn to dusk on any Tuesday, Thursday, or Saturday, and, as of 1893, on Friday evenings.[17] They included eight varieties of vegetables; six kinds of foul; meats such as beef, pork, and mutton; seven different cereals; fresh and salted butter; eggs; raw and spun wool; soap; honey; maple sugar; potatoes; tobacco; straw; hay; and hides.[18]

In the late nineteenth century, Saint-Hyacinthe's central market was the hub of a commercial district that stretched outwards from the market site between Saint-François and Saint-Simon streets, and along Cascades and Saint-Antoine streets in the lower town. Urban development and demographic growth meant increased demand for consumer products of all kinds, particularly as wage labour and the need to purchase, rather than produce, most essential goods became a way of life. The appearance of a wide range of increasingly specialized shops – many of them with premises on Cascades Street – must be seen in that context (Illustration 5). The presence of a local bourgeoisie with money to spend on such items as food, wine, clothes, and financial services was also part of the equation, as was the positioning of Saint-Hyacinthe within a transportation network that stimulated local demand for rooms, drinks, meals, and other services.

By comparing a local street and business directory from the 1850s with one from the turn of the century, it is possible to get an idea of the kinds of commercial and service establishments that emerged during this period of transition, and of their location in the town. The directories compiled in 1857 and 1902 have been examined in this way, with special attention paid to businesses of particular types.[19] A blunt comparison of the overall numbers gives the impression of minimal change in this 45-year interval. In 1857, 100 businesses were counted in the selected sectors, or one for every 37 local residents. At the end of the century, 240 such businesses were counted, or one for every 38 local residents. At first brush, then, rapid demographic growth, rather than economic structural change, would seem to account sufficiently for the expansion of small commercial and service businesses during this period. In 1857, furthermore, these establishments were already concentrated on the four streets branching out from the market square. That is, two-thirds of the businesses identified for 1857 were situated on Cascades, Saint-Simon, Saint-François, and Saint-Antoine streets. By 1902, this proportion had declined only slightly (from 66% to 63%), reflecting the continued importance of the city's commercial core, as well as the appearance not only of new poles of activity around the railway stations but also of small shops – especially grocery stores – in neighbourhoods throughout the expanding town.[20]

A closer look at the types of businesses listed in these directories, however, provides a better idea of the kinds of changes occurring in the local economy. Food stores are an instructive example. In 1857, only two establishments were listed as dealing exclusively in "groceries," and only 20 – one for every 185 residents – sold some category of food or drink. Most people who sold groceries combined this trade with other pursuits, in general stores and other kinds of establishments. François Cadoret, for example, was a trader dealing in "dry goods, hardware, groceries, produce, etc." at the corner of Cascades and Saint-François streets on the market square.[21] More unexpected, perhaps, are the examples of Jean-Baptiste Laurence, identified as a "grocer and joiner" living at the corner of Saint-Antoine and Concorde streets; and André Sinotte, a "grocer and shoemaker" living at Sainte-Anne and Saint-Antoine streets, a block west of the market.[22]

By 1902, this picture had changed considerably. The number of general stores in Saint-Hyacinthe had actually declined, from 28 in 1857 to 18 in 1902, despite the substantial increase in population. Conversely, the number of more specialized dealers in food and drink had risen from 20 to 94 (one per 98 residents).[23] The presence of some 27 grocery stores, only seven of which were located in the commercial core, suggests the new importance of the neighbourhood corner store in this community.[24] There were 38 butchers, compared to only four in the 1850s; most occupied stalls in the central market, with some declaring residential addresses outside the city, in parishes such as Saint-Simon, Sainte-Madeleine, and Sainte-Rosalie. Fewer bakeries were in evidence per capita than in 1857, suggesting perhaps a larger scale of bread production in a smaller number of concerns. But more stores specialized in confections and candies, sometimes in combination with fruits, tobacco, or other products.[25] Moreover, there were merchants listed who dealt in far more specialized product lines than any mentioned in the 1857 directory. W.H. Meldrum and A.F. Duclos, for example, were egg exporters with premises at the corner of Saint-Antoine and Mondor; Joseph Maranda dealt in poultry, butter, and cheese from a space in the central market; and Charles Peloquin was an "apiarist [and] fruit and vegetable canner" who sold honey and preserves, also in the central market.[26]

After food and drinks, clothing was the most important category of goods exchanged in Saint-Hyacinthe's shops. Here again, trends in the number of shops may be deceptive. In 1857, 18 tailors, dressmakers, hatters, milliners, and the like were listed in the local directory. By 1902, this number had reached 35: barely doubling in a period in which population had increased by a factor of 2.5. What was the reason for this? In a period during which more and more people worked for wages, it seems unlikely that local families would have become less dependent on exchange networks for such basic needs.[27] Moreover, although the directories alone do not substantiate it, most of the businesses identified for 1857 would have been small concerns dealing in custom-tailored clothing. These shops had not disappeared by 1902. Instead, larger concerns could be found alongside them, selling ready-made clothes at prices within the range of working-class budgets. Thus, while only one "merchant tailor" is identified among all the shops in this sector in 1857, that number had risen to six by 1902. One of them, M.O. David & Co., advertised itself as "merchant tailors and [dealers in] ready-made clothing," with premises on Saint-Simon Street.[28] It would be surprising, indeed, if at least some of the other merchant tailors listed in 1902 were not also doing a volume business in mass-produced garments.

The definition of essential goods in this community must certainly include fuel and construction materials: the raw materials of winter survival and year-round shelter. In 1857, some Saint-Hyacinthe residents may have been able to supply their needs for firewood, lumber, and the like by using informal economic networks, without recourse to local merchants. Others would have done business with the farmers and traders who dealt in exactly these kinds of supplies at the newly established haymarket in *Quartier* 1. In effect, only one cordwood dealer was listed in the Saint-Hyacinthe directory for 1857 – Jean-Baptiste Bouchard, at the corner of Cascades and Concord streets – and not a single dealer in sawn lumber of any description. By 1902, however, Saint-Hyacinthe residents could buy firewood from seven different dealers, coal from three, and sawn lumber from five. Merchants sold these products in various combinations. Clément Rouleau & fils, with extensive premises on Laframboise Street near the Grand Trunk station, sold "coal and wood, wholesale and retail"; one can speculate that the railway was among their important clients. Léon Palardy sold lumber and firewood on Saint-Antoine Street. And several local merchants eschewed the sale of cordwood in favour of more fully manufactured wood products, such as boards, shingles, door and window frames, mouldings, and furniture. Isidore Laporte, for example, advertised as a "commerçant de bois de sciage de toutes sortes, lattes, clapboard, porteaux, piquets, etc. Spécialité: charpente et bardeaux."[29] The appearance of such a substantial number of new businesses in this sector of the local economy surely reflects the incapacity of older structures (essentially, informal networks and the haymarket) to meet the needs of this growing community for fuel and building materials. For in addition to building homes and keeping them warm in the winter, these entrepreneurs began to participate in a wider range of activities. These included building and heating churches, schools, factories, and other institutions; and supplying fuel to railway locomotives and the fixed steam engines that now dotted the industrial landscape.

Other kinds of specialized shops made their appearance in this community during the last decades of the nineteenth century. In the context of rising literacy levels, for example, two booksellers and two newspaper agents were open for business by 1902, where none had been in evidence in 1857. Three of these four shops were located on Cascades Street, the main commercial artery. In the area of personal services, 11 barbers were listed in 1902, as opposed to just one, 45 years earlier. Moreover, whereas in 1857, such laundry services as may have been available were not listed in the street directory – neither, surprisingly, was a single washerwoman or *blanchisseuse* listed in the 1861 census – by 1902, Saint-Hyacinthe had two steam laundries and two "Chinese laundries," all in the commercial core. The appearance of such establishments suggests the commercialization of certain kinds of domestic work, particularly for bourgeois families who could afford to have their clothes washed by others.[30]

Service-related establishments, such as hotels, boardinghouses, and restaurants, also increased in number during the later nineteenth century, although their rate of growth did not outstrip that of the local population. Whereas the 1857 directory listed 12 hotels, four boardinghouses, and one saloon, the 1902 directory mentioned 17 hotels, nine boardinghouses, and two restaurants, many located in the area around the central market, with secondary concentrations in the neighbourhoods of the three railway stations.[31] Nor did the number of workers in the communications and transportation sector increase, when measured on a per capita basis, although certain qualitative changes in this area do merit attention. In 1857, the Saint-Hyacinthe directory listed seven carters and three Grand Trunk Railway workers. By 1902, this sector was much more diversified – with six carters, six railway employees, three telegraph agents, and the local manager of the Bell Telephone company.[32]

More striking, finally, were the quantitative changes in the financial services sector. In 1857, Saint-Hyacinthe's residents included four insurance agents, acting on behalf of five different companies; however, no local bank, or branch of any other bank, was in place. Forty-five years later, the town had 10 insurance agents, some of whom, such as D.S. Bray, represented a single company (in his case, Metropolitan Life of New York), while others, such as F. Bartels and George Henshaw, represented as many as 10 or 11. Henshaw's clients had access to policies issued by a range of British, American, and Canadian firms, including Atlas, Confederation Life, Lloyd's, London

Guarantee and Accident, Maritime of Liverpool, Thames and Mersey, and the Travellers Company of Hartford Connecticut. Unlike retail stores, insurance agents did not tend to cluster along the town's four main commercial streets. Instead, many did business from statelier premises in the upper town, or on Saint-Denis Street – a short spur, climbing from the market square to Girouard Street, that was also home to the town's two telegraph offices. In addition to its many insurance agents, Saint-Hyacinthe by 1902 could also lay claim to a local bank, the Banque de Saint-Hyacinthe, with offices on Cascades Street. Established in 1874, this bank, over the subsequent 35 years, served in part to channel local and regional savings into industrial development projects.[33] By 1902, Saint-Hyacinthe also had branches of the Banque Nationale (also on Cascades) and of the Eastern Townships Bank, located on Girouard Street in the upper town.[34]

Even from this quick comparison, it is fair to conclude that the range of goods and services available for sale in Saint-Hyacinthe increased dramatically in the 45 years between 1857 and 1902. The period witnessed an absolute decline in the local presence of that least specialized of mercantile establishments: the general store. Indeed, when measured on a per capita basis, there were substantially more grocery stores, butchers, confectioners, fuel and building supply dealers, laundries, barbers, booksellers, banks, and insurance agents in town at the turn of the century than had been present during the 1850s. Expansion also occurred in other sectors – clothing dealers, hotels, and boardinghouses, for example – which, when measured in terms of number of establishments, did not seem to outstrip demographic growth. But this growth was nonetheless substantial and may have accompanied the other economic phenomena, such as an increase in the scale of operations in certain businesses – larger hotels, bigger stores dealing in ready-made clothing, for example – that were occurring during this period but could not be detected using this method. All these observations point to the same conclusion. Saint-Hyacinthe was at a phase in its transition to industrial capitalism during which more and more people were relying on its growing network of increasingly specialized commercial and service establishments to fulfil their many needs – for everything from food and drink, through new clothes and clean laundry, to firewood and building materials.

THE RISE OF INDUSTRY

As we saw in the previous chapter, Saint-Hyacinthe's population grew rapidly in the second half of the nineteenth century. Particularly from the 1870s on, the town was able not only to retain its locally born population but to attract migrants from the countryside. The reason was simple. By mid-century, Saint-Hyacinthe's bourgeoisie had begun to hitch its wagon to the rising star of industrial capitalism. By the last quarter of the century, the town was no longer simply a regional *entrepôt*. It was an important industrial centre whose factories attracted – and created – a burgeoning population of wage-labouring families.

The transition, however, did not occur overnight. In the 1850s, a decade of commercial and institutional expansion, manufacturing in Saint-Hyacinthe remained broadly pre-industrial in character. Artisans working in small shops with leather, wood, stone, and iron produced a wide range of goods for the regional farming population, much as they had done since the early days of the village. The *Canada Directory* of 1851 lists 29 such artisans, including two iron founders and four blacksmiths. Metal workers were particularly important, as the presence of an axe factory suggests. Surprisingly, in a town that would later be dominated by the leather trades, no shoemakers were listed in the 1851 directory.[35]

Seven years later, a new edition of the *Canada Directory* described the town's manufacturing concerns in the following way: "Saint-Hyacinthe contains a fine stone and brick grist mill, the property of the Hon. L.A. Dessaulles and S. Monk Esq.; a sawmill, with turning and planing machines, the property of Messrs. Nagle; carding mills, foundries, an organ-building establishment, tanneries; and many extensive manufactories of various kinds."[36] The gristmill mentioned here was the descendant of the seigneurial mill that had been in operation at the rapids since the 1770s. The carding mills had been present in 1851 (two wool-carders are mentioned in the directory for that year). The foundries and tanneries were there as well, again on the basis of the 1851 directory. The Casavant organ manufactory, established late in the 1840s, was missed in 1851, no doubt because it was located just outside the town limits. Whether the Nagle sawing and planing mill predates 1850 as well is unclear.

In the 1850s, Saint-Hyacinthe's manufacturing sector expanded along traditional lines. Artisans' shops and a few larger enterprises continued to provide the region's rural population with goods made from iron, wood, and leather, and with milling services for their grain. No major injections of capital or technology occurred, and there was little development that can properly be called "industrial." The largest shops in existence at the start of the 1860s were those associated with metallurgy.[37] Most of these probably employed no more than five or 10 workers using traditional methods. In Saint-

Hyacinthe as in other parts of North America, elements of the craft system persisted in this industry until a much later date.[38]

One can be quite precise about the development of Saint-Hyacinthe's manufacturing sector in the 1860s, thanks mainly to the availability of the industrial census for 1871. A detailed look at that document provides, as well, a base from which to examine the much more significant industrialization of the ensuing 30 years (see Table 2-1). The census takers found 95 "industrial establishments" in Saint-Hyacinthe in 1871.[39] All but a handful were artisan's shops employing less than 10, and in most cases less than five, hands. Over three-quarters of the establishments were located in the first census division, which was comprised of *Quartiers* 3 and 4 and which included the town's main water-power site.[40]

Several important manufacturing concerns were established in the years just prior to the 1871 census. Prominent among these was the foundry established by Augustin Chagnon in 1870. In 1871, Chagnon employed 20 men, more than any other local metal goods producer. His shop was unique in Saint-Hyacinthe in that it was organized on the principle of the "industrial village." Located in a rural setting on the northwestern outskirts of town, Chagnon's complex included not just the metal shops but also residential buildings for his employees and their families.[41] An 1875 Saint-Hyacinthe directory described the operation as follows: "des forges, des fonderies, une fabrique de bouilloires et d'engins, des ateliers pour tourner le fer pour les patrons, soier et blanchir le bois etc. ... On y fabrique enfin le plus vulgaire ustensile de cuisine jusqu'à l'engin le plus compliqué et le plus puissant."[42]

The most important industrial concern to appear in the 1860s, however, was the boot-and-shoe factory established by Louis and Victor Côté, in 1865 (Illustration 7). Victor Côté, a leather merchant, began commercial operations in Saint-Hyacinthe in the 1850s.[43] Louis Côté, an inventor of shoe-manufacturing machinery, was to become one of the town's most prominent industrial capitalists, as well as its mayor for several years in the 1880s.[44] The factory the Côtés started in 1865 had a long life in the community – surviving the 1876 fire, Victor's departure in 1877, economic downturns in the 1870s and 1890s, and several moments of internal restructuring. In 1871, in its location at the corner of Cascade and Piété streets, it was described as a "wholesale manufacturer of all descriptions of boots and shoes."[45] Its labour force consisted of 43 men, 22 boys (less than 16 years old), and 24 girls.[46] With fixed and variable capital valued at over $80,000, production of over 75,000 pairs of boots and shoes each year, and wages of over $20,000 (an average weekly wage of $4.38

Table 2-1

Industrial Establishments in Saint-Hyacinthe, 1871: Number of Shops, Number of Workers, and Average Number of Workers Per Shop, by Productive Sector

Sector	A Shops	B Workers	B/A Workers per Shop	Percentage of Workers in Shops of Five or Less
Leather	14	136	9.7[a]	24
Metals	11	66	6.6	35
Clothing	15	54	3.6	89
Food & drink	19	41	2.2	100
Transportation equipment	5	23	4.6	35
Printing	2	23	11.5	0
Textiles	5	22	4.4	55
Wood	10	21	2.1	100
Construction	3	14	4.7	50
Other	11	45	4.1[b]	36
Total	95	445	4.7	47

Source NA, Manuscript census, 1871, Saint-Hyacinthe, divisions 1 and 2, schedule 6, "Industrial Establishments"

Notes

[a] Includes Côte shoe factory. Average number of workers would be 3.6 were this establishment excluded.

[b] Includes Ouvroir Sainte-Geneviève, which produced woollen cloth and soap (see Illustraton 10). Ignoring this establishment gives an average number of workers of 1.6.

for employees of all categories), it was easily the largest industrial enterprise in Saint-Hyacinthe at the beginning of the 1870s.

Five concerns, besides the Chagnon foundry and the Côté shoe factory, employed 10 or more workers in Saint-Hyacinthe in 1871.[47] Isaïe Fréchette's iron foundry, also apparently new to the community, employed 15 men and two boys in 1871. The industrial census describes the shop as a *boutique de machinerie* specializing in *instruments d'agriculture*. But Jacques Ferland has pointed out the close ties between Fréchette and Louis Côté in the patenting, and probably in the manufacture, of shoe-manufacturing equipment.[48] Ferland's hypothesis – that Fréchette was engaged in the design and manufacture of this type of machinery for local producers and the Canadian and export markets – is supported by the description of the shop contained in the local directory for 1875: "une usine considérable ...; ils fabriquent surtout des machines pour moulins, notamment des moulins à bardeaux supérieurs à tout autre, leur outillage est des plus complet [sic] et ils peuvent entreprendre n'importe quelle espèce de machinerie."[49]

Another relatively large-scale concern was the steam-powered printing shop operated by Camille Lussier, editor and publisher of *Le Courrier de Saint-Hyacinthe*. Here, nine men, two women, and six boys operated the presses on which not only the newspaper but also a good deal of the city's intellectual production were printed.[50] Similar in scale, though surely not in its level of mechanization, was Joseph Larivière's carriage-making shop which employed 13 men and two boys in 1871. This was the largest of five such shops in the city, establishments which, according to the author of the 1875 directory, were in a position to furnish "n'importe quel genre de voiture depuis la charette la plus simple jusqu'au carosse le plus élégant."[51]

Victor Côté and Georges-Casimir Dessaulles were local capitalists with diversified manufacturing interests. In addition to his partnership with Louis Côté (often identified, incorrectly, as his brother), Victor Côté was the proprietor of six establishments, employing over 20 workers. Most of his employees were men engaged in leather production: Côté ran small shoemaking and saddlery shops as well as a steam-driven tannery. But three men and two women also worked in his flour, carding, and fulling mills.

The principal owner of milling equipment in town, however, was Georges-Casimir Dessaulles (Illustration 9). Dessaulles had inherited a quarter of the seigneurie of Saint-Hyacinthe in a *partage* made by his mother in 1852.[52] One of Saint-Hyacinthe's leading industrialists, he was elected mayor in 1868 and would retain the post through much of the later nineteenth century. In 1871 he owned three water-powered mills (flour, carding, and fulling), all of which were located at the site of the *moulin banal*. By far the most valuable of the four establishments was the former seigneurial gristmill, which was worth $35,000 in 1871. Dessaulles employed seven men, two women, one boy, and two girls in the three mills, in addition to the five men and five women who worked in the woollens manufactory. Average weekly wages (for all categories of worker) were $3.73 in the flour, carding, and fulling mills, and $4.61 in the woollens operation (this discrepancy is explained by the absence of children in the latter shop).[53]

One further establishment employed over 10 workers in Saint-Hyacinthe in 1871. Run by the Grey Nuns of the Hôtel-Dieu, the Ouvroir Sainte-Geneviève had 10 women, 15 girls, one man, and three boys working in the production of woollen fabric and soap in 1871 (Illustration 10). The *ouvroir* had been founded in April of 1864 "dans le but de procurer aux femmes pauvres de l'ouvrage quand elles n'en trouvent pas au dehors."[54] The women's wages were extremely low and were obviously insufficient to provide a livelihood outside the institution. Total annual wages paid at the beginning of the 1870s were $600, or 40 cents per week per worker.

It is misleading, of course, to treat the *ouvroir* as a purely industrial establishment. Although it did have a productive function, it was mainly a social institution designed to provide shelter for needy women, while simultaneously reinforcing certain moral principles, including the value of work. But by the mid 1880s, it had developed another function, similar to that of the *salles d'asile* in Montreal.[55] The *ouvroir* was described in a local 1886 directory as an institution "where are admitted aged women who, having no home, are still able to work; where are also received, during the day, the infant children of poor women who are obliged to leave their homes and do work outside."[56] Although this "daycare" function may simply have been overlooked by authors of earlier accounts, it may well have developed in the period after 1870, as part of the institutional response to new conditions created by industrial capitalism.

In 1871, then, the level of industrial activity in Saint-Hyacinthe was moderate. A handful of establishments employed 10 or more workers and only one, the Côté shoe factory, employed over 50. In virtually every sector, most manufacturing concerns were organized as small shops, along broadly artisanal lines. Indeed, 82 of the 95 "industrial establishments" listed in the 1871 census employed five workers or less. Under half of the town's manufacturing workers (47%) worked in these smaller shops – a reflection of the presence, in specific sectors, of a number of medium-sized concerns and one large firm. Nevertheless, such activities as clothing production, baking, butchering, brewing, furniture making, cooperage, blacksmithing, and saddlery maintained both their importance in the local economy and their artisanal character.[57]

Given the absence of further industrial censuses, it is difficult to be as exact about manufacturing establishments in Saint-Hyacinthe at dates other than 1871. Yet it was in the last three decades of the nineteenth century that the town's industrial vocation really emerged. During this period, according to one estimate, the number of local industrial workers increased by a factor of six, from about 300 in 1871 to over 1,800 in 1901.[58] Some of this increase stemmed from expansion in industrial sectors in which the town already had a presence: leather, metallurgy, woollen textiles, and the clothing industry. But attempts by the local bourgeoisie to attract investment, particularly in new branches of textile production, proved important as well. Certain projects, such as the proposal in 1872 to establish a silk ribbon manufactory using French capital and technology, were outright failures.[59] But others, such as the knit-goods factory that was established in 1881, became permanent fixtures in a town whose citizens were increasingly dependent for survival on wages derived from industrial work.

Industrial development in Saint-Hyacinthe was promoted by a local elite that equated the town's interests with the expansion of manufacturing activity, organized along capitalist lines.[60] Rudin has shown the extent to which municipal boosterism prevailed in the 1870s and 1880s, both in the thinking of the local bourgeoisie and the actions of the municipal council. After 1870, city council encouraged industrialists through a policy of long-term tax exemptions and, increasingly in the 1880s and 1890s, municipal bonuses.[61] In the 1870s, as we have already seen, the population of Saint-Hyacinthe increased by over 40%. This growth was related to a wave of industrial development that attracted workers, and thus generated positive migratory balances. The decade was not all of a piece, however. Economic expansion in the early 1870s gave way to a serious recession as the decade drew to a close.

In his personalized, highly opinionated history of Saint-Hyacinthe, C.-P. Choquette characterized the early 1870s as a period of "fiévreuse activité industrielle."[62] Other sources reinforce this impression. The Chagnon foundry, established in 1870, was paying $10,400 in wages to its 30 employees by 1873, and was producing $40,000 worth of iron products each year.[63] In 1873, the Dessaulles woollens mill was reorganized as "La Compagnie Manufacturière de Saint-Hyacinthe." Backed by such prominent local business people as Dessaulles, Victor Côté, Romuald Saint-Jacques, Augustin Papineau, and Joseph Barsalou, the mill – sometimes referred to as "la manufacture d'étoffe" – expanded its workforce from 12 in 1873 to 150 in 1882.[64]

Incentives offered by city council had a role in the growth of the early 1870s. In 1874, 10-year tax exemptions were granted to one established firm (the Chagnon foundry) and two new ones: the tannery opened by Silas Duclos and Paul T. Payan on William Street, and the McMartin-Hamel shoe company.[65] The Duclos-Payan tannery was to become a fixture in the town.[66] But the McMartin-Hamel shoe factory failed in 1875, despite the receipt of a $2,000 municipal bonus, in addition to the tax holiday, to cover the cost of its move from Montreal.[67] Still in the leather industries, it is worth stressing the growth of the Côté shoe factory during the 1870s. Without any form of municipal subsidy, this factory expanded from 89 workers in 1871 to almost 200 by 1883.[68]

The second half of the 1870s, however, was a period of economic difficulty in Saint-Hyacinthe, as in the rest of Quebec. The years from

1873 to 1879 saw the most serious economic crisis of the later nineteenth century, and Saint-Hyacinthe's nascent industrial sector was anything but immune to the macroeconomic forces underlying this recession.[69] Local factors exacerbated the situation as well. Jean Francoeur has stressed the atmosphere of frequent catastrophes which, in his view, slowed industrial development during this period.[70] The Chagnon foundry, for example, burned in August of 1875, as did the Larivière carriage-making shop in November of 1876. Much more disastrous was the major fire that consumed three-quarters of the lower town on 3 September 1876, taking with it the shoe factory and tannery run by the Côté family, and the sawmill run by Ignace Gosselin, not to mention the 600 or so residences also consumed in the blaze (see Illustration 12).[71]

Industry fared poorly in this context of international recession and local disaster. As already noted, the McMartin-Hamel shoe factory failed in 1875, as did its locally controlled successor some years later. Victor Côté's tannery was not rebuilt after the 1876 fire. Camille Lussier's *Courrier de Saint-Hyacinthe* failed by the end of the decade and its assets were sold to Pierre Boucher de la Bruère. Choquette characterizes the period as one of *malaise*, during which local manufacturing industries languished and capitalists awaited the outcome of the 1878 federal election, which would determine tariff levels. By the end of the decade, the only industrial enterprises in regular operation were the Côté shoe factory; the Duclos-Payan tannery; the L.P. Morin woodworking shop, set up in the boom of the early 1870s; and the Casavant organ manufactory on the northeastern edge of town.[72]

But if the pace of industrial development in the 1870s was halting, the same cannot be said of the 1880s. During this decade, a number of factors, including an expanding national economy and a proactive municipal council, helped local manufacturers to nearly double their annual output.[73] In the local economy, as on the national level, the period was one of consolidation and concentration. The total number of manufacturing establishments did not increase appreciably in the decade (from 114 to 116), although the number of large-scale concerns certainly did. So did the size of the industrial work force. In the 1880s, as two major factories saw the light of day, at least 600 industrial jobs were created. And the average number of workers in each shop rose from seven in 1881 to over 12 in 1891.[74]

Municipal council used tax revenues to help finance this wave of expansion. Debates over the desirability of industrial bonuses – as mayor, shoe manufacturer Louis Côté had been a fierce opponent – had been resolved by 1881, the year in which $12,000 was granted to the American-based Abel Hosiery Company to establish a knit-goods factory in the town. This firm used a type of mechanized knitting frame invented by its founder to turn out "webbed goods, such as gloves, mittens, stockings, shirts, and drawers."[75] The company had difficulties in Saint-Hyacinthe in its early years. The early 1880s witnessed the accidental death of Mr Abel and two failed attempts to secure additional bonuses from the local government. In 1885, according to Rudin, "the firm faltered and had to be reorganized as the Granite Mills."[76] But by 1886, *le tricot*, as the mill was known locally, was in full production, employing some 300 hands in the manufacture of socks and underwear (Illustration 13).[77] City council granted four more bonuses to industrialists during the 1880s. Three of these went to firms that failed soon afterwards.[78] But a $14,000 bonus granted in 1883 led to the arrival in Saint-Hyacinthe of the Séguin-Lalime shoe factory, formerly of Saint-Jean, and its installation on the industrial waterfront site formerly occupied by the McMartin-Hamel concern. Like the Granite Mills, this company was employing some 300 workers by the end of the decade.[79]

Local directories and guides written in the 1880s emphasized the increasingly industrial character of the town, sometimes in colourful terms, but usually with a "boosterist" agenda. The following description comes from a street directory published in 1887:

Pas moins de douze établissements importants fournissent de l'ouvrage à plus de 1,500 employés de tout âge et des deux sexes à des prix rémunérateurs – aussi est-il intéressant de voir ces essaims d'industriels se diriger vers leurs usines, ou en revenir, à certaines heures du jour. Il faut aussi tenir compte des nombreuses industries moins considérables qui emploient un bon contingent de travailleurs.

Nos magnifiques et puissants pouvoirs d'eau ... fournissent la force motrice à pas moins de douze industries et la vapeur fait le reste. C'est à dire que plus de vingt-cinq engins fonctionnent journellement et souvent la nuit pour permettre de répondre à toutes les commandes.[80]

A more elaborate guide published in 1886 mentions the town's chief manufacturing concerns, in addition to providing engravings of most of them. The establishments listed are the two shoe factories, operated by the Côté family and Séguin-Lalime; the Granite Mills knit-goods factory, managed by the brothers Ferdinand and Maurice Boas; the woollens mill run by la Compagnie Manufacturière de Saint-Hyacinthe; five metallurgical shops; three door-and-sash manufactories; six carriage shops; two organ builders; two printers shops; a furniture factory; and the Duclos and Payan tannery.[81]

Saint-Hyacinthe's industrial expansion in the 1880s, then, was substantial. And the early 1890s were years of still more significant growth, even though the national economy was in recession. But in the last five years of the century, it became apparent that local manufacturers, boosted by municipal subsidies, had overextended themselves. After 1895, as Rudin suggests, "while the rest of the nation was experiencing recovery ... Saint-Hyacinthe industries were forced to cut back on their payrolls in order to survive."[82]

The boom of the early nineties was assisted by the continued largesse of municipal authorities. Bonuses were used both to attract new concerns and to allow existing ones to expand. The main example of the first case involved the Eastern Townships Corset Company (Illustration 14), which was lured away from Sherbrooke in 1891 with the offer of a $15,000 subsidy.[83] Its labour force was estimated at 150 to 200 in 1894.[84] More money was spent expanding established concerns, however, than on attracting new concerns. Particularly significant was a $60,000 bonus, granted to the Boas brothers in 1894, to increase the workforce at the Granite Mills from 300 to 800. The character and extent of the renovations undertaken with that money are described in a guide published in 1894: "Le Granite Mills fait d'immenses travaux au pouvoir d'eau, et est à installer des turbines qui donneront mille forces de pouvoir. De vastes usines sont à construire et les affaires de cette importante maison qui a absorbé la compagnie manufacturière seront triplés aussitôt que les constructions seront terminées."[85] Two other concerns, both shoe factories, took advantage of municipal bonuses to expand their operations in the early 1890s. Aided by a subsidy of $15,000, Séguin-Lalime "ont construit un immense établissement sur la rue Cascade, dans lequel ils espèrent doubler sinon tripler leurs opérations" (Illustration 15).[86] In fact, this company was able to expand its workforce from 300 to 500 hands.[87] Another bonus, of $3,750, allowed the slumping Côté shoe factory to expand appreciably between 1890 and 1894 and to increase its workforce from 130 to 200.[88]

Saint-Hyacinthe's manufacturing sector grew considerably in the first half of the 1890s. But many local producers began to experience difficulties by the middle of the decade. Séguin-Lalime, for example, was already in trouble by 1895. Over the next six years, it reduced its payroll to 200, only to close completely in 1902. By the late 1890s the Boas brothers, as well, were struggling. Their response was similar: sweeping layoffs in the years leading up to 1899, when the Granite Mills was finally shut down. Although it managed to remain open, the Côté shoe factory slashed its payroll in the later 1890s, and was still in trouble at the turn of the century.[89] Clearly, Saint-Hyacinthe's industrialists, and especially its industrial workers, were faring badly by the late 1890s. The local conjuncture was one of wholesale layoffs and important plant closings, even as the national economy entered the expansive period of the Laurier boom. In the final years of the century, population growth skidded to a halt. Drawn by opportunities for wage labour in industry, new arrivals had helped swell the local population by 44% between 1890 and 1898. But the local recession reversed the trend dramatically and saw the town lose 13% of its population between 1899 and 1902.[90]

In the early years of the twentieth century, Saint-Hyacinthe's bourgeoisie struggled to restore the boom conditions of the 1880s and early 1890s. The local government continued to use its taxing power to bolster manufacturing industries. But it could do little more than re-establish some of the major firms of the 1890s on a more modest footing. In 1899, for example, city council served as a major player in the sale of the Granite knitting mills to an American-based syndicate called "Canadian Woollen Mills." In exchange for the promise to pay $150,000 in wages each year, the local government offered this prospective buyer attractive terms on the repayment of the $60,000 owed by the Granite Mills to the municipality. The deal was made and the factory reopened in 1900. Absorbed by Penmans of Canada in 1903, it employed about 600 workers in the years leading up to World War I.[91]

The municipal government also played a role in the reopening of the former Séguin-Lalime shoe factory. The city had taken possession of the company's assets because of an outstanding $15,000 debt. To keep the factory running, council made an attractive offer to the Ames-Holden shoe company of Montreal. In 1903, Ames-Holden was essentially given the Séguin-Lalime property on Cascades Street (worth $50,000) plus a bonus of $8,000 and a 10-year tax exemption. In exchange, the company was required to pay $400,000 in wages over the ensuing 10 years. By 1913, the factory was operating at, or near, former levels: 455 workers were earning $200,000 per year in wages.[92]

On the whole, then, the initial years of the twentieth century were a time of modest recovery and stabilization. Civic authorities made repeated attempts to attract new industries to the community. But only one new firm of any significance – an organ company that employed 20 hands in 1914 – was established. Attempts to breathe new life into existing industrial facilities were more successful. In addition to the two major initiatives just discussed, the municipality granted $30,000 in bonuses to the Côté shoe factory and $15,000 to the Paquet-Godbout door-and-sash firm in the early 1900s. By 1913, these two companies together employed about 450 workers.[93]

A CHANGING LABOUR MARKET

The rise of industry in the later nineteenth century represented a profound and permanent transformation. The arrival of large, mechanized factories run along capitalist lines had a major impact on the labour market in this community and, inevitably, on social relations. From here on in, a majority of families would depend on wages for survival – an unstable economic relationship that would shape many other aspects of their lives.[94] But for a small minority, industrial capitalism meant new opportunities to accumulate wealth, and to spend it in ways that were increasingly specific to a privileged class.

To better understand the social changes that accompanied industrial development in Saint-Hyacinthe, it is helpful to compare the occupations of people living in the town in 1861 with those of people living in the same geographic area – the original four *quartiers* of Saint-Hyacinthe – in 1891.[95] Such an analysis (see Table 2-2) reveals that Saint-Hyacinthe's paid labour force was more predominantly young, unmarried, and female in 1891 than it had been in 1861.[96] These trends reflect the demand within Saint-Hyacinthe's major industries – particularly those in the clothing and textile sectors – for young, single women as wage labourers. In the manufacturing sector, the increased presence of women was felt especially strongly. In 1861, only six women were employed in this sector for every 100 men; by 1891, this ratio had risen to 34 per 100.

While it is clear that the number of women in the waged labour force had increased, much of the industrial development in this period occurred in leather-related industries, where the labour force was mostly male. By 1891, leather workers easily constituted the largest fragment of the local industrial sector, employing almost half (47%) of all manual workers engaged in manufacturing. More specifically, in 1861, four years prior to the arrival of the first boot-and-shoe factory, the leather trades were entirely dominated by men. By 1891, the sector had expanded dramatically, going from 46 to 510 workers. Although almost 100 women were now working in the industry, 82% of the manual workers involved in leather production mentioned in the 1891 census were still men. As this discussion shows, Saint-Hyacinthe's labour force between 1861 and 1891 was strongly differentiated by gender. It is therefore appropriate to think in terms of specifically male and female segments of the labour market. Each of these segments was profoundly affected by the industrial transition of the later nineteenth century. Though closely intertwined, they can best be examined separately.

Some 800 men living in Saint-Hyacinthe households declared occupations in 1861. Thirty years later, over 1,500 male residents of

Table 2-2
Occupational Structure: Saint-Hyacinthe, 1861 and 1891[a]

	1861			1891		
	N	%	Sex Ratio[b]	N	%	Sex Ratio
AGRICULTURE	3	0.3	0	26	1.3	0
MANUAL WORKERS IN URBAN TRADES	497	55.5	26	1,328	67.1	42
Production	340	37.9	6	1,075	54.3	34
Transportation	35	3.9	0	67	3.4	0
Services	118	13.2	228	174	8.8	222
Other	3	0.3	0	8	0.4	0
LABOURERS	169	18.9	0	132	6.7	0
NON-MANUAL	227	25.3	8	493	24.9	20
Professions	30	3.3	0	35	1.8	0
Commerce	101	11.3	6	227	11.5	14
Manufactures	1	0.1	0	18	0.9	0
Services	39	4.4	22	82	4.1	32
Status declaration	56	6.3	6	110	5.6	38
Other	0	–	0	21	1.1	31
UNCLASSIFIED	6	–	–	34	–	–
TOTALS[c]	902	–	15	2,013	–	32

Source Manuscript census, Saint-Hyacinthe, *Quartiers* 1 to 4, 1861 and 1891
Notes
[a] Occupations declared by the non-institutional population of the original territory of Saint-Hyacinthe (*Quartiers* 1 to 4), 1861 and 1891, with sex ratios in each occupational category.
[b] These are femininity ratios, defined as women per 100 men.
[c] Classified declarations only are used to calculate percentages; that is, 896 for 1861 and 1,979 for 1891.

the original four *quartiers* of the town made such declarations to the census taker. About two-thirds of these men were married: 68% in 1861 and 66% in 1891. This tiny drop in the proportion of married men in the local labour force mirrors a slight, but perceptible, increase in the number of young, single men among those living and working in the community. Men under 25 years of age – many of them unmarried – constituted 26% of the labour force in 1861 and 28% in 1891.

Table 2-3 gives the distribution by economic sector of the male workers in the original territory of Saint-Hyacinthe in 1861 and 1891. The most fundamental distinction expressed in the table is that of manual and non-manual workers. The proportion in each of these major categories remained relatively constant across the 30 years.

Table 2-3
Occupational Structure: Saint-Hyacinthe Men, 1861 and 1891[a]

	1861		1891	
	N	%	N	%
AGRICULTURE	3	0.4	26	1.7
MANUAL WORKERS IN URBAN TRADES	394	50.7	932	62.1
Production	320	41.2	803	53.5
Leather	46	5.9	419	28.0
Construction	68	8.8	63	4.2
Wood	103	13.3	113	7.5
Food & drink	23	3.0	38	2.5
Metals	55	7.1	75	5.0
Clothing	18	2.3	30	2.0
Textiles	5	0.6	37	2.5
Other	2	0.3	28	1.9
Transportation	35	4.5	67	4.5
Carters	34	4.4	54	3.6
Railway workers	1	0.1	7	0.5
Other	0	–	6	0.4
Services	36	4.6	54	3.6
Domestic	33	4.2	8	0.5
Other	3	0.3	46	3.1
Other	3	0.4	8	0.5
LABOURERS	169	21.8	132	8.8
NON-MANUAL	211	27.2	411	26.9
Professions	30	3.9	35	2.3
Doctor	9	1.2	16	1.1
Lawyer	9	1.2	10	0.7
Notary	9	1.2	4	0.3
Other	3	0.3	5	0.3
Commerce	95	12.2	200	13.3
Marchand	32	4.1	43	2.9
Commerçant	21	2.7	42	2.8
Accountant	1	0.1	21	1.4
Clerk	38	4.9	85	5.7
Other	3	0.3	9	0.6
Manufacturers	1	0.1	18	1.2
Services	32	4.1	62	4.1
Government	18	2.3	17	1.1
Education	3	0.3	4	0.3
Hotels/inns	8	1.0	21	1.4
Other	3	0.3	20	1.3

Table 2-3 (continued)

	1861		1891	
	N	%	N	%
Status declaration	53	6.8	80	5.3
Bourgeois	45	5.8	53	3.5
Other	8	1.0	27	1.8
Other	0	–	16	1.1
UNCLASSIFIED	6		29	
TOTAL[b]	783		1,530	

Source Manuscript census, Saint-Hyacinthe, *Quartiers* 1 through 4, 1861 and 1891

Notes

[a] Occupations declared by the non-institutional, male population of the original territory of Saint-Hyacinthe, 1861 and 1891.

[b] Classified declarations only used to calculate percentages. That is, 777 for 1861 and 1,501 for 1891.

About 70% of the employed male population was engaged in manual occupations at both census dates.[97] However, although constant in time, this proportion was not constant in space. Even in 1861, well-defined working-class and bourgeois areas can be discerned by examining male job titles in the manuscript census. Further downstream and located mainly on the low-lying alluvial plain, *Quartiers* 1 and 2 had a high proportion of manual workers: over 80% in 1861 and about 76% in 1891. *Quartiers* 3 and 4 – further upstream and situated for the most part on higher ground – were more bourgeois in character. Fully 36% of the men in this area declared a non-manual occupation, both in 1861 and 1891.

As this period of industrial transition progressed, more and more working-class men in Saint-Hyacinthe became involved in leather production. Table 2-3 shows a dramatic increase in the number of men declaring manual occupations in the leather sector. As a proportion of all male workers, those in the leather industries rose from 6% in 1861 to 28% in 1891, by which time a number of industrial tanneries and boot-and-shoe factories were in full operation. In absolute terms, the number of men doing manual jobs in leather production increased by a factor of almost 10: from 46 in 1861 to 419 in 1891.

A closer look at male job declarations in the leather trades reveals the extent of the changes in production that had affected the sector by 1891. In 1861, 46 leather workers declared four distinct occupations: shoemaker (32 cases), saddler (10 cases), tanner (three cases), and leather cutter (one case). In 1891, in boot-and-shoe production alone, 281 men made 24 different occupational declarations, most referring to narrowly defined tasks. As we shall see shortly, this multiplication of job titles reflects mechanization, the subdivision of the work process, and the dilution of craft skills: well-documented processes for the Quebec boot-and-shoe industry of this period.[98] Similarly, at least 15 separate job titles were declared by 107 male tannery workers in the 1891 census for Saint-Hyacinthe.[99]

As the increasingly mechanized leather industries grew, other sources of manual employment for Saint-Hyacinthe men declined in their relative importance; only textile production gained ground. This is consistent with what we have learned of local economic history from descriptive sources. Of 38 male textile workers listed in 1891, eight were working at the woollens mill of the Compagnie Manufacturière de Saint-Hyacinthe, while 22 were employees of the Granite Mills knit-goods factory.[100] The proportion of general labourers in the male workforce declined sharply, possibly because of the increasing complexity of the urban economy and the greater specificity of work roles (and therefore occupational titles) under industrial capitalism. On the non-manual side, the most striking change between 1861 and 1891 was the increase in the number of individuals who could be classified as "manufacturers": from one organ builder in 1861 to 18 producers of at least eight different types of commodity in 1891.[101]

We have seen that Saint-Hyacinthe's labour force became increasingly feminized in the years between 1861 and 1891. Yet most of the women enumerated in those years declared no paid employment. Those who did were usually young and single. In both 1861 and 1891, 58% of the women who declared occupations were under the age of 25; about four-fifths were under age 40. Unmarried women made up about 80% of those who reported paid work at both census dates; married women and widows each represented about 10% of the women in the formal labour force. The fact that so few married women declared occupations to census takers in 1861 and 1891 may mean either that married women did not often work for wages or that census enumerators neglected to mention it when they did.[102]

Over four times as many women declared paid work in 1891 as had done in 1861. This was a result not only of demographic growth, but of the expansion of employment for women in Saint-Hyacinthe's leather, clothing, and textile industries. Women workers in this community were more densely concentrated in manual occupations than were men. As Table 2-4 shows, 87% of the women who reported jobs in 1861, and 83% of those who did so in 1891, were engaged in some sort of manual work.[103] With the industrialization of the intervening

Table 2-4
Occupational Structure: Saint-Hyacinthe Women, 1861 and 1891[a]

	1861		1891	
	N	%	N	%
MANUAL WORKERS IN URBAN TRADES	103	86.6	396	82.8
Production	20	16.8	272	56.9
Leather	0	–	91	19.0
Food & drink	1	0.8	1	0.2
Clothing	19	16.0	84	17.6
Textiles	0	–	87	18.2
Other	0	–	9	1.9
Services	82	68.9	120	25.1
Domestic	82	68.9	95	19.9
Other	0	–	25	5.2
NON-MANUAL WORKERS	16	13.4	82	17.1
Commerce	6	5.0	27	5.6
Marchande	6	5.0	4	0.8
Commerçante	0	–	6	1.3
Accountant	0	–	1	0.2
Clerk	0	–	16	3.3
Services	7	5.9	20	4.2
Education	5	4.2	11	2.3
Hotels/inns	2	1.7	9	1.9
Status declaration[b]	3	2.5	30	6.3
Other, non-manual	0	–	5	1.0
UNCLASSIFIED	0		5	
TOTAL[c]	119		483	

Source Manuscript census, Saint-Hyacinthe, *Quartiers* 1 through 4, 1861 and 1891
Notes
[a]   Occupations declared by the non-institutional, female population of the original territory of
      Saint-Hyacinthe (*Quartiers* 1 to 4), 1861 and 1891.
[b]   All these women were *rentières*.
[c]   Classified declarations only used to calculate percentages. That is, 119 for 1861 and 478 for
      1891.

period, however, the structure of occupations for working-class
women changed dramatically. In 1861, prior to the arrival of factory
industry in Saint-Hyacinthe, almost 70% of women in the formal
labour market were domestic servants. By 1891, when the most

impressive wave of the town's industrialization was in full swing, that proportion had declined to 20%. Although the absolute number of women employed as domestics in the community had increased during this interval (from 82 to 95), they were now far outnumbered by the almost 300 women working in production. As a proportion of all women engaged in paid labour, manual workers in the manufacturing sector increased from 17% in 1861 to 57% in 1891.

As noted, this change was related to growth and restructuring in the leather, clothing, and textile sectors. No woman was working in the leather trades in 1861; by 1891, 91 were so occupied, 83 of them in the local boot-and-shoe industry. Female textile workers also emerged on the scene after 1861. Although none showed up in Saint-Hyacinthe that year, 30 years later 87 were counted, 74 of them employed at the Granite Mills. Clothing workers – mainly dressmakers and seamstresses – were relatively numerous at both dates. They represented 16% of the women in the formal work force in 1861 and 18% in 1891.

The main trends in women's occupations in Saint-Hyacinthe during this period, then, were a decline in the relative importance of domestic service and an increase in the importance of manual labour in the local manufacturing industries, and more particularly in boot-and-shoe and knit-goods production.

BOOTS, SHOES, SOCKS, AND UNDERWEAR: LIGHT INDUSTRIES IN SAINT-HYACINTHE

Toward the end of the nineteenth century, the town of Saint-Hyacinthe had begun to offer a particular type of industrial employment to individuals and families from the surrounding region. No cotton mill was in place, as in Montreal or Valleyfield at a similar date. But the local woollens mill and particularly the knit-goods factory did employ hundreds of young men, and especially young women, in the production of flannel cloth and machine-knit socks and underwear. Nor did the level of boot-and-shoe production compare to that of Quebec City. But here again, local tanneries and shoe factories employed hundreds of workers in jobs that often required little training, that did not lead to the mastery of a craft, and that featured low wages and high levels of attrition. Knitwear and shoe production came to dominate the Saint-Hyacinthe economy in the later nineteenth century. By looking in detail at these particular industries and their workers, we can begin to appreciate more fully the specific set of opportunities and constraints, faced by individuals and families in this community, as a result of the rise of industrial capitalism.

Knitwear production

The mechanized production of knit or "webbed" goods was unique among the textile industries in that its output was not simply lengths . of woven cloth, but completed garments such as hosiery, underwear, and gloves. This sector has been largely neglected by historians of industrialization in Quebec, mainly because it was not as important in the nineteenth century as cotton or woollen textiles. The knitwear industry was not, however, absent from the province. As early as 1846, a Boston entrepreneur named Jonas Lee established a knit-goods mill in Sherbrooke which, for a short time, produced shawls, shirts, underwear, and socks on 13 knitting machines, using woollen yarn from the neighbouring Lomas mill. And in 1872, a group of local businessmen in nearby Coaticook, with the aid of a municipal bonus, founded a company called Coaticook Knitting that specialized in underwear production. The company thrived as a locally owned business for 20 years, until 1892. At that point, it was bought by Penmans, Canada's largest knitwear producer; in 1899 Penmans expanded operations at the Coaticook mill.[104]

The history of the knit-goods industry elsewhere in Canada, however, has been well studied. The main contribution comes from Joy Parr, whose work focused on the Paris, Ontario, mill established by John Penman in the 1860s and, particularly, on the labour process and gender roles in this community between 1880 and 1950.[105] Parr's rich analysis sheds new light on sexual segregation in the workplace, on the deliberate gendering of work roles in a context of technological change, and on the consequences of "women's work" for the organization of domestic economies and for the development of notions of masculinity and femininity.[106] Although it has much broader implications, her study is extremely helpful in understanding knitting technologies and the division of labour in the Canadian knit-goods mills during the 1880s and 1890s, when this industry began to play a major role in the Saint-Hyacinthe economy.

As we have seen, the knit-goods industry arrived in the town of Saint-Hyacinthe in the early 1880s. By this time, knitting frames had had a long history, particularly in the British Midlands, where a strong craft tradition had emerged around the production of stockings and other garments using these human-powered machine tools. As E.P. Thompson has shown so clearly in the British case, merchant hosiers had already begun to introduce cheaper goods and more exploitative labour practices at the turn of the nineteenth century, provoking stiff resistance from the traditional framework knitters, or "stockingers."[107] And, as Parr has written, further shifts in the organization of production occurred at mid-nineteenth century, both in Britain and North America, as capital pushed framework knitting out of small workshops into the factory. Rarely used in the domestic industry, circular knitting frames became the rule in the new, industrial knitting mills. Lighter and easier to use than the "flatbed" frames used by traditional stockingers, they were specifically designed to be used by women. Furthermore, "[t]he rotary motion of the circulars was adapted to steam power sooner and more successfully than was the alternating clatter of the stockinger's frame."[108] Later in the century, more fully automated circular machines were developed which, by incorporating a programmable reciprocating action, enabled the production of an entire sock or stocking from top through heel and toe. Knitting mills began, as well, to use "round underwear frames [which] made changes in dimension and splices without operator intervention." The result was an ever-greater degree of automation as the century drew to a close and an even greater emphasis on inexpensive, unskilled, largely female labour than had been the case a decade or two earlier.[109]

It is not entirely clear where Saint-Hyacinthe's Abel Hosiery Company (later Granite Mills) fits into this story of transition from the stockinger's shop to mechanized factory production. It is evident, however, that mechanization and the division of labour in this industry were well advanced by 1881, when the local knit-goods mill was established with American capital and technology and a substantial cash bonus from the local council.[110] The American knitting machines invented by Abel and installed at the new mill were probably mechanized circular frames of the variety that producers in Britain and North America, using a low-paid, mainly female labour force, had found so suitable to the mass production of items such as socks and underwear.[111] Like other American knitting frames used in Canada, they were probably designed on the "universal principle" and therefore were able to shift quite easily from one line of production to another – a real advantage in the small Canadian market.[112] Moreover, like other investors in the light industries being established in Quebec's cities and small towns, the industrial capitalists who established Abel Hosiery and, later, those who kept it afloat under the name "Granite Mills," must have seen real advantages in local labour-market conditions. In particular, they would have been drawn to Saint-Hyacinthe by the presence of a large local pool of young women from working families. These women could be induced, for 40 or 50 cents per day, to work 10 to 12 hours tending knitting machines, mending dropped stitches, folding and packaging garments, or performing any other of the many detailed tasks involved in transforming raw fibres into finished socks and underwear.

Two sources from the late 1880s and early 1890s allow us to be somewhat more precise about who did what in the Granite Mills knit-goods factory. For reasons that will become clear shortly, testimony collected in Saint-Hyacinthe in April, 1888, by the Royal Commission on Relations of Capital and Labour, focused largely on working conditions in the knitting mill.[113] And a closer look at the 1891 manuscript census for *Quartiers* 1 to 4 allows us to identify 96 individuals who, based on their declared occupations, definitely worked there.[114] Combined with a reading of Parr and other secondary sources, these documents give us a glimpse inside the Granite Mill and provide at least a sketch of who and what were involved in the various stages of knit-goods production in Saint-Hyacinthe.[115]

Many tasks had to be accomplished between the arrival of raw wool at the knit-goods factory and the shipping out of finished garments. Certain operations, moreover, were still being put out to domestic workers in the late 1880s. Maurice Boas, the plant manager, declared to the Royal Commission in 1888 that Granite Mills employed over 300 workers, of whom more than 100 worked outside the factory.[116] The available sources are unclear as to which phases of production were accomplished by outworkers. Most likely, they included finishing operations such as tying off, working back in, or simply cutting the many loose threads produced during the machine-knitting process. Undershirts and long johns such as those produced in Saint-Hyacinthe would also have needed plackets sewn on the front. This type of work might well have been done by women working at home.[117]

The first stage in knitwear production at the Saint-Hyacinthe mill was yarn preparation: the transformation of bales of raw wool into spools of yarn that could then be loaded onto knitting machines. In general, knit-goods factories used many types of fibre, including cotton and finer materials such as silk and lace. But wool was the stock-in-trade at the Saint-Hyacinthe mill, which employed an initial group of workers in carding, dying, and spinning woollen yarn. The carding room in Saint-Hyacinthe employed both men and women. Two local men in their early thirties reported the occupation "carder, knitting mill" to the 1891 census takers.[118] And Philomène Desgranges had reported to the Royal Commission in 1888 that she worked 12-hour shifts in the Granite Mills carding room, earning 50 cents a day for her efforts.[119] The wool had also to be dyed – gruelling, hot work that was assigned to men like Cyprien Robidoux, who in 1888 earned one dollar per day for drying wool in a hot-room section of the dye house.[120] Spinning was another male preserve within the knitting mill, although relatively few such high-status jobs would have been available. A single "spinner, knitting mill" – a married man aged 30 – identified himself as such to 1891 census takers in the four original *quartiers* of Saint-Hyacinthe.

The next stage in knitwear manufacture was to use the knitting machines to convert spools of yarn into quantities of knit fabric. With circular knitting frames, the finished fabric took a tubular form, the diameter depending on the size of the machine: wide for the torso of an undershirt; narrow for a sock. And the specific shape – whether there were tapers or turns, for example – depended on adjustments such as those made possible by the reciprocating action mentioned earlier. In the original four *quartiers*, "knitting-machine operator" or "knitter" was the most frequently declared specific occupation related to knitwear production. Twenty-five women and five men were so employed in 1891, confirming Parr's observation for the East Midlands and southwestern Ontario, that "knitting was both men's and women's work and exceptional in the hosiery industry as a mixed-gender occupation."[121] Besides their role tending the machines, these knitters shared their youth: all but one, a 54-year-old single woman, was aged 23 years or less; and 16 of the girls and three of the boys were aged between 13 and 19. This certainly suggests a relatively advanced stage of automation in machine knitting, where minding the machines required relatively little skill or strength and could be assigned to the most inexperienced, lowest paid workers.

Amédée Lapierre was one such worker who gave evidence at the Royal Commission hearings in 1888. He had been hired three years earlier at the age of 18, to work in the machine department at a rate of 33⅓ cents per 11-hour day.[122] By 1888, Lapierre had become a very productive machine operator indeed, to the point where, in January, his supervisor took him off the piece rates (so much per hundred pounds of knit fabric) that had enabled him to earn $1.25 per day, to impose a daily rate of $1.00 for his work in the manufacture of shirts, underpants, and mittens.[123] Although most of the knitters in the mill were girls and young women, then, Granite Mills chose to retain a certain number of young men as machine knitters, perhaps, as in Paris, in order to be able to run a night shift. Lapierre reports working through the night on at least two occasions. But it was also because young men had to be trained on the knitting machines if they were to serve later as higher-status fixers, responsible for the care and maintenance of the knitting machines.[124] The knitting room, moreover, was a training ground for young women as well, the most skilled of whom, to the extent that they remained in the factory, might well move on to more demanding jobs such as seaming and mending.

Parr's description of the day shift in the knitting room of Penmans in Paris, although it applies to a later period, may well apply, in its broad outlines, to the Saint-Hyacinthe factory in the 1880s and 1890s. In her description, three people were in charge of the machines:

Female machine minders kept the equipment cleaned and oiled, and the yarn cones filled, inspecting each sock or stocking as it came off the machine for flaws caused by developing machine faults ... [A] floor fixer supported each pair of knitter-minders, intervening when the minder had shut down the machine, changing needles, setting up new patterns, retiming the cylinder before the restart ... A mechanic supported the fixers. He worked out the sequences in the jacks and chains for new patterns and conducted or guided fixers through major repairs.[125]

Turning machine-knit sections of fabric into finished garments, known as "finishing," was the third phase of production in the Saint-Hyacinthe knitwear factory. The type of finishing process used determined the comfort and quality of the article, as well as the amount of skilled labour required for its production. Producing inconspicuous, comfortable seams involved a painstaking, eye-straining procedure known as "looping," by which skilled workers, usually women, linked together stitches on the edges of garment sections: on the open toes of socks, for example; or on the arm and body of an undershirt. Rougher, less comfortable seams could be produced by simply sewing the sections together; this took less time and could be done much more cheaply.

It is difficult to determine which of these finishing methods predominated in Saint-Hyacinthe. No "seamers" or "loopers" identified themselves as such to the 1891 census takers. The young women pictured in Illustration 17 may well have been loopers, engaged in the detailed, demanding occupation of finishing the toes of woollen socks. But this image is from the first decade of the twentieth century, after Penmans had acquired the mill and by which time the operation may have evolved. One 22-year-old woman did identify herself as a "finisher" in 1891, however, while two young women operated sewing machines in the knitting mill, which may suggest the use of cheaper finishing methods. Some of those who identified themselves simply as "workers in a knit-goods mill" – 34 women and six men – would probably have been involved in finishing operations. But it is impossible to say exactly how many.

The presence of "cutters" in the factory – two were located in the 1891 census – also suggests the cheaper method of making seams. Hormisdas Cordeau, a *tailleur* at Granite Mills who gave testimony to the Royal Commission, worked at piece rates, earning up to $1.50 per day when work was good, enough to keep his family of four children in modest sufficiency. But, he lamented, "c'est venu que l'ouvrage était tellement méchant, qu'on ne pouvait rien gagner. On appelle l'ouvrage méchant, celui dans lequel l'étoffe est toute percée, où on est obligé de prendre beaucoup de temps."[126]

Cordeau's complaint, that the fabric he was asked to cut was full of holes and dropped stitches, was directed, it would seem, against the machine tenders, whose work included catching such flaws before they occurred; and against specialized "menders," or *repriseuses*, whose job it was to pick up and repair dropped stitches after the garments had come off the machines. Two women – a 38-year-old married woman and a 17-year-old single girl – reported their occupation as "mender" to the 1891 census takers.

Moreover, the part of the operation called "mending," became the object of an important controversy on the Saint-Hyacinthe shop floor, one which was abundantly reported to the Royal Commission in 1888. Albina Lorange was one of a dozen young women who walked out of the mill on 20 March 1888. She explained her reasons to the commission a month later: "J'ai laissé le moulin en dernier lieu le vingt mars, parce qu'ils nous obligeaient à repriser les coins des bas et on étaient pas capables, au prix qu'ils nous donnaient, de faire cet ouvrage-là."[127] Her colleague Alphonsine Blanchette tells essentially the same story. She left the mill because the foreman of the mending and finishing departments[128] had insisted that she mend not only dropped stitches but the heels and toes of knit socks: "[p]arce qu'ils nous avaient dit de repriser les points clairs le même jour et on est parti."[129] In a heated exchange, the plant manager, Maurice Boas, told a different story to commission members, who were extremely critical of the labour practices in this mill. His version was that the foreman had simply instructed the women to do their work properly: "He simply asked them to do their work correctly," he stated, adding a few minutes later that "[t]here is only one way of mending them, and that is to mend them, if that is any description for this Court."[130] But this vague response to persistent questioning revealed nothing so much as Boas' own ignorance of the details of knitwear production and his desire to cut production costs.

More convincing is the testimony of Hermine Lemoine, another worker who walked out on 20 March, who was asked by commission member Jules Helbronner to explain the nature of the work speed-up that provoked the walkout:

Q. – Comme ni M. Boas, ni la Commission connaît assez les bas, voulez-vous expliquer à la Commission sur quoi est venue la difficulté au sujet des bas?

R. – C'est qu'il voulait nous faire repriser les rétrécis des talons et du bout du pied, quand il n'y avait pas de mailles d'échappées. Quand il y avait des mailles d'échapées, on pouvait les repriser comme d'habitude; mail il voulait nous faire repriser les rétrécis pour le même prix et on a refusé de les repriser et on est parti.

Q. – Alors, si je comprends bien, le travail que vous faisiez d'abord et pour lequel vous étiez payée, c'était de repriser les trous?

R. – Repriser tous les trous.

Q. – Et le travail qu'on a voulu vous faire faire, c'était de repriser les trous et de plus les parties claires?

R. – Oui, les rétrécis clairs qu'on appelle.[131]

One reading of this testimony is that menders were being asked, in addition to their normal job of repairing holes, to do what would normally be the job of another specialized worker: to finish socks by seaming the heels and toes, and without any increase in their piece rates. This would be a substantial speed-up, indeed, and could easily explain why these young women felt they had no other choice but to walk off the job.

Finishing knit goods was difficult, detailed work that was much more difficult to mechanize than knitting. While, in the long run, it may have created many skilled factory jobs for women – as it did in Paris, Ontario – it also involved a number of tedious, repetitive operations that had to be done by hand. The 14-year-old girl whose job in 1891 was to clip the threads of waste that joined finished socks together like sausage links (*défaire les bas*) provides a good example of this; as does the young boy whose job it was to turn the socks, which came off the machines inside out, the right way around (*virer les bas*). So, too, do the "boarders" – the young men who, using wooden frames and steam, gave the socks their final shape and whose rates had been drastically cut in the weeks prior to the arrival of the Royal Commission in Saint-Hyacinthe. Amédée Pallardy, for one, had been working as a *mouleur de bas* when, in early April of 1888, Granite Mills management cut the piece rates for this work from 3 cents to 1½ cents per dozen.[132] Pallardy estimated that he could shape between 50 and 55 dozen socks per 10-hour day, if the work was available (although this was generally not the case). Rather than accepting the 50% pay cut, Pallardy quit his job to seek work elsewhere, only to be replaced by two lads of 13 and 14 who earned daily wages of 30 and 40 cents for the same work.[133]

In most phases of production, then, Granite Mills relied on a workforce in which girls and young women predominated. Of the 96 knitwear workers identified using the 1891 census, 74 were women and girls, most of whom were young – the average age was 21 and the youngest girl in the mill was 13 – and all but five of whom were unmarried.[134] This company profited from a labour-market situation in which many girls and young women sought waged employment in order to supplement fragile family economies. Although there were some exceptions, few worked beyond their early twenties, and fewer still continued working once they were married. Mill managers knew they were operating in a situation in which the supply of unskilled, relatively short-term labourers was abundant. And they designed their wage rates and other practices accordingly. Fines, arbitrary regulations, work speed-ups, and the withholding of wages until the middle of the next month – implying a wait of up to six weeks between being hired and receiving one's first pay packet – were among the abuses uncovered by the members of the Royal Commission. Not surprisingly, mill managers justified their policies with the starkest free-market arguments. When confronted with the fact that Granite Mills had recently slashed its employees' wages, Maurice Boas replied simply, "There is no price that cannot be reduced."[135] While it shows the importance of the skills acquired by the young women in the finishing room who, at 21 or 22, already had several years of experience in the factory, Boas' reaction to the menders' strike of March 1888 – which was to fire them all and to withhold their back wages – also reveals the surplus of young women willing to take on factory work and the advantage this afforded to capitalists in the local labour market. "This strike put us to a great deal of inconvenience, and loss of time, in order to teach the new help," Boas explained to the Royal Commission. "We have no difficulty in getting new help, as there are plenty of people in St. Hyacinthe [sic] to do the work, and who are anxious to be employed ... The applications were more numerous than the positions we had to fill, but unfortunately they had no skill in the work."[136]

Shoe production

Unlike knitwear manufacture, boot-and-shoe production in Quebec is one of the most thoroughly studied sectors of the industrializing urban economy in the nineteenth century. The work of Joanne Burgess is the most helpful in understanding the evolution of technology and the labour process in factories such as the one established in Saint-Hyacinthe by Louis Côté and his associates in the 1860s.[137] Using the example of Montreal, she has identified many of the changes in the production of boots and shoes – changes which capitalists imposed in order to increase volume and reduce per-unit labour costs, and which spelled the end of craft production and the rise of the factory in this sector.[138]

The transformations began in the early part of the century, prior to the introduction of machines, when merchant shoemakers began to produce for inventory (rather than to order) and to institute a division of labour. In 1849, the first machine tool was introduced, probably a leather-rolling machine, by the firm Brown and Childs. The event provoked a strike by journeymen shoemakers who believed, correctly, that the new machinery constituted a threat to their craft skills, their livelihood, and ultimately their way of life.[139] During the 1850s, sewing machines were introduced into shoe production, revolutionizing the "binding" or "closing" operations which had been assigned to women working at home, and which could now be repatriated to the central workshop.[140] But attaching the soles and heels to machine-sewn uppers – the process known as "bottoming," "making," or, in French, *montage* – continued to be a traditional operation. It was one that was still being put out to craft workers working at home or in small workshops, at least until the 1860s, when the introduction of sole-sewing machines enabled capitalists to centralize and mechanize this final phase of boot-and-shoe production.[141] In Montreal, then, true factory production in the boot-and-shoe industry emerged in the second half of the 1860s. It was marked by two new developments: the introduction of steam power, which would ultimately be applied to all phases of production; and the transfer of "bottoming" into the central workshop, made possible by the use of sole-leather sewing machines, of which there were 30 in Montreal by 1872.[142]

Louis Côté established his Saint-Hyacinthe establishment in the mid 1860s, just as these final shifts in the transition from craft shop to factory were occurring. It is not clear exactly what machinery was in place in 1865 or how much work was being put out to craft workers. But the Côté factory seems unlikely to have lagged too far behind its Montreal and Quebec City competitors in applying machinery to shoe production. Côté was himself a prolific inventor of shoemaking machinery. He filed his first Canadian patent, in 1870, for a sole trimming-and-finishing machine (Illustration 19). In the ensuing 35 years, Côté filed 31 more patents, many of them for improvements to mechanized equipment used in the production of counters, or heel stiffeners, to which he gave a distinctive "clam shell" pattern for strength.[143] Côté's motives were like those of other inventors of "labour-saving machinery" in this period: to increase productivity and reduce labour costs by displacing skilled workers. He laid them out starkly when he filed his 1870 patent for the sole trimmer: "The object of this machine is to dispense with the greater part of the manual labour now required in cutting, trimming, cambering, and moulding the soles and heels of boots and shoes and polishing the same on the edge and *to enable unskilled hands to do that work perfectly*."[144] Like the sole-sewing machines introduced a few years earlier, this machine was specifically designed to render the hard-earned craft skills of shoemakers obsolete. Journeyman shoemakers working at home were to be either thrown out of work or forced to compete with untrained workers for factory jobs as machine tenders. Not surprisingly, this created downward pressures on salaries; it also provided the context for organization and defensive strikes by craft associations such as the Knights of Saint Crispin in the late 1860s.[145]

By the early 1890s, unskilled hands, including many young children, had been operating increasingly sophisticated shoemaking machinery in the Côté factory for some 25 years. Côté's was no longer the only such factory in town. But there is no reason to think that the organization of production was substantially different in the competing firm of Séguin-Lalime, which had been in operation locally since 1883. Both concerns were fully mechanized boot-and-shoe factories of the kind which were only just emerging in the 1870s but which, by the time of the 1891 census, were the rule in the Canadian shoe industry. All phases of boot-and-shoe manufacture had been centralized in factories, which housed increasingly sophisticated machinery, connected to steam engines by complex and dangerous webs of belts, gears, and pulleys. And both employers used an advanced division of labour to keep labour costs to a minimum, assigning certain tasks to men, others to women, and still others to children.

As with the knitwear industry, we can learn more about the social relations of shoe production by examining the Saint-Hyacinthe evidence given in 1888 to the Royal Commission on Relations of Capital and Labour, and by scouring the 1891 census for the occupations of local people employed in boot-and-shoe production. The balance between the two sources, however, is different. Compared to Granite Mills, the Royal Commission paid relatively little attention to the Saint-Hyacinthe shoe factories. Only a handful of witnesses were called and no explicit suggestion of questionable labour practices was made (although the age of certain workers, as we shall see, was a matter of some concern). Perhaps the commissioners thought it unseemly to delve too deeply into the business affairs of their former colleague, Louis Côté. Côté, who had been named to the commission in November of 1887, was replaced in March of 1888, barely a month before the Saint-Hyacinthe hearings, apparently due to illness.[146] Evidence pertaining to the local shoe industry from this source, then, is scanty. On the other hand, some 364 people living in the four original *quartiers* of Saint-Hyacinthe declared occupations related to shoe production in 1891. They constitute a substantial base from which to attempt to understand the inner workings of the Saint-Hyacinthe boot-and-shoe industry toward the end of the nineteenth century.

In 1891, boot-and-shoe production employed more people than any other sector of the Saint-Hyacinthe economy. The 1891 census reveals that 281 men and boys and 83 women and girls living in the original territory of the town worked in either the Côté or the Séguin-Lalime shoe factories. The average male worker in the industry was 28 years old and more likely than not to be married. But substantial numbers of teenaged boys worked in the factories as well: almost one-quarter of male shoe-factory employees were less than 18 years old.[147] Girls and women were less numerous in the shoe factories; the 1891 census search turned up 83. They were also substantially younger than the men and much less likely to be married. Although several women workers were in their thirties and one in her forties, only one married woman – a 20-year-old *couturière* – was located in the census for the original territory of Saint-Hyacinthe. The average age of female shoe-factory workers was 18, reflecting the presence of large numbers of young girls: 42 were under 18 years old in 1891, of whom 17 – one-fifth of female shoe-factory workers in the town – were under 15.

Two of the young girls employed in the Louis Côté shoe factory were among the witnesses at the Saint-Hyacinthe hearings of the Royal Commission in April of 1888. Corinne Côté was 12 years old, earned one dollar per week doing various jobs in the factory, and, according to her testimony, had been working in the plant since the previous spring.[148] Quebec's 1885 Factories Act "made it illegal to employ a boy under 12 or a girl under 14 without a certificate from the child's parents authorizing him or her to work."[149] The commissioners did not press the question of whether or not Corinne had her parents' written authorization to work in the shoe factory; one wonders whether this was to allow Louis Côté to save face. Still, few working children in this period would have done so without their parents' consent, a point made clearly enough by the next witness. Rosanna Plamondon was a 14-year-old girl who had been working in the Côté factory for some two years, not only with her father's consent but as his helper. Because her labour power was pooled with that of her father, she could not even tell the commissioners how much she earned per week. "Je ne puis pas dire," she replied to Jules Helbronner, "parce que je travaille pour papa."[150]

Burgess has used an 1864 guide to Montreal businesses to identify three basic stages in the production of boots and shoes: preparing and cutting the leather, sewing together the pieces for the uppers ("closing"), and pegging or sewing the uppers to the soles and heels ("making").[151] A quarter century later, the essential steps in shoe-making had not changed. But, following the industrial capitalist logic of mechanization and the deskilling of craft work, the number of detailed tasks that could be assigned to underpaid, unskilled wage labourers had multiplied. In 1891, scores of boot-and-shoe workers still declared themselves to be, simply, "shoemakers" or "apprentice shoemakers."[152] This may reflect both the persistence of a craft identity among certain workers and a certain degree of semantic slippage on the part of factory workers (who did, after all, make shoes) and census takers. The dominant impression from the 1891 occupational titles, however, is one of a progressive subdivision of the labour process, aided by increasingly sophisticated machines, which led to the creation of many new and increasingly narrow specializations.

In the Montreal shoe factories of the mid 1860s, the preparation and cutting of leather had been men's work. It had also been substantially mechanized. Steam-powered machines were already in use for preparing, rolling, and doubling the leather, while others were used to cut soles and prepare heels.[153] Mechanized early on, it seems unlikely that these operations changed substantially in the ensuing 25 years. In 1891 in Saint-Hyacinthe, only two occupations were unambiguously associated with this phase of the process. Fourteen male workers identified themselves as "cutters, shoe factory"; eight of these were teenagers, including one who declared himself to be an "apprentice cutter."[154] Moreover, four men and one teenaged boy identified themselves as being in charge of "sole leather." Four more men who declared themselves to be "crimpers" might also be associated, broadly, with leather preparation, suggesting that this part of the production continued to be a male preserve, as it had been in the 1860s.

Several leather cutters were among the shoe-factory workers who gave testimony to the Royal Commission in 1888. Among them was Octave Delage, who worked 60-hour weeks as a leather cutter at the Séguin-Lalime factory, earning either $9 or $10, depending on the season, for his efforts. An experienced cutter, Delage reported that greener hands in the same department earned $6 per week, while apprentice cutters generally started at $1. By his account, there were nine workers and 12 apprentices in the department where he worked. Asked about the nature of these "apprenticeships," Delage's responses are revealing, if not surprising: "Q. – Est-ce qu'ils on un système d'apprentissage, est-ce qu'ils prennent des apprentis? R. – Ils prennent un grand nombre d'apprentis, mais pas par contrat. Q. – S'engagent-ils à montrer complètement aux apprentis leur métier? R. – Pas que je sache, monsieur."[155] At the time of his testimony, Delage had barely one week left on the verbal contract into which he had entered a year earlier. He seemed oddly sanguine about the fact that, despite widespread acknowledgment of his excellence as a worker, his contract was to be terminated on 1 May 1888. His employers had been explicit about the reasons for his dismissal: "C'est parce que je suis membre d'une association ouvrière ... On me l'a dit."[156]

In the 1860s, the sewing together of sections of leather to form uppers (the operation known as "closing") had been done mainly in the factory, by girls and women using sewing machines (which were not necessarily steam activated) and other, more specialized machines. At the time, this second stage in the manufacturing process employed almost all the women present in the Montreal factories.[157] In Saint-Hyacinthe in 1891, this pattern seems to have persisted. Twenty-eight of the female shoe-factory workers located in the census were "sewers" or "sewing-machine operators"; a further eight gave job declarations that included the word "uppers" (*empeignes*), while another four worked with unidentified machines that seem likely to have been sewing machines. This makes a total of 40 girls and women, ranging in age from 12 to 35 years, who were almost certainly involved in "closing" operations. The fact that 29 of the female shoe-factory workers identified did not specify the nature of their employment – one assumes that many of them were also doing this kind of work – means that three-quarters (40 of 54) of the female shoe-factory workers who made a detailed job declaration in 1891 were assembling uppers.

Pegging or sewing the soles to the uppers, or "making," was the third stage in the shoe-production process and, as we have seen, the last to be mechanized. Burgess describes the mid 1860s as a transitional phase. The McKay sole-sewing machine had just appeared, and machines existed in some shops to peg the uppers to the soles. But most of the "making" was still assigned to workers in their homes or in smaller shops, to be performed by hand with traditional tools.[158] Shortly thereafter, mechanized sole-sewing machines came into general use and this stage of the manufacturing process was integrated into larger and larger factories.[159]

By the early 1890s, a substantial proportion of the male workers employed in shoe production, at least in Saint-Hyacinthe but surely in other places as well, operated sole-sewing or sole-pegging machines situated within the factory walls. Forty-six male workers, ranging in age from 15 to 48 years, declared themselves to be "makers" (*monteurs*) in 1891, while another four teenaged boys gave the occupation *apprenti-monteur*. This represents 35% (50 of 144) of the male shoe-factory workers whose jobs were described in any detail by the census takers in 1891; that is, those who declared an occupation other than shoemaker, apprentice shoemaker, or shoe-factory worker. "Making" boots and shoes, then, was an exclusively male occupation which, like leather cutting, retained at least the vestiges of an apprenticeship system. Teenaged boys would be trained on the job to use sole-pegging and sole-sewing machines, whose efficient use required a degree of skill. Experienced makers could earn $10 per week in 1888, according to Joseph Côté, a shoe-factory foreman who testified before the Royal Commission. Less skilled hands might earn as little as five dollars per week.[160]

Burgess' account of the phases of shoe factories in the 1860s makes no mention of what would seem, by the 1890s, to be the final phase of mechanized shoe-production in Saint-Hyacinthe: "finishing." One suspects that this was because, in the 1860s, the skilled workers responsible for "making" the shoes – whether in the factory or as outworkers – would have also been charged with trimming away excess sole leather, polishing the sides of the soles and heels, and performing other tasks required to put made boots and shoes into saleable condition. By 1891, however, perhaps as a result of the application of new technologies such as Côté's sole-trimming and finishing machine, "finishing" had become a separate, all-male occupation within the factory. Twenty-one male shoe-factory workers, ranging in age from 15 to 59, declared themselves to be "finishers" in 1891, while another four boys were described as "apprentice finishers." There were also specific jobs associated with polishing and packaging the shoes, and with stock handling. Most of these – except for polishing, where some girls and older men were employed – were occupied by teenage boys.

Saint-Hyacinthe's shoe industry, then, was like the knit-goods factory in that it provided a certain number of jobs to women, mainly as sewing machine operators in the intermediate phase of shoe production known as "closing." Even more than in knitwear, however, these jobs were assigned to girls as young as 10 years old who were not expected to stay in the factories beyond their early twenties. This, as we shall see in the next chapter, was the average age of marriage for working-class women in this town. Clearly, this was no coincidence. Female workers in this industry were even younger that at Granite Mills – 18 as opposed to 21 – and it was rare, indeed, to find a married or widowed woman working in the Côté or the Séguin-Lalime factories.

Men, on the other hand, outnumbered women by a ratio of over three to one in the shoe factories and were responsible for most other phases of shoe production: from leather preparation and cutting through "making" and finishing the shoes. Boys entered at an early age and, in their initial months and years of work, were considered apprentices and paid accordingly: as little as one dollar per week. Shoe-factory operators like the Côtés and Séguin-Lalime used the artisanal vocabulary of apprenticeship to valorize the acquisition by young lads, not of the arts and mysteries of the shoemaker's craft, but of the truncated set of skills required to effectively run increasingly sophisticated machinery, some of it of local invention. Once learned, these skills allowed experienced cutters, makers, and finishers to earn as much as $10 per week in the local factories when work was available. In general, however, weekly take-home pay was substantially lower than this. Dissatisfied workers could quit and take their skills to other factory towns, as many did. They could also draw on long-standing traditions of craft solidarity to organize against further dilution of skills and in defence of their standards of living. Some, like Octave Delage, found out that the price of such resistance could be high. By the turn of the century, however, organized labour militancy was well established in the Saint-Hyacinthe boot-and-shoe industry. Jacques Ferland's inventory of strikes in Quebec in this industry between 1880 and World War I includes four from Saint-Hyacinthe, all of short duration, over issues such as repeated pay cuts (1898), the firing of a foreman in the leather-cutting department (1899), the hiring of a non-union machinist (1900), and the requirement to work on a holiday (1904).[161]

Saint-Hyacinthe's two main "light" industries, knit-goods and footwear, complemented each other. They offered employment possibilities to married, male "breadwinners" and to young men and boys who, by starting as apprentices in the local shoe factories, could acquire real skills that afforded them not just income potential but also the possibility of mobility. They also provided jobs for girls and young women. These young women, while they too acquired marketable skills as machine knitters, menders, and closers, were treated by capital as temporary workers – not apprentices – and expected to leave the wage-labour market, as most apparently did, before the age of 25. This pattern of employment, imposed by capital in its search for cheap, stable sources of labour power, fit with the expectations of the local population. But it also created a cruel paradox within the labour market. Given the low wages paid even to skilled adult male workers, many families relied on the labour of secondary workers – usually unmarried children aged 13 to 25 – for daily survival. Unfortunately, it was precisely this pattern of family employment which provided factory operators like Côté and the Boas brothers with access to such an abundant pool of unskilled labourers and – to the extent that they were bothered by such matters – with a justification for their low-wage policies.

Without an industrial census for any date other than 1871, it is impossible to be as precise as one would like about the development of manufacturing in Saint-Hyacinthe in the half century or so after 1850. The broad lines of the town's industrialization in this interval can nonetheless be discerned. Particularly in "light" industries such as leather goods and knitwear, machine-assisted, industrial capitalist production arrived in the 30 years after the establishment of the Côté shoe factory in 1865. Although interrupted by the recession of the late 1870s, its expansion was substantial, particularly in the 1880s and the first half of the 1890s. This transformation was engineered in part by an aggressive local bourgeoisie. But its most profound effects were felt by the labouring people of the town, a growing proportion of whom depended on the wages they took home from larger and larger shops, organized along capitalist lines.

Industrial expansion – particularly between 1871 and 1895 – brought an important shift in the town's occupational and social structure. The leading sectors in the economic transition were the leather trades, particularly boot-and-shoe production and tanneries; and textiles, represented locally by an important knit-goods factory and a smaller woollens mill. Industrialization in these sectors totally transformed the local labour market. In 1861, only 51 individuals (all of them male) declared employment in either leather or textile production. Thirty years later, 634 people, 178 of whom were women, worked in these two sectors. Most of these people were industrial wage labourers: proletarians who lacked control over shop, tools, raw materials, and the other means of production. This control was now vested squarely, if sometimes precariously, in the hands of a local bourgeoisie that was increasingly aggressive in its quest for new sources of capital and profit.

Saint-Hyacinthe's population did not become entirely dependent on factory work during this period. Important and related transitions were underway in other sectors of the local and regional economies as well. Agriculture became more specialized and more commercial. Saint-Hyacinthe's role as regional *entrepôt* translated into railway building and the rapid expansion of local exchange institutions, such as the public market. All kinds of goods and services, from lumber to insurance, became available in the increasingly specialized businesses that spread out from the market square. Smaller shops continued to thrive in certain manufacturing industries, even as large factories geared to wider markets appeared on the scene in the 1870s, 1880s, and 1890s. Capital concentration and the arrival of machine-assisted production in certain sectors did not inhibit the multiplication of small-scale, traditionally organized units in others. In Saint-Hyacinthe as elsewhere, industrial capitalism arrived on a staggered timetable, quickly recasting some manufacturing activities, while leaving others relatively untouched.[162]

But for all its nuances, the industrial capitalist transformation was no less dramatic. As the town and its industrial base grew, a majority of its expanding population came to rely on wages for survival. The insecurity of wage dependency, in a context where unstable markets could provoke pay cuts, layoffs, and plant closings, cannot be emphasized strongly enough. Factories, with their steel skeletons and austere brick facades, with their low wages and strict capitalist work discipline, had redefined the life of this community by the 1880s.[163] And the implications for ordinary people, in terms of the ways in which they worked, lived, and struggled, were significant indeed. As we shall see, the consequences of industrial capitalism in Saint-Hyacinthe extended even to the most intimate areas of human relations, as individuals strove to create and to maintain viable and meaningful familial relationships, in material circumstances that had been altered forever.

13 Granite Mills knit-goods factory, pictured in the 1886 promotional album *St. Hyacinthe Illustré/Illustrated.* That year, *le tricot* employed some 300 men and women in the mechanized production of socks and underwear. (*St. Hyacinthe Illustré/Illustrated* [1886], 5)

14 The Eastern Townships Corset Company. Lured from Sherbrooke in 1891 with a cash bonus, this factory was located just to the north of the Grand Trunk railway tracks. This building too is still standing. (ASHRSH, Collection Hélène Nichols (BFG 44); U. Fournier, St. Hyacinthe, Éditeur, no 4)

15 The Ames-Holden Shoe Company of Montreal took over the financially troubled Seguin-Lalime factory on Cascades Street in 1903. By 1913, it employed some 455 workers. (ASHRSH, Collection Hélène Nichols (BFG 44); U. Fournier, St. Hyacinthe, Éditeur, no. 10)

16 Yarn room at the knit-goods factory, ca. 1903. By this time, Granite Mills had gone bankrupt and the Saint-Hyacinthe factory had been acquired by Penmans Manufacturing Company. The mill remained one of the town's most important industrial employers throughout the first half of the twentieth century. (ASHRSH, section B, series 14, album 4)

17 Women at work in the knit-goods factory, ca. 1903. These women are either knitting on small circular frames or, more likely, working as "loopers" finishing the toes of woollen socks. Most of the workers in the knit-goods factory were women and girls. (ASHRSH, section B, series 14, album 4)

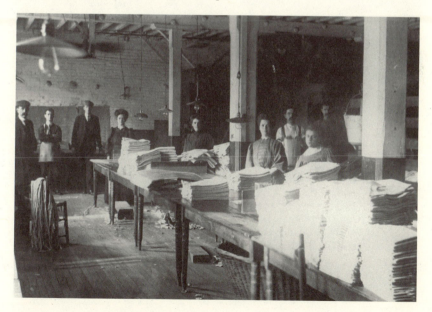

18 Women's responsibilities in the knit-goods mill included folding the finished garments, such as the long johns and undershirts pictured here. (ASHRSH, section B, series 14, album 4)

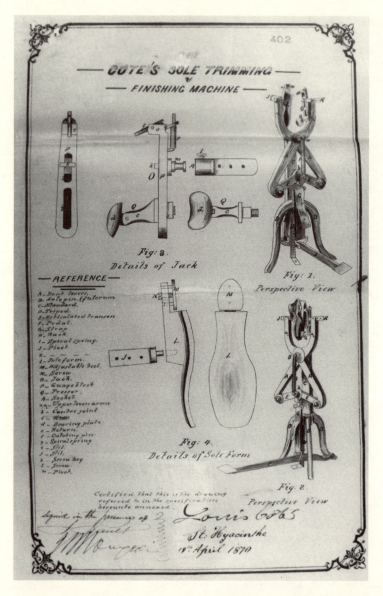

19 Louis Côté's "sole trimming-and-finishing machine," as illustrated in his 1870 submission for this, his first Canadian patent. (Canadian Intellectual Property Office, Canadian patent number 402, 1870. Photograph by Vanessa Reid)

20 Bird's-eye view of Saint-Hyacinthe in 1910. (NA "Cité de St-Hyacinthe 1910," NMC C18055, H3/340/Saint-Hyacinthe/1910)

21   This plain brick building served as a pro-cathedral for the diocese of Saint-Hyacinthe from August 1854 until the completion of a permanent structure in 1880. Situated on land donated by the Dessaulles family, it was the site of many of the weddings discussed in chapter 3. The building was later used as an organ factory and, at the time of this photograph, as a hospice. (ASHRSH, section B, series 14, album 1, "Hospice St. Charles, St-Hyacinthe, Que.," The Valentine and Sons Publishing Co. Ltd.)

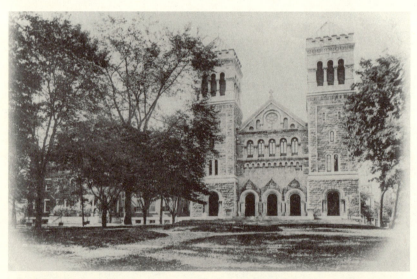

22   Built between 1878 and 1880, this is the original Saint-Hyacinthe cathedral. It is visible in Illustration 20, as is the single spire of Notre-Dame-du-Saint-Rosaire, located just across Bourdages Street to the southwest. The cathedral's square towers were replaced in the major renovation accomplished between 1908 and 1911. (ASHRSH, Collection Hélène Nichols (BFG 44); Pinsonneault, édit., Trois-Rivières, Quebec)

3 To Have and to Hold: Marriage and Family Formation in Nineteenth-Century Saint-Hyacinthe

Marriage was among the most important transitions experienced by individuals in nineteenth-century Quebec, as it is for men and women in all societies. It set up the material, affective, and symbolic conditions for the daily lives of a majority of adults. It established complex webs of social interaction involving not just husbands and wives but wider networks of kin and community. Furthermore, marriage created the only socially sanctioned context for sexuality and reproduction.[1] For all these reasons, marriage deserves the attention it has received recently from historians.[2]

In Saint-Hyacinthe, people adapted marriage to the new urban and industrial realities of the later nineteenth century in various ways. Most importantly, a new, socially differentiated pattern began to emerge. Increasingly, marriage meant one thing to the members of Saint-Hyacinthe's comfortable elite, and quite another to the manual workers employed at the Côté shoe factory or the Granite Mills knit-goods plant. After 1850, distinct patterns of family formation came to characterize the local bourgeoisie, the growing working class, and the farming population living in the nearby countryside.

The changes that occurred were closely tied to shifts in the access young men and women had to the material underpinnings of married life. In agricultural communities, people needed land to form a family; in craft communities, a skill. But as the industrial-capitalist transition progressed, these older economic realities receded and were replaced with new ones – grounded for most on wage labour; for others on professional activities, business acumen, or inherited property. In this very real sense, then, the realities of matrimony and family formation were modified as local society was transformed by industrial capitalism in the later nineteenth century.

Many aspects of marriage in Saint-Hyacinthe, some dynamic and some more stable, are examined in this chapter. We begin with a general profile of three cohorts of men and women who married at the cathedral between 1854 and 1891 and whose married lives will be our focus for the rest of the book. This is followed by a discussion of the seasonal and weekly calendar of matrimony, which shows that despite the subtle impact of industrial capitalism, the conservative influence of the religious calendar was tenacious and, on the whole, more important. The chapter concludes with an analysis of men's and women's marriage ages in this manufacturing town. And it is here that the strongest evidence of a new, socially differentiated pattern of marriage and family formation emerges.

HUSBANDS AND WIVES

Who were the men and women who married at the Saint-Hyacinthe cathedral in the second half of the nineteenth century? What did they do for a living? Where did they come from? Were they single or widowed, educated or illiterate? In this section, these questions will be answered for 295 couples formed between 1854 and 1861, 277 formed between 1864 and 1871, and 340 formed between 1884 and 1891.[3] The exercise has two basic objectives. One is to show the extent to which these particular couples reflect the composition of the local population. The other is simply to introduce readers to the 912 couples whose domestic and reproductive lives will be investigated in the rest of this book.

Socio-economic status is an appropriate starting point for such a portrait. Saint-Hyacinthe's parish registers contain a wealth of occupational information about the husbands in the three cohorts. Husbands' occupations are noted in 84% of the marriage acts in the three cohorts.[4] Using declarations from civil acts (mainly baptisms) passed in the first five years of a marriage, it was possible to increase the total number of husbands for whom occupational information was available to 829, or 91% of the husbands in the three cohorts.[5]

Saint-Hyacinthe-le-Confesseur was a mainly urban parish from its inception. Yet the occupations declared by the men who married there reflect the close proximity of the countryside and the role of the town as regional *entrepôt*. *Cultivateur* was the occupation most frequently declared by husbands in each of the three cohorts (see Table 3-1); almost one-quarter of the husbands in the three cohorts

Table 3-1

Occupations of Husbands in the Three Marriage Cohorts

	Cohort A		Cohort B		Cohort C	
	N	%	N	%	N	%
AGRICULTURE	70	28.7	67	26.8	65	19.5
MANUAL WORKERS IN URBAN TRADES	102	41.8	94	37.6	173	51.8
Production	94	38.5	82	32.8	150	44.9
Leather	16	6.6	20	8.0	63	18.9
Construction	20	8.2	18	7.2	8	2.4
Wood	31	12.7	21	8.4	29	8.7
Food & drink	7	2.9	7	2.8	12	3.6
Metals	15	6.1	12	4.8	18	5.4
Clothing	2	0.8	2	0.8	8	2.4
Textiles	2	0.8	1	0.4	2	0.6
Other	1	0.4	1	0.4	2	0.6
Not specified	0	–	0	–	8	2.4
Transportation	7	2.9	6	2.4	9	2.7
Carters	7	2.9	2	0.8	5	1.5
Railway workers	0	–	3	1.2	4	1.2
Other	0	–	1	0.4	0	–
Services	0	–	5	2.0	11	3.3
Other	1	0.4	1	0.4	3	0.9
LABOURERS	38	15.6	29	11.6	26	7.8
NON-MANUAL	34	13.9	60	24.0	70	21.0
Professions	7	2.9	15	6.0	15	4.5
Doctors	2	0.8	5	2.0	3	0.9
Lawyers	2	0.8	6	2.4	7	2.1
Notaries	2	0.8	4	1.6	2	0.6
Other	1	0.4	0	–	3	0.9
Commerce	17	7.0	28	11.2	34	10.2
Marchand	10	4.1	15	6.0	11	3.3
Commerçant	3	1.2	4	1.6	4	1.2
Accountant	0	–	2	0.8	8	2.4
Clerk	3	1.2	6	2.4	11	3.3
Other	1	0.4	1	0.4	0	–
Manufacturers	0	–	1	0.4	3	0.9
Services	5	2.0	6	2.4	4	1.2
Government	1	0.4	4	1.6	0	–
Education	1	0.4	1	0.4	0	–
Hotels/inns	3	1.2	0	–	2	0.6
Other	0	–	1	0.4	2	0.6

Table 3-1 (continued)

	Cohort A		Cohort B		Cohort C	
	N	%	N	%	N	%
Status declaration	5	2.0	8	3.2	12	3.6
Bourgeois	3	1.2	6	2.4	11	3.3
Ecuyer	1	0.4	0	–	0	–
Other	1	0.4	2	0.8	1	0.3
Other	0	–	2	0.8	2	0.6
UNCLASSIFIED	1		0		0	
NO INFORMATION	50		27		6	
TOTAL[a]	295		277		340	

Source Family Reconstitution Files.

Note

[a]   Percentages have been calculated with the number of husbands for whom an occupational declaration was available and could be counted in the denominator. That is, for Cohort A, 244; for Cohort B, 250; and for Cohort C, 334.

were farmers.[6] Many of these men came from outside the parish to marry Saint-Hyacinthe women. Joseph Arpin, for example, was a farmer from Saint-Ephrem d'Upton who in February of 1855 married Marguerite Girard of Saint-Hyacinthe.[7] But a sizeable number were residents of that part of the parish situated outside the town of Saint-Hyacinthe: those rural tracts incorporated in 1861 as the municipality of Saint-Hyacinthe-le-Confesseur.[8] This was the case of Norbert Goyet, for instance, *cultivateur, de cette paroisse*, who married Zoé Gagnon at the Saint-Hyacinthe cathedral in August of 1866.[9]

Whether or not they tilled the land, most of the men who married in this parish were manual workers of one kind or another. Those who worked in urban-manual occupations predominated, which is no surprise given what we have seen of the occupational structure of the town. Nor is it surprising that most of these workers were involved in manufacturing; that is, 40% of the husbands in the first two cohorts and 50% of those in the third had manual jobs in sectors related to the transformation of leather, wood, iron, and other raw materials. This increase, of course, reflects the growth of the local manufacturing sector and the increased importance of industrial workers in the local occupational structure by the 1880s.[10] At the same time, the proportion of general labourers, both in the marriage register and in the census lists, declined.[11] *Journaliers* such as Marcellin Dion, who married Octavie Harnois in May of 1888, could still be found among the husbands in the third cohort. But Dion was an exception in this as in other respects (most notably in that he was marrying his brother's widow).[12] By this time, most manual workers were declaring more specific occupations, rather than identifying themselves as labourers.

Although the great majority of Saint-Hyacinthe husbands were manual workers of one description or another, this predominance was not total. Fourteen percent of the men who married in the 1850s and over 20% of those who married in the 1860s and 1880s were professionals, merchants, industrialists, teachers, shopkeepers, civil servants, and others in non-manual occupations. These proportions are lower than those of the bourgeois and petit-bourgeois professions in the town. But this difference is easily explained by the fact that Saint-Hyacinthe's young women often married farmers from the surrounding region, or even from further afield.[13] Among the non-manual workers in the three cohorts, we find prominent local figures such as Victor Côté; Georges-Casimir Dessaulles; and Honoré Mercier, at this point a young lawyer who married twice at the cathedral (in the 1860s and early 1870s).[14] But there are also humbler folk such as hotel-keeper Prosper Reeves; general merchant Hilaire Mathieu from nearby Saint-Barnabé parish; and Théophile Dupont, a merchant's clerk who married Albina Chagnon, daughter of foundry owner Augustin Chagnon, in October of 1867 and became involved in his father-in-law's business, notably as a bookkeeper.[15]

Overall, then, the discrepancies in the distribution of occupations between the men in the three marriage cohorts and those identified by census enumerators in the town of Saint-Hyacinthe are small. They derive from the difference between the territorial limits of the parish (which contained an agricultural population) and the town (which did not) and from the fact that Saint-Hyacinthe's young women attracted so many farmers from the surrounding agricultural region. This is no surprise at all, really, and merely serves to underline the importance of Saint-Hyacinthe as a key regional *carrefour* in this period.

Unfortunately, almost nothing is known about the occupations of the women who married in Saint-Hyacinthe in the second half of the nineteenth century. Professional information is available for only nine of the 912 wives in the three marriage cohorts. They include seamstress Adéline Leduc, who married local carriage-maker Eusèbe Bourgeois in February 1869; teacher Albina Laflamme who, one week later, married Noé Cadoret, a bricklayer; and Malvina Brodeur, a dressmaker who, although she was living in Holyoke, Massachussets, took her wedding vows with labourer Octave Brien *dit* Desroches, also from Holyoke, at the Saint-Hyacinthe cathedral in February, 1888.[16] For purposes of demographic analysis, however, this handful of cases is very little to go on. It is difficult indeed, for example, to say what proportion of the young brides in Saint-Hyacinthe in the 1880s had spent time working as knitters at the Granite Mills or as closers in one of the local shoe factories. One suspects that many did, but it is impossible to offer this as anything more than an hypothesis.

In the absence of this information, it was necessary to draw on their fathers' occupations, as reported in the marriage acts, to get some sense of the women's social and economic background. Such declarations were available for 40% of the women who married in Cohort A, 65% of those in Cohort B, and 74% of those in Cohort C. Though their uncritical use is problematic, these declarations none-theless provide a general idea of the status and class position of the women who married in Saint-Hyacinthe during this period.[17] By comparing husbands' occupations with those of their wives' fathers, it is also possible to estimate levels of social and occupational endogamy in Saint-Hyacinthe.

Table 3-2 shows that an increasing proportion of the women who married in Saint-Hyacinthe in the later nineteenth century were from urban backgrounds, whether working-class or bourgeois. In the 1850s, the number of farmer's daughters was almost double the number who had been raised in urban-manual families, as one might expect in such an early phase of the town's expansion. The gap narrowed over the next 30 years, to the point where, by the 1880s, more wives were of urban-manual origins (35%) than from farm families (31%). The proportion of brides from non-manual back-grounds increased as well, from 14% in the 1850s, to 22% in the 1860s, to 27% in the 1880s.[18]

There was a simple generational logic at work here. The town's substantial growth between mid-century and the 1880s meant that an increasing proportion of the women who married there had been raised locally, in households dependent on urban activities rather than farming for survival. A majority of the brides of the 1850s and 1860s married men who worked in the town, whether in manual or non-manual occupations. Twenty or thirty years later, the daughters of this generation began to think about marriage. More likely than their mothers to have been raised in an urban setting, they more often married men who were factory workers, clerks, or professionals rather than farmers.

The analysis of the occupational background of the men and women in the three cohorts is taken a step further in Table 3-3. Al-ready, a certain social differentiation in patterns of family formation

Table 3-2
Occupations: Fathers of Wives in the Three Cohorts

	Cohort A		Cohort B		Cohort C	
	N	%	N	%	N	%
AGRICULTURE	56	47.1	77	43.0	78	31.1
URBAN MANUAL	29	24.4	43	24.0	88	35.1
Production	24	20.2	37	20.7	71	28.3
Transportation	4	3.4	6	3.4	17	6.8
Other	1	0.8	0	–	0	–
LABOURERS	17	14.3	19	10.6	18	7.2
NON-MANUAL	17	14.3	40	22.3	67	26.7
Professions	1	0.8	6	3.4	8	3.3
Commerce	4	3.4	13	7.3	12	4.8
Services	4	3.4	5	2.8	17	6.8
Status declaration	8	6.7	15	8.4	29	11.6
Other	0	–	1	0.6	1	0.4
UNCLASSIFIED	0		0		2	
NO INFORMATION	176		98		87	
TOTAL[a]	295		277		340	

Source Family Reconstitution Files.
Note
[a] Note: percentages are given as a proportion of those for whom occupation is known and has been classified. That is: Cohort A – 119; Cohort B – 179; Cohort C – 251.

in Saint-Hyacinthe is apparent. Social and occupational endogamy – the propensity to marry within one's own social or occupational group – was much higher in certain segments of society than in others.[19] In the case of farm families, for example, levels of endogamy remained high throughout the period. Seven of every 10 farmers married the daughters of other farmers, even though only four of 10 brides in the three cohorts came from a farming family.[20] Similarly, about half of the men in non-manual occupations married women from similar backgrounds, even though such women represented under one-quarter of all brides.

At the other end of the social scale, the level of endogamy among labourers' families actually increased between the 1860s and the 1880s. Although the small numbers involved dictate caution, it is just possible that as the *journaliers* became a smaller and smaller group in this town they also became more tightly knit. Their increasingly

Table 3-3
Social and Occupational Endogamy

Husband's Occupational Category	Cohort	Wives' Fathers	
		Distribution in Marriage Cohorts (%)	Proportion in Same Category as Husband (%)
Agriculture	A	47.1	80.0
	B	43.0	68.1
	C	31.1	64.4
	Total	38.4	69.7
Urban-manual	A	24.4	45.2
	B	24.0	30.6
	C	35.1	43.7
	Total	29.1	40.6
Labourers	A	14.3	38.5
	B	10.6	36.8
	C	7.2	58.3
	Total	9.8	43.2
Non-manual	A	14.3	50.0
	B	22.3	58.5
	C	26.7	49.0
	Total	22.6	52.8

Source Family Reconstitution Files
Note
    This table is based on the 513 cases where both the husband's and the wife's father's
    occupations are known.

closed marriage circle certainly seems to have set them off from the bulk of the working class. Men in urban manual-trades showed a different pattern. By the 1860s, they were only slightly more likely to marry women from a similar background than might be predicted from the distribution of such women among all brides. This relatively low level of endogamy persisted into the 1880s and stands in contrast to the higher levels of the 1850s.

Social endogamy was high within the local bourgeoisie and in the farming population. It also seems to have been high among general labourers. But if so, this was surely for a different set of reasons. Men and women from non-manual and farming backgrounds seemed to prefer not to marry outside their social groups. Labourers and the daughters of labourers, on the other hand, may not have had the opportunity to do so even if they so wished. But no such social barriers restricted access to the urban working class. Increasingly, women from a wide range of socio-economic backgrounds married urban manual workers. But few working-class women were likely to move in the other direction.

This analysis highlights the relationship between family formation and class formation in an unexpected way. As Charles Tilly has argued, a proletariat grows not just through expropriation, as in the Marxist schema, but through natural increase as well. Here in Saint-Hyacinthe, there seems to have been a pattern of class formation in which men who were already proletarians helped ensure the continued growth of the working class by marrying women from other social groups. Of course, these women may already have been wage labourers themselves, something which only information on the occupations of the brides in the three cohorts could clarify. One might speculate, and with some confidence given what we have seen of the local economy in this period and the figures presented in Table 2-4, that an increasing proportion of them were.[21]

Saint-Hyacinthe's marriage registers contain clues as to the geographic origins of these husbands and wives, as well as the professional information just discussed. It is already apparent that many of the men who married at the Saint-Hyacinthe cathedral between 1854 and 1891 had come from outside the parish. Most of the grooms, however, were local residents, as were the great majority of the brides. In over half of the marriages in the three cohorts, both parties lived in the parish; in a further 29%, the wife only was a local resident.[22] Those Saint-Hyacinthe men who married women from other communities – and there must have been many – most often did so in their brides' home parishes. Such couples, many of whom surely established residences in Saint-Hyacinthe, would fall through the cracks of the cohort family-reconstitution method adopted here.

Table 3–4 shows the number of husbands and wives in each cohort who were parish residents at the time of their marriage. This was the case for four-fifths of the women in Cohort A, and for over 85% of those in Cohorts B and C. In contrast, only 55% to 60% of the men in the three cohorts were residents of the parish. Thus, although Saint-Hyacinthe women were always more likely to choose their husbands locally, about three in 10 in each cohort married men from outside the parish.[23] Some of these men settled locally, but most simply returned with their brides to their home parishes. We have already met Joseph Arpin, the farmer from Saint-Ephrem d'Upton who married Saint-Hyacinthe resident Marguerite Girard in 1855. My systematic search of the local parish registers and manuscript census in the ensuing half-century turned up no further trace of this couple who, in all likelihood, had settled on Joseph's farm in Saint-Ephrem.[24]

Table 3-4
Distribution of Husbands and Wives by Place of Residence (Parish of Saint-Hyacinthe or Other)

| | HUSBANDS | | | | | |
| | Cohort A | | Cohort B | | Cohort C | |
	N	%	N	%	N	%
Parish	153	54.8	165	60.0	201	59.3
Outside the parish	126	45.2	110	40.0	138	40.7
Information missing[a]	16		2		1	
Total	295		277		340	

| | WIVES | | | | | |
| | Cohort A | | Cohort B | | Cohort C | |
	N	%	N	%	N	%
Parish	225	80.6	235	85.5	297	87.6
Outside the parish	54	19.4	40	14.5	42	12.4
Information missing[a]	16		2		1	
Total	295		277		340	

Source Family Reconstitution Files
Note
[a] These cases not counted in calculation of percentages.

Saint-Hyacinthe, as we have seen, was a developing commercial *entrepôt* – a railway link and a market town, as well as a manufacturing centre – in the second half of the nineteenth century. It also seems to have occupied a central place in a regional network of matrimonial exchange. This is a role which can be easily demonstrated with anecdotes, but which also merits systematic attention. The number of men in the three cohorts who came from outside the parish to marry is summarized visually in Figure 3-1.[25] Two things emerge from this analysis: the regional character of the Saint-Hyacinthe marriage market, and the wider reach of the town's influence. As the map suggests, over half (53%) of the non-resident men who found their brides in Saint-Hyacinthe came from neighbouring parishes in Saint-Hyacinthe and Bagot counties. Neighbouring parishes such as Notre-Dame-du-Rosaire in Saint-Hyacinthe county and Sainte-Rosalie and Saint-Dominique in Bagot county were especially well represented. Fully two-thirds of the non-resident husbands in the three cohorts (68%) came from a total of five counties in the immediate vicinity of Saint-Hyacinthe (Bagot, Saint-Hyacinthe, Shefford, Verchères, Rouville).

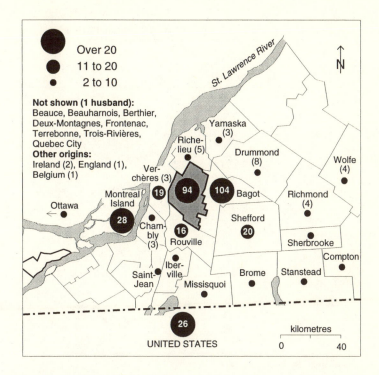

Figure 3-1 Geographic origins of non-resident husbands, three cohorts combined. Source: Family Reconstitution Files

Yet Saint-Hyacinthe did exert a certain pull even beyond these fairly narrow limits. Men living in the Eastern Townships, in the northeastern part of the United States, and on the island of Montreal all came to Saint-Hyacinthe to marry. Exchanges with areas to the south – with counties in the Townships and with the United States – seem to have peaked in the 1860s. An examination of seven Townships counties (Shefford, Richmond, Wolfe, Brome, Compton, Missisquoi, and Stanstead) together with the city of Sherbrooke shows that this region accounted for 10% of the non-resident husbands in the 1850s, 14% in the 1860s, and 8% in the 1880s. Similarly, only 2% of the husbands from outside the parish lived in the United States in the 1850s; this proportion increased to 12% in the 1860s, and declined again to 8% in the 1880s. In contrast, the proportion of husbands from the island of Montreal grew steadily across the period. Non-resident husbands from the Montreal area increased from 3% in the 1850s, to 8% in the 1860s, to 11% in the 1880s.[26]

Table 3-5
Resident and Non-Resident Husbands, by Occupational Group[a]

	Cohort	Residents N	Non-Residents N	Proportion of Residents[b] %
Agriculture	A	17	50	25.4
	B	24	43	35.8
	C	16	49	24.6
	Total	57	142	28.6
Urban-manual	A	85	16	84.2
	B	69	24	74.2
	C	137	35	79.7
	Total	291	75	79.5
Labourers	A	26	12	68.4
	B	25	4	86.2
	C	17	9	65.4
	Total	68	25	73.1
Non-manual	A	10	23	30.3
	B	37	22	62.7
	C	31	39	44.3
	Total	78	84	48.1

Source Family Reconstitution Files

Notes

[a] Based on 820 husbands for whom residence and occupation are known.

[b] Calculated as the number of residents divided by the total number for whom place of residence prior to marriage is known.

As already suggested, many of the men who came from outside the parish to marry local women were, like Joseph Arpin, farmers. In fact, most of the farmers who married at the cathedral in this period were non-residents. As Table 3-5 shows, 142 of the 199 farmers who married in the three cohorts (71%) were from outside the parish; the rest would have been from the rural part of Saint-Hyacinthe-le-Confesseur. In contrast, only one-fifth of the urban-manual workers and one-quarter of the labourers who married at the cathedral were from outside the parish. More than half of the husbands in the non-manual category were local residents, except in the expansive 1850s when a clear majority came from outside the parish.

Saint-Hyacinthe's pull on the agricultural population of the surrounding region, then, was considerable. As an expanding commercial and industrial centre, the town played an important role as the centre of social relations for farming communities all over this area. Public markets, general and more specialized stores, the railway, a courthouse, educational institutions – all were located in Saint-Hyacinthe and drew country people there for business and for social occasions. Clearly, some young men included courting in the range of activities they undertook in town, perhaps on market days. This should be no surprise at all.

The fact that Saint-Hyacinthe-le-Confesseur was a cathedral parish may also have contributed to the influence it exerted on the surrounding region. One factor that would have drawn certain non-resident couples to the cathedral was the need for episcopal dispensations to counteract prohibitions against consanguineous or affine unions.[27] Florentin Vigéant, for example, a Montreal merchant, needed such a dispensation to marry Eugénie Roy, the widow of his brother Jean, a founder who had been living in the United States. With the bishop's permission, the couple married at the Saint-Hyacinthe cathedral in 1885, some 17 years after Eugénie's first wedding, which had also taken place at the cathedral. In this case, neither the husband nor the wife was a resident of Saint-Hyacinthe, which may suggest that they married there because they needed the bishop's blessing.[28] Dispensations of this kind, whether for consanguinity or affinity – and sometimes for both – were granted much more frequently in the 1880s than they had been in the 1850s and 1860s.[29] Whether this was a result of social change or simply a reflection of an increased concern with the regulation of this type of union on the part of the church remains unclear.[30]

Another area in which the bishop of Saint-Hyacinthe would have been called upon to intervene was in what were referred to as "rehabilitations." Ten of the couples who married between 1854 and 1861 were seeking the Church's recognition of unions that had in fact existed for some time. The circumstances under which marriages might have had to be rehabilitated are somewhat obscure, except where a prohibition of consanguinity or affinity had been discovered after the initial wedding, in which case the ceremony would have had to be repeated.[31]

These cases, however, were truly exceptional. Most of the Saint-Hyacinthe brides and grooms in this period, as one might expect, married under more conventional circumstances. Most of the grooms were bachelors, for example, and most of the brides were spinsters, to use the contemporary expression. As Table 3-6 shows, about seven in ten unions in each of the three cohorts were first marriages for both parties. A further 15% were first marriages for the wife only, 10% were remarriages for both parties, and 3% were remarriages for the wife only.[32]

Table 3-6
Distribution of Couples by the Civil Status of Each Spouse, by Cohort

		A	B	C	Total
First marriage for both	N	214	202	233	649
parties (bachelor-spinster)	%	72.5	72.9	68.5	71.2
First marriage for wife	N	46	37	55	138
only (widower-spinster)	%	15.6	13.4	16.2	15.1
First marriage for husband only	N	5	9	12	26
(bachelor-widow)	%	1.7	3.2	3.5	2.9
Remarriage for both	N	21	28	39	88
parties (widower-widow)	%	7.1	10.1	11.5	9.6
Missing data	N	9	1	1	11
	%	3.1	0.4	0.3	1.2
Total		295	277	340	912

Source Family Reconstitution Files

It is important to disaggregate these data by gender, as remarriage was a very different adventure for men and women in this period. Doing so shows that 86% of the brides in the three cohorts were previously unmarried, compared to only 74% of husbands. This means that roughly twice as many widowers as widows married at the Saint-Hyacinthe cathedral in each of the three periods studied.[33] This is consistent with research on widowhood and remarriage, which shows clearly and consistently that widowers tended to remarry in greater proportions, and after a shorter interval, than widows.[34] The situation in Saint-Hyacinthe was no different. Honoré Mercier was an exceptional figure in many ways, but not in this. When, in May of 1871, he married Marie Virginie St-Denis, bringing with him four-year-old Eliza, the daughter of his first wife, Léopoldine Boivin, whom he had married in 1866 and who had died prior to November 1868, he was acting exactly like most young widowers – but rather fewer young widows – of his generation.[35]

Finally, were Saint-Hyacinthe's brides and grooms well enough educated to affix their signature to the marriage register? And did the social and economic changes of this period include an increase in literacy rates in this community? Although some debate exists about methods in this area, the ability to sign such a register is usually taken as an adequate measure of individual literacy, and as a particularly good measure of trends in literacy over time.[36] This information, which was collected for previously unmarried husbands and wives in

Table 3-7
Signature Rates

| Cohort | Proportion Signing Marriage Register (%) | | | |
| | Men[a] | | Women[b] | |
	%	N	%	N
A (1854–61)				
Agriculture	32.0	50	52.1	48
Urban-manual	48.2	85	57.1	28
Labourers	20.8	24	15.4	13
Non-manual	82.6	23	93.3	15
No data	50.0	32	46.4	110
All occupations	45.3	214	50.5	214
B (1864–71)				
Agriculture	41.9	43	59.0	61
Urban-manual	57.9	76	82.9	41
Labourers	19.0	21	31.3	16
Non-manual	97.5	40	87.1	31
No data	40.9	22	58.5	53
All occupations	58.4	202	65.8	202
C (1884–91)				
Agriculture	75.7	37	84.9	53
Urban-manual	82.0	128	90.7	75
Labourers	50.0	16	47.1	17
Non-manual	95.7	46	94.6	56
No data	83.3	6	78.1	32
All occupations	81.5	233	85.4	233

Source Family Reconstitution Files

Notes

[a]   Previously unmarried husbands, grouped by occupation.

[b]   Previously unmarried wives, grouped by father's occupation.

the three marriage cohorts, is presented in Table 3-7.[37] As the table shows, signature rates in Saint-Hyacinthe did indeed follow the well-documented upward trend for the period, which was directly related to the spread of primary education. As Allan Greer and others have demonstrated, Quebec's literacy levels increased dramatically in the second half of the nineteenth century, especially in urban areas.[38] Among both men and women who married at the Saint-Hyacinthe cathedral between 1854 and 1891, the increase in signing capacity was steep and uninterrupted. Forty-five percent of men signed the register in the 1850s, a proportion that grew steadily – to 58% in the 1860s and to 82% in the 1880s. Among the wives, the proportion signing the register was consistently several percentage points higher. It was also subject to the same upward trend: half of the women signed in the 1850s, two-thirds in the 1860s, and 85% in the 1880s.

Table 3-7 also contains an occupational breakdown of these signature rates. The ranking of the four occupationally defined groups was rigidly consistent. Labourers and the daughters of labourers were the least likely to be literate; men and women from non-manual backgrounds had the highest signature rates, while those in the urban-manual and farming categories occupied the middle ground. The gaps between the most and the least literate groups, however, were narrowing in this context of rising literacy. Men and women from working-class and farming backgrounds made spectacular gains in the period, substantially reducing the differential between themselves and the almost universally literate, non-manual elite. *Journaliers* and their families remained distinct in this, as in other respects. Barely half of the husbands and wives in the "labourer" category signed the marriage register as late as the 1880s, by which time over 80% of the general population was able to do so.[39]

Patterns in the professional, geographic, civil-status, and literacy profiles of these 912 couples, reveal no major surprises. They do, however, give a clear sense of who married whom in late-nineteenth-century Saint-Hyacinthe. Most of the husbands were either local manual workers or farmers from the surrounding region, although the Saint-Hyacinthe bourgeoisie was well represented as well. Young men tended to marry women from a similar background, and this was particularly true if they were at the richer or poorer extremes of the economic scale. Though remarriage was an important reality for some, the majority of husbands and the vast majority of wives had never been previously married. Finally, an increasing proportion of brides and grooms were literate enough to sign the marriage register, although clear class and gender differences did persist in this area.

THE MARRIAGE CALENDAR

When did people in Saint-Hyacinthe prefer to marry? On Saturday afternoons in June? Or at some other point in the week and year, at a time prescribed by custom but nonetheless responsive to the new exigencies of commercial and industrial development? Local marriage registers contain detailed information on the timing of matrimony in the week and year (although they are less helpful on time of day). Shifts in the day or season at which marriages were celebrated may reflect new rhythms of life associated with the generalization of factory work and other important trends, agricultural specialization being one example. Continuities in these matters would demonstrate the persistent influence of other factors: the Church and its prohibitions, for example, or the *curé* and his humours.

With respect to the timing of weddings in the week, the pattern was one of near absolute continuity. The principal days for weddings throughout the later nineteenth century were Mondays and Tuesdays; over 80% of the marriages in the three cohorts occurred on one of these two days.[40] Weddings were virtually never celebrated on Fridays or Sundays. Saturday weddings – the norm that has developed in the twentieth century – accounted for only 4% overall, with a very slight upward trend.[41] Wednesday and Thursday weddings were somewhat more common, accounting for about 6% each.

Industry and urban development seem to have had little or no effect on the weekly round of weddings in Saint-Hyacinthe. Priests, who had much to say about when ceremonies would take place, planned in accordance with the religious calendar and their own availability. Saturday remained a day of work rather than rest and recreation, so that the more recent preference for this day would have made no particular sense. Overall, the Catholic tradition of Monday and Tuesday weddings, which as Jean-Pierre Bardet observes dates back to the 1720s, persisted in this industrializing community.[42]

The distribution of marriages through the year seems to have been more sensitive to socio-economic change. Figure 3-2 traces the percentage distribution of weddings by calendar month for the three cohorts.[43] As one can immediately see, major troughs in all three curves occur during the months of March and December; at no time did weddings celebrated in either of these months exceed 4% of the annual total. These slow periods in the year correspond, of course, to Lent and Advent: seasons of fasting and other kinds of sacrifice (including, at least in theory, sexual abstinence) in the Catholic religious calendar. Their persistence as slow periods throughout the later nineteenth century in Saint-Hyacinthe is unquestionable.[44]

But a comparison of the three curves also shows certain discontinuities. Seasonal peaks and troughs were noticeably less pronounced in the 1880s than they had been in the 1850s and 1860s. At least in relative terms, winter seems to have declined as the preferred season for matrimony. February, for example, was a month of intense nuptiality in the 1850s and 1860s, but not in the 1880s. Conversely, the post-Lenten recovery was much steeper and more sustained in the latter period than in the former two. As a result, April and May had higher than average numbers of weddings in the 1880s for the first time. At no time did many marriages occur in the mid-summer months, although there was always a resumption in September. But

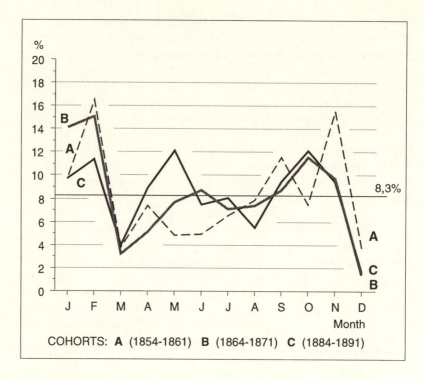

Figure 3-2 Distribution of marriages in the year, by cohort.
Source: Family Reconstitution Files

here, too, the patterns varied. In the 1850s, the number of weddings fell sharply in October, only to rise to a peak in the month of November, before dropping to low Advent levels. In the 1860s and the 1880s, most autumn marriages occurred in October. November was a month of more moderate activity in which levels were already beginning to fall to their pre-Christmas levels.

By the 1880s, then, a flattening out of the marriage calendar could be seen in Saint-Hyacinthe, as winter weddings receded and April and May took on a new importance. This may have resulted from the increasingly urban character of the parish and the corresponding decline in the relative significance of agriculture to its economy. The importance of the calendar of agricultural labour to the seasonal distribution of weddings is one of the best loved truisms in historical demography. One would expect to see this relationship dissipate in a community that was increasingly urban and proletarian in character. But the situation in Saint-Hyacinthe was more complex than the truism would suggest. Farmers as well as urban dwellers participated in the trend away from winter, toward spring, marriages.[45] Did transformations in agriculture modify the seasonal round of work sufficiently to allow the farming population to participate in a trend toward spring marriages that had originated in the town? Perhaps. Alternatively, farmers may have been more likely by the 1880s to turn to non-farm, wage-earning activities outside the region during the winter months.[46] If so, the old tradition of January and February weddings would necessarily have fallen by the wayside.

In Saint-Hyacinthe, then, links between economic structural change and the evolving calendar of matrimony are difficult to discern. As with the distribution of weddings during the week, patterns were determined in part by religious prohibition of certain seasons. But within these parameters a certain levelling out can be observed, especially in the relative decline of winter and the rise of spring as preferred seasons for matrimony. These trends may well reflect changes in the seasonal patterns of work, both in agriculture and in urban occupations. They provide a hint of the many ways in which fundamental social and economic change was reshaping family formation in Saint-Hyacinthe and in Quebec as a whole during this period.

AGE AT MARRIAGE

Age at marriage is one of the central topics in historical demography. Marriage ages are sensitive to a wide range of factors, including cultural traditions, social norms, religious prescriptions, and material circumstances. They are influenced by economic opportunity and by household circumstances, by personal choice, and by family and community pressure. Furthermore, marriage ages are profoundly gendered; in virtually every society where this has been studied, women marry several years earlier than men.[47] Women's marriage ages, moreover, are particularly important from a demographic perspective, because of their direct influence on general fertility levels, particularly within non-contraceptive populations.

Marriage age is often described as a kind of demo-economic linchpin, articulating systems of production and reproduction to each other. Research into the proto-industrial phase of capitalist development in Europe, for example, suggests that new opportunities for wage labour removed obstacles to early marriage in certain regions. Early marriage, through its positive influence on birth rates, produced rapid demographic growth in those regions and, as the new economic structures spread, in Europe as a whole.[48] Joan Scott and Louise Tilly express a general consensus on this issue by characterizing marriage age as "perhaps the most sensitive indicator of the relationship between resources and population" in early modern England and France.[49]

Economic conditions, then, affect the decisions men and women make about if and when to marry. So, too, do social and economic differences. This is because the opportunities available to young people can change dramatically over time and vary widely between social groups. The structure of economic opportunity – in the form of land, skills, education, professional training, or access to a wage – plays a major role in influencing the age at which men and women decide to establish households and form families.[50]

In an important sense, however, the question of when one marries is subordinate to the question of whether one marries. Marriage age, in other words, is part of the larger question of nuptiality. As we saw in chapter 1 (Table 1-3), marriage rates in the parish of Saint-Hya-cinthe-le-Confesseur were falling in the second half of the nineteenth century, from about nine per thousand in the 1860s and 1870s to seven per thousand in 1901. Provincial levels in the same interval were lower, but also falling: from eight per thousand in 1861 to six per thousand in 1891 and 1901.[51] These crude marriage rates, however, are flawed measures of the level of nuptiality, mainly because they take no account of the age and sex structure of the populations being compared. Unfortunately, this information is largely unavailable for Saint-Hyacinthe during the period in question: after 1861, published census data was aggregated only at the level of the county.[52]

County-level indices of female nuptiality for all regions of Ontario and Quebec, however, have been calculated by Marvin McInnis. McInnis estimated the proportion of married women among those aged 15 to 45 in all counties of the two provinces in 1851 and 1891.[53] His data show a general downward trend, though the intensity, and even the direction of the trend vary from one region to another. In Montreal, for example, the trend was slightly upward, from 49.5% in 1851 to 50.4% in 1891.[54] In the other major Quebec cities, particularly Quebec, the trend was strongly downward, as it was in the mainly rural counties surrounding Saint-Hyacinthe: Bagot, Rouville, and Shefford. In Saint-Hyacinthe county itself, levels were noticeably lower and the downward trend, though present, was attenuated; for example, in 1851, 55.7% of the women aged 15 to 45 were married, compared to 54.2% in 1891.[55]

Age at first marriage is a more precise and revealing measure of nuptiality than marriage ratios. Moreover, it can be evaluated rather thoroughly for industrializing Saint-Hyacinthe, using data generated

in the family-reconstitution study. This study relied heavily on declarations of age found in the manuscript census and in death certificates. Since uncritical use of such declarations involves unacceptable
risks, some discussion of the way these data were collected, tested,
and ultimately used is necessary. Most of this discussion has been
relegated to the methodological appendix.[56] But to summarize briefly, the marriage ages discussed here are, in most cases, estimates
based on anywhere from one to five declarations of age. These declarations were made by individuals to census takers and by family
members to the priests charged with writing burial acts. For each
declaration, an implied birth year was calculated by subtracting the
stated age at the time of the event (census or burial) from the date of
the event. In cases where several age declarations were available, the
implied birth years thus generated were compared to each other,
their consistency evaluated, and where necessary, a selection made.[57]
These birth-year estimates were assigned codes that reflect their
reliability, defined in terms of the amount of age information available and its internal consistency.

At an earlier stage of the analysis, these estimation codes were
used as a sorting criterion. Each set of marriage ages was presented
twice, once using all the available age information, and a second time
using only those marriage ages judged the most reliable.[58] In the
current analysis, this double-barrelled approach has been abandoned, mainly because the slight differences between the two series
were found to be statistically insignificant. The numbers of more
reliable "best" age values available for each cohort and occupational
category are nonetheless reported in the tables.

The analysis presented here is of age at *first* marriage, following a
convention in historical demography for which there are strong
substantive and practical reasons. Substantively, comparing first and
subsequent marriages is like comparing apples and oranges. The
material circumstances of the bride and groom and the cultural
meanings attached to the wedding may be profoundly affected by
whether or not it was a remarriage. In practical terms, examining the
ages of widows and widowers is complicated by the fact that marriage
acts do not generally differentiate between those remarrying for the
first time and those remarrying for the second (or subsequent) time.
Nor can an analysis of the average age at marriage of widows and
widowers account for other critical variables, particularly the age of
the surviving spouse at the death of his or her partner.[59]

Table 3-8 presents the available data on age at first marriage for
men who married in the parish of Saint-Hyacinthe during the three
periods under review. The most striking thing about these husbands

Table 3-8
Men's Age at First Marriage, Parish of Saint-Hyacinthe

	Mean	Median	Mode	Standard Deviation	Number of Cases	Number of "Best Values"[a]
1854–61	23.4	23	23	4.33	122	67
1864–71	24.2	23	21*	5.72	128	93
1884–91	24.0	23	20	6.02	149	75

Source Family Reconstitution Files

Notes

[a]   Best values: Known birthdate or at least two age declarations (census or burial), two of which yield birth-year estimates that agree to within a range of two years.

*   More than one modal value.

is their youth. The mean age at first marriage for men in Saint-Hyacinthe ranged between 23.4 and 24.2 years, with very little variation. And the median marriage age for men was 23 years in each of the three cohorts. In contrast, as Table 3-9 indicates, the singulate mean age at first marriage for men in all of Quebec increased from 26.5 years in 1861 to 27.2 years in 1891.[60] Men in Saint-Hyacinthe, then, consistently married some three years earlier than the provincial average.[61] Also apparent from the table is the absence of any significant trend in marriage age across the three cohorts. Interestingly, men in Saint-Hyacinthe did not follow the provincial trend toward later marriage, which is apparent in Table 3-9 and which affected regions as diverse as Montreal and the Saguenay.[62]

When these figures are broken down by occupational category, however, the picture that emerges is somewhat different (Table 3-10). The mean values for the 1850s are difficult to interpret, but the median values would certainly suggest very little variation in marriage age among men in the different kinds of occupations. A clear pattern of social differentiation emerges in the 1860s, however, and persists into the 1880s. One can think of this pattern as three-tiered. Labourers married earliest in the 1860s and the 1880s: mean values were between 21 and 22 years. Urban-manual workers were slightly older, with mean marriage ages ranging between 23 and 24. The uppermost tier – the men who waited the longest before marrying – was occupied by farmers and those in non-manual occupations. These men married substantially later; the mean values are between 25 and 26 years of age.[63] In later nineteenth-century Saint-Hyacinthe, then, farmers and non-manual workers married up to three years later than manual workers in urban occupations, who themselves married a year or two later than *journaliers*.

Table 3-9
Singulate Mean Age at First Marriage for Men: Quebec (Total), Montreal, and the
Saguenay Region: 1852–1891

	Quebec (total)	Montreal	Saguenay
1852	25.5	25.5	24.6
1861	26.5	26.5	25.3
1871	26.8	26.2	25.4
1881	26.8	26.5	25.4
1891	27.2	27.9	25.9

Source: Pouyez, Lavoie et al., *Les Saguenayens*, table 6.10, 270

Table 3-10
Men's Age at First Marriage by Occupational Category

	Mean	Median	Mode	Standard Deviation	Number of Cases	Number of "Best Values"[a]
1854–61						
Agriculture	23.2	23	21	4.51	30	19
Urban-manual	23.1	23	23	3.20	56	30
Labourers	24.7	23.5	20	4.63	14	8
Non-manual	25.0	23	23	5.02	11	5
1864–71						
Agriculture	26.0	25.5	21	6.13	26	20
Urban-manual	24.0	22	23	6.20	53	37
Labourers	21.7	21	20*	4.95	17	13
Non-manual	25.2	25	23	4.63	26	19
1884–91						
Agriculture	25.6	25	25*	5.72	18	8
Urban-manual	23.5	22	20	6.23	98	51
Labourers	21.2	20	20	2.17	9	3
Non-manual	26.0	24.5	24*	5.77	24	13

Source Family Reconstitution Files
Notes
[a]   Best values: Known birthdate or at least two age declarations (census or burial), two of which
      yield birth-year estimates that agree to within a range of two years.
*   More than one modal value.

We can briefly look at the trends in each occupational category,
and introduce some examples, in order to get a better sense of what
was occurring in Saint-Hyacinthe with respect to men's age at marriage during this period. In the first place, farmers were marrying two
to three years later in the 1860s and 1880s than they had in the
1850s. For instance, Lévi Loranger, a farmer from Notre-Dame-de-

Saint-Hyacinthe who married Obéline Scott in September of 1865, was 27 years old at the time, just slightly above the average for farmers in this marriage cohort.[64] Farmers who married in the third cohort, in the 1880s, continued to do so at a relatively advanced age, particularly compared to the town's urban manual workers. Although the link must remain hypothetical, it is possible that this trend toward delayed marriages – in this regard, Saint-Hyacinthe's farmers echoed men elsewhere in Quebec – had to do with the agricultural changes of the period. As we have seen, Saint-Hyacinthe County was quickly reaching the limits of its potential for agricultural expansion, at least in terms of the number of working farms. Access to farming as an occupation was therefore becoming increasingly difficult for young men in the countryside. In addition to the resulting pressure for out-migration, this restriction of economic opportunities may well have meant a decision to delay marriage for those who stayed.[65]

In contrast to farmers, the marriage age of urban manual workers – by far the most numerous group in the study – remained very low indeed during this interval. The mean age at first marriage for husbands in this category ranged between 23 and 24 years throughout the period, with no significant trend. Median ages were slightly lower, at 22 years in the 1860s and 1880s cohorts, suggesting the frequency with which manual workers in their late teens and early twenties married in this community. For example, Arthur Renaud married in May of 1889 at the age of 19; Johnny Champigny married two months later at the age of 18; a year after that, Omer Dufresne, aged 20, married at the Saint-Hyacinthe cathedral. The examples could be multiplied. Interestingly, Arthur, Johnny, and Omer shared something else besides their youth. They all worked in the local leather industries. Arthur and Johnny were both shoemakers, according to the priests who filled out their marriage certificates; however, the census taken two years later revealed that both worked in local shoe factories. Omer was identified as a *corroyeur* in his marriage certificate, which suggests tannery work. But he must have wound up in the Côté or the Séguin-Lalime shoe factories, for he stated his occupation as *cordonnier* in eight civil acts passed between 1892 and 1902, only to resurface as a carter in 1904.[66]

These stories illustrate the pattern of earlier marriage in the urban working class, as identified in Table 3-10. Reasons for the pattern are not hard to find. Young men employed in the local tanneries, shoe factories, and knitting mill needed fewer material resources in order to marry. They formed families on the basis of their access to a wage rather than accumulation of capital or skill. Particularly if they had begun to work at the age of 14 or 15, as many did, they may well have reached their maximum wage-earning potential – never very high – by the age of 19 or 20. At any rate, they would certainly not have expected their earning power to increase by more than a dollar or two per week by the time they reached their mid-twenties. Having accepted wage labour as a way of life, such men reached a point where they felt they could "afford" to marry earlier in life than either farmers or young men building careers in commerce or the professions.

Though by the 1880s we are looking at only a handful of general labourers, it is clear that their marriage age had been in sharp decline since the 1850s. The mean age at first marriage for *journaliers* fell from 24.7 in the 1850s, to 21.6 in the 1860s, and finally to 21.2 (based on just nine cases) in the 1880s. This shift was almost certainly related to the changing opportunities for labourers in Saint-Hyacinthe. In the 1850s, a *journalier* who married in the parish might well have been an agricultural worker, perhaps a prospective farmer who had been awaiting his opportunity to acquire land while helping his parents on the family farm. Later marriage under these circumstances would not be unexpected. Indeed, what is unexpected is the frequency with which Saint-Hyacinthe *journaliers* in the 1850s waited until after their 25th birthday to marry. Lévi Morin, Adolphe Tremblay, Théophile Desmarais, and Narcisse Demarais were all labourers who married at the cathedral between 1856 and 1860. None of these four were less than 27 years of age.[67] By the 1880s, on the other hand, a *journalier* in Saint-Hyacinthe was much more likely to be an unskilled wage labourer in a large factory. It would be no surprise, then, if he timed the formation of his family in a way similar to other urban manual workers, who by and large married early. Joseph Lafleur, who married in 1886 at age 19, and Ozias Casavant, who married in 1887 at age 20, were fairly typical (except that Joseph's bride, Exilda Phlibotte, was four years older than he). Both were identified as *journaliers* in the marriage register. Subsequent parish and census documents, however, show that both worked in local factories, rather than agriculture. According to the 1891 census, Joseph was working in one of the shoe factories in 1891. And Ozias declared a range of industrial occupations between 1887 and 1899, including *corroyeur, tanneur, cordonnier,* and *employé au tricot.*[68] It is difficult to imagine a more urban, proletarian itinerary.

The age data for husbands in the non-manual category remain to be examined. During the period, mean age values were consistently high, at between 25 and 26, and rising very gradually. Men who declared non-manual occupations always married later than the cohort average. Their mean marriage age was higher by 1.6 years in the 1850s, 1.0 years in the 1860s, and 2.0 years in the 1880s. Thus, Honoré Mercier was relatively young, by the standards of his social class, when in 1866, as a 24-year-old lawyer, he married Léopoldine Boivin in 1866. More typical was Joseph Alexandre Aimé Beauchamp, a veterinary doctor, who married Marie Elmina Mathieu in 1887 at the age of 26. Merchants as well as professionals delayed marriage into their mid to late twenties during this period. This is amply attested to by the examples of Prosper Meunier *dit* Lapierre, who was 29 when in 1865 he married the schoolteacher Eugénie Marchessault; and Hector Pagnuelo, a merchant grocer who, at 27, married Blanche Sicotte, daughter of the Quebec Superior Court judge Louis Victor Sicotte in 1886.[69]

As we can see, then, the ages at which men first married trace a clear pattern of social differentiation in Saint-Hyacinthe during the second half of the nineteenth century. The aggregate trend toward later marriage that has so often been documented for Quebec in this period seems to have missed Saint-Hyacinthe entirely. Mean and median marriage ages for the three cohorts remain roughly equal, at between 23 and 24 years. However, a close look at the Saint-Hyacinthe data reveals socially specific trends that may be of even greater interest. In this particular town, farmers and members of the local bourgeoisie were participating in the provincial trends toward later marriage by the 1860s. On the other hand, the average age at first marriage for urban-manual workers, a category dominated by Saint-Hyacinthe's industrial working class, remained very low. And general labourers were marrying earlier at the end of the period, when factory work was the norm, than they had been at the beginning, when it was not.

This pattern of substantially earlier marriage in the urban manual and labourer categories fits well with some widely held views about the link between family formation and economic autonomy. Professionals, merchants, and others in non-manual occupations needed time to establish themselves in business, or to acquire the education necessary to practise medicine or the law. Farmers might need to delay marriage until they could acquire sufficient capital (in the form of land, livestock, and equipment) to support a young family. Clearly, these economic obstacles to early marriage did not operate in the same way within the urban working class. As a result, urban-manual workers continued to marry early, even as men working in other sectors of the economy delayed family formation. General labourers – propertyless and wage-dependent by definition – were behaving like the urban-manual workers by the 1860s, and marrying even earlier by the 1880s.

Table 3-11
Women's Age at First Marriage, Parish of Saint-Hyacinthe

	Mean	Median	Mode	Standard Deviation	Number of Cases	Number of "Best Values"[a]
1854–61	21.5	20	19	5.07	146	84
1864–71	22.4	21	18*	6.18	141	100
1884–91	22.9	21	18	6.98	183	103

Source Family Reconstitution Files

Notes

[a]   Best values: Known birthdate or at least two age declarations (census or burial), two of which yield birth-year estimates that agree to within a range of two years.

*   More than one modal value.

Table 3-12
Singulate Mean Age at First Marriage for Women: Quebec (Total), Montreal, and the Saguenay Region: 1852–1891

	Quebec (total)	Montreal	Saguenay
1852	23.7	23.1	18.9
1861	24.5	25.4	21.2
1871	24.9	25.0	22.3
1881	24.8	24.2	23.2
1891	24.7	25.8	23.1

Source: Pouyez, Lavoie et al., *Les Saguenayens*, table 6.10, 270

Women marrying for the first time in Saint-Hyacinthe did so at an even earlier age than their husbands, at an average age that was about three years younger than the provincial level. Table 3-11 presents the available data on age at first marriage for women in the three Saint-Hyacinthe cohorts. Women in this parish married at between 21 and 23 years of age,[70] well below the singulate mean age at first marriage for Quebec women, which was between 24 and 25 years through most of this period (see Table 3-12). These levels are also slightly below the threshold of 23 years which John Hajnal has stated as the lower limit of the "European marriage pattern."[71] Saint-Hyacinthe women, then, married very early by Western European (and North American) standards.

The table also suggests that women in the parish toward the end of the nineteenth century were marrying over a year later than had been the case in the 1850s. From 21.5 years in the 1850s, the mean age at first marriage for Saint-Hyacinthe women increased to 22.9 in the 1880s. Local brides shared in the trend toward delayed marriage that characterized Quebec society as a whole, as a comparison with Table 3-12 shows. But they continued to marry some two years earlier than the provincial average, and some three years earlier than Montreal women in the same period.[72]

To what extent did her social position affect the timing of a woman's transition to married life? A look at the occupations of the brides' fathers provides some hints (Table 3-13). As with male marriage ages, there is a striking pattern of differentiation among the four occupationally defined categories. In the 1850s, women's marriage ages were uniformly low, the mean age in each category being between 18 and 20 years during this early period. By the 1860s there was a new pattern – in which, on average, the daughters of farmers and non-manual workers married at 24 or 25 years of age, while the daughters of urban-manual workers and general labourers married between ages 20 and 21. This pattern persisted into the 1880s, except for the fact that the means for daughters of urban manual workers and labourers had risen slightly in the interval. In other respects, the figures were similar to what they had been 20 years earlier: daughters of non-manual workers and farmers married at an average age of about 24, while women from an urban-manual or labouring background married, on average, at about age 21.

A few examples will illustrate the emerging pattern. The daughters of farmers in the 1864-71 period provide an interesting place to begin. We have already met Adéline Leduc, the seamstress who married Eusèbe Bourgeois in 1869. At 25 years of age, Adéline was a year older than the average age of farmer's daughters who married in Saint-Hyacinthe during this period. Eusèbe, a carriage maker, was precisely the average age for urban-manual workers, which meant that, at 24, he was a year younger than his wife.[73] This would be unremarkable, except for the fact that at least nine other farmer's daughters also married younger men in this period. Émilie Languirand, for example, was the 24-year-old daughter of farmer Pierre Languirand. In 1869, she married Pierre Millette, another local farmer, aged 19 years.[74] These examples reinforce what the mean marriage ages suggest: women from agricultural backgrounds married late in the 1860s, whether because they chose to work before marriage or for other reasons. That they should so often have married men younger than themselves is something of a surprise. But given the variations that are hidden by the averages and the fact that labourers and other men in manual occupations tended to marry so early, it stands to reason that some women, like Adéline and Émilie, would have chosen to marry younger men.

Fewer surprises are found among the daughters of urban-manual workers and general labourers who married in the parish during the 1860s. The statistics demonstrate that the daughters of such men

Table 3-13
Women's Age at First Marriage by Father's Occupational Category

	Mean	Median	Mode	Standard Deviation	Number of Cases	Number of "Best Values"[a]
1854–61						
Agriculture	19.9	19	21	3.31	29	17
Urban-manual	18.5	18	17 *	2.04	19	8
Labourers	20.3	19.5	18*	3.72	12	7
Non-manual	20.2	20	20	2.15	10	8
1864–71						
Agriculture	24.0	22	22	7.59	47	35
Urban-manual	20.0	20	18	3.03	31	23
Labourers	21.2	21	17*	4.81	13	7
Non-manual	24.7	24.5	20*	6.09	20	13
1884–91						
Agriculture	24.3	22	18	8.14	43	19
Urban-manual	21.4	20	18	5.43	63	39
Labourers	21.2	18	17	6.34	11	7
Non-manual	24.1	22	19*	7.97	46	28

Source Family Reconstitution Files

Notes

[a] Best values: Known birthdate or at least two age declarations (census or burial), two of which yield birth-year estimates that agree to within a range of two years.

* More than one modal value.

married early, between 20 and 21 years of age, on average. There are plenty of examples one could select in support of the numbers. Albina Robitaille's father, a Saint-Hyacinthe tailor, had already died when in 1870, at age 18, she married a 23-year-old shoemaker, Henri Champagne.[75] And Julie Proulx was also 18 on her wedding day in January of 1866. She was the daughter of Saint-Hyacinthe labourer Olivier Proulx and her groom was Alexandre Fortier, another local labourer, aged 22.[76] As for the daughters of the bourgeoisie, two women who married 20 years later, in Cohort C, serve to illustrate a pattern of later marriage that was by then well established. Blanche Sicotte, the judge's daughter whom we have already met, was 26 when she married Hector Pagnuelo in 1886. For her part, Auglore Messier was a merchant's daughter who was also 26 years of age when she married the lawyer Jacques Octave Beauregard, a year her junior, in 1890.[77]

Fleshed out with these examples, the data in Table 3-13 demonstrate the emergence, from the 1860s on, of a pattern of social differentiation in women's ages at marriage in Saint-Hyacinthe. This pattern saw daughters of men engaged in non-manual occupations and in agriculture marry three to four years later than the daughters of urban-manual workers and *journaliers*. Bourgeois women, like the bourgeois men they most often wed, generally married several years later than their working-class counterparts. And brides from an agricultural background were generally older than the daughters of urban-manual workers, by a similar margin. One explanation of the latter pattern may be that many of the farmer's daughters who married in Saint-Hyacinthe were recent migrants to the town. Young single women who had come from the countryside in search of employment in domestic service, commerce, or industry might be expected to marry later than non-migrant women.[78] As to bourgeois women, their reasons for delaying marriage probably related to the high levels of social endogamy in this group. Although direct evidence is not available, it is possible to imagine a pattern of long engagements in which women essentially waited for their fiancés to acquire the training or capital necessary for family formation.

Clearly, this pattern of socially differentiated marriage ages was a new phenomenon in the period under review. By the 1860s, the propertied elements in this community had begun to behave quite differently from the working class. Surely the new economic and social relations emerging in the period, particularly the appearance of well-defined bourgeois and wage-labouring elements in the local population, had much to do with this change. Further analysis of the family-reconstitution data will show the extent to which this trend toward social differentiation occurred in other areas, such as household composition and fertility.

So far, we have considered a woman's marriage age only as a function of her socio-economic status, as reflected – adequately enough, one hopes – by her father's occupation. But there were obviously many other influences on a woman's choice about when and whether to marry. One of the most important of these was whether or not she participated in the formal labour market. As we have seen, however, Saint-Hyacinthe's parish registers are all but silent on the subject of women's paid labour. Of all 912 brides in the three cohorts, information is available for only nine concerning age at (first) marriage and labour-force participation prior to the wedding.[79] The behaviour of these women does not look exceptional when one considers the three teachers who married in the 1860s at ages 20, 22, and 24 respectively, or the 21-year-old tannery worker who married at the beginning of the 1890s.

On the other hand, a pattern of delayed marriages does seem to emerge when one looks specifically at the five seamstresses in the group. Spread across two cohorts, these five women had an average age at first marriage of 26 years. Three of them – Arzélia, Sophronie, and Victoria Tremblay – were sisters, whose parental household situation was particularly bleak. Their father, a labourer, had died in 1874 when they were between 8 and 16 years of age. In 1881, they were living with their widowed mother and two single women, aged 27 and 49. All six women in the household reported the occupation *couturière* to the census taker.[80] None of the three Tremblay sisters would marry before age 25. Arzélia was 28 when she married machinist Ferdinand Guerin in 1884; Sophronie was 25 when she married Arthur Dufresne, a shoe-factory worker, in 1888; and Victoria was 26 in 1891 when she married a shoemaker of her own, Wilfrid Dumaine.[81] All three, of course, were well above the average age at marriage for labourer's daughters in this period, which was about 21 years.

The case of the Tremblay sisters hints at the impact of women's wage labour on marriage ages. It also shows how domestic circumstances might either prevent a woman from marrying, or delay the event.[82] In poor households, young women who could contribute their domestic labour and bring in a wage were valued assets. An adult daughter's contribution to the family economy became even more important in the event of parental death or disability. In households where the principal wage earner – generally the father – had died or become too ill to work, the labour of older daughters (and sons, for that matter) could be essential to the family's survival.[83] Like the Tremblay sisters, many young women in such situations would have hesitated to form new families, knowing that their labour power and their emotional support were indispensable to their widowed mothers with households full of younger children.

One final line of analysis is in order before concluding this discussion of marriage ages. We have seen that, on average, men married about two years later than women. But this tells us nothing about the age difference between marriage partners, except that (statistically) the husband was likely to be somewhat older. We have also seen that certain women, particularly those from an agricultural background who married in the 1860s and who were themselves aged 24 or more, chose younger men more frequently than we might have expected. But what of the more general patterns? Were men from certain occupational groups more likely to marry women who were closer in age to themselves? And did these age differences vary over time?[84] To find out, it is necessary to examine age differentials on a couple-by-couple basis, rather than to simply compare aggregate figures.[85]

The results of this analysis are found in Table 3-14. As in the independent analysis of men's and women's marriage ages, a clear pattern of social differentiation emerges. The age difference between farmers and their wives expanded slightly in the period. It was relatively high – on the order of three to four years – for each of the three cohorts, edging closer to four years for the first time in the 1860s. The same is true of the non-manual group, where the average age differential was exactly four years for each of the two later periods. In the urban-manual group, however, husbands and wives tended to be closer in age. Stable at about three years in the 1850s and 1860s, the average age gap had declined to two years by the 1880s. The numbers for labourers and their wives, although very small, are intriguing. They declined from a level higher than that of farmers (3.6 years) in the 1850s to a level below even that of urban-manual workers (1.3 years) in the 1880s.

As with men's and women's marriage ages, then, the difference in age between brides and grooms was socially specific. Age gaps were much more clearly differentiated in the 1860s and 1880s than they had been in the 1850s. From the 1860s on, labourers and urban-manual workers were considerably closer in age to their wives than non-manual workers and farmers: roughly the pattern identified by Bardet for Rouen. There may be a simple explanation for these trends. After all, to the extent that husbands were older – as they were within the bourgeoisie and the farming population – they would have had a greater opportunity to select younger women to marry. In other words, a six-year age gap between a 28-year-old lawyer and his wife was, on the whole, more likely than the same gap between a 19-year-old factory worker and his wife. It would be possible to construct a more romantic explanation, of course. Might there have been, for example, a fundamental shift in the nature of marriage within the urban working class, perhaps involving the emergence of a more "companionate" form of marriage, based mainly on mutual attraction and love? At the same time, could the persistence of May-December unions within the bourgeoisie and the farming population – and this is not even considering remarriages, where age differences were even greater – suggest the maintenance of a more calculated, rational approach to matrimony among the propertied elements of society? Possibly. But on the whole, the mathematical argument seems the sounder.

Subject to the conservative influence of institutional and ideological structures in place for generations, certain aspects of matrimony in

Table 3-14
Mean Difference Between Husband's and Wife's Marriage Age[a]

	Mean Age Difference	Number of Cases	Standard Deviation
1854–61			
Agriculture	3.1	30	0.8
Urban-manual	3.1	54	0.6
Labourers	3.6	13	1.2
Non-manual	3.3	11	2.1
1864–71			
Agriculture	3.8	25	1.3
Urban-manual	3.0	48	0.9
Labourers	2.1	16	1.3
Non-manual	4.0	21	0.9
1884–91			
Agriculture	3.8	16	1.2
Urban-manual	2.0	92	0.4
Labourers	1.3	6	1.3
Non-manual	4.0	23	1.4

Source Family Reconstitution Files

Note

[a] First marriages for both parties, by cohort and husband's occupational category, calculated using all available age values.

nineteenth-century Saint-Hyacinthe changed very little in the second half of the nineteenth century. We have seen the uniformity with which marriages were celebrated only on certain days of the week, and not at all during periods of religious abstinence. Certainly, as this example shows, the Catholic Church maintained its control over the ritual of matrimony. Marriage at this level was a sacred institution linked to a popular conception of morality that was sanctioned and enforced by the church and its laws. Industrial capitalism was unable to disrupt these patterns significantly, at least not in a period as short as a generation or without considerable resistance and retrenchment. This was, after all, a period during which the Catholic Church was growing stronger in Quebec, not weaker.

If the rituals and ideology of matrimony remained intact, the economic and social realities that informed and conditioned family formation were transformed in industrializing Saint-Hyacinthe. By the 1850s, the village on the Yamaska had become an important market town and administrative centre. By the late 1860s, industrial capitalism – embodied mainly in the Côté shoe factory – had arrived. By the late 1880s, the arrival of new factories and the expansion of older ones meant unprecedented numbers of local men, women, and children working for wages. These sweeping changes had an impact on all aspects of social relations, including marriage.

In the 1850s, soon after the arrival of the railway, young farmers from the surrounding region had already begun to court and marry Saint-Hyacinthe women, as they would do throughout the rest of the century. Most of the men and women who married at the Saint-Hyacinthe cathedral, however, were local residents. Their changing profile reflects the influence of industrial capitalism on local social structure. By the end of the 1880s, a clear majority of the men who married at the cathedral were manual workers in specific urban occupations, most of them in the growing manufacturing sector. Many of the women may have been industrial workers as well, although there is no way of verifying this from their marriage acts. Certainly, they were more likely than their mothers to have been raised in urban households, most of which were headed by manual workers.

How did the changing economic and social realities of later nineteenth-century Saint-Hyacinthe affect peoples' choices about family formation? The answer to this question depends almost entirely upon factors such as occupation and social class. Increasingly, the members of the four socio-economic groups distinguished in this chapter formed their families in different ways, on the basis of divergent sets of economic opportunities and constraints. Some of these differences were created, while others were enhanced in the transition to an industrial-capitalist economy.

The first hint of a differential model of family formation appears in patterns of social and occupational endogamy. Here, class formation and family formation were linked through socially specific rules of spouse selection. Social endogamy in the bourgeois and agricultural segments of local society both restricted access to these groups and ensured the growth of the working class. Similarly, occupational endogamy within labourers' families both maintained and reflected the social distance between *journaliers* and urban workers with specific trades. The reality of these social distinctions is reflected in literacy levels which, although they were converging in the period, maintained a consistent ranking that translates, clearly enough, the social and economic hierarchies in this community.

But the strongest evidence of a socially differentiated pattern of family formation comes from the analysis of marriage age. Several kinds of social differentiation with respect to age at marriage had developed by the 1860s. On average, men in the bourgeois and agricultural categories waited several years longer than labourers and urban-manual workers. Similarly, the daughters of farmers and non-manual workers married considerably later than the daughters of urban-manual workers and *journaliers*. Furthermore, urban-manual workers moved closer in age to their brides, while age differences in the non-manual and agricultural categories remained wide.

These patterns reflect the close and well-established relationship between economic autonomy and family formation in historic populations. Farmers and their brides, who were very often the daughters of other farmers, needed access to sufficient land to support a family before they could contemplate marriage. Whether that land was acquired through purchase or through some form of inheritance (including *donations entre vifs*), a waiting period might well be involved. This was especially true in the context of the agricultural changes underway in the region during this period, which saw the emergence of larger, more specialized, market-oriented farms, but also a decline in the total number of farms. Similarly, professionals, merchants, and others in non-manual occupations needed time to acquire an education or sufficient capital to go into business on their own account. Certain bourgeois standards, moreover, had to be met in the new household; many nineteenth-century marriage contracts – increasingly middle-class instruments – required the husband to support the wife at a level in keeping with her class background.[86] That meant savings, and savings took time.

A woman's socio-economic background influenced her marriage age as well. Here, however, the link to economic autonomy is more difficult to distinguish. What seemed to be emerging by the 1860s was a new social norm of later marriage among women from propertied backgrounds. Whether these women were simply waiting for their prospective husbands (in most cases from a similar background) to acquire the capital necessary for family formation, or whether a more subtle mechanism was at work is not immediately clear.

It is perfectly clear, on the other hand, that men who worked in urban manual trades married very early throughout this period, as did women whose fathers worked in such occupations. This would not have been expected if the urban-manual workers marrying in Saint-Hyacinthe during this period had been independent craft producers, whose long apprenticeships had exerted upward pressures on marriage age in pre-industrial societies, Quebec included.[87] Nor does it fit particularly well with the aggregate trends toward later marriage that have been documented for Quebec and other parts of Canada in the later nineteenth century. Rather, it is a pattern which echoes that of the early capitalist wage workers studied by the architects of the proto-industrial model in Europe. While Saint-Hyacinthe's manual workers did not marry earlier as opportunities for wage labour became more abundant after 1865 – in fact, it is hard to

imagine them marrying much earlier than they had in the 1850s –
nor were they affected by the pressures to delay marriage that were
affecting other groups in the local and provincial populations. Look
at Hector Pagnuelo, for example, who was busy building his grocery
business and Joseph Beauchamp, who was studying and working to establish his veterinary practice; both were still bachelors at age 25. At
the same age, factory workers such as Joseph Lafleur, Ozias Casavant,
and Arthur Renaud had already been married men for six or seven
years.

23 Wedding portrait. This unidentified couple was photographed by Saint-Hyacinthe photographer Fred Jaret around the turn of the century. Wearing a plain, dark dress, the wife holds a rolled document, perhaps their marriage contract. The husband's worn shoes and powerful hands hint at a life of manual work. (ASSH, section A, series 17, dossier 24.6)

24 Wedding portrait. another unidentified couple, this one somewhat more elaborately turned out, poses for a photographer. (ASSH, section A, series 17, dossier 24.6)

25   This large Victorian house, right next to the cathedral at 750–780
Hôtel-Dieu, was built between 1854 and 1859. It was the residence of
Georges-Casimir Dessaulles and his family when they were enumerated
by the 1871 census taker (see chapter 4). Henriette Dessaulles wrote
her diaries here; Maurice Saint-Jacques, the young lawyer whom she would
marry, was a close neighbour. (ASHRSH, section B, series 14, album 3)

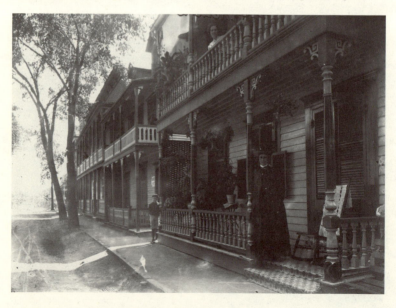

26   Housing in Saint-Hyacinthe at the turn of the century. Residential buildings
such as these would have housed several working families in relative comfort.
(ASSH, section A, series 17, dossier 18)

27 Looking up Bourdages Street at the turn of the century, one is struck by the close proximity of industry and worker housing. The knitting mill sits directly across from a row of residential buildings which is distinctive for its variety. Older houses with pitched roofs – which may well have been divided up into apartments – sit alongside more recently built blocks of flats. (ASSH, section A, series 17, dossier 18)

28 A mixed residential and commercial street in Saint-Hyacinthe at the turn of the century. Here again, note the predominance of two- and three-storey blocks of flats. (ASSH, section A, series 17, dossier 18)

29 A working-class street in the lower town, looking up toward Cascades Street and beyond. The plain brick buildings on the left would have had interior staircases leading to apartments on the upper two storeys. (ASSH, section A, series 17, dossier 18)

30 Children pose outside their home: a rundown block of flats in the lower town. (ASSH, section A, series 17, dossier 18)

31 A portrait of a bourgeois family taken at the Victor Morin studio on the *Place du Marché*. The woman appears to be several years younger than her husband. Is she also expecting their third child? (ASSH, section A, series 17, dossier 24.7)

32 A young mother poses with her three small children for Saint-Hyacinthe photographer Victor Morin in 1894. (ASSH, section A, series 17, dossier 24.8)

33 This Saint-Hyacinthe family posed for the camera near the turn of the century. (ASSH, section A, series 17, dossier 24.7)

34 A stereotypical Quebec family: mother, father, and their 15 children, of whom three had in this case joined religious orders. Although not "typical," such families were not uncommon in the rural areas around Saint-Hyacinthe in the later 19th century. But in the town itself, such extremely high fertility was becoming increasingly rare. (ASSH, section A, series 17, dossier 24.7)

4 Families at the Threshold: Newlyweds, Household Structure, and Proximity to Kin

André Scott, a 23-year-old farmer, and Lumina Lagacé, aged 19, were married in the Saint-Hyacinthe cathedral on 27 January 1859. Two years later, the couple and their 13-month-old daughter were enumerated in the district of Saint-Hyacinthe-le-Confesseur. The young family, which in a matter of weeks would expand to four members with the birth of a second daughter, occupied their own household in this rural district. But even though they were alone together in their one-storey wooden house, they were surrounded by kin. In the next house visited by the census taker, for example, was the family of a 30-year-old farmer named Antoine Scott, very likely André's brother.[1]

Georges-Casimir Dessaulles' second marriage, to Frances Louise (Fanny) Leman, was celebrated at the cathedral in January of 1869. The prominent industrialist and member of the seigneurial family was 41 years old at the time, the father of three young children, and the mayor of Saint-Hyacinthe. In May of 1871, when the Dessaulles household was visited by the census enumerator for *Quartiers* 3 and 4 of the city, the family was one of the wealthiest in town. The mayor owned 430 hectares of land, including 20 lots in town, with two houses, four shops or manufactories, and eight barns or stables. The household was also more complex in its composition than most. Fanny Leman, who at 25 was 16 years younger than her husband, had given birth to the couple's first child, a daughter named Fanny Rosalie, in November of 1869. Young Rosalie joined a household that already included Dessaulles' three children from his previous marriage: Arthur, Henriette (the diarist), and Alice, aged 12, 11, and 9 years, respectively. Also present were the mayor's new mother-in-law (the widow Honorine Papineau Leman, aged 53) and two domestic servants – both unmarried women in their mid-thirties, one French-Canadian, the other Irish.[2]

When Hilaire Allard married Joséphine Tanguay in June of 1890, he was an 18-year-old leather cutter in the local boot-and-shoe industry; she was the 19-year-old daughter of another shoemaker. Apparently, this young couple did not have the resources to set up their own household immediately after their wedding. Ten months after the marriage, on 20 April 1891, a census enumerator counted them as members of the household headed by Joséphine's father, Alfred Tanguay. The family occupied a two-storey wooden house containing seven rooms, located in *Quartier* 2 of the town of Saint-Hyacinthe. The dwelling – a spacious one by working-class standards – housed a total of eight individuals: Joséphine's parents Alfred and Emérance Tanguay, both aged 43; her three unmarried siblings, aged 17, 13, and 8; and her maternal grandmother, Emérance Courtois, a 76-year-old widow. Two weeks after the census was taken, the family circle grew to include a fourth generation: Joséphine Tanguay gave birth to her first child, a daughter named Marie Eulalie Eva, on 3 May 1891.[3]

These three cases illustrate the variety of domestic arrangements made by recently married couples in Saint-Hyacinthe in the second half of the nineteenth century. Such living arrangements were the results of individual and family decisions, made on the basis of a distinct set of requirements and constraints. Informed in part by custom, these choices were also made in the context of changing social and economic conditions. Social class, employment opportunities, the availability and cost of housing, the proximity of relatives who might either lend a hand or require assistance: all contributed to set the limits within which young couples manoeuvred to secure acceptable shelter.

Household composition has been a staple in the diet of family historians since the 1960s, when people like Peter Laslett first began applying quantitative methods to the study of domestic life in past times. This effort challenged an element of received wisdom: the notion that a once widespread pattern of complex households disappeared with the rise of industrial capitalism and urban life. Laslett and his colleagues used census-type documents to show that simple, nuclear households had been present and, indeed, predominant in a wide range of pre-industrial settings. The idea that the appearance of such households was recent – a result of the disruptive effects of cities and industrial work – was therefore widely discounted.[4]

Laslett's position, and particularly his methodology, have not gone unchallenged. Studies by Lutz Berkner and others suggest that a large proportion of pre-industrial households went through phases of extension at particular points in the family life cycle.[5] The method of focusing on households observed in census "snapshots" of historical reality had missed this aspect of family dynamics. Households in past times were not fixed in their structure; rather, in the phrase of Tamara Hareven and John Modell, they were "malleable," taking on new members as the needs and resources of the simple family and the extended kin group dictated. Furthermore, they continued to do so in urban, industrial settings, as the work of Hareven, Modell, Michael Anderson, and many others showed.[6]

The study of these issues has continued to evolve since Laslett first challenged the notion of a shift from an extended to a nuclear model during industrialization. One of the most useful insights is the importance of variations in household structure across the family life cycle. Howard Chudacoff's work on American cities in the later nineteenth century, for example, shows that many recently married couples either relied on kin for assistance in household arrangements or provided assistance to less fortunate members of their extended families. Chudacoff pointed out the particular propensity of young married couples to live in complex households, focusing on the "extraordinary variety and frequency of household extension" that characterized the domestic arrangements of newlyweds in nineteenth-century American cities such as Providence, Rhode Island.[7] These arrangements benefited not only the young couple but the kin with whom they lived. This early phase of the family cycle, then, was "a time when a young couple needed assistance, material and emotional, in adjusting to a new pattern of life. But it was also a time when a new household was established, thereby providing an additional place where others – siblings, widowed parents, and non-kin in need of housing – could be lodged."[8]

Chudacoff's emphasis on the importance of the earliest phase in the life cycle for household extension echoed points that had been made in the European literature, by Berkner and Anderson especially. Another point reminiscent of Anderson is a broadening of the notion of "family extension" – to include not just co-residence, but close spatial proximity between newlyweds and kin. Indeed, Anderson's epigram, "kinship does not stop at the front door" could well be taken as the motto of much of Chudacoff's work.[9]

With the work of these scholars in mind, this chapter explores the domestic arrangements made by recently married couples in Saint-Hyacinthe in the second half of the nineteenth century. The analysis is based on a matching of the couples in the three marriage cohorts with manuscript-census lists for the Saint-Hyacinthe area: a procedure that was an essential step in the cohort-based family-reconstitution strategy. The households we will visit are those occupied by Saint-Hyacinthe couples on the date of the first census following their weddings.[10] The chapter has three specific objectives: to describe and measure the household strategies used by recently married couples in Saint-Hyacinthe; to evaluate the extent to which kinship ties influenced those strategies; and to interpret trends and patterns in kin co-residence and proximity in terms of the economic and social changes affecting this community during the second half of the nineteenth century.

As we shall see, autonomous, simple-family households such as André Scott and Lumina Lagacé's were established by the majority of couples who married and settled in later nineteenth-century Saint-Hyacinthe. But a significant minority lived in households that included other kin, especially widowed parents and younger siblings. Domestic servants and other non-kin could also be found in many households, especially those of more affluent families like the Dessaulles. Especially from 1871 onward, and independently of whether they shared their lodgings with members of their extended families, many young couples had kin nearby, often in separate households within the same building. Very few recently married couples lived in households headed by others, although more – like Hilaire Allard and Joséphine Tanguay – did so toward the end of the period than at the beginning. Throughout this period, Saint-Hyacinthe newlyweds were more likely to harbour widowed parents or younger siblings within their new homes than to depend on more established family members for support in the area of housing.

NEWLYWEDS IN SAINT-HYACINTHE

Residential strategies early in the life cycle have been studied for almost half (42%) of the couples in the three marriage cohorts. Those who settled either in the parish of Saint-Hyacinthe-le-Confesseur (including the town) or in the neighbouring parish of Notre-Dame-du-Rosaire were traced to the manuscript census in the course of the family-reconstitution study. Of the 912 couples in the three cohorts, 386 were identified in the first census enumeration following their weddings.[11] The rate of record matching improved over time, somewhat surprisingly since one of the key linkage criteria (the wife's surname) disappeared from the census schedules in 1871.[12] This seems to suggest that couples who had married at the Saint-

Hyacinthe cathedral were increasingly apt to settle in the town and its vicinity as the industrial transition progressed. In 1891, the local economy was in a phase of expansion and the prospect of jobs in the knitting mill, the shoe factories, and the new corset factory would certainly have provided sufficient explanation for such a trend.

Which couples set up house in Saint-Hyacinthe and which did not? As suggested in chapter 3, the decisive factor in this regard was whether the husband had lived in Saint-Hyacinthe prior to the wedding. Newly formed families were much more likely to settle in Saint-Hyacinthe if the husband was already a local resident.[13] Conversely, very few non-resident men established households in Saint-Hyacinthe. Although they have not been traced beyond the immediate Saint-Hyacinthe area, most would surely have returned with their brides to begin married life in their home parishes. The case of Joseph Arpin, the farmer from Saint-Ephrem d'Upton who married Marguerite Girard in 1855 and then disappeared from our study area, was far from unique.[14] Of the 374 couples in which the husband was not a resident of the parish, only 60 (16%) were found in the Saint-Hyacinthe area at the time of the next census.

The occupational distribution among husbands traced to the census is similar to that in the three marriage cohorts. In 43 cases, spread evenly across the three cohorts, the census identified husbands linked from the marriage acts as farmers. This level (11%) is lower than that observed for the three marriage cohorts, but much higher than the very low proportion of farmers (under 2%) in the town of Saint-Hyacinthe in 1861 and 1891.[15] Much larger proportions of the husbands traced to the census either declared specific manual occupations or identified themselves as labourers: 73% in 1861, 59% in 1871, and 71% in 1891. Although these levels exceed the corresponding proportions in the marriage cohorts, they are in line with those in the local population, where over 70% of employed men were in manual occupations unrelated to agriculture.[16] As to non-manual occupations, they appear among the linked couples in almost exactly the same proportions as in the three marriage cohorts.[17]

In effect, matching marriage acts with the first subsequent census represents a narrowing of our focus. We are now concerned not with the 912 couples who married at the cathedral in the three selected intervals, but with those couples – some 386 in all – who, once married, established households in the Saint-Hyacinthe area. This implies a focus on those couples with husbands who had lived in the parish prior to the wedding, since these were the ones most likely to settle locally. Among the husbands, there is also a concentration of urban-manual workers and a relatively small number of farmers, reflecting the occupational structure of the town and the fact that so many farmers came from outside the parish to marry local women. None of these differences are to be regretted. Arguably, although fewer in number, the couples linked from local marriage registers to the census are more representative of the population of Saint-Hyacinthe than the 912 unions analyzed in chapter 3. Not only did these men and women marry at the cathedral, but they established households in the town or its immediate vicinity, and remained there at least long enough to appear in a census enumeration. Many of them must have had deep roots in the community and close kin near at hand, with whom to co-operate in matters of housing, as in other areas, should they so choose.

Further descriptive information on the couples traced from marriage acts to the next subsequent census is contained in Table 4-1, which gives the composition of the "conjugal families" traced to the census lists.[18] This breakdown not only clarifies the extent to which mortality intervened between the marriages under review and the subsequent census, but also gives an idea of the variety of the family situations experienced by recently married couples in Saint-Hyacinthe.

Almost all of the couples traced from the marriage registers to the census were still "intact," in the sense that husband and wife were alive and living together. Less than 4% of the unions had been ruptured by the death of one or other spouse. This low level of mortality is not surprising, given that the cohorts were composed mainly of young adults, enumerated, on average, three to four years after their marriages.[19] Honoré Mercier's case – having married in 1866, he was already widowed when the census takers found him in 1871 – was unusual.[20] In effect, almost all recently married husbands and wives lived together, although evidence from 1861 suggests that this was not always the case. Three of the husbands in the 1854–61 cohort were declared "absent" at the time of the enumeration. They may have been temporarily absent, perhaps because of some form of seasonal labour, such as logging.[21]

Most couples remained together in the short interval between the wedding and the next census. Very few were split either by death or by any form of voluntary separation. Over 80% of the conjugal families traced to the census in Saint-Hyacinthe consisted simply of a married couple either with no children, or with a child or children present. The latter situation was the more common, since as noted, an average interval of three to four years separated marriage and census enumeration: ample time for the birth of a child, or even two.

Table 4-1
Portrait of Conjugal Families Linked to Census Lists, by Cohort[a]

	A	B	C	Total
Intact couple, no children	28	25	40	93
Intact couple with own children present	66	73	85	224
Stepfamilies[b]	13	14	27	54
Ruptured unions[c]	5	4	6	15
Total	112	116	158	386

Source Family Reconstitution Files

Notes

[a] Families linked from marriage acts to the next census.

[b] Intact couples in which one party or both has co-resident children from a previous marriage, with or without additional children from the present union.

[c] Mainly widows and widowers, with or without children. Also includes three cases from the 1861 census in which the husband was declared "absent."

In cases where the husband or wife had previously been married, the composition of the conjugal family was generally more complex. Remarriage created new families consisting of husband, wife, children from previous unions, and any children born to the new union. Fifty-four of the families in the three cohorts were of this blended variety, referred to here as "stepfamilies." Because more men than women remarried, it was most frequently the husbands' children who were brought into new unions.[22] The case of Sophie Bourgeois makes the point rather well. When the census takers caught up with the family in 1861, she had been married to innkeeper Abraham Monet since 1854. Besides their own three young children, the couple lived with Abraham's two teenaged sons from his former marriage, to Rose Lussier.[23] The examples could be multiplied but the point to be made is that remarriage for men was at least in part a means of making sure that necessary domestic work, including child care, got done. The greater frequency of remarriage for widowers also implies, from a child's perspective, that stepmothers must have significantly outnumbered stepfathers in nineteenth-century society.[24]

In all, 371 of the 386 conjugal families traced to the census were made up of intact couples, with or without their own children. But the majority of these couples were already parents. Some of the husbands and wives had been married before, and some brought children from their former unions into the new household. Most of the discussion in the remainder of this chapter will focus on these 371 intact couples linked from the three marriage cohorts to the subsequent manuscript census. This is not to suggest that the residential strategies of young widows and widowers are not interesting. They certainly are. Young widows and widowers, in fact, seem to have relied more heavily than intact couples on the kin group for support in the area of basic shelter. My limited data suggest that recently widowed individuals most often lodged with their parents or with other relatives. Seven of the 12 widows and widowers linked to the census were living in households headed by others, usually kin, rather than in independent dwellings. As will be shown shortly, less than 10% of intact couples used that strategy to deal with the basic problem of shelter.

HOUSEHOLD STRUCTURE

What were the domestic arrangements made by couples in the Saint-Hyacinthe area in the early years of their married life?[25] In this industrializing community, young married couples almost invariably set up independent households when they got married, or very soon thereafter. As Table 4-2 shows, of the 371 couples traced to the first subsequent census, all but 28 headed their own, independent households.[26] This simple fact – that over nine-tenths had established independent households by the time of the first census following their weddings – is important, not least because it underscores the point made in the previous chapter about the contingent relationship between economic autonomy and family formation.[27]

The fact that a small minority did not head their own households, however, reinforces the idea that ties of kinship were important to young couples just starting out. Twenty-four of these 28 couples were living with kin when the first census after their wedding was taken.[28] Most – 20 of 24 – were living with the parents of one spouse or the other. This was the case, for example, of Amedée Millier and Joséphine Sinotte, who were married at the cathedral in July 1889 and who, when enumerated in the spring of 1891, were living with their eight-month-old daughter Rose in the household headed by Joséphine's father, Benjamin Sinotte, a supervisor in one of the local shoe factories.[29] Perhaps surprisingly, however, no obvious preference appears for either the wife's or the husband's family.[30] One might have expected women's parents to predominate, as in Amedée and Joséphine's case, if only because a higher proportion of brides than grooms had been residents of Saint-Hyacinthe prior to marriage. But this was not the case. A few couples, moreover, had neither established their own households nor moved in with kin. Of these, two were lodging in a hotel; one was boarding in a private home; and another had found work, husband and wife together, in domestic service.[31]

Table 4-2
Household Structure: Intact Couples Linked to Subsequent Census, by Cohort

		A	B	C	Totals
1a	Heads of simple households,	49	75	94	218
	no extras	45.8%	67.0%	61.8%	58.8%
1b	Heads of simple households,	14	13	22	49
	with extras	13.1%	11.6%	14.5%	13.2%
2a	Heads of complex households,	29	16	15	60
	no extras	27.1%	14.3%	9.9%	16.2%
2b	Heads of complex households,	10	3	3	16
	with extras	9.3%	2.7%	2.0%	4.3%
3	Sub-nuclear: inmates in	5	4	15	24
	households headed by kin	4.7%	3.6%	9.9%	6.5%
4	Inmates in households	0	1	3	4
	headed by non-kin	–	0.9%	2.0%	1.1%

SUB-TOTALS

		A	B	C	Totals
1	Heads of simple households	63	88	116	267
		58.9%	78.6%	76.3%	72.0%
2	Heads of complex households	39	19	18	76
		36.4%	17.0%	11.8%	20.5%
3+	Inmates in households headed	5	5	18	28
4	by others	4.7%	4.5%	11.8%	7.5%
TOTALS		107	112	152	371

Source Family Reconstitution Files.
Note

Couples in categories 1 and 2 head their own households. Those in categories 3 and 4 do not. "Extras" are defined as non-kin co-residents, usually boarders, servants, and employees. Category 4 exists because, in a few cases, linked couples were identified as "extras" in households headed by others.

Against this backdrop, in which most newly married couples established independent households throughout the period, there was a perceptible increase in the number who lived with others, especially kin, after 1871. The number of recently married couples living in these situations was very low indeed (under 5%) in 1861 and 1871. And although the absolute numbers remained rather small ($^{18}\!/_{152}$), the proportion increased to almost 12% in 1891.[32] The limited number of observations here certainly suggests that this apparent increase may be nothing more than a statistical anomaly. But the increase might also be placed in the context of certain pressures associated with the rise of industrial capitalism that had begun to be felt by the early 1890s.

One of these was certainly the pressure on the housing stock created by the economic and demographic expansion of the 1880s. This was a preoccupation of the Royal Commission on the Relations of Capital and Labour when it visited Saint-Hyacinthe in 1888. Many workers, such as Cyprien Robidoux, were asked whether they could afford to own their own homes, and, if not, whether rents had risen in recent years. Most replied that they rented and that affordable lodgings were increasingly hard to come by. Robidoux, who worked in the Granite Mills, paid four dollars a month for the rooms he rented on Saint-Michel street, where he had lived for five months with his wife and four children. Five years earlier, in his estimation, the same lodgings would have cost $2.50.[33]

Although recently married couples only rarely lived in households headed by others, then, more seem to have done so in 1891 than in 1861 or 1871. Part of the reason may have been the rising cost of working-class housing in the years leading up to the taking of the 1891 census. Couples who could not afford to set up housekeeping on their own would have fallen back on relatives, most often parents or in-laws. The youth of these individuals, who were usually seeking temporary shelter in a *very* early stage of their married lives, must also be stressed. On average, they had been married 30 months at the time of the census; the wife was 25 years old and, in most cases, had not yet given birth to her first child.[34] In contrast, women in independent, simple-family households had been married an average of 43 months, were about 28 years old, and were likely to have had at least one child, if not two.[35]

Table 4-2 provides a breakdown of all couples linked from the marriage registers to the next census, by cohort and household type. Across the three cohorts, over 70% of these newly formed households were simple in structure.[36] A fair question might be whether this should be regarded as a small or large number. Direct comparisons are possible between my 1871 figures and those for two working-class neighbourhoods on the outskirts of Montreal in the same year. Seventy-nine percent of recently married couples in Saint-Hyacinthe in 1871 lived in simple households, the highest proportion detected for any one census year. The equivalent figure for the general population of Saint-Jean-Baptiste, on the northern fringe of the city, was 78%, while in the "Bas-du-village" section of Saint-Augustin, just to the west of Montreal, the proportion was 83%.[37] The majority of recently married couples in Saint-Hyacinthe lived in simple households then, and the proportion that did so was comparable to the proportion of such households in two working-class suburbs of Montreal.[38]

The fact that up to four-fifths of recently married couples in Saint-Hyacinthe lived in simple households, usually without any non-kin extras such as boarders and servants, certainly underscores the importance of the "nuclear" household in this community. Whether this was a new development or a long-standing pattern is an important, but somewhat recalcitrant, question. Much depends on the 1861 census, which is especially difficult to interpret.[39] If my reading of that source is correct, the proportion of simple households would have increased from just under 60% for Cohort-A couples to almost 80% for Cohort-B couples. It would then have declined very slightly but remained above 75% for couples who married during the expansive 1880s.

It is tempting, indeed, to argue that this is what happened. It is possible, for example, to suggest that in 1861, the housing available in Saint-Hyacinthe had not yet caught up to demand, forcing young couples to make other arrangements, mainly involving co-residence with kin. But given the methodological adjustments that were necessary to harmonize the 1861 census with subsequent lists, it seems imprudent to do much more than speculate about these matters, even though this analysis of the 1861 census should *maximize* the number of simple households identified in that year.

Because the 1861 figures are so fragile, the interesting possibility that the subsequent decade saw a dramatic decline in the importance of complex households, at least for newlyweds, should not be overstated. What is abundantly clear, however, is that independent, simple households were the rule in all three cohorts. At the same time, an important minority of couples established households in which they also sheltered kin. None of the couples were found to be sharing households with unrelated couples: a pattern once considered important by many authors discussing nineteenth-century Canadian towns and cities.[40] Those few who did not head a household, as we have seen, were mainly staying with the parents of one spouse or the other, probably as a temporary arrangement in the earliest months of marriage.

Who were the family members living with those couples who had managed to establish households of their own? The picture that emerges here, as in Chudacoff's work, is of young couples dealing from a position of relative strength. Many of the co-resident family members were the widowed parents of one spouse or the other; others were unmarried younger siblings or cousins. Wives' and husbands' relatives were equally likely to co-reside with the newly established family. Many of these individuals no doubt made substantial material contributions to the new household. But it seems likely that the flow of advantages went mainly the other way: that parents and unmarried siblings benefited more from these arrangements than did the newlyweds.

In the three cohorts, 76 young couples headed complex households; of these, 66 lodged persons whose relationship to the married couple could be identified.[41] In almost half of these households (27 of 66), a widowed parent of one spouse or the other was lodging with the recently married couple. Family members, and adult children in particular, were the main source of support for older people in Saint-Hyacinthe during this period.[42] And it is no surprise that this support extended to shared lodgings. A household like that of Saint-Hyacinthe notary Esdras Bernier and his wife Alida Marchessault fits well with expectations about co-operative relationships between adult children and widowed parents. Esdras and Alida had married in November 1865 in their early twenties. When they were visited by the census takers in 1871, they lived in Notre-Dame-de-Saint-Hyacinthe with their two young daughters and Alida's widowed mother, Judith Marchessault, who was 55.[43] Nor were such arrangements limited to the more affluent members of the community. Consider the experience of Alphonse Desjardins, a machinist, and Cédonie Brouillard, who were married in January 1887. In 1891, they were 25 and 24 years old respectively, living in a household of which Alphonse was the head, in the company of their two young children, Alphonse's 44-year-old mother Rosalie, and three of his siblings. The young machinist's earnings would have been supplemented by those of his widowed mother and his sister Délima, who were both dressmakers, and that of his brother Charles Émile, an apprentice shoemaker.[44] This example further supports our quantitative analysis, which reveals that the next most important group of co-residents was unmarried lateral kin: probably siblings in most cases. These were found in 21 of the 66 households and most were younger than the newlywed couple under scrutiny.

Age, in fact, was a clear distinguishing feature of the kin living with recently married couples in Saint-Hyacinthe. Of the 101 related persons identified in these 66 households, 31 were less than 20 years old; 13 of these were orphans or half-orphans aged 13 years or less. In the same group of 101 co-residents, 37 were aged 60 years or more. Thus at least 50 of the 101 kin co-residents (13 children and 37 aging parents, most of them widowed) can be classed more or less confidently as dependants. The 18 youths aged between 14 and 19 years might also be so considered, except that many must have been expected or constrained to contribute their labour power – in the form of a wage or as apprentices or domestic workers – to the new household. This was certainly the case of Délima and Charles Émile Desjardins, whom we have just met and who were aged 17 and 14, respectively, when enumerated in 1891.[45] Unmarried collateral kin (aged 20 to 59) must have done the same.

This analysis again reinforces the argument that economic autonomy remained a crucial precondition for family formation as Saint-Hyacinthe residents lived through the industrial transition. The great majority of couples who settled locally had established independent households by the time of the first census following their wedding. Only about 8% lived in households headed by others. Furthermore, of those who had established households, an important minority were in a position to shelter additional family members in their homes.[46] One should perhaps not underestimate the reciprocal nature of these arrangements. Young husbands, although named as household heads, may for example have been living in premises owned by a widowed parent or in-law. Recently married couples who undertook to shelter a 12-year-old child may have expected, and received, certain benefits that remain hidden in the census. But the major impression is of young people establishing new and independent households that might then play a role in domestic strategies involving the wider kin group. Where to lodge a widowed parent or an orphaned nephew? Recently married couples in Saint-Hyacinthe seem to have been well positioned to help provide answers to these kinds of questions. To borrow Chudacoff's image, these were "new branches on the family tree," on which its needier members might hope to find at least a temporary perch.

It is important to ask whether these household patterns had a class or occupational component. Table 4-3 contains an occupational analysis of household structure for recently married couples in the three marriage cohorts. Households headed by merchants, professionals, clerks, and others in non-manual occupations appear to have been more likely to shelter both co-resident kin and non-kin extras than those headed by farmers, labourers, and manual workers in urban trades. One-third of all households in the non-manual category were complex in structure, compared to only one-quarter of those headed by urban-manual workers, and barely one-fifth of those headed by farmers. The predominance of simple households among farmers certainly calls for reflection. One might expect to observe the opposite if a rural pattern of complex households were in the process of yielding to a more "nuclear" urban norm.[47]

Non-manual households stand out even more sharply when we examine the presence of non-kin extras in the household. Not

Table 4-3
Household Structure by Occupational Category: Three Cohorts Combined

	Farmers		Urban-Manual		Labourers		Non-Manual	
	N	%	N	%	N	%	N	%
1a Heads of simple households, no extras	32	74.4	125	61.9	29	60.4	32	42.1
1b Heads of simple households, with extras	2	4.7	25	12.4	4	8.3	18	23.7
2a Heads of complex households, no extras	5	11.6	26	12.9	10	20.8	18	23.7
2b Heads of complex households, with extras	3	7.0	7	3.5	1	2.1	4	5.3
3 Subnuclear: inmates in households headed by kin	1	2.3	16	7.9	3	6.3	4	5.3
4 Inmates in households headed by non-kin	0	–	3	1.5	1	2.1	0	–
Simple family households (1a, 1b)	34	79.1	150	74.3	33	68.8	50	65.8
Complex family households (2a, 2b, 3)	9	20.9	49	24.3	14	29.2	26	34.2
Heads of households with no extras (1a, 2a)	37	88.1	151	82.5	39	88.6	50	69.4
Heads of households with extras (1b, 2b)	5	11.9	32	17.5	5	11.4	22	30.6
TOTAL[a]	42		202		48		76	

Source Family Reconstitution Files.
Note
[a] Professional information missing for two households (total examined here is 369).

surprisingly, domestic servants and other employees were found much more frequently here than in working-class or agricultural settings. But, in line with what Bettina Bradbury has observed for Montreal, boarders and lodgers were also more likely to live in bourgeois and petit-bourgeois households than in those of manual workers.[48] When journalist and publisher Camille Lussier and his wife Marie Kérouack were enumerated in 1871, they had been married for seven years and already had three children. But there were a total of nine people living in their Saint-Hyacinthe household: the couple, now aged 36 and 27; the three children, aged between two and six; Camille's widowed mother Josephte Lussier, aged 72; two young women identified as servants (Zoé Laroque, aged 20, and 16-year-old Éliza Berthiaume); and Alfred Bernier, a 26-year old lawyer. As the numbers seem to indicate, this degree of household complexity – involving a conjugal family of five, a widowed parent, two servants and, apparently, a lodger – was unlikely, indeed, to occur anywhere else but within the local bourgeoisie.[49]

Table 4-4 adds a spatial dimension to this analysis. Here, the information on household structure is presented by geographic zone rather than occupational group. The results tally with those just presented. Households were most likely to be augmented with non-kin extras in *Quartiers* 3 and 4, where most of the town's élite was concentrated. Patterns in the predominantly working-class *Quartiers* 1 and 2, and in the mainly agricultural zone outside the city limits were simpler. They were also remarkably similar. In both areas, about three-quarters of recently formed households were simple in structure and less than 15% contained boarders, lodgers, servants, apprentices, or other employees.[50]

Who exactly were these non-kin "extras"? It was possible to identify a total of 65 households in the three cohorts that were augmented by the presence of persons other than family members (Table 4-4).[51] Of these, 30 contained boarders or lodgers, 18 contained domestic servants, 11 contained apprentices or other employees, while six contained some combination of these three types of extras. Distributing these last six around to the other categories gives 33 households with boarders or lodgers, 23 with domestic servants, and 15 with apprentices or other non-domestic employees.

As one expects, certain types of extras were concentrated in the more predominantly bourgeois area of the town. Of the 33 households that contained boarders or lodgers, 19 (58%) were located in *Quartiers* 3 and 4, where less than a third of all couples linked from the marriage acts to the census lived.[52] Domestic servants were also concentrated in this more affluent zone: just over half (12 of 23) of the households with servants were located, like the Dessaulles and Lussier homes, in *Quartiers* 3 and 4. The rest of the "non-kin extras" identified in these three cohorts were apprentices and other employees who lived with their masters or employers.[53] This practice seems to have been in decline in Saint-Hyacinthe during this period, as one might expect given the rise of industrial capitalism and the increased separation between home and workplace that accompanied it. Apprentices and other non-domestic employees were present in almost half ($^{11}/_{24}$) of the households augmented by non-kin in 1861. But this figure was very much lower in both 1871 ($^{1}/_{16}$) and 1891 ($^{3}/_{25}$).

The households of recently married couples in Saint-Hyacinthe, then, were most often simple in structure. About three-quarters of

Table 4-4
Household Structure by Geographic Zone: Three Cohorts Combined

	Quartiers 1 and 2		Quartiers 3 and 4		Outside City Limits	
	N	%	N	%	N	%
1a Heads of simple households, no extras	112	64.0	51	44.7	55	67.1
1b Heads of simple households, with extras	14	8.0	29	25.4	6	7.3
2a Heads of complex households, no extras	31	17.7	16	14.0	13	15.9
2b Heads of complex households, with extras	6	3.4	5	4.4	5	6.1
3 Subnuclear: inmates in households headed by kin	11	6.3	10	8.8	3	3.7
4 Inmates in households headed by non-kin	1	0.6	3	2.6	0	–
Simple family households (1a, 1b)	126	72.0	80	70.2	61	74.4
Complex family households (2a, 2b, 2c)	48	27.4	31	27.2	21	25.6
Heads of households with no extras (1a, 2a)	143	87.7	67	66.3	68	86.1
Heads of households with extras (1b, 2b)	20	12.3	34	33.7	11	13.9
TOTAL	175		114		82	

Source Family Reconstitution Files.

the newlyweds lived in their own independent households with no co-resident kin. Those who did live with kin were more likely to be providing support to older or younger relatives than leaning on parents or in-laws for help. More detailed attention to the very early months of marriage, however, might reinforce the impression that the latter practice was not unknown. It would also be interesting to explore the possibility that those young couples who did turn to parents for help might in many cases have been in situations of extraordinary need. How typical, for example, was the case of Alma Hogue and Emery Petit who, in the spring of 1891, 18 months after their marriage, were living with their three-month-old daughter Laura in the household headed by Alma's father? The census alone might suggest that this was an ordinary case of early life-cycle cohabitation. But the parish records add another perspective, for they reveal that Alma died barely a month after the census was taken, as did her baby, two months after that.[54] Had the woman moved her family in with her parents not because of a predictable life-cycle squeeze but because she was seriously ill and needed extra support to care for her young child? There is no way to say for sure but it seems at least a likely hypothesis.

RESIDENTIAL PROXIMITY

Nineteenth-century censuses provide indices not only of household structure but of the physical distance maintained between newly married couples and their relatives. A full treatment of this subject would require attention to the presence of kin in the same street, neighbourhood, and town as the couple in question. But interesting hints as to where such a study might lead can be gained from the examination of the extent to which recently married couples lived in the same building – or census *house* – as other members of their extended families.[55] While the households of newlyweds were generally independent and simple in structure, Saint-Hyacinthe was like other industrializing communities in that kinship did not end "at the front door." Many young couples chose to live in close proximity to kin after marriage, very often occupying distinct lodgings within the same building.

Obviously, no such arrangement was possible in cases where young families owned or rented a single-dwelling house.[56] As Table 4-5 shows, this was the most common situation for recently married couples in Saint-Hyacinthe. Over half of the families located in the census occupied distinct houses. This proportion increased in the period, from about 50% in 1861 and 1871 to over 60% in 1891.[57] These proportions varied in space as well. As we have seen, social structure was not uniform within the town, with greater concentrations of manual workers living in *Quartiers* 1 and 2. Nor was it uniform between urban Saint-Hyacinthe and the surrounding countryside, with its predominantly agricultural population. As well, there were important differences in the built environment and the cost of housing among the various zones, differences that influenced where and how young couples chose to live.[58]

Not surprisingly, recently married couples in the rural areas around Saint-Hyacinthe were more likely than town dwellers to live in distinct houses. Of those in Notre-Dame-du-Rosaire and Saint-Hyacinthe-le-Confesseur, 63% lived in this fashion. The only surprising thing here is that the proportion is not as high as one might have expected. Those living in predominantly working-class *Quartiers* 1 and

Table 4-5
Type of House Occupied and Presence of Kin in Contiguous Households, by Cohort[a]

	A		B		C		Total	
	N	%	N	%	N	%	N	%
Single-family house	54	50.5	58	51.8	96	63.2	208	56.1
Multiple-family houses								
a) No kin present	37	34.6	17	15.2	27	17.8	81	21.8
b) Kin present	16	15.0	37	33.0	29	19.1	82	22.1
TOTAL	107		112		152		371	

Source Family Reconstitution Files
Note
[a]   Intact couples linked from marriage acts to first subsequent census, by cohort.

2 of the town were the least likely to occupy – much less own – their own homes: only 41% across the three cohorts did so. In the relatively comfortable *Quartiers* 3 and 4 of the town, a higher proportion (56%) lived in distinct houses, only some of which were as opulent as the Dessaulles house, pictured in Illustration 25. It was here in the stronghold of the local bourgeoisie that the increasing preference for single-family houses was most apparent, as the ratio of young couples living in them rose from 45% in 1861 to 62% in 1891.

These variations are echoed when the same data are analyzed along occupational lines. Independently of the geographic variable, couples in which the husband was engaged in commerce, a profession, or another non-manual occupation were easily the most likely to live in distinct houses: 74% did so, compared to 61% of farmers, 48% of labourers, and only 41% of manual workers in urban trades. Again, there is no surprise here. Farmers and non-manual workers were more likely to occupy separate houses than manual workers because they were considerably more likely to own real property, whether in the countryside or in town. Urban wage labourers, on the other hand, more commonly lived in rented apartments, flats, and sections of houses than did farmers, merchants, and professionals.

But demographic factors had a part to play here as well. All else being equal, couples who had been married longer and whose families were therefore larger were more likely to occupy separate houses – a reflection of their greater need for family space.[59] And couples in which neither spouse had been married previously were much less likely to live in a separate house than couples in which one partner (or both) had been widowed.[60] Widows and widowers, of course, were usually older, and many had previously established dwellings in which to lodge their newly formed, sometimes rather complex, families.

The rest of these couples – some 163 – lived in buildings that housed more than one family. Although much of the built environment of this period has been destroyed by fires, the census and photographic records suggest strongly that some form of duplex or triplex must have been an important element of local domestic architecture. Also present, although less common, were larger tenement buildings, some with six or more apartments. Of all couples in the three cohorts who lived in multi-family houses, two-thirds lived in two-family houses, suggesting the importance of duplexes. One-fifth were in buildings that housed three families, while the rest (13%) lived in houses containing four or more domestic groups.

Illustrations 26 through 30 depict some of the various kinds of buildings that would have lodged more than one household in nineteenth-century Saint-Hyacinthe. Many were in close proximity, indeed, to the factories in which so many of their occupants worked. Illustration 27, for example, shows housing on the northeast side of Bourdages Street; directly across the street is the southwestern wall of the knit-goods factory. Multi-family houses in Saint-Hyacinthe ranged from comfortable, well-maintained duplexes on tree-lined residential streets (Illustration 26); to more modest, three-storey buildings on muddy, commercial streets (Illustrations 28 and 29); to stark, dilapidated apartment blocks such as that shown in Illustration 30. It is easy to imagine a family such as that of Victor Bienvenu living in such a building. Victor was a tannery worker who married Victoria Gosselin in April of 1888. When the census takers caught up with them three years later, they were living with their two young children in a two-storey house that had 12 rooms, but in which five other families also had lodgings.[61]

As one would expect, the predominantly working-class north-eastern half of the city (*Quartiers* 1 and 2) had more than its share of multiple-family houses. Fewer than half of the linked couples in the three cohorts were traced to this zone (47%); yet 54% of the couples living in two-dwelling units, 63% of those in three-dwelling units, and fully 77% of those in houses containing four or more households were located in *Quartiers* 1 and 2. These numbers give a good idea of the crowded conditions in this particular area. The working-class families who lived in the lower town, close to the river and to the factories where many worked, also lived in much closer proximity to their neighbours than did other members of the community. Zotique Gauthier, for example, was a shoe-factory worker who, in 1888, lived with his family in a four-room flat without running water for which he paid $5 per month.[62] His situation, like Victor and Victoria Bienvenu's, would have been fairly typical of the growing working class at this juncture.

Among the young couples who lived in duplexes, tenements, and other multi-family buildings, however, it is possible to detect a strong pattern of residential proximity to kin. As Table 4-5 shows, when recently married couples lived in apartments and flats rather than distinct houses, the chances were about even that the buildings they lived in also lodged other members of their extended families. One-half of the couples living in multi-family houses, in other words, had relatives living in at least one of the other households in the building. This proportion varied significantly across the three cohorts, however, peaking in 1871 and falling off afterwards. Fully one-third of the recently married couples traced to the 1871 census lived in buildings that also lodged extended family members.

Both situations – living in multi-family buildings, with and without relatives in separate lodgings under the same roof – can be illustrated with examples from the 1871 census. Thomas Comeau was a tannery worker who married Mélanie Lussier in Saint-Hyacinthe in May 1868. In 1871, the couple's household included their two young daughters, Anna and Emma, and Thomas's younger brother, Louis, also a tannery worker. Listed as the head of a separate *family* within the same *house* – in other words, a separate household within the same building – was the widower Abel Côté, a 42-year-old carpenter living with his five children, aged nine to 19. From all appearances, the two families were unrelated.[63] Paul Ferland and Alphonsine Juneau, on the other hand, represent the pattern that was the more common in 1871: the presence of kin within the same building. Alphonsine had been the 15-year-old daughter of a local baker when she married Paul, a cabinetmaker, in 1867. In 1871, they were enumerated, with their two children, as one of two households in a house located on Sainte-Marie street in Saint-Hyacinthe. The three members of the other household were Alphonsine's father, Jean-Baptiste Juneau; her mother, Angèle Marcil; and her younger brother, Cléophas Juneau, a 16-year-old tailor.[64]

Another way of evaluating these patterns is to count the "contiguous" households located in all multi-family buildings and to calculate the proportion that contained kin. In this study group, 163 couples lived in multi-family houses, which contained a total of 255 contiguous households. An important percentage (about two-fifths) of these contiguous households contained at least one person who could be identified as a relative. These numbers surely reflect a wide range of realities: some young couples probably rented rooms or apartments from parents, siblings, or other relations. Others may have used kinship ties to gain access to premises owned by third parties, receiving information about availability – and perhaps a good word with the landlord – from relatives already established in buildings owned by others. But without further data from evaluation roles, directories, leases, and other sources, distinguishing among these various practices is impossible.

It is possible, however, to say something about the couples who used them. As with multiple-family houses generally, working-class families predominated among those with kin in the same building. Manual workers were at the head of 76% of the families lodged in buildings that contained other kin. This was about one-quarter of all manual-workers' families traced to the census. A further 16% of the households in this category were headed by farmers; this represents a surprisingly high proportion (30%) of farmers' families linked to the census. Certainly, the residential strategies they employed would have been different from those of the urban working class, primarily because of the importance of land and its transmission between generations.[65] But the results, in terms of maintaining proximity to kin, seem in many cases to have been similar. As to bourgeois couples, given their strong propensity to live in single-family houses, only very few (less than 10%) had kin living in contiguous dwellings.

Extended-family members who lived in distinct, contiguous households were usually on a much different footing than those identified as co-resident with the recently married pair. The crucial difference was that most of those in contiguous households were themselves members of intact conjugal families. They were very often the parents or married siblings of the recently married pair, usually with their own children present. Four-fifths of these households contained married couples, half of whom were the parents of one spouse or the other. Noé Girouard's family was fairly typical, although, at 18 years of age, Noé was a very young man to be married and a household head. Nonetheless, in May of 1891, the tannery worker was enumerated as the head of a household that included himself, his 19-year-old wife Marie Deslauriers, and their one-month-old son Henri. Also present in the house was another household, headed by Noé's 45-year-old father, a general labourer; it included his mother and four of his siblings, three of whom worked in local tanneries and shoe factories.[66] Contiguous households that lodged a widowed parent were less common: only 13 of the 97 households under scrutiny did so, and two of the parents had remarried. This pattern stands in marked contrast to that identified for co-resident kin, who were mostly widowed parents or unmarried younger siblings.

Living with kin in contiguous dwellings, then, had a different meaning for young married couples than sharing a household with a family member. In the former case, newly formed families either co-operated on an equal footing or stood to benefit from advantages offered by their kinsfolk. Usually married couples, often the parents of the young husband or wife, these relatives had resources and information to offer a pair of newlyweds. In cases where young couples shared their household with kin, however, they seem mainly to have been offering support to less advantaged relatives – most often widowed parents, younger siblings, or both – rather than using kin networks to help them through rough patches of their own.

Linking marriage acts to the first subsequent census provides a number of insights into the household strategies used by recently married couples in Saint-Hyacinthe; it also underlines the continued importance of kin in these matters. The international literature suggests that this phase of the life cycle was a particularly important one for household extension and other forms of co-operation with kin, such as residential propinquity. The analysis presented here neither confirms nor contradicts that proposition. But it does allow a number of important points about young couples, their residential arrangements, and their kin networks to be made.

Household formation in this community was predicated on the accumulation of the capital, skill, or access to a wage required to set up an independent household. Over nine-tenths of the couples in this study group headed their own households by the time of the first census after their weddings. The fact that fewer did so in 1891 than had in 1861 or 1871, however, may warrant some emphasis. Part of the reason, I have suggested, might be found in the rising cost of living and the scarcity of affordable housing in the late 1880s and early 1890s. But it is also possible that the time-honoured link from economic autonomy to family formation may have been loosening. Certainly, many couples who married in the years just before 1891 would have done so in anticipation of an independence based on expected wages in the local industries. But should these expectations have been dashed, even temporarily – should a factory worker lose his job, for example, or have his wages cut below a level that could support two adults and perhaps an infant – the recourse to immediate family for a roof and bed, if only for a little while, might have come quickly enough. So, too, would young couples have leaned heavily on family networks in times of sickness and death, as Bettina Bradbury's work has shown and as the case of Alma Hogue illustrates so poignantly.[67]

Still, most recently formed families did live in independent households in 1891, just as they had in 1861 and 1871. There were important social differentials in household structure, however, just as in marriage age. Household complexity was greatest among those in non-manual professions, where extended-family members might have been somewhat more likely to perch, although the statistical basis for this conclusion is fragile. But bourgeois households most certainly harboured disproportionate numbers of boarders, servants, and other non-kin extras. In the single-family houses they most often occupied, bourgeois families had both the space in which to accommodate relatives and lodgers and the resources necessary to hire domestic servants.

Working-class households were most often simple in structure; they were unlikely to be augmented, either by kin or non-kin. But unlike those of farmers and non-manual workers, many working-class households were embedded in multi-family houses, of which there were more in *Quartiers* 1 and 2 than in other parts of the town. Often, as in the cases of Paul Ferland and Alphonsine Juneau and of Noé Girouard and Marie Deslauriers, these working families had kin as their closest neighbours, occupying distinct but contiguous dwellings on the same premises.

The differences between co-resident kin and those living in contiguous households suggest different kinds of social relations. Co-resident kin seem to have lived in a situation of at least partial dependency. Many were the widowed parents and unmarried younger siblings of the recently married husbands and wives. Such persons could not easily have established independent households. Their reliance on the newly formed couple, in a society in which family, community, and parish provided virtually all social services, was patent. Kin living in contiguous households, on the other hand, were free agents. They were much more likely to be members of intact conjugal families, more fully capable of providing for themselves, and perhaps in a better position to provide various forms of assistance to a young couple just starting out.

The fact that both of these patterns coexisted in Saint-Hyacinthe is ample testimony to the continued importance of kin as a network of social relations and as a source of material support, even as industrial capitalism reshaped this community. This analysis, then, provides further support to what is now a well-established thesis. Rather than destroying the extended family, industrial capitalism created a context in which people used their existing social networks – much of them kin-based – in new, creative ways.[68] What is also clear is that social class made an enormous difference in the kinds of kin-based strategies that were adopted. While young bourgeois couples were often called upon to lodge a dependent relative – most often a widowed parent – the urban working class adopted a pattern of close residential proximity between independent, but related, households.

While the extended family continued to play a major role in housing strategies, then, it did so in ways that were increasingly class-specific. Social differentiation occurred here, just as it did in the timing of matrimony, both in the life cycle and in the calendar year. And as we shall see, family life had begun to change in other ways, as industrial capitalism created incentives for fertility reduction, even within a Catholic population which faced intense ideological pressure in the opposite direction.

5 Interesting Conditions: Fertility and Family Size in Transition

The focus of this chapter is on fertility and fertility control in a context of fundamental economic and social change. The analysis is built around three questions. First, did fertility decline in Saint-Hyacinthe during the period of the town's nineteenth-century industrial transition? Second, were fertility levels socially and occupationally specific? Third, if fertility levels did begin to fall in this industrializing town, what was the reason? What was the logic, in other words, linking the emergence of a particular kind of industrial capitalism with the demographic trend toward smaller families?

To pose these questions is to attempt to operationalize a series of hypotheses about industry and its impact on reproduction in later nineteenth-century Quebec. It is important to get beyond linear accounts of the demographic transition in which industry and urban life, through obscure mechanisms, triggered fertility decline. There is a need, rather, to recover something of the complexity of a process that had household economics at its core, but which was also affected by cultural attitudes, religious beliefs, and the gendered dynamics of family decision making.

The documentary foundation of this chapter is a close examination of the age-specific fertility behaviour of some 386 women in the three marriage cohorts: those who remained in Saint-Hyacinthe through a significant portion of their child-bearing years and whose children were baptized at the cathedral.[1] The results, to be presented in detail shortly, show a decline of approximately 20% in marital fertility between the Saint-Hyacinthe women who married between

1854 and 1861 and those who married between 1884 and 1891. On average, as we shall see, women who married toward the end of the century gave birth to two to three fewer children than those who married in the 1850s.

Despite widely circulated stereotypes about the perennially prolific Quebec family, this observation in fact reinforces what we already know about fertility trends in the later nineteenth century. In 1968, Jacques Henripin demonstrated a 17% drop in Quebec's general fertility rate across the period 1851 to 1891.[2] He argued that for the first 20 years of this period, most of the decline was due to falling marriage rates; but that after 1871, it was the net decline in fertility within marriage that was more important.[3] There are also studies suggesting that the fertility decline in the Saint-Hyacinthe area may have been precocious, compared to other predominantly French-speaking parts of the province. Quebec's fertility levels in this period, as Marvin McInnis has shown, were strongly differentiated by region. His figures depict a nineteenth-century fertility decline that was largely restricted to the urban centres and to certain rural counties, many of them with large English-speaking populations. But in Saint-Hyacinthe county, where very few anglophones indeed resided, marital fertility nonetheless fell by 21% between 1861 and 1891, one of the sharpest declines detected for any Quebec county.[4]

On the important question of occupational and class differences in fertility behaviour during this period, there is much less work upon which to build. Research on this issue in Quebec has often minimized the influence of social and economic factors, conentrating instead on linguis'ic, religious, and cultural differences. The beginnings of a fertility decline within the French-speaking, Catholic population of nineteenth-century Quebec, then, is overshadowed by the early and quite extraordinary transition occurring in the United States and among Canadians of British origin. Much of the literature on Quebec fertility is blind to differentials other than those between aggregate French-Canadian levels and those of the mainly Protestant anglophones in Quebec and elsewhere in Canada.[5]

A clear need exists, then, for studies that look beyond cultural differences to illuminate social and economic influences on reproductive behaviour. One way to undertake such a study is to examine patterns of fertility in historical situations where socio-economic differences between cultural groups were slight.[6] Another way is to concentrate on class, occupational, regional, and urban/rural differentials within the French-Canadian population.[7] Much of what has been written on Quebec fertility in the nineteenth century focuses on farm families, if only because such families dominate the aggregate statistics most readily available for the period. Relatively little attention has been paid to the emerging urban bourgeoisie, or to the numerically more important working class. It is crucial at this stage in the debate to know whether their reproductive patterns set them apart from each other and from rural dwellers, and if so, why.[8]

This is the approach adopted in the present chapter, which focuses on the fertility behaviour of a group of couples who shared a religion, a language, and a community, but who belonged to different social and occupational groups. Marital fertility levels in Saint-Hyacinthe, as we shall see, followed a pattern of differential decline. Many Saint-Hyacinthe women – especially those who married in the 1860s and later – made successful attempts to control their fertility. But although bourgeois families were the first to adopt family limitation strategies, by the end of the century, the wives of Saint-Hyacinthe's manual workers had begun to practise fertility control as well.[9]

What explains the pattern of fertility decline observed in Saint-Hyacinthe? How, if at all, was it linked to the emergence of industrial capitalism and to the particular kind of material conditions that emerged in this town? Most of this discussion will come in its place, once the demographic data have been presented in detail. But some attention to the complex relationship between fertility behaviour and socio-economic change – a relationship that has fascinated and puzzled students of "the demographic transition" for at least three decades – seems necessary at the outset.[10]

Authors in this tradition have assumed that economic structural transformations were somehow responsible for fertility decline, although the precise mechanism linking the two has proven very difficult to articulate.[11] Early statements of the demographic transition model oversimplified the matter by ascribing changing patterns of reproduction to industrialization and urbanization or, alternatively, to "modernity." More recent theories reflect the inability of these extremely broad concepts to convey the diversity and complexity of historical fertility situations.[12] Widely held assumptions have been challenged by economists, historians, anthropologists, and others who have noted the unwillingness of both historical and contemporary populations to behave in the expected ways.[13] But a fascination remains with economic structure and with the countless ways in which it can, and does, affect reproductive behaviour: with the relationship between production and reproduction, to borrow that apt phrase from the anthropologist Jack Goody.[14]

Efforts to understand the fertility transition in Quebec have emphasized cultural influences on reproductive behaviour but, sometimes tacitly, have usually accepted the logic of the traditional demographic transition model. Henripin, for example, adopted a more or less classic version of the demographic transition, in which urban and industrial development led to declining levels of mortality, then fertility.[15] Since, in his view, the impact of urban and industrial development on Quebec women after 1850 was slight, his main concern was to explain why Quebec couples *resisted* the pressure to reduce family size, particularly when English-Canadian fertility was falling on cue.[16]

Though her study was not primarily demographic, Bettina Bradbury added an interesting wrinkle to this debate by arguing that the links from economic change to a new demographic pattern were far more complex than traditional demographic transition theory had suggested. In her words,

Recent research in demography and demographic history is making clear how changes in economic circumstances were reflected in modifications of patterns of marriage and family formation. Detailed knowledge of local economies has been necessary to show such changes. The divorce of people from ownership of their own productive units seems to have engendered the most dramatic change in marriage and reproductive strategies, not industrialization or urbanization as had traditionally been argued.[17]

On the other hand, McInnis (an economist) takes a more or less thoroughly cultural perspective. He tends to attribute nineteenth-century fertility decline in counties such as Saint-Hyacinthe and La Prairie to their proximity to Montreal, soft-pedalling the influence of material factors on reproductive behaviour. In a 1987 paper, he argued that the fertility transition in French Canada "gives every indication of having been a diffusion process, radiating outward from Montreal."[18]

Gérard Bouchard's contribution to this debate has been to build a model of family reproduction around the experience of the Saguenay region. In the Saguenay, fertility decline came late. Indeed, Bouchard treats persistent high fertility as a crucial element of the regional model of family reproduction, which he calls "co-integration." This, it must be remembered, is a region in which most of the population was engaged in agriculture well into the twentieth century, and in which the industries that did develop were resource-based, capital intensive, and dependent on an almost exclusively male labour force. The combination of agriculture and heavy industry in this region provided a much different material basis for family reproduction than the shoe- and knit-goods factories of a town such as Saint-Hyacinthe.[19]

Overall, Quebec is no different from the other societies that have experienced substantial fertility decline since the eighteenth century. It is fine and useful to make comparisons with other societies, or among cultural communities within a given society. But, above all, fertility levels must be treated as the result of choices made, and sometimes not made, by women and men in response to aspects of their environment, and especially to the particular sets of economic opportunities and constraints that they experienced and perceived.

This, at least, is the approach adopted in the present chapter. Fertility decisions, it is assumed, were informed in large measure by material conditions, which explains the decision to study them in a context of emergent industrial capitalism. But as Bradbury argues, the decline of household production and the rise of wage labour may have been much more important than diffuse, abstract processes such as industrialization, urbanization, and modernization. Capitalism, by removing production from the household to the marketplace, tended, at least in the long term, to render obsolete one of the most apparent economic incentives to high fertility: the family's need for a labour force.[20] Certainly these fundamental economic shifts were well under way in nineteenth-century Saint-Hyacinthe. But on the other hand, Saint-Hyacinthe was a community in which a particular pattern of industrial capitalism emerged, one which was widespread in Quebec and which was predicated on labour-intensive industries. To the extent that wages remained low, school attendance remained irregular, and families pooled their labour power in order to survive, capital may have continued to pay a certain dividend for large families, even as fields and farmhouses gave way to factories and cold-water flats.

Examining fertility trends and differentials in Saint-Hyacinthe, then, can illustrate the extent to which men and women adjusted their reproductive strategies to suit a new set of economic and social conditions, one characteristic of later nineteenth-century Quebec. Any such response was certainly filtered through other dynamic aspects of contemporary reality, such as religion, cultural tradition, education, and gender relations. But the fundamental role of material factors – including class position and access to property, the vagaries of the capitalist waged-labour market, and the cost of food and housing – should never be underestimated in evaluating the root causes of fertility decline.

FERTILITY DECLINE IN SAINT-HYACINTHE

The pattern of falling fertility in later nineteenth-century Saint-Hyacinthe is clearly legible in Table 5-1 and Figure 5-1. The data are

Table 5-1
Age-Specific Marital Fertility Rates[a]

| Cohort | Age Category | | | | | | (Total) |
	15–19	20–24	25–29	30–34	35–39	40–44	15–44
A (1854–61)	429	524	478	433	396	174	417
B (1864–71)	522	505	474	391	312	145	380
C (1884–91)	512	488	417	300	220	103	332

Source Family Reconstitution Files

Note

[a]   Live births per thousand women in the specified age category per year.

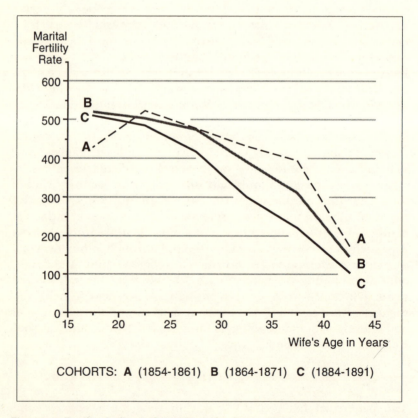

Figure 5-1 Fertility decline in Saint Hyacinthe. Source: Table 5-1

age-specific marital fertility rates, calculated for women in the three marriage cohorts according to procedures described in detail in the appendix.[21] We see that fertility rates in Saint-Hyacinthe fell progressively in this period, for every category of married women except the youngest. Wives under 20 years of age were noticeably more fertile toward the end of the century than they had been in the 1850s.[22] Otherwise, scanning from the youngest age group to the oldest, we see an increasingly sharp drop in marital fertility. The decline between the first and third marriage cohorts ranges from about 7% in the 20 to 24 age category to over 40% for women aged 35 years or more. The 20% drop in the fertility of all married women – from 417 per thousand in the 1854–61 cohort, to 332 per thousand in the 1884–91 cohort – is clear evidence of the beginnings of a fertility transition in this industrializing community with its French-speaking, Catholic, increasingly proletarian population.[23]

Table 5-2 and Figure 5-2 help to put these figures into perspective. They present a comparison between fertility rates in Saint-Hyacinthe and those from other communities where similar measurements have been made. When examined alongside those of a strongly contraceptive population – such as that of Britain in the 1920s – marital fertility rates in nineteenth-century Saint-Hyacinthe seem high indeed. Even the third cohort of Saint-Hyacinthe women, those married from 1884 to 1891, bore about 50% more children than these twentieth-century British women aged 20 to 24 years, and over 200% more than those in their early thirties.

More appropriate, perhaps, are comparisons with the other French-Canadian populations shown in the table and figure. As the table shows, fertility levels were extremely high in New France.[24] Rates for married women over 30 were even higher in early eighteenth-century Canada than among the Hutterites, who according to demographers represent a theoretical maximum. Compared to the early French-Canadian population, the fertility of Saint-Hyacinthe women who married in the 1850s was already at a reduced level. The crucial difference was among those over 30, where levels in the eighteenth century had been so high. For Saint-Hyacinthe women in Cohort A, marital fertility rates for women over 30 were, by age group, 10.5%, 3.4%, and 24.7% lower than in eighteenth-century Canada.

By the standards of Quebec's nineteenth-century population, Saint-Hyacinthe was not exceptional in this respect. Indeed, the reduction of marital fertility in the 30 to 44 age group was a trend felt even more strongly in Quebec as a whole than in this local setting, at least prior to the 1850s.[25] Until this time, the forces that wrought this change had been working more slowly in Saint-Hyacinthe than

Table 5-2
Age-Specific Marital Fertility Rates: Three Saint-Hyacinthe Marriage Cohorts and
Eight Other Populations

		Age Category					
		15–19	20–24	25–29	30–34	35–39	40–44
a)	Hutterites, 1920s marriages	NA	550	502	447	406	222
b)	Canada, 1700-50	493	509	496	484	410	231
c)	Canadian nobility, 18th-century marriages	447	534	507	424	351	172
d)	Saguenay region						
	1840–59 marriages	NA	467	441	411	366	228
	1885–89 marriages	NA	505	466	431	356	193
e)	Saint-Hyacinthe						
	1854–61 marriages	429	524	478	433	396	174
	1864–71 marriages	522	505	474	391	312	145
	1884–91 marriages	512	488	417	300	220	103
f)	Quebec (province)						
	1851 estimate	510	508	486	420	289	152
	1921 estimate	510	490	425	340	225	118
g)	Great Britain, c. 1920	NA	320	165	90	50	20

Sources

a) Henripin and Lapierre-Adamcyk, *Eléments de démographie*, 205

b) Henripin, *La population canadienne*, 60

c) Gadoury, "Comportements démographiques et alliances de la noblesse" [unpublished CHA paper], table 4, 32

d) Roy, "Paramètres sociaux de la fécondité saguenayenne"

e) See Table 5-1

f) Estimates made by Henripin, published in *Tendances et facteurs de fécondité*, 382

g) Henripin and Lapierre-Adamcyk, *Eléments de démographie*, 205

elsewhere. Fertility rates in Cohort A remained higher than the Quebec aggregates in most age categories.[26] And apart from those in the 40 to 44 age group, women who married in Saint-Hyacinthe in the 1850s seem to have been even more fertile than those who wed in the newly colonized Saguenay region between 1840 and 1859.[27]

Fertility levels in Saint-Hyacinthe declined markedly between the first and third cohorts in this study: between the lifetimes of women who married during the wave of institutional development of the 1850s and of those who formed their families during the unprecedented industrial expansion of the 1880s. Much of this decline involved women over 30: the fertility of married women in each of the over-30 age groups fell by between 30% and 45%. Yet levels for women in their teens and twenties remained high. The result is a marital fertility curve (for Cohort C) very similar to that based on Henripin's estimates for Quebec population in 1921 (see Figure 5-2).

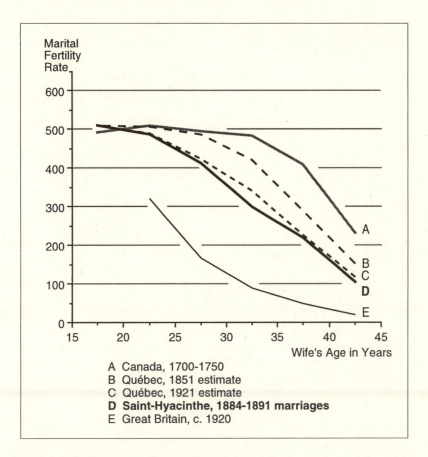

Figure 5-2 Age-specific marital fertility rates: Saint-Hyacinthe 1884–1891 and four other populations. Source: Table 5-2

While these figures may have lagged behind aggregate fertility trends in the decades leading up to the 1850s, then, they suggest that Saint-Hyacinthe women had become trend-setters during the next half century.

The pattern that was emerging so clearly in later nineteenth-century Saint-Hyacinthe spoke of a particular type of fertility control within marriage: the type that John Knodel has defined as "family limitation."[28] Falling fertility rates in the over-30 age groups suggest successful attempts to stop bearing children, but only after a certain number had already been born. Family limitation emerged in Quebec over a long period; on an extremely uneven timetable; and with wide variations by social class, region, and ethnicity.[29] Its accelerated emergence in Saint-Hyacinthe after 1860 – years which saw

Table 5-3
Age-Specific Marital Fertility Rates, by Wife's Age at Marriage

Women's Marriage Age	Age Category (years)						Woman-Years Observed
	15–19	20–24	25–29	30–34	35–39	40–44	
Cohort A							
15–19	429	515	410	408	299	130	519.5
20–24		537	492	419	383	203	465.5
25–34			(588)	485	(545)	(235)	169.0
Cohort B							
15–19	527	416	413	262	241	98	567.5
20–24		569	515	470	367	220	604.0
25–34			(534)	405	329	109	268.0
Cohort C							
15–19	512	509	397	277	291	(200)	705.5
20–24		460	415	256	196	85	780.5
25–34			(531)	411	180	55	289.0

Source Family Reconstitution Files
Note

Marital fertility rates for women married prior to age 15 or after age 34 have not been included. Two categories of marriage age (25–29 and 30–34) have been combined in this table. All rates shown are based on at least 30 observed woman-years. Lorraine Gadoury implies that rates based on less than this number are suspect. See Gadoury, "Comportements démographiques et alliances" [CHA paper], table 4, 32. In the present table, rates based on less than 50-woman-years are in parentheses.

fundamental changes in the local economy – invites more detailed attention to fertility trends and differentials in this community.

Age-specific marital fertility rates are closely related to the age at which women married. In Table 5-3 and Figure 5-3, separate sets of fertility rates are presented for women marrying prior to age 20, those marrying in their early twenties (20 to 24), and those marrying between ages 25 and 34. These figures reveal an interesting evolution which is best understood as a response to the following question: Which women were more likely to slow down or stop bearing children after the age of 35, those who married early or those who married late? At the beginning of the period, the women who had married prior to age 20 were the least fertile in the 35 to 39 and 40 to 44 age categories. This is the pattern one would expect in a population that did not practise any form of fertility control. Among women marrying in Cohort B, the pattern of lower fertility after 35 for women who had married early persisted. But women who had married after age 25 were now more likely to stop child-bearing early than those who had

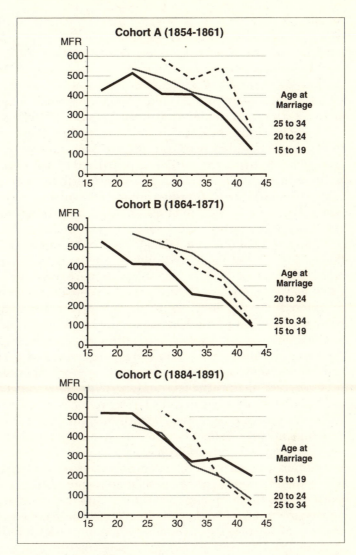

Figure 5-3 Age specific marital fertility rates (MFR) by wife's marriage age. Source: Table 5-3

married between the ages of 20 and 24. By the time of the 1880s cohort, the pattern observed 30 years earlier had been inverted. Women who married prior to age 20 were the most likely to continue having children after age 35. Those who married between ages 20 and 24 had fewer children, and those who married after age 25 had the fewest of all.

This analysis has at least two important implications, the first of which is quite specific. Data from the 1884–91 cohort point to the existence of two distinct reproductive patterns in Saint-Hyacinthe. Certain women married young and continued to bear children until a relatively advanced age: a pattern we can qualify as "traditional." Other women married later and discontinued their child-bearing activity early. Their family sizes would have been reduced to something approaching "modern" levels, both by later marriage and by fertility control within marriage. Régina Bachand can be taken to represent the "traditional model." She married railway worker Alfred Brodeur in September 1890 at age 18; gave birth to a son in January of 1892; and continued bearing children at regular intervals until, in January of 1914, at the age of 42, she gave birth to her fourteenth and last child (another son).[30] And we have already met Sophronie Tremblay. She was one of the daughters of the labourer's widow who helped support her family by working as a seamstress while she was growing up. As we have seen, Sophronie married relatively late, in 1888, at age 25, to shoe-factory worker Arthur Dufresne. All things considered, we should perhaps not be surprised that her child-bearing career was relatively modern. She had married late and did not bear her first child, a daughter, until she was 28 years old, in December 1891. She bore a son in 1894; daughters in 1895 and 1897; and a set of twins, both girls, in December of 1899 when she was 36 years old. After five pregnancies and six children – admittedly a lot by late twentieth-century standards – her reproductive years were over.[31]

This comparison highlights the second, more general implication of the quantitative analysis these examples are meant to illustrate. In the long term, general fertility levels probably declined in a scissors-like motion. Certain women, such as Sophronie Tremblay, were shortening their periods of procreation at both ends, through both later marriage and the "stopping" behaviour known as family limitation.[32] At the same time, other women, like Régina Bachand, retained the pattern of early marriage and more or less unrestricted fertility. The co-existence of these two patterns in industrializing Saint-Hyacinthe suggests something of the socially differentiated character of fertility decline in this community, a topic which will soon be explored in greater depth.

The overall trend toward fertility restriction in later nineteenth century Saint-Hyacinthe can be illustrated in two further ways. In the first place, as more and more women attempted to stop having children prior to menopause, there was a lengthening of the interval between the births of the last two children.[33] This final birth interval increased from an average of 30.8 months for couples in the first marriage cohort, to 33.5 months in the second cohort, and 38.2 months in the third.[34] At the same time, the average age of the mother at the birth of her last child declined. From an average of 40.3 years in Cohort A, a woman's age at the birth of her youngest child fell steadily, to 39.1 years in Cohort B, and 37.9 years in Cohort C.[35] The average woman who married in the 1880s, then, completed her family over two years earlier than a woman from her mother's generation who had married in the 1860s. This is rather dramatic evidence of the type of control over marital fertility I have been suggesting.[36]

How did all of these trends affect family size in Saint-Hyacinthe? One way of answering this question is to simply observe the number of births per marriage in the 102 *completed* families in the three cohorts.[37] Calculated on this basis, the average number of children born to Saint-Hyacinthe women fell from 8.3 in Cohort A, to 7.6 in Cohort B, and, again (much more sharply) to 5.7 in Cohort C.[38] Because of the number of cases, these averages must be treated with caution. But they do tend to confirm the general trend already noted in this chapter; that is, that families were smaller at the end of this period, by about two children, than they had been at the beginning.

Given the limited number of completed families in the study, it is helpful to support this assertion with a synthetic measure of average family size, based on marital fertility rates and other data. Such a measure, by incorporating information from all 386 family reconstitution files in the fertility analysis, provides a more accessible measure of fertility than the age-specific rates themselves. By setting women's marriage age at the cohort mean and assuming both partners survived through the wife's 45th birthday, cohort- and age-specific marital fertility rates can then be applied to a hypothetical woman whose imagined reproductive life represents the "average" behaviour of the cohort.[39]

The average family sizes estimated on this basis follow a similar path to those observed in completed families. Starting from a level of 8.8 children per couple in the 1854–61 cohort, this index fell to 8.0 for unions formed between 1864 and 1871. The same precipitous decline as observed with completed families then occurred: due to falling marital fertility rates, especially in the over-30 age group, this particular estimate of average family size fell to 5.9 for the 1884–91 cohort.[40] The hypothetical "average" woman who married in Saint-Hyacinthe in the 1880s, then, would have given birth to almost three fewer children than a representative of the 1854–61 cohort.

So far, we have been concerned only with the numbers of children born to married women in Saint-Hyacinthe. In order to understand the logic of fertility trends in this community, it is also important to know something about the chances these infants had for survival. Marriage age and marital fertility, after all, were not the only influences on family size in late nineteenth-century Saint-Hyacinthe. Infant and child mortality also had an impact.

Table 5-4 provides some of the available information on infant and child mortality in the three Saint-Hyacinthe marriage cohorts, and compares it to published estimates for Quebec during this period.[41] The level of infant mortality is dramatic. Infant mortality quotients remained very high – generally above 250 per thousand – in a period when provincial levels were declining: to about 150 per thousand by the 1891 generation. This was a period during which Quebec's urban and rural infant mortality levels were sharply differentiated, mainly due to sorely deficient hygiene and poor living conditions in the cities. Saint-Hyacinthe, despite its moderate size and proximity to the countryside, was situated squarely on the urban side of this mortality divide. With infant mortality reaching 286 per thousand in the 1884–91 cohort – a figure over 85% higher than the provincial quotient in the same period – Saint-Hyacinthe was just as unhealthy a place for infants under a year old as Montreal.[42]

Child mortality, as well, took its toll on Saint-Hyacinthe's families during this period. Here again, levels were above those experienced by the population of Quebec as a whole.[43] If one ignores the exceptionally high figure of over 200 deaths per thousand detected in Cohort B, however, it is possible to argue that child mortality in Saint-Hyacinthe was declining on a course roughly parallel to the Quebec figures. The Cohort-B figure can be regarded as exceptional because serious epidemics in 1882 and 1885 – the second of which was certainly smallpox – took a heavy toll on the local youth, at exactly the time when the children of couples married between 1864 and 1871 would have been most susceptible.[44]

Part of the reason for the alarming levels of child, and particularly infant, mortality was the poor quality of the water supply in Saint-Hyacinthe. This public health issue, in fact, became a subject of some controversy in the mid 1880s. Industrialist Louis Coté (Illustration 8) was both mayor and president of the Compagnie de l'aqueduc – a private utility – when, during the spring of 1884, critics began to complain that the intake pipe for the city's drinking water had been placed too close to sources of industrial and domestic effluent. Public health was threatened and Côté was vigorously criticized in council and in the local press, to the point where he offered his resignation as mayor (it was refused).[45]

Table 5-4
Infant and Child Mortality

Part 1. Infant and Child Mortality Quotients, Children Included in the Saint-Hyacinthe Fertility Study, by Cohort, with Corresponding Quebec Levels

	Infant Mortality Quotient[a]	Child Mortality Quotient[b]
Saint-Hyacinthe		
1854–61 Cohort	.278	.167
1864–71 Cohort	.244	.204
1884–91 Cohort	.286	.139
Quebec[c]		
1861 Generation	.178	.140
1871 Generation	.165	.129
1891 Generation	.154	.112

Part 2. Infant and Child Mortality Quotients in Saint-Hyacinthe as Ratios of Provincial Levels (Provincial Quotient in Corresponding Generation = 100)

Cohort	Infant Mortality	Child Mortality
A	156	119
B	148	158
C	186	124

Sources Family Reconstitution Files; Bourbeau and Légaré, Evolution de la mortalité
Notes
[a] Deaths under one year per 1,000 live births.
[b] Deaths at ages one to 15 per 1,000 live births.
[c] Average of values given for male and female children, from mortality tables in Bourbeau and Légaré, Evolution de la mortalité, 112, 113, 115.

Clearly related to environmental factors, infant mortality was one of the most serious social and demographic consequences of urban development during this period, in Saint-Hyacinthe as in other Quebec cities. High infant mortality, moreover, encouraged high fertility through a well-known mechanism. Infant deaths – which interrupt breast-feeding, thereby eliminating the contraceptive effect of lactation – tend to result in shorter birth intervals and, therefore, more births over time.[46] Saint-Hyacinthe's falling fertility levels are perhaps the more remarkable for this reason. The point of the present discussion, however, is not to explore this relationship in depth. It is to suggest, rather, the extent to which infant and child mortality could stand between fertility levels and size of families in this nineteenth-century community.

We know that about one-quarter of all the children born to women included in the fertility study died in the first year of life, and

Table 5-5
Four Estimates of Average Family Size, by Cohort

		A	B	C
1	Completed Families	8.3	7.6	5.7
	(N=102)	(20)	(37)	(45)
2	Average number of children born (ANC)[a]	8.8	8.0	5.9
3	Children surviving infancy[b]	6.3	6.1	4.2
4	Children surviving to 15 years[c]	4.8	4.4	3.4

Source Family Reconstitution Files

Notes

[a] ANC = Total Marital Fertility Rate/1000, holding female marriage age constant at mean cohort value (rounded to 22 years for cohorts A and B, and 23 for cohort C).

[b] ANC, minus children dying before their first birthday, estimated according to cohort-specific infant mortality quotients (see Table 5-4).

[c] ANC, minus children dying before their 15th birthday, estimated according to cohort-specific infant and child mortality quotients (see Table 5-4).

that another 15% died between ages one and 15. Two further measures of family size in Saint-Hyacinthe have been generated that incorporate these mortality figures. First are estimates of the total number of children who would have survived to one year; second are estimates of those children surviving to 15 years among those born to the hypothetical "average" women discussed earlier. As Table 5-5 shows, when one considers the effects of high infant and child mortality, a gently rising age at marriage for women, and a drop in marital fertility (especially in the over-30 age group), family sizes in Saint-Hyacinthe toward the end of the nineteenth century begin to appear small indeed. From a level of 6.3 in the first cohort, this estimate of the average number of children surviving infancy falls to 4.2 for women who married in the 1880s. Of these, only 3.4 (down from 4.8) would, according to this synthetic measure, have survived to the age of 15 years.

These sorts of statistical averages, of course, hide at least as much as they reveal. They help us to understand general trends but can obscure the behaviour of individual women and families. Although the average number of children born to Saint-Hyacinthe women who married in the 1880s was around six, and the average number that survived infancy was just over four, few women would have had exactly that experience. Reproductive life stories such as that of Corine Mongeau illustrate this point very clearly. The daughter of a Saint-Hyacinthe "shoemaker" – which generally, in this community, meant a factory worker – Corine was 18 when she married local mason

Zéphirin Henry in May of 1887. Over the next 24 years, she gave birth to 13 children, more than twice the cohort average. The first of these, a son, was born exactly seven months after the wedding, which seems to suggest a prenuptial conception.[47] Corine had her last child, also a son, some 24 years later, in April of 1911 at the age of 42. But of all these 13 children – and this is the point of the story – six died in the first year of life, while two more died before reaching their second birthdays. Although her fertility was high, Corine's family size – if we measure by the number of children surviving to age 15 – was only five, which was just slightly above the average for women in this cohort.[48] Worlds apart was the life of Hélène Elizabeth (Lizzie) Buckley, a local bourgeoise who, at 22, married François Jules Laframboise, accountant for the Banque de Saint-Hyacinthe and the son of a Superior Court judge, in September of 1886. Lizzie gave birth to six children over the next 16 years: precisely the average for this marriage cohort. However, all her children survived infancy; in fact, no burial certificates were found for any of her children, suggesting that they all lived to be adults. She was 39 when she gave birth to her last child, a little girl, in October of 1903. Although Lizzie's fertility was about half Corine's, then, she actually raised more children to adulthood (six, as opposed to five) than her working-class neighbour.[49]

These examples, in addition to revealing the variety of experiences that can be masked by the statistics, hint at some of the variations that characterized the fertility and reproductive behaviour of Saint-Hyacinthe women in the later nineteenth century. But we need to examine these questions systematically. Were smaller families, and especially the deliberate restriction of family size, the preserve of a particular segment of Saint-Hyacinthe's population, perhaps an elite group as in so many other contexts? Were fertility levels, in other words, socially and occupationally specific, and, if so, along what lines?

DIFFERENTIAL DECLINE

Asking the question of whether or not fertility in Saint-Hyacinthe was socially specific forces certain adjustments. Our methodological "lens" must be more sharply focused if these more detailed and differentiated images are to emerge. The ideal apparatus for understanding differential fertility in Saint-Hyacinthe would be a set of age-specific marital fertility rates for each occupational group within each cohort. But the amount of information available in certain categories does not always allow the calculation of such rates.[50]

Table 5-6
Fertility Rates by Husband's Occupation[a]

		Age Category						
	Cohort	15–19	20–24	25–29	30–34	35–39	40–44	[Total] 15–44
Farmers	A	–	(593)[b]	–	–	(400)	(296)	–[c]
	B	–	(632)	(640)	(480)	(308)	(200)	[472]
	C	–	(553)	(565)	(533)	(345)	(250)	[489]
Urban-manual	A	414	511	460	380	351	140	391
workers	B	543	465	468	377	327	182	387
	C	514	485	404	289	228	112	328
Labourers	A	–	–	(429)	(462)	(537)	(191)	[417]
	B	–	(625)	(378)	(320)	(178)	(138)	[325]
	C	–	–	–	–	–	–	–
Non-manual	A	–	(621)	(621)	698	(629)	(333)	[600]
	B	–	561	455	422	319	60	347
	C	–	481	433	294	165	0	310
THREE-COHORT AGGREGATES								
Farmers		–	598	598	500	333	197	474
Urban-manual		494	488	439	339	289	140	363
Labourers		–	(596)	400	379	313	148	347
Non-manual		(426)	540	478	436	304	80	381

Source Family Reconstitution Files

Notes

[a] Age and occupationally specific marital fertility rates, by cohort, with three-cohort aggregates.

[b] Age-specific rates based on under 30 woman-years are in parentheses; those based on under 10 years have been omitted.

[c] Overall marital fertility rates based on under 150 woman-years are in square brackets; those based on less than 50 years have been omitted.

Such cohort- and socially-specific rates as can be considered reliable are given in Table 5-6. The aggregate (three-cohort) rates presented at the bottom of the table represent a partial, less than satisfactory solution to the problem of small numbers. Examining these aggregates, however, helps identify some persistent fertility differentials in Saint-Hyacinthe. As Figure 5-4 shows, for example, farmers' wives had appreciably higher fertility than women in other categories. The 19 farm families in the three cohorts – admittedly a very small group – displayed an overall marital fertility rate of 474 per thousand: 31% above the level in the urban-manual category and 24% higher than the rate for women in the non-manual group.

A farm/non-farm differential in fertility makes intuitive sense and resonates with much of the existing literature on this topic.[51] It seems unlikely, then, that farm families participated in the trend toward reduced fertility that characterized this heterogeneous, but predominantly urban parish in the later nineteenth century. Women like Amanda Scott – who in 1888 at age 18 married Ferdinand Viens, a farmer from the rural part of Saint-Hyacinthe-le-Confesseur parish – were not uncommon in the *rangs* surrounding the town at the end of the nineteenth century. Amanda gave birth to 15 children in the ensuing 20 years, all but four of whom survived to age 15. Strangely, and sadly, of the 11 surviving children, four more died before the age of 20.[52]

Though they provide an illustration of the farm/non-farm differentiation, the three-cohort rates plotted in Figure 5-4 also give some false impressions that only a diachronic analysis can correct. The aggregate figures suggest that families headed by men in non-manual occupations, with an overall marital fertility rate of 381 per thousand, were larger than urban-manual families, for whom the corresponding rate was 363 per thousand. Except possibly in the first cohort, however, this was not the case at all. The relative levels of marital fertility in the local bourgeoisie and the urban working class shifted in important ways during this period, as a closer look at the overall rates given in the right-hand column of Table 5-6 reveals.

A curious feature of this series is the exceptionally high level of marital fertility among women in the non-manual category who married between 1854 and 1861. This figure (600 per thousand) can surely be rejected as a cohort- and occupationally specific measure of marital fertility, since it is based on only 14 women, observed over a total of 130 years. But these 14 high-fertility women cannot be excluded from the aggregate rates displayed in Figure 5-4. They do much to help create the false impression that, overall, bourgeois families were larger than working-class families in this industrializing community.

Let us assume that the real level of marital fertility for bourgeois women in Cohort A was 417 per thousand: the level observed for the entire cohort.[53] Starting from this hypothetical level, marital fertility in the non-manual category would have declined by 17% to 347 per thousand in Cohort B, and by another 11% to 310 per thousand in Cohort C. Under these assumptions, the marital fertility of bourgeois women would have declined by 25% across the period, to a level some 7% below the general rate for all women in Cohort C.

The data for the wives of urban-manual workers also show a decline, but on a much different timetable. There was very little

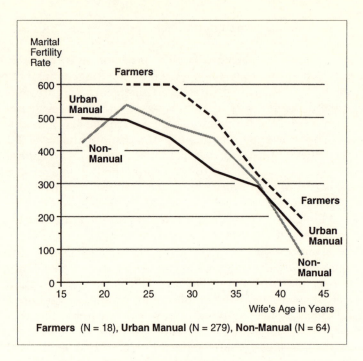

Figure 5-4 Age and occupationally specific marital fertility rates, three-cohort aggregates (labourers excluded). Source: Table 5-6

reduction in working-class fertility between the 1850s and 1860s marriage cohorts – perhaps not surprisingly given the relatively short time span and the fact that the social and economic transition was at such an early stage. But marital fertility in this category did decline – by some 15% – between Cohorts B and C, to a level slightly below that of the full cohort in the final period.[54]

It is clear enough, then, that bourgeois fertility began to fall before that of working-class women in Saint-Hyacinthe. The observed figures for the 1854–61 cohort are based on only a few cases. But they certainly seem to suggest that, at this juncture, bourgeois families were no smaller than those of manual workers; they may even have been larger. By the 1864–71 cohort, a new pattern of differentiation had emerged. Fertility in the non-manual category had fallen to a level some 10% below that of the working class, which had barely budged in the interval. And between the 1860s and the 1880s, the trend to lower fertility within marriage generalized. Bourgeois and working-class fertility rates were, respectively, 11% and 15% lower in Cohort C than they had been in Cohort B. But some of the differential established in the earlier period was maintained. Bourgeois women

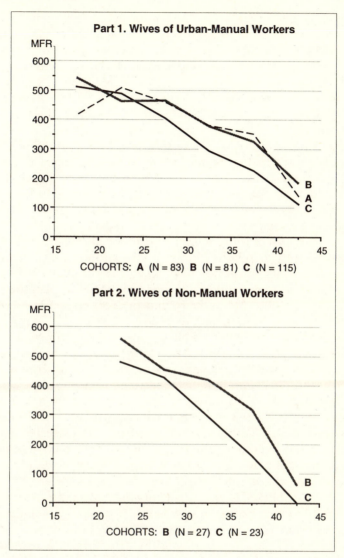

Figure 5-5   Age-specific marital fertility rates by occupational group and cohort.
Source: Table 5–6

marrying between 1884 and 1891 had about 5% fewer children than those whose husbands were manual workers.

Some of this information is presented graphically in Figure 5-5. There are no reliable age-specific rates to help us trace the decline in bourgeois fertility between 1854–61 and 1864–71. But the graphs plotted here emphasize the role of family limitation (in Knodel's sense) in the generalized drop in marital fertility between Cohorts B and C. The fertility of working-class women aged 30 to 34 and 35 to 39 fell by 23% and 30%, respectively. The corresponding declines for bourgeois women were 30% and 48%.[55] Many more women than previously, in manual and non-manual families, stopped bearing children in their thirties, and sometimes even in their late twenties. Catherine Dufort, for example, married a local doctor, Gaspard Hyacinthe Turcot, in June of 1886 at age 19. By the time she was 29, in 1896, she had borne the last of her five children.[56] Some may also have been spacing births, perhaps by breast-feeding longer, which would have had the added benefit of reducing infant mortality. Again, Catherine Dufort's case is illustrative. Her average birth interval was 24 months and she lost no children in infancy, suggesting that, with or without her husband's medical advice, she was using lactation to keep her children healthy and to gain some measure of protection against repeated pregnancies.[57] If others were doing the same thing, this would go a long way toward explaining the slight reductions observed in the fertility rates of younger married women, particularly within the bourgeoisie.

So far, it has been possible to suggest the presence of fertility differentials between farm and non-farm women, and between the wives of manual and non-manual workers in the town. Farm women – at least those few who have been observed here – do not seem to have restricted their fertility in the period under review. In the town, however, both bourgeois and working-class women did. Bourgeois women such as Catherine Dufort and Lizzie Buckley, like members of elite groups in other contexts, seem to fit the mould of fertility "forerunners" who adopted family limitation early on. But by the 1880s marriage cohort, working-class women, such as Sophronie Tremblay, had begun to use what must have been for many the most sensible reproductive strategy, despite strong ideological pressures against any form of fertility restriction.

Are there any more hints to be gained from occupational data that might tell us which women, particularly within the working-class majority, limited their family size, and which did not? Were the wives of wage labourers, for example, any more or less prone than the wives of independent artisans to do so? Was there, in other words, a relationship – positive or negative – between the level of proletarianization and fertility decline?

Two approaches to the occupational data for husbands in the "urban-manual" category permit a preliminary exploration of these questions. In the first place, workers who consistently declared the same occupation (other than *cultivateur* or *journalier*) were distinguished from those who declared a variety of occupations in the course of their careers. This was a quick way of separating out artisans (who would generally remain in a single trade) from wage labourers (who might tend to be more occupationally mobile). A more systematic way would be to link these family reconstitution files to other documents, especially municipal tax roles, directories, and notarized contracts. Practical constraints, however, mitigated against using this strategy. Instead, I assumed that occupational stability would be positively correlated with craft skills and perhaps with the independent status of an artisan, and that mobility would be correlated with wage work.

We can compare the occupational itineraries of Joseph Lussier and Joseph Blanchard to see how this worked in practice. Lussier's occupation was recorded in the parish register some 21 times between July 1871 and May 1904. Each time, he was described as a *menuisier*, a construction trade that was little affected by the changing relations of production in the period. Blanchard, on the other hand, declared himself a *cultivateur* in his marriage act; but in 12 subsequent civil acts passed between May 1886 and May 1919 he gave eight distinct job titles: *cordonnier* (five times), *cultivateur* (twice), *sellier, journalier, facteur, employé de manufacture, employé au tricot,* and *emballeur* (once each). If Lussier worked for wages, he at least had a skill that seems to have translated into steady work in the same trade; he may also have worked on his own account. Blanchard, on the other hand, had no steady occupation; he had clearly become an industrial wage labourer by the end of his career, as is, in this case, so apparent from the job titles themselves.[58]

A contrasting pattern between workers who consistently declared the same occupation and those who were occupationally mobile is apparent in Table 5-7. Fertility levels declined in both these segments of the working class between the 1864–71 and 1884–91 cohorts. But the decline was much more precipitous among the wives of occupationally stable manual workers. These families were about 10% larger than the average for all manual workers in the first two cohorts. By the 1884–91 cohort, however, marital fertility in this segment of the working class had declined rapidly – to a level some 7% below that of all urban-manual families. Indeed, marital fertility for wives of stable manual workers had fallen to a level – 305 per thousand – even below that recorded in the same cohort for bourgeois women. Among the wives of occupationally mobile workers, fertility levels fell much more slowly, albeit from a substantially lower initial level. The small numbers involved render

Table 5-7
Marital Fertility Rates, Wives of Three Categories of Urban-Manual Workers

	Cohort	Overall Marital Fertility Rate (15–44)	Number of Woman-Years Observed	Number of Women	Percentage of Rate for Wives of all Urban-Manual Workers
1 One profession	A	431	290	28	110
declared consistently	B	419	219.5	22	108
	C	305	472.5	40	93
2 More than one	A	373	651.5	55	95
profession declared	B	377	742.5	59	97
	C	339	981	79	103
3 Manual workers in the	A	395	263	15	101
leather trades, at some	B	421	299	20	108
point	C	347	671	59	106

Source Family Reconstitution Files

Notes

Manual workers in category 1 consistently declared the same occupation in all parish register acts and census lists (*journaliers* and *cultivateurs* excluded). Some obvious occupational equivalences were accepted. *Maçon* and *tailleur de pierre*, for example, were considered identical for these purposes. Manual workers in category 2 declared a variety of occupations in the various documents. These first two categories are mutually exclusive. The third category distinguishes all manual workers who at any time declared an occupation related to shoemaking, tanning, or saddlery. It contains members of both of the other two groups.

these conclusions fragile.[59] But the suggestion that the wives of independent artisans may have adopted fertility control more readily than those whose husbands had to rely on wages to support their families is at least an interesting hypothesis.

A second way to attempt to distinguish Saint-Hyacinthe's wage-labouring families is to focus on families in which the husbands had, at some point, worked in the leather trades. Many of the leather workers who married in the 1860s and the great majority of those who married in the 1880s would have worked for wages in the city's industrial tanneries and boot-and-shoe factories. The case of Jérémie Cloutier illustrates this point admirably. Cloutier was a farmer when he was married, in 1858, at the age of 21. But he declared the occupation "shoemaker" (*cordonnier*) in three successive civil acts, grouped closely in a 12-month period starting in August 1875. Clearly, the word "shoemaker" in late nineteenth-century Saint-Hyacinthe could mean a number of things. The person described as such might still be an independent artisan, running a small shop, working on custom orders, and doing repairs, perhaps with the assistance of an apprentice. But by the

1870s, the far greater likelihood was that a person described as a shoemaker in the parish register was in fact a shoe-factory worker.[60] By the mid 1870s, most shoe-production workers were employed in one of two factories: the one run by the Côté family, or the troubled McMartin-Hamel plant that would fail in 1875 only to be reopened by local investors as La Compagnie de Chaussures de Saint-Hyacinthe. Jérémie Cloutier, then, is extremely unlikely to have been an independent artisan. He had declared eight distinct occupations before describing himself as a shoemaker for the first time in 1875 at the age of 38 years. This is certainly not a pattern one would anticipate from a skilled craftsman. Rather, it reflects insecurity of employment and the frequent obligation to try something new: perhaps among the most salient characteristics of proletarians.[61]

Focusing on the families of even the most temporary leather workers (Table 5-7) reinforces the impression gained by looking at the relationship between occupational mobility and fertility. Among the wives of leather workers, fertility declined in this interval to rates comparable to those found for occupationally mobile manual workers (which many of them, like Cloutier, were). The decline, however, was muted compared to that of women in other occupationally defined groups. Fertility rates in the 1884–91 cohort were about 6% above the general rate for families of urban-manual workers, and fully 12% above the non-manual level.

Joseph Blanchard, whom we have met, was both occupationally mobile and, between 1888 and 1897, a worker in the Saint-Hyacinthe leather trades. He was very obviously an industrial wage labourer, even though, like Cloutier, he reported his occupation as "farmer" when he was married, to a young woman from Sherbrooke, Sophronie Henry, in May of 1886 (they were 29 and 26 years old, respectively). The family set up housekeeping in Saint-Hyacinthe's *Quartier* 2, in a two-storey wooden house which also accommodated two other families. By 1891, Joseph was working in a shoe factory – he reported his occupation as "cordonnier" – and there were three children in the household. As we have seen, Jérémie moved from job to job, working as a labourer, a delivery man, a knitting-mill employee, and even returning briefly to farming in the years between 1891 and 1919. Sophronie, in the mean time, managed the family economy, performed domestic labour, and bore children. When the census takers called in April of 1891, she must have been very pregnant, indeed, with her fourth son, Victor Albani, who was born on 19 April of that year.[62] She bore six more children in the ensuing 12 years; her last, a daughter, arrived in October of 1903 when Sophronie was 43 years old. Of her 10 children, all but two survived the dangerous first year of life, although one daughter died at the age of 12. With 10 live births, eight children surviving infancy, and seven surviving to age 15, then, Sophronie – despite what might be described as a late start – was well above the average for her marriage cohort in all these respects. In short, she seems very unlikely to have been taking active measures to attempt to reduce or restrict her fertility.[63]

The family of Camille Gosselin and Rosina Bernier, on the other hand, illustrates the pattern I have proposed for occupationally stable manual workers (outside the leather trades). Camille was a 30-year-old baker and Rosina was the 23-year-old daughter of a baker when they married in Saint-Hyacinthe, like Jérémie and Sophronie, in May of 1886. In 12 subsequent civil acts and two census enumerations, Camille consistently identified himself as a baker. There can be little doubt that he was an independent tradesman; in 1891, for example, he declared to census takers that he employed two workers during the year. And in 1901, the family was enumerated as living in a rented brick house on Saint-Antoine Street, one of the town's main commercial arteries. Camille reported himself to be both an "employee" and "working on his own account" to the 1901 census takers, suggesting, perhaps, that his independence was not as total as it had been in previous years. Although comfortable by working-class standards, the Gosselin family could by no stretch of the imagination be considered affluent. Camille declared his annual income to be $600, the equivalent of a weekly income of about $11.50: more than most boot-and-shoe and knitwear workers, but not as much as the $18 weekly wage of a highly skilled cabinetmaker working at the Casavant organ-building establishment, just outside the city limits.[64]

Camille and Rosina did not have a small family by today's standards. Rosina gave birth to seven live infants and had one stillbirth between April 1887 – 11 months after the wedding – and October of 1898, when she was 34 years old. Besides the stillbirth, only two of Rosina's children died young; she lost a nine-month-old son in August 1890 and a three-year-old daughter in December 1891. Five children, then, survived to age 15. The fact that the stillbirth of her eighth child marked an early end to her child-bearing years may suggest that this difficult delivery, ending in tragedy, had left Rosina sterile. On the other hand, the stillbirth may have been a warning to the couple to either take measures to restrict their fertility or else risk Rosina's death the next time around. If this second hypothesis is correct – and it is impossible to be absolutely certain – Camille and Rosina would appear to have been taking matters into their own hands by effectively avoiding further pregnancies over the next 10 years.[65]

These individual cases, once again, are meant to illustrate several broad trends observed within the population, and particularly the labouring population, of this community. To return to those trends, fertility did decline across the board within the Saint-Hyacinthe working class in the late nineteenth century. Because of limitations in the quantitative data, it is more difficult to detect differences among economic sectors, or shared patterns among those with a similar relationship to the means of production. But it does appear that families in which the husband consistently reported the same trade contributed disproportionately to the fertility decline. Such families, it is assumed, enjoyed steadier incomes and, in at least some cases, the ownership of their craft shops or other productive units. In contrast, fertility among the wives of workers in the local leather sector, where industrial capitalism had made some of its most significant inroads, declined at a slower rate than that of the working class as a whole.

So far in this section, marital fertility rates have been used to evoke differences between social groups and the evolution of those differences over time. Because of methodological constraints, it is difficult to go much further down this road. Differential analysis of completed family size, the final birth interval, and the mother's age when she stopped bearing children are all rendered hazardous by the small numbers involved.[66] It is possible, however, to generate differential estimates of average family size, using the age-specific marital fertility rates given in Table 5-6 and the women's marriage ages reported in chapter 3, grouped this time by husband's (rather than father's) occupation. By applying differential quotients of infant and child mortality, cohort and occupationally specific measures of family size can also be generated. Table 5-8 gives these estimates for all farm families in the three cohorts together, for the urban-manual families in each of the three cohorts, and for the non-manual families in Cohorts B and C.

As we have already seen, particular patterns of age at marriage and of marital fertility characterized farm families, the working class, and the bourgeoisie in Saint-Hyacinthe during the later nineteenth century. The handful of agricultural families stands out in many ways. Marital fertility seems to have remained high among farmers' wives throughout the period under review. When aggregate (three-cohort) fertility rates and a marriage age of 22.0 years are applied (again, the three-cohort mean), the result is an average

Table 5-8
Family Size Estimates, with Infant and Child Mortality Quotients, by Occupational Group

Grouping (Wives of ...)	Women's Mean Age at First Marriage[a]	Marital Fertility Rate	Average Number of Children Born[b]	Infant Mortality Quotient[c]	Estimated Child Mortality Quotient[d]	Children Surviving Infancy[e]	Children Surviving to Age 15[f]
Farmers, three cohorts combined	22.0	474	9.6	.150	.178	8.2	6.5
Urban-manual workers							
Cohort A	21.3	391	8.5	.288	.162	6.0	4.7
Cohort B	21.5	387	7.9	.240	.204	6.0	4.4
Cohort C	21.9	328	6.4	.295	.139	4.5	3.6
Non-manual workers							
Cohort A	21.9	–	–	.274	.210	–	–
Cohort B	25.1	347	6.1	.252	.181	4.5	3.0
Cohort C	25.9	310	3.8	.282	.141	2.7	2.2

Source Family Reconstitution Files

Notes

[a] Mean age for wives of men in these categories. Note that these values vary from those in Table 3-13, where women's ages are grouped by the profession of their father, not their husband.

[b] Total Marital Fertility Rate / 1000, holding marriage age constant at cell value (see note a).

[c] Deaths under one year per thousand live births.

[d] Deaths between ages one and 15 years, per thousand live births.

[e] Average number of children born, minus deaths under one year.

[f] Average number of children born, minus deaths under 15 years.

of 9.6 children born to women in this category. Amanda Scott, whom we have met, lived with her husband on a farm in the first *rang* of Saint-Hyacinthe-le-Confesseur, from their marriage in 1888 to her premature death in 1909 at the age of 39. By any standard, the 15 children to whom she gave birth in her 21 years of childbearing constituted a large number. She was by no means alone among the prolific farm women living near the town of Saint-Hyacinthe at the turn of the century. But she was also exceptional in that, because of her early marriage and despite her premature death, she brought five more children into the world than the "average" farm woman of this period.[67]

In the urban working class, where more quantitative evidence is available, subtle shifts in the demographic determinants of family size were at work. Between the 1854–61 and 1864–71 cohorts, marriage ages rose very slightly, while marital fertility remained constant. The result would have been marginally smaller families; our method suggests a decline from 8.5 to 7.9 children. As already suggested, however, the more important shifts for working-class families occurred after the 1860s, when the real fundamental changes in the local economy were occurring. Again, marriage age rose slightly. But the decisive shift was the reduction in marital fertility, which saw the average number of children born to a working-class family drop to 6.4. Despite her late marriage, then, Sophronie Tremblay, the seamstress who in 1888 had married a shoe-factory worker and who gave birth to six children over the ensuing 11 years, can be taken as an "average" woman of her class at the turn of the century with respect to reproduction.[68]

Bourgeois women marrying in the 1860s and the 1880s had smaller families than working-class women, both because they more often married later and because they were more likely to practise fertility control. Women's age at first marriage in the 1864–71 cohort was already some three years above the urban-manual level, and marital fertility rates were significantly lower. While marriage ages remained high between 1884 and 1891, marital fertility among bourgeois women declined still further. As a result, the estimate of the average number of births in families where the husband had a non-manual occupation fell from 6.1 to 3.8 during this interval.

Euphémie Gauthier may not have been one of Saint-Hyacinthe's pre-eminent *bourgeoises*. One doubts whether she would have been invited to outings with the Dessaulles, Buckley, and Laframboise families. Euphémie was the daughter of shoemaker Nazaire Gauthier, born in the United States in the late 1860s, probably while her father was sojourning in an American shoe factory. In 1889, at age 21, she married Prosper Reeves in Saint-Hyacinthe. Prosper was a clerk in his father's hotel – the Vermont Central on Laframboise Street near the Grand Trunk Station – until he took over the business in the 1890s. Euphémie, although she married earlier than most wives of non-manual workers in this period, nonetheless exemplifies the more modern reproductive pattern that was spreading in this town, especially within the local bourgeoisie. In fact, she was much more modern than most women of her generation. In all, she was to have three daughters, Eva, Rosalie, and Jeanne, at long intervals between 1890 (when she was 22) and 1905 (when she was 37). The age difference between Rosalie and Jeanne (who would marry a local doctor in 1932) was a full 10 years, suggesting a decade of successful attempts to avoid pregnancy. One can speculate that the birth of Jeanne in 1905, when the older girls were already 15 and 10 years old respectively, was either a "surprise" or the result of a conscious effort on the part of Euphémie to bring one more baby into her busy world – the hotel business, after all, was no sinecure – while she was still able. Without other kinds of sources, of course, we will never know.[69]

As suggested earlier, infant and child mortality levels were important components of family size. Were there social and occupational differences here as well? With respect to infant mortality, urban versus rural residence was a more important factor than the father's occupation. The farm families in the three cohorts had much better rates of infant survival than urban families, whether working class or bourgeois. The infant mortality quotient for the farm families was .150, compared to .276 for urban-manual families and .266 for non-manual families. This fits, of course, with what we know about rural-urban differences in the province and about the especially precarious conditions in which infants lived in this particular town. Over time, both urban groups conformed to the pattern identified for the full cohorts: high initial levels (Cohort A), followed by lower levels in Cohort B, with a return to high levels – over .280 for both groups – in Cohort C.[70]

Coherent patterns in child mortality are harder to discern. Children aged one to 15 were more resistant than infants to the negative effects of urban life on human health. Child mortality quotients, therefore, do not reveal the same farm/non-farm dichotomy as do figures on infant mortality.[71] Moreover, child mortality in both the urban manual and non-manual categories declined substantially between the second and third cohorts, in a period when infant mortality was rising. More detailed study would be necessary to confirm one further hypothesis: that the epidemics of the 1880s hit the working class harder than the bourgeoisie. The very high child-mortality quotients found for urban-manual families formed between 1864 and 1871 suggest that they did.

What impact did these differential levels of infant and child mortality have on family size? The figures just presented permit the calculation on a differential basis of the two measures of family size used earlier: children surviving infancy and children surviving to 15 years (see the two right-hand columns of Table 5-8). Assuming the validity of these synthetic measures, the assertions they support can be made in simple terms. Of the 10 or so children born to the "average" farm family in Saint-Hyacinthe during this period, eight would have survived infancy and six or seven would have reached their fifteenth birthday. Working-class mothers generally gave birth to fewer children. Across the period, they also lost an increasing proportion to death in the first year, although fewer died between ages one and 15. Those who married in the 1850s and 1860s would have seen six children survive infancy, and five reach the age of 15. Fewer children born to working-class couples who married in the 1880s – between four and five, on average – reached the age of one year, although lower child mortality rates meant that as many as four of these survived to adulthood. Bourgeois families, which we can begin to observe in the 1860s cohort, were smaller to start with and anything but immune to infant and child mortality. Through later marriage and fertility control, the average number of births in such families had already been reduced to six in the 1864–71 cohort. Four or five of these would have survived infancy, while only three would still have been alive at age 15. Of the four or so children born to the "average" bourgeois woman married between 1884 and 1891, only three survived infancy, while as few as two might have lived into their late teens.

In later nineteenth-century Saint-Hyacinthe, then, the families of men in non-manual occupations – to whom I have been referring as "bourgeois" families – took an increasingly modern approach to reproduction. Their decisions to marry relatively late and/or to practise some form of fertility control within marriage made for smaller families. So did the consistently high levels of infant and child mortality associated with poor urban hygiene in general and, in the case of Saint-Hyacinthe, with a contaminated water supply (which became a highly charged political issue in the mid 1880s). These factors combined to reduce the effective size of the average bourgeois family (those surviving to adulthood) to between two and three children by the turn of the twentieth century.

Working-class families were also getting smaller, even though marriage was still early and family limitation less widespread than within the local elite. As suggested above, the more financially secure segments of the working class – those whose occupational stability might be read as resistance to proletarianization – were quickest to reduce their fertility. Ironically, occupationally mobile families and those who relied on wages from the leather industries – those who would appear to be the least able to "afford" additional children – were the most likely to have them.

Farm families, on the other hand, do not seem to have changed their reproductive behaviour very much during this period, except to the extent that both men's and women's marriage ages rose, for reasons discussed in chapter 3. This would have caused only a slight decline in the average size of the farm family. And as data for a small group of families suggest, marital fertility remained high among farmers' wives in the immediate vicinity of Saint-Hyacinthe, despite the proximity of the town and any "modernizing" influence it might have had. Additional children continued to be, and to be perceived as, economic assets on the farm, even as agriculture became more specialized and market oriented, and as the chances of establishing one's sons and daughters in the regional farm economy declined. This is to say nothing of religious and moral arguments against fertility control, which remained strong in this community and were perhaps more faithfully heeded in the countryside than in the town.

Clearly, a substantial decline in marital fertility occurred in this growing French-Canadian town, and during a period that coincides with important economic, social, cultural, and institutional changes. This reduction was accomplished primarily through the "stopping" mechanism that Knodel calls "family limitation"; that is, fertility rates fell disproportionately in the over-30 age groups, and the age at which women stopped having children altogether declined by several years. This transition seems to have begun in the bourgeoisie and to have spread unevenly into the working class. Working families in which the husband had a stable occupation seem to have been more prone than the occupationally mobile to limit childbearing. The few farming families in the study seem to have remained relatively untouched.

As fertility declined, so too did family size, which, while affected by later marriage and lower marital fertility rates, was further reduced by high levels of infant and child mortality. Overall, more than 40% of children born in this community had died before reaching the age of 15 years. By the 1884–91 marriage cohort, then, the number of children born in the "average" Saint-Hyacinthe family had been reduced to less than six, and the number surviving to adulthood had dropped to less than four.

Such is the broad pattern that has been observed. The thorny problem of interpretation remains. How did a pattern of socially differentiated fertility decline reflect new economic structures, cultural inputs, and the balance of gender relations? Our answer to this complex question must necessarily be partial and speculative. This study has provided evidence of a particular pattern of demographic behaviour. But penetrating beyond the observed behaviour to the historical structure of individual and collective motivations proves more difficult.

The assumption throughout this chapter, and this book, has been that material considerations need to be placed at the centre of any proposed explanatory framework. But at first brush, the position of bourgeois women as fertility "forerunners" in Saint-Hyacinthe – an observation that fits well with the broader literature on this topic – seems to contradict any direct economic explanation of fertility decline. One could argue that middle-class families could best afford additional children and that those in the wage-labouring population had the most to gain from adopting controls on fertility. If people stopped having children because they could not afford them, why – to put it more bluntly – did richer people stop first?

Some might argue that the reasons for the relatively precocious middle-class recourse to family limitation, and for the maintenance of comparatively high fertility levels in the working class (in a context of aggregate decline), were inherently cultural. Cultural patterns, norms, or attitudes might diffuse more quickly within the better educated bourgeoisie, while traditional behaviour might persist in the popular classes, even if outside observers considered that behaviour to be economically unsound. The young Saint-Hyacinthe *bourgeoise* Henriette Dessaulles, for example, held just such a view of the faulty economics of working-class fertility in Saint-Hyacinthe. She also displayed her confusion about sex and reproduction when she confided to her diary in January, 1881. "I suppose that Jos [her friend] doesn't know any more about it than I do," she wrote,

but her words ... imply that people only have children when they really want to. That does make sense, but on the other hand, the way things happen in poor families makes me wonder if this is so. Last week at the X's, the mother and father were down in the dumps because they are going to have a sixth child, while the other five already don't have enough to eat. Surely, when there is no work, that is too many children for their means. But isn't it up to them, then, to decide not to have any more?"[72]

Henriette's musings are echoed in the familiar argument that treats the maintenance of relatively high fertility during Quebec's industrial transition as an essentially cultural phenomenon. From this perspective, moral and especially religious pressures are seen to have propped fertility up to higher levels than were strictly rational in the new economic context. In this view, working-class families, many recently urbanized, were inclined to behave nostalgically, in ways that were more appropriate to the economic realities of a bygone generation, and against their better interests. Sure of the felicity of the Church's teachings and perhaps unaware of alternative approaches to reproduction, many were unprepared to make deliberate choices about reproduction and content to do things in the traditional way, despite perhaps serious economic consequences. Fertility in nineteenth-century Quebec is most often interpreted in this way. The strong opposition of the Catholic clergy to contraception is repeatedly invoked as the most effective cultural "prop" to the traditional pattern of large families.[73]

This explanation, built on cultural rather than economic factors, has some force. It would certainly seem to account for the social differentials in fertility behaviour observed in Saint-Hyacinthe. But there are complexities that it misses. Cultural factors, in the first place, do not always act as "props" to fertility. In some instances, they may even reinforce the economic incentives to family limitation. Urban communities in nineteenth-century Quebec, for example, were in frequent contact with world views other than those built on the traditional pillars of family, farm, and faith. Communities in which economic structural change was occurring were also the most susceptible to processes of "cultural diffusion," whereby attitudes favourable to fertility control are seen as being channelled in from the outside.[74] There may have been many Euphémie Gauthiers, then, who, as an American-born French Canadian, had some experience of another culture, one in which bearing large families was not constructed by powerful elites as a religious duty and a symbol of national pride.[75]

But, more seriously, the argument based on cultural props also violates what John Caldwell has proposed as a fundamental demographic principle: that "all societies were economically rational" in their fertility behaviour.[76] Using this idea as a point of departure, it is possible to argue that the socially differentiated pattern observed in Saint-Hyacinthe had an economic as well as a cultural logic.

There is really no difficulty in finding an economic rationale for fertility reduction in the local élite, where "cultural diffusion" was also most likely to operate. Bourgeois families were particularly concerned about matters relating to property transmission and inheritance. Fewer children meant a reduced risk of conflict and, perhaps more importantly, precluded the fragmentation of large estates into many smaller pieces. Bourgeois children may also have represented a greater economic investment to their parents than did working-class children. Indeed, if the net cost of children over the life course is compared to the revenue they generate for the parental household – essentially Caldwell's "wealth-flows" calculus –

the fact that middle-class children were relatively more expensive to their parents emerges clearly enough. The example of education illustrates this point. Since young middle-class children were more likely than their working-class counterparts to be in school, they constituted a drain on their parents' resources at an age when the children of urban-manual workers, like those of farmers, were already making a contribution to the family economy in the form of their labour.

At the same time, the cultural props argument ignores several important ways in which wage-labouring families benefited from high fertility. We have seen that working-class children in Saint-Hyacinthe began contributing to the family economy at an early age. Young Rosanna Plamondon, who worked at her father's side in the Côté shoe factory in the 1880s, was one of thousands of girls and boys during this period who brought additional cash home to wives and mothers, who, in turn, had to convert it into food, clothing, and shelter. Before they were old enough to work, the care of children could be spread out among other women – older sisters, aunts, grandmothers, and neighbours – freeing their mothers up for other duties. Their education was relatively inexpensive, since schooling was rudimentary and short-lived. They continued to help maintain the family economy, with domestic labour or the remittance of a wage packet, through adolescence, provided they were among the bare majority of all children born who survived to age 15. As adults, they surely provided support to aging parents by sharing housing or living close by, as shown in the previous chapter, and as caregivers in illness and death. The economic incentives to reduce family size, then, particularly when so few survived to adulthood, were perhaps less apparent among wage-earning families than Henriette Dessaulles and others believed. In maintaining relatively high fertility, members of the working class were not necessarily acting – unthinkingly or nostalgically – against their own better interests.

Still, many working-class women, like Sophronie Tremblay, did take measures to reduce their fertility. It would have been fascinating to be able to measure the extent to which those who worked in the Granite Mills, in the shoe factories, or (as did Sophronie) as seamstresses prior to marriage were more likely to have smaller families. One of the major implications, after all, of the "light-industry" model of industrial development, as described in chapter 2, was that working-class girls and young women could expect to spend several years as wage labourers before marriage. They could also, of course, choose not to marry at all and to remain in the mills indefinitely, acquiring skills and responsibility along the way. Mademoiselle Virginie Léonard did not give (and was not asked) her age when she testified at the Royal Commission hearings in 1888. And I cannot say for sure that she never married. But her duties and salary certainly suggest that she had made a career out of her job at the Duclos-Payan tannery. She was the forewoman of a department in which she supervised 20 young women, earning $10 per week, which was more than most men.[77] In Saint-Hyacinthe, there must have been many examples of women who chose careers, in industry and elsewhere, over marriage and child rearing. There must also have been many who chose to work for wages in their teens and early twenties and left the mills when they married. Along the way, they doubtless acquired confidence in their own abilities, the habits of independence and of resistance to authority – recall the 1888 menders' strike in the knitting mill – and perhaps a network of women friends whose ideas on sex, marriage, and reproduction may have differed from those of their mothers, their *fiancés*, and their parish priests.

With these arguments and hypotheses about the impact of industrial capitalism on fertility in place, it is interesting to look at other factors that may have entered into the equation. Gender relations, in particular, must be seen as central to the issue of fertility and fertility control. Indeed, to advance the argument that fertility declined because of decisions people made is to beg the question of who made those decisions and for what reasons. Backing away from Caldwell's calculus, one might certainly argue that it was *men* who had an interest in maintaining high fertility, whether to defend the existing balance of wealth flows between generations or for some other reason. But women had the more active role in fertility control, and their motivation to do so may have sprung from entirely different sources.[78] Some would have attempted to have fewer children, literally, out of fear for their lives; particularly in cases – and I have suggested that Rosina Bernier may have embodied one such instance – where the health risks associated with further child-bearing were significant. Others would have simply recognized the strain on fragile family economies that was represented by additional babies, no matter what the perceived long-term material benefits of large families. If women were gaining autonomy within conjugal relationships, perhaps asserting the independence they had learned in the workplace, they may have been increasingly able to set this kind of reproductive agenda.

To the extent that families remained patriarchal and authoritarian, however, men may have dictated the strategies they considered appropriate to their economic activities: more children, perhaps, if they required a large family labour force; fewer if they believed additional children would represent an economic burden in the long run. At least some men, moreover, were certainly locked into ideological constructions of masculinity in which large families were a symbol of virility and a source of self-esteem, and in which unrestricted sexual access to their wives – reified into a woman's "conjugal duty" by the Catholic Church – was a basic entitlement. Still, this was a period in which women began to seek opportunities other than those provided by the traditional role of wife and mother. The avenues they followed might lead them far away from prescribed maternal roles, sometimes into the factories, sometimes into the professions (such as journalism, as in the case of Henriette Dessaulles), and sometimes into the expanding religious communities that Marta Danylewycz has reinterpreted as the expression of a more or less latent feminism.[79] The crucial point here, then, is to be found not so much in the specific sexual and reproductive agendas of men and women, as in the idea that the balance of decision-making power within conjugal relationships might have varied over time, and might itself have been sensitive to social and economic transformations. This balance helped to determine what decisions about sex and child-bearing were made, by whom they were made, and why.[80]

From this perspective, the precocious assertion by bourgeois women in Saint-Hyacinthe of their reproductive freedom is even less surprising. Lemieux and Mercier have stressed the idea that women who practised family limitation around the turn of the century often did so out of concern for their health, and to avoid the risks associated with repeated child-bearing.[81] Compared to women of other socio-economic groups, bourgeois women of Saint-Hyacinthe would have been more aware of basic information about health and reproductive technologies, better educated, and in touch with the liberal ideas on fertility and sexuality that so directly contradicted those of the clergy. But working-class women, too, seem to have been interested in limiting their fertility, despite what one can only imagine to have been the opposition not only of the clergy but of their husbands.

All of this raises questions about the structure of authority and decision making within Quebec families experiencing the transition to industrial capitalism. Men and women often had divergent interests in matters related to fertility and reproduction. But whose interests were translated into action, and how? Did women seek to minimize the labours associated with high fertility, both in terms of child-bearing and domestic work? Did men, as patriarchs, continue to view additional children, and particularly sons, as economic assets, even when farm life had given way to a family wage economy? And how were these kinds of material concerns negotiated in the emotionally charged context of the family to produce decisions about whether, when, and how to have sex?

These are big questions, for which the differential demographic analysis just reported provides no definite answers. Other research avenues need to be explored, if the gendered dynamics of fertility decisions in this context are to be fully understood. Tamara Hareven has written that even in the context of the patriarchal household, "strategies of family limitation were commonly left to the initiative of women, especially at a time when such matters were not discussed openly."[82] This is an intriguing thought, but one which seems to imply a certain stasis. What if gender relations *were* changing in late nineteenth-century Quebec? Might women have had more and more success in setting the sexual and reproductive agenda within conjugal relationships? If so, this might go a long way toward explaining the particular patterns of fertility decline in an industrializing community such as Saint-Hyacinthe.

6 Conclusion: The Art of the Possible

The research that led to this book began with a set of questions about industrial capitalism and the demographic transition, about the impact of economic change on population patterns, and about the role of the family in mediating those relationships. It focused attention on family and population in one of Quebec's industrializing towns, Saint-Hyacinthe, in the second half of the nineteenth century. This particular town was both typical and unique in its experience of the industrial capitalist transition. It owed its commercial and administrative importance both to the arrival in the late 1840s of what soon became the Grand Trunk Railway and to its position at the heart of a thriving agricultural region. In the years after 1865, industrial capital created an important wage labour market in this community, grounded essentially on labour-intensive "light" industries such as leather products and knit goods. Social relations were profoundly affected – as bourgeois and working-class elements in the local population became increasingly well defined and separate; and as labouring families came to rely on the inadequate and uncertain wages of their men, women, and children for daily survival. Most of the discussion has been about the impact of these changes on patterns of family formation in this community. Did young people marry earlier or later as the pattern of economic opportunity shifted? Did newlyweds draw more or less heavily on kin in working out their household arrangements? And did married couples alter their approach to fertility and family size to fit their new material circumstances?

The answers to these questions all lead to the same general conclusion. Although the impact of the new economic realities on family formation was profound, it was also profoundly differentiated. Saint-Hyacinthe families were divided by status, wealth, occupation, and by the other correlates of social class; factors such as the neighbourhood and the type of house they lived in, as well as the number of years their children spent in school. And class differences were mirrored in demographic behaviour. Local farmers, in a context of contracting opportunity, delayed marriage, as did members of the bourgeoisie, while working-class men and women continued to form their families at a very early age. Young bourgeois couples might well provide shelter to a widowed parent or a younger unmarried sibling, or augment their households in other ways; by taking in boarders, for example, and by hiring domestic servants. But although they were deeply imbricated in kinship networks, working-class couples were less likely to share their limited domestic space in these ways. More often, they moved in around the corner or down the hall from parents and other relatives. Reproductive choices were also made in light of socially specific material circumstances, as the distinct timetables of fertility decline among bourgeois and working-class women in this community demonstrate. It is difficult to deny the material basis of these various kinds of differentiation, even if the specific economic logic of a given behaviour pattern – slower fertility decline in the working class, for example – was sometimes complex and hidden from view.

Occupation, in addition to social class, may have had an important influence on patterns of family formation. But because men's occupations were classified in such a way as to permit comparisons between four broadly defined social groups, the implications for family formation of specific types of economic activity (other than farming) have been missed. It is difficult to say with certainty, for example, if the families of life-long tailors and iron moulders were organized differently than those of men who moved from agriculture to the shoe factories; or to say whether merchants' wives were more inclined to restrict their fertility than the wives of doctors, lawyers, or notaries. Given the small number of families reconstituted for any one trade or profession, this level of precision was impossible in the present study. Nor, unfortunately, have we been able to make a systematic study of women's work outside the home, which, on the basis of other studies and of anecdotal evidence, probably influenced both the age at which women married and the nature and motivation of their reproductive choices.

But despite these limitations, the story of how Saint-Hyacinthe families lived their multiple transitions in the nineteenth century has a lot to teach us. Most apparently, it can teach us about the complexity of the relationship between economic and demographic change. Consider, for example, the impact of urban life – a separate reality from industrial capitalism, although intimately linked to it – on family formation. Saint-Hyacinthe, after all, did not become a manufacturing centre overnight. In the early 1850s, it was already a commercial and administrative town of over 3,000 inhabitants, with important religious institutions, a railway station, a busy market, and several dozen craft shops. When the parish register of Saint-Hyacinthe's cathedral was opened in 1854, urban conditions were already well established. To the extent that urban life affects patterns of family formation, then, couples who married in the 1850s and 1860s had already lived through an important transformation.

There is no doubt, moreover, that urban conditions *did* affect patterns of reproduction, in Saint-Hyacinthe as elsewhere. Infant mortality is a case in point. Levels were much higher in the town than in the surrounding countryside, apparently for ecological rather than strictly economic reasons. Infant deaths tended to contribute to high fertility by interrupting lactation, producing shorter birth intervals and therefore more children. In the light of this essentially urban demographic situation, the fertility decline that occurred in Saint-Hyacinthe is all the more noteworthy.

New family strategies, then, may already have been emerging in the 1850s, as rural migrants adjusted to the unfamiliar conditions of the town. By the 1880s, many of the men and women who married at the cathedral were second-generation town dwellers at least. As they formed families in one of the most expansive periods in local economic history, their domestic and reproductive strategies took the new industrial realities into account. However, urban conditions, in what was now a town of almost 7,000 inhabitants, still remained as a kind of *toile de fond*.

The relationship between economic and demographic change, moreover, raises a whole set of issues around causality and context. In this book, I make no claim for a direct and automatic link between industrialization, urbanization, and demographic change. However, in Saint-Hyacinthe at least, it is now clear that the rise of industry did create conditions in which new domestic and reproductive strategies became appropriate for individual families. Industrial capitalism allowed bourgeois families like the Dessaulles and even the Reeves – whose hotel business would certainly have profited from the city's role as a manufacturing centre – to accumulate the capital that paid for the homes, education and other amenities that set them apart from the popular classes. It placed young women in the industrial workplace, sometimes from the age of 10. There, they acquired the skills needed to mend the seams of knitwear or to cut heel counters from strips of leather, as Virginie Léonard did, and proudly, in the Payan-Duclos tannery in the late 1880s. In the process, many learned to assert their independence and to challenge authority. And it created the sorts of family-wage economies in which the balance between needs and resources was always delicate, and in which child labour, early marriage – which meant fewer adults to feed and clothe in the parental household – co-operative housing strategies of many kinds, and reduced fertility might well be considered and adopted as essentially economic strategies for making ends meet.

In Saint-Hyacinthe, then, industrial capitalism created conditions in which certain types of familial and demographic change became almost inevitable, without necessarily constituting their immediate cause. This nuance is important. Interpreting industrial capitalism as context recognizes the fact that people made domestic and reproductive choices, but not without a certain set of economic realities as background. Later marriage in the urban bourgeoisie, for example, was linked to the desire to accumulate education, position, and household capital; to the rising expectations, in other words, of the next generation of "community leaders." But within that set of constraints, individuals had options: not to marry at all, perhaps; or to marry early or "unwisely" and take whatever material consequences ensued. People's domestic and reproductive strategies, in other words, were informed rather than determined by material considerations. It is at this point that one must introduce cultural attitudes, religious conventions and restrictions, human sentiment, gender relations, and the possibly determinant influence of whim and folly into the discussion. But the boundaries set by constantly changing sets of material constraints, opportunities, and circumstances must not be forgotten.

This study also points to several directions for further research – some obvious, some less so. One avenue, which has been virtually untravelled either by demographers or historians, involves what I refer to in chapter 3 as "stepfamilies."[1] In Saint-Hyacinthe, linking marriage registers to the manuscript census revealed the striking frequency with which widows, and especially widowers, who remarried brought children from previous unions into their newly formed families. Georges-Casimir Dessaulles and Honoré Mercier were only the most prominent of the many men in this community whose first wives died prematurely and who, in remarrying, entrusted *les enfants du premier lit* to the care of their new wives. Such households, and the new step-relationships they entailed, are usually missed in research on the history of domestic life, in Quebec as elsewhere. This is regrettable, because of the quantitative importance of the experience (in a period when levels of adult mortality and remarriage were relatively high); because of the fascinating array of fears and misgivings that surrounded it; and because of the increased prevalence of new kinds of blended and reconstituted families, to use the modern vocabulary, in very recent times.[2]

A more obvious research avenue emerges from the fertility analysis presented in chapter 5. Saint-Hyacinthe, while it may have resembled many Quebec towns in the nineteenth century, had a specificity which must be remembered and respected and which may well extend to its reproductive history. The character of Saint-Hyacinthe's industrialization – the presence of light industries, of which many, such as the Granite Mills, drew on a female labour force – suggests the possibility of similar patterns in Valleyfield and Sherbrooke, but differing ones in Trois-Rivières and Hull, where forest-based industries predominated. The location of the town on the Grand Trunk Railway, partway between Montreal and the northeastern United States, certainly provided commercial advantages. But it also ensured a certain contact with the newer ideas of the age, to an extent that might not have been true in other communities of a similar size. Nor should we forget the reputation of Saint-Hyacinthe as a centre of intellectual exchange and as fertile soil for liberal ideas. All these factors may have helped to create conditions in the town favourable to demographic change, and particularly to fertility decline.

The study of a single community, whether or not that community is in some sense typical or representative, does not permit comprehensive answers to many of the questions raised here, particularly those dealing with Quebec's fertility decline. Further study of the fertility of Quebec women in the late nineteenth and early twentieth centuries is necessary. And such a project is currently underway. Built around a series of detailed analyses of Quebec regions and localities chosen for their contrasting economic and cultural profiles, this project combines traditional demographic analysis with attention to the kinds of narrative sources (letters, diaries, interviews) which must be consulted, if the kinds of difficult interpretive questions raised in chapter 5 are to be answered more fully. The idea is to continue the search for a better understanding of the respective influences of economic, cultural, and other factors (including gender relations) on the fertility of Quebec women in a wide variety of settings, and over a much longer period than that examined in this book.[3]

There have been sweeping changes in economic structure, demography, cultural norms, and gender relations since Honoré Mercier, Régina Allard, Jérémie Cloutier, Philomène Kérouack, André Scott, and Sophronie Tremblay lived, married, and raised their families in nineteenth-century Saint-Hyacinthe. Yet as a new century dawns, work and family continue to rank among the most prominent day-to-day concerns for most individuals. Decisions about marriage and child-bearing are major life events which, increasingly perhaps, must be made with one eye on the budget. Marriage may less often be formalized by a religious ceremony; but it still must be grounded on some kind of earning capacity, or at least on the expectation of earning capacity in the future. Setting up an independent household is less likely to be timed to coincide with family formation. Yet leaving home is still an important life-course transition that presupposes a certain degree of economic autonomy for young people, although it does not usually mean breaking all ties with kin. And whether, when, and how often to bring children into the world are among the most important decisions that women in the 1990s, with or without the collaboration of a husband or partner, must make. Material opportunities and constraints are particularly important considerations in this area, as debates over daycare show so clearly. Increasingly, women are choosing to fit their fertility into life courses in which education and employment, rather than marriage and motherhood, are the central themes. As a result, the average age of a woman at the birth of her first child has risen steeply in recent years. At the same time, the multiplication of new reproductive technologies since the invention of the contraceptive pill in the 1960s has provided women not only with the means of exercising more sexual freedom than ever before, but also of putting their new fertility strategies into practice.

Decisions about marriage, domestic arrangements, and child-bearing cannot be seen as knee-jerk reactions to economic structural change and shifting labour-market conditions. This would be an untenable position indeed, allowing little room for falling in love; for family conflict, religious beliefs, sexual mores, cultural attitudes, and personal idiosyncrasies; or, indeed, for individual agency. But to suggest that people make such choices without an eye on economic realities would be equally foolish. In our postmodern world, family life is just as clearly contingent on access to the material bases of daily life as it was during the transition to industrial capitalism a century ago. It remains, like other kinds of politics, the art of the possible.

Appendix

Family Formation in Focus:
An Essay on Methods

The dissertation upon which this book is based had some 75 pages of methodological appendices, explaining all aspects of the cohort-based family reconstitution technique, right down to the colours used to code the research forms. That degree of detail is unnecessary here, although those interested may, of course, consult the relevant sections of the dissertation.[1] What follows, then, is a general description of the research strategy and a discussion of the tactics used to deal with four special problems: the use and classification of occupational titles; the calculation of marriage ages on the basis of age declarations; the recreation of household boundaries from census lists; and the calculation of marital fertility rates in a situation of high geographic mobility.

FROM PARISH REGISTERS TO COMPUTER PRINTOUTS

In order to examine the effects of industrial capitalism on demographic behaviour in nineteenth-century Quebec, I decided first to concentrate on the population of Saint-Hyacinthe. Other communities experiencing industrial development during this period, such as Saint-Jean, Chambly, and Valleyfield, were considered. The choice fell on Saint-Hyacinthe because it had all the features I was looking for: industrial development along the lines of light-industry model; a not too unwieldy size; proximity to Montreal (where I lived); a fairly well-developed historiography; and an active regional historical society and archives.

The next step was to narrow the focus in two specific ways. First, I decided to concentrate on a single parish: Saint-Hyacinthe-le-Confesseur, the cathedral parish established in the 1850s. For a study of urban demography, the choice of the cathedral parish was an obvious one, since its territory included the town of Saint-Hyacinthe in its entirety, at least until the late 1880s (see Figures 1-3 and 1-4). Second, to further trim the size of the population, I adopted a marriage-cohort approach to family reconstitution. Three marriage cohorts were selected so as to include families formed at progressive stages of the town's industrial transition.

Data collection and provisional record linkage were undertaken concurrently, first in the parish registers, then in the manuscript census. For the parish register phase, I worked at the Archives nationales du Québec, Montréal (ANQM) with the courthouse copy, for the period prior to 1876. For the subsequent period, which extended to 1919 for the baptisms of children (none was found after 1914) and to 1948 for burials, I worked in the presbytery of the Saint-Hyacinthe cathedral with the curé's copy. The parish register work was done in seven steps:

1 Information from the marriage acts of couples in Cohort A, (1854–61) was recorded on paper forms. Each marriage was assigned a code to be used throughout the research to identify the couple in question. Some of the basic information from these forms was entered into a dBASE III computer file, which was then used to generate two alphabetical master lists, one ordered by the husband's surname, one by the wife's. These lists were used in all subsequent record linkage operations.

2 A systematic search was conducted in the registers of the cathedral for civil acts related to Cohort-A couples for the period 1854–63. Record linkage was nominative, manual, and assisted by another set of codes, intended to reflect the strength of the proposed links.[2] Verification of those links was part of the process of compiling family files, to be discussed later. A separate, colour-coded form was used for each type of civil act. The various types of acts, defined by their relationship to the couples in the three cohorts, were the following:
   a. Baptisms of children
   b. Burials of children
   c. Burials of husband or wife
   d. Remarriages of husband or wife
   e. Marriages of children.

3 Marriages for Cohort B (1864–1871) were recorded and the names of the husbands and wives added to the master lists. The 277 couples in this cohort represent all marriages celebrated at the cathedral during this interval.

4 The systematic search (step 2) was resumed and broadened to include civil acts related to Cohort B, all for the period 1864–1883.

5 Marriages for Cohort C were recorded and added to the master lists. The 340 marriages in this cohort constitute a 75% systematic sample of the 450 occurring in the period 1884–91. Three in every four marriages, in other words, were retained for the study. This selection was made in order to keep the size of the three cohorts approximately equal (at about 300).

6 The systematic search (step 4) was resumed and broadened to include acts related to the couples in all three cohorts, for the period 1884–1919.

7 A search was conducted for the burial acts of husbands and wives in all three cohorts during the period 1920–48. This search was complicated by the fact that four new parishes were detached from the territory of the cathedral during this period. Burials in the Saint-Hyacinthe-le-Confesseur register were scanned for the period 1920–48. Those in the four new parishes were scanned from the various dates of the opening of their registers through 1948. This operation turned up the burials of five members of Cohort A, 35 of Cohort B, and 104 of Cohort C.

Having completed the research in the parish registers, I next began tracing the couples in the three marriage cohorts to the manuscript census for the Saint-Hyacinthe area. This was a way of collecting additional information, especially about age and household structure. The procedures resembled those just described for the parish registers, especially in terms of the concurrent collection of data and record linkage. They can also be described as a series of steps:

1 The 1861 manuscript census for the City of Saint-Hyacinthe *and* the rural municipalities of Saint-Hyacinthe-le-Confesseur and Notre-Dame-de-Saint-Hyacinthe were read and compared to the master lists of husbands and wives in Cohort A. Enumerations suspected of corresponding to couples in the cohort were identified. Detailed information about their families, and summary information about other families residing in the same building (census *house*) were transcribed onto a specially designed form.

2 The 1871 census was treated in the same way, except that the names in the schedules were compared to the master lists for both Cohort A and Cohort B. Information about couples from both cohorts was retained and transcribed onto special forms.

3 Marriages from Cohorts A and B were linked to the 1881 census schedules, and the relevant information transcribed exactly as in step 2.

4 Couples in all three cohorts were matched with the 1891 manuscript census schedules for the districts named in step 1, and the same information recorded.

5 Couples in Cohort C were matched with the 1901 manuscript census schedules in the same way.

It is worth noting that the geographic territory covered by the census search extended beyond the boundaries of the parish, into Notre-Dame-de-Saint-Hyacinthe (for boundaries, see Figure 1-4). This was a way of maximizing the information recovered, especially with regard to the ages of the men and women in the three cohorts. The principles of record linkage applied here were the same as those used in the parish-register work. As before, links proposed in the course of data collection were verified at a later stage, when family files were being compiled.

In the case of the 1901 census, the data collection and record linkage were undertaken *after* the completion of the research for the dissertation. Because the 1901 schedules were not available at the time, these steps were not included in the original research design. This work, completed in 1995 with the assistance of Julien Bréard, has substantially improved the quality of the data for couples in Cohort C, particularly with respect to marriage age. It has also provided an additional control for geographic mobility, thus solidifying the fertility analysis in chapter 5.

Once the data collection was complete, the next step was to sort the various coloured forms into family files and to undertake the verification procedures needed to validate the record links proposed during data collection. Manual sorting of 10 types of forms (six from the parish registers and one from each of the manuscript censuses between 1861 and 1891) took about a month. Verification procedures were of two kinds: internal and external. Each of the proposed record links was first evaluated in terms of its consistency with other suggested links in the family file. After this internal verification, ambiguous links remained in a total of 97 family files, or about 11% of the total. All the remaining ambiguous links were then checked, using a variety of sources and methods, most of them genealogical.[3] This external verification reduced the number of family files still containing ambiguous links to 22, or just over 2% of all files in the three cohorts (8 in Cohort A, 9 in Cohort B, and 5 in Cohort C).

All the data collection and record linkage for this book was done manually, with only minor computer assistance in the form of two dBASE III files used to generate alphabetical lists. However, most of the analyses performed on the files, once constituted and validated, were automated. For these purposes, it was necessary to generate a computerized database suitable for the demographic analyses. The tools selected for these purposes were the ORACLE relational database management system and an IBM mainframe computer, both "accessed" – to use the appropriate neologism – through Hélène Langlois of the Services de l'informatique at the Université du Québec à Montréal. The basic principle was to recreate, in electronic form, the structure of a *fiche de famille*, as described in the manuals written by Louis Henry and E.A. Wrigley.[4] The database contained five tables, each related to each other through a common variable: the unique code assigned to each couple. Thus, rather than condensing all the information relative to a given couple on a single sheet of paper, the information concerning that couple was spread about in the five tables. The common linkage code provided the logical unity for a set of information that corresponds quite closely to that accommodated by traditional family reconstitution forms.[5]

Once the data collection was complete, the record linkages established and verified, the family files validated, and the database structure designed, I conducted the final phase in the research (prior to the analysis) – data entry. This stage, much like assembling the family files, was straightforward but time-consuming.[6] The only real challenge was to establish the correspondence among the various civil acts related to individual children. This was a type of record linkage that had not been accomplished at the point of data collection, nor during the assembly of files.

Generally, matching baptism acts to burial acts was done on the basis of the child's name and sex, as declared in both documents; and of the correspondence between the date of birth declared in the baptism and the age declared in the burial certificate. Links from baptisms to marriage acts were made in a similar way, the only difference being the lack of a precise declaration of age in the marriage certificates. Some ambiguities nonetheless arose, especially in cases where burial or marriage acts were found for which no obvious corresponding baptism could be identified. As a rule, age and sex were considered to be the most reliable data in sorting out these ambiguities. A male child named Emile who died in August of 1873 at the age of three months, for example, was linked with a boy baptized in the month of May in the same family, even if the boy's given name at baptism was Joseph. Sometimes, information from the manuscript census was used to clarify cases where a nominative variation or an inaccurate age declaration was suspected. Children identified exclusively in the census schedules, however, were not recorded in the database.

HANDLING OCCUPATIONAL TITLES

Like most studies in social and demographic history, this one makes extensive use of the job titles recorded in acts of baptism, burial, and marriage, and in the manuscript census schedules. These declarations had to be sorted into coherent, systematically defined socio-economic categories. As sources of information about wealth, status, and social class, they are imperfect, as is any system of classification that attempts to make sense of them. But without them, the historical study of population patterns, family life, economic and social structure, and a hundred other topics would be next to impossible.

The first principle I applied in developing a system for classifying occupations was that the categories had to be broad enough to permit a coherent, differential analysis of demographic behaviour. Given the modest number of usable *fiches* in each cohort, a highly detailed occupational grid would have reduced the number of cases in each category to an unacceptable level. With this in mind, I considered a number of different sorting criteria. The one selected was the nature of the effort required on the job. The most fundamental distinction in the classification scheme used here, then, is between occupations that required sustained *manual* work and those that did not.

The resulting typology has four categories; three refer to different types of manual occupations, while the fourth contains all non-manual occupations. The first category, *agriculture*, contains mainly farmers (*cultivateurs*), but also some rural manual workers who were clearly identified as such (those that declared their occupation as *garçon de ferme*, for example). Next comes the largest of the four categories, *urban-manual*, which, in fact, contained most of Saint-Hyacinthe's employed population.[7] It covers all manual occupations not explicitly related to agriculture; it therefore allows all manual workers in urban trades and industries to be treated together.

A third category of manual workers, defined as *labourers*, was developed out of respect for the particular local context. Most of the discussion in the book focuses on the Parish of Saint-Hyacinthe-le-Confesseur, which contained a rural population in addition to that of the town of Saint-Hyacinthe. For this reason, it was deemed important to distinguish farm and non-farm families at most stages of the analysis. But it was also necessary, given the importance of agriculture in part of the parish, to handle individuals who described themselves as *journaliers* with care. Some may have worked as farm labourers; others must have worked in town, as unskilled labourers in construction or in the factories. Since these important distinctions could not be made on the basis of job titles alone, labourers were assigned to a separate category.   Finally, all occupations in which the principal effort required was *non-manual* were grouped together. These included the professions, large and small merchants and shopkeepers, and service occupations such as teaching. Also included here were people who declared a status (such as *écuyer*, *bourgeois*, or *rentière*) rather than an occupation.

Occupational groupings are imperfect proxies for social classes. The distance between social and occupational groupings, moreover, depends on one's definition of what it means to belong to a particular class. If urban residence and a manual occupation are deemed sufficient to define membership in the working class, for example, there is then no real difference between the occupational category and the social class, so defined. But if propertylessness and wage dependence are also important criteria, as they should be, then one must be more circumspect. Small masters continued to run independent shops; carters owned their horse and *charette*, and blacksmiths their forges in later nineteenth-century Saint-Hyacinthe. The fact that such people owned their means of production and worked on their own account would certainly exclude them from a strictly defined working class or proletariat.

On the other hand, most craft and industrial workers in nineteenth-century Saint-Hyacinthe would certainly have declared what I refer to as urban-manual occupations. My tendency, then, has been to finesse the important theoretical distinction between social class and occupational category and to interchange the terms "urban manual" and "working class" more or less freely.[8] Similarly, I often identify individuals who declared non-manual occupations and their families as "bourgeois" or "middle class." This compromise is grounded in considerations of both substance and style. A local bourgeoisie certainly existed in this period, made up of families such as the Dessaulles, the Côtés, the Kérouacks, the Morisons, and the Naults. These people would certainly have declared non-manual occupations.[9] And rather than overburdening the reader with phrases such as "families of men in non-manual occupations," I have often preferred to use, more simply, "bourgeois families," or "middle-class families." Certainly some clerks and small shopkeepers are misrepresented in this way, as are many innkeepers, whose affinities may have been more with the working class than with the local elite. But most of those men who declared non-manual occupations in Saint-Hyacinthe, and especially those who consistently declared non-manual occupations (the category was defined in this way for the fertility analysis in chapter 5), were decidedly bourgeois.

The idea of this classification scheme was to try to approximate local class structure, while respecting the presence of a farming population in the parish. The fit, admittedly, is only approximate. But the social coherence of this occupational grid seems to have been borne out by a number of the analyses presented in the book. Despite the fact that literacy levels in the parish were converging, for example, members of the four categories consistently stood in the same relationship to each other with respect to their capacity to sign the marriage registers. As we saw in chapter 3, those in the non-manual category were consistently the most literate, followed by urban-manual workers, farmers, and labourers, in that order (see chapter 3, Table 3-7). Besides what it tells us about literacy, this analysis seems to suggest that my occupational classification system provides a reasonably coherent picture of social differences in this community.

Such, then, is the basic scheme. But in this book, occupational titles are used in a variety of ways. Besides giving an idea of the structural changes occurring in the local economy (chapter 2), they also serve as a way of classifying families in three successive phases of socio-demographic analysis (chapters 3, 4, and 5). In each case, details and nuances could be discussed, and some specific problems mentioned.

Occupational declarations – those from the manuscript census schedules of 1861 and 1891 – were first used in chapter 2, to evoke the changing labour market in late nineteenth-century Saint-Hyacinthe. Men and women who lived in the original territory of the town and who declared an occupation were grouped into the four occupational categories (agriculture, urban-manual, labourers, and non-manual). Since so many declarations were available (902 for 1861 and 2,013 for 1891), a more detailed breakdown was also possible. Thus urban-manual workers were distributed into three sectors (production, transportation, and services) and into a number of subsectors within these areas. Similarly, non-manual occupations were classified by sector: professions, commerce, services, etc. (see Tables 2-2, 2-3, and 2-4).

This was the only phase of the research in which a significant number of women's occupational declarations were available. The occupational typologies employed for the men and women were identical. Certain types of occupation (such as the professions) were inaccessible to women, however, and were excluded from the presentation of this data (Table 2-4). Also excluded were the categories "agriculture" and "labourers," but solely because no women in Saint-Hyacinthe declared themselves to be *cultivatrices* or *journalières*. Men's and women's manual occupations, as declared in the 1891 census, were also called upon, in a subsequent section of chapter 2, to assist in an evaluation of the division of labour within certain local industries. Local residents who could be identified as knit-goods and shoe workers were distinguished and their sometimes quite detailed job titles analyzed, in order to better understand who did what in the factories.

In chapter 3, occupational declarations made in marriage acts were the basis of an analysis of the socio-economic background of the husbands and wives in the three cohorts. The same detailed grid used in chapter 2 was applied to occupational declarations made by husbands (Table 3-1). When husbands' occupations were missing from the marriage acts, information was recovered from the next civil act involving the couple (usually the baptism of a child), provided that that act occurred in the ensuing five years. The absence of job declarations for most of the women who married at the cathedral meant a grouping by their fathers' occupations, using the same detailed grid applied to the husbands (Table 3-2). Differential analyses of social endogamy, residence prior to the wedding, signature rates, and marriage age: all used these occupations, grouped into the four broad occupational categories, as sorting criteria.

In chapter 4, the four basic categories were again in use. Numbers were smaller, however, so that no more detailed distributions could be examined. In the analysis of household structure, the sorting criterion was the husband's occupation *as declared to the census taker*. Data from the marriage acts, then, had to be revised to account for occupational mobility that had occurred in the intervening period. The interval from wedding to census varied from a few days to seven years. Many of the husbands changed occupations in that period; a certain number even moved between the broadly defined categories.

In the differential analysis of fertility reported in chapter 5, the husband's occupation was the main sorting criterion. A woman's fertility, in other words, was studied with reference to what her husband did for a living. This might be thought unjust, except for the fact that a relationship clearly existed between the two variables. I will return to this point shortly.

Besides the scarcity of job declarations by women, other difficulties emerged in handling the occupational information for the fertility analysis. The thorniest of these, ironically, was a kind of embarrassment of riches. Because of the nature of the research, a long series of occupational declarations was available for certain men. It was not at all unusual for individuals to change jobs frequently, or even to "migrate" between occupational categories in the course of their married lives. Jérémie Cloutier, for example, declared himself a farmer at his wedding in July 1858, and again at the baptism of his first-born son in April 1859. In this particular case, I recorded nine further baptisms, five burials of children, and two census declarations between 1861 and 1876. Cloutier declared an occupation in 11 of the civil acts and on both census returns. He was at various times described as *journalier, boucher, gardien de pont, commis marchand, hôtelier, boulanger, commerçant*, and *cordonnier*. This kind of detail is fascinating for students of occupational mobility, but a problem in a fertility analysis in which each couple must be assigned to a unique socio-economic category. Cloutier, on the basis of a single declaration, might have been classed in any one of the four categories!

The solution adopted for this problem had two elements. First, each declaration was assigned to its corresponding category, and the individual assigned to the category containing the most declarations (the modal *category*, rather than the modal *occupation* was used). Jérémie Cloutier described himself as a shoemaker three times; a labourer three times; a farmer and a butcher twice each; and as a baker, merchant's clerk, hotelkeeper, shopkeeper, and bridge guard once each. This amounts to two declarations in the "agriculture" category, six in the "urban-manual" category, three in the "labourers" category, and four in the "non-manual" category. My decision to place him in the "urban-manual" category was based on the modal value in this distribution.

Second, to be classified as farmers or labourers, individuals had to declare that occupation *exclusively*. In the case of farmers, this convention was adopted so as to allow lifetime cultivators to be distinguished from farmers' sons and occasional fieldworkers who would ultimately live mainly from urban wages. In the case of labourers, it seemed pointless to maintain the distinction between this group and urban-manual workers in cases where individuals could be observed moving in and out of various urban occupations.

Occupational mobility was also used as a criterion in the analysis of the fertility of the wives of urban-manual workers. Workers who consistently declared the same occupation, it was proposed, may have belonged to a more comfortable segment of the working class. I also hypothesize that most independent craft producers – skilled artisans in trades that were not immediately threatened by industrialization – may have been in this category. Arguably, workers who frequently changed occupations were following professional itineraries more typical of wage labourers. In another stage of the analysis, men who had at any time worked in the leather trades were isolated from the rest of the urban-manual group, on the assumption that those people were the most likely to have had some experience of factories. Many of the large-scale producers in town, particularly those which employed large numbers of men, were either boot-and-shoe factories or industrial tanneries.

As we have seen, any occupational classification scheme of this nature poses a number of difficulties, some of which are harder to resolve than others. The case of Jérémie Cloutier, cited in chapter 5, illustrates one of the central problems in analyzing occupational titles in a context of emergent industrial capitalism. Although Cloutier declared on several occasions that he was a "shoemaker," he does not appear to have picked up the trade before the mid-1870s, when he was already 38 years of age. We can be very confident that he was a shoe-factory worker and not a skilled leather artisan; in fact, a similar assumption was integrated into the analysis of 1891 shoe-factory workers presented in chapter 2. But Cloutier's case highlights some of the complexities that hide behind the analysis of occupational titles. Changing relations of production transformed the content and character of many occupations in nineteenth-century Quebec. In Saint-Hyacinthe, the changes were felt especially strongly in the leather sector. Language, perhaps especially the language used by the parish priests who officiated at civil acts, was slow to catch up. Interestingly, the language used by census takers was more technical and precise. The *curé* always referred to shoemakers and almost never to shoe-factory workers. The census takers, as we have seen, were often much more specific, describing individuals as "employé: manufacture de chaussures," and then describing their function.

Another recalcitrant problem in this exercise was the absence of information on women's employment and the necessity of analyzing their marital and reproductive activity in terms of their fathers' or their husbands' occupations. I found it awkward to be so frequently discussing the marriage ages of the "daughters of manual workers," or the fertility of "farmers' wives." Such usages reflect the nineteenth-century notions of women's subordinate status that were built into the documents. Priests, census takers, and other (male) generators of sources, routine and otherwise, defined women's roles in terms of their relationships to men, whether fathers or husbands.

My discomfort with treating women's marital and reproductive activity primarily in terms of men's occupations, however, was mitigated somewhat by the belief that women's social and economic roles in the nineteenth century *were* influenced by their relationships to men. That a young woman was the daughter of an urban-manual worker, for example, would have been an important fact in her life, affecting not only her marriage "prospects," but the nature of her household responsibilities, how much education she received, and whether she was likely to work for wages. It would surely be preferable to know whether or not she did work outside the home prior to marriage and, if so, in what capacity; her father's occupation is no proxy for that very precise piece of information. But it had an important influence on her social and economic position nonetheless.

Similarly, the analysis of fertility by the husband's occupation reflects an inescapable gender bias in the sources. Married women's paid work may have been a crucial determinant of marital fertility. But the parish registers and the manuscript census are virtually silent on the subject.[10] Here, again, there are substantive reasons for using "husband's occupation" as a sorting criterion. Just as "the daughter of a manual worker," carried social and economic meaning, so did "the wife of a farmer." Being the wife of a farmer was an occupation, not just a status, and among the many responsibilities was the reproduction of the labour force for the family farm.[11] Being the wife of a lawyer was also a job, but of a much different kind. Tending to the physical and emotional needs of the husband, creating the private domestic space that became known as the home, and producing children, but perhaps not so many as would constitute a drain on the family budget: these were among the main functions of the bourgeois wife in the late nineteenth century.[12]

I have argued that women's reproductive strategies reflected the economic constraints and opportunities they experienced. Women's material circumstances were most often influenced by the type of family economy they managed and in which most of their work was done. The difficulty of saying very much about women's paid labour and its effect on fertility is regrettable. But the fact remains that men's occupations in the nineteenth century had a structuring influence on family economies and, I have argued, on women's reproductive work. Classifying families along these lines for the purpose of fertility analysis, then, is both useful and necessary.

USING DECLARED AGES

The parish priests who wrote Catholic marriage acts in nineteenth-century Quebec made no mention of either the age of the bride and groom or their birthdates.[13] Under these circumstances, having adopted a marriage-cohort approach to family reconstitution, I had two options. Given sufficient time and resources, I could have traced the baptism acts of all the husbands and wives in the cohorts, using standard genealogical techniques. Failing this, I could have made careful use of age declarations found in the manuscript census and in burial acts, estimating birthdates (or at least birth years) on this basis. This was the option adopted for the present study. The procedure was as follows.

First, all available age declarations for each husband and wife were collected from both the census and burial acts. Individual age-information files were thus generated as part of the process of reconstitution. Second, each individual's age file was examined carefully, with a view toward generating the best possible estimate of his or her birth year. A file might contain no information at all; this was, in fact, the case for 400 of the 912 husbands in the three cohorts and for 379 of the wives. It might also contain a precise birthdate: this was mainly true of individuals in the third cohort who were sons or daughters of couples in the first two cohorts. Some birthdates have been recovered in other ways, but the total is still only 59 of the 1,824 marriage partners in the three cohorts. Three-fifths of the files contained from one to five age declarations. Given the well-known fragility of declared ages, these had to be handled with extreme care.

Before any decisions were made about estimating birthdates on the basis of these declarations, a number of tests were undertaken.[14] Those files where precise birthdates *and* one or more declarations were available were given special attention. Of 32 census declarations that could be tested in this way (all but one from the 1891 census), 17 were exactly accurate (to the year) and 27 were accurate to within plus or minus one year. None of the remaining five declarations was more than three years off the mark. Twenty-two burial declarations were assessed in a similar way, with equally encouraging results: 15 were accurate to the year and a further five showed discrepancies of only one year.

Census and burial age declarations were also examined for evidence of rounding. Ages ending in zero were found in the census more frequently than one would expect if no rounding had occurred, especially among older individuals. Fifteen percent of husbands and wives in their thirties and forties declared ages ending in zero (based on 704 declarations), while 19% of those aged 50 and over did the same (227 cases).[15] Accordingly, census declarations ending in zero were treated as particularly fragile, especially where older people were concerned.

Finally, and decisively, special attention was paid to the extent to which the various declarations made by the same individual corroborated each other. Birth years were calculated from each available declaration and then compared visually on a case-by-case basis. The principle applied here was that while a single age declaration might be wildly inaccurate, two or more declarations that indicated roughly the same birthdate were extremely unlikely to be so.

Once these tests were completed, individual decisions were made about the likeliest birth year, and codes were assigned to reflect how those decisions had been made. These birth-year estimation codes consisted of two parts: a one-digit hierarchical code that broadly reflected the quality of the estimate; and a three-digit code that carried detailed information about the way the estimate was made, including the total number of declarations, the range of implied birth years, and the criterion applied in the final decision. In a general way, and in accordance with the principle stated in the preceding paragraph, the *modal* value was selected where this value was clear, though more arbitrary criteria had to be introduced where it was not.

For purposes of simplicity, we can restrict our attention here to the one-digit hierarchical codes, which provide a quick summary of the age information used in this book. Five codes were developed, presented here in descending order of the reliability of the birth-year estimates to which they pertain:

0 – Birthdate is known; no need to estimate birth year;

1 – Two or more declarations, where any two yield estimates with a range of 0 to 2 years;

2 – Two or more declarations, where any two yield estimates with a range of 3 years;

3 – Two or more estimates, where no two yield estimates with a range of less than 4 years;

4 – One declaration only.

Types 0 and 1 are referred to in the text as "best values," meaning either that a precise birthdate is known or that there is close agreement between two or more declarations in the files. A clear majority (624 of 1,045) of the marriage ages used in the present study are of these more reliable types. A small minority (50) are of types 2 and 3, while the rest (371, or about 36%) are based on only one declaration.[16]

In the dissertation upon which this book is based, the distinction between "best values" and "all values" is maintained throughout the discussion of marriage, in order to reflect the more fragile nature of types 2, 3, and 4 marriage-age estimates while not losing this information entirely. Slight differences in mean marriage ages for men and women emerge in each cohort, and in each occupational group within each cohort, depending on whether these measures are calculated with only the "best value" age declarations (types 0 and 1) or with all the available age information. Subsequent testing, however, using Levene's test for equality of variances to compare type 0 and 1 estimates with type 2, 3, and 4 estimates, has shown that the differences between the two series are not statistically significant.[17] In light of this finding, the parallel calculation of two separate sets of mean marriage ages, using first "best" and then "all" age estimates, was abandoned. All available age estimates, then, are currently included in the analyses, even those based on a single declaration. The number of the more reliable "best" values in each cohort and category, however, is reported in the tables.

If approached carefully, marriage ages calculated from census and burial declarations can be a reasonably sound body of information. In those cases where declarations could be compared to precise birthdates, the accuracy of the stated ages was found to be rather good. Where multiple declarations were available, there seemed to be a high degree of internal consistency among the stated ages. The methods just explained are, therefore, a viable alternative to full family reconstitution in the measurement of age at marriage and of other demographic phenomena in late nineteenth-century Quebec.

HOUSES, FAMILIES, AND HOUSEHOLDS

One of the ongoing debates in Canadian family history deals with which of two categories used by nineteenth-century census takers, the *house* or the *family*, best corresponds to the co-resident domestic group.[18] In a paper published in 1983, Gordon Darroch and Michael Ornstein examined a sample from the 1871 census of over 3,000 households in the four Canadian provinces. Their findings seemed to confirm the general picture proposed by Peter Laslett and supported by the work of Michael Katz, David Gagan, and Chad Gaffield: 75% of households had a simple-family structure.[19] Difficulties arise, however, with the 8% of households that these authors classified as being "composed of unrelated, co-residing families." Darroch and Ornstein assumed that the census category *house* most closely approximated the households they were interested in studying. Subsequent research, however, has shown that, at least in urban Quebec, this may have led to an exaggeration of the importance of non-kin co-residence during this period.

In her initial treatment of similar data for two working-class wards of Montreal between 1861 and 1881, Bettina Bradbury grappled with the same difficulty. Bradbury concentrated on families that took in boarders and shared residential space, seeing these practices – along with gardening and stock-raising – as important non-wage survival strategies for families of the period. In Montreal, boarding was more common in professional and petit-bourgeois households than in those of the working class, particularly after 1861. "House sharing," however, was another matter. Bradbury argued that "'doubling up', subletting rooms to other families or renting one to two

rooms from landlords who had divided up their dwellings all helped reduce
... a family's major and most fixed of costs – the rent."[20]

Bradbury made this argument despite her awareness of the ambiguous
nature of the definitions of *house* and *family* employed by census takers in
1871. By checking census lists against municipal evaluation roles and city
directories, she confirmed her suspicion that the enumerator's notion of a
house did not necessarily correspond to the idea of a household, as Darroch
and Ornstein had assumed. Her note of caution on this point is worth citing
at length:

> In attempting to match census returns with city directories and
> evaluation roles, it became clear that some houses that were apparent-
> ly "shared" by families were actually separate tenements, with residents
> who were independently assessed by the city for water rates and
> occasionally even given a separate address in the city directory. With-
> out a full-scale and highly detailed study tracing the size and layout of
> every house, it appears difficult to determine exactly which families, or
> what percentage apparently sharing housing on census day were
> actually doing so. Nor is it possible to tell what proportion sublet part
> of their own dwelling as a survival strategy, and what proportion was
> forced to crowd together in substandard living conditions as a result of
> a landlord's subdivision of space. And there is no way of showing how
> often sharing resulted in extreme overcrowding.[21]

Because of these ambiguities in the census, Bradbury's analysis was of "the
extent of sharing that would have existed had the census definition [of the
house] reflected reality"; that is, the reality of the household or co-resident
domestic group.[22] She used qualitative evidence of squalid and overcrowded
conditions in Montreal's working-class neighbourhoods to bolster her
argument for frequent house sharing among working-class families. She also
demonstrated the effect of the life cycle on this type of household arrangement: young, recently married couples did, indeed, tend to share housing
more often than older couples with more children present. Still, questions
remain about the reality behind what Bradbury describes as "house sharing."
Was she really looking at situations in which two, three, or more families
crowded into dwellings intended for a single family? Or was there more
evidence for lower levels of doubling up and a greater tendency to let or
sublet parts of residential buildings that, in fact, constituted distinct dwellings, though the enumerator did not conceive of them as separate *houses*?

Recently, Bradbury has substantially revised her position on house
sharing, largely in response to Gilles Lauzon's careful critique of the way she,
Darroch and Ornstein, and others used census schedules to understand

household structure.[23] Lauzon examined a working-class neighbourhood on the western edge of Montreal, and although he did not manage to "trace the size and layout of every house," he did unearth enough detail about a sufficient number to handicap any interpretation that equated multi-family *houses* with shared households. Examining the 1871 census manuscripts for the Village of Saint-Augustin, Lauzon discovered a pattern similar to those found by Darroch and Ornstein and Bradbury: many *houses* were occupied by multiple, apparently unrelated *families*. But rather than drawing the usual, tempting conclusion (high rates of "household sharing," or "house sharing," to use Bradbury's more cautious phrase), Lauzon pushed the analysis, tracing families located in a small sector of Saint-Augustin to marriage registers, evaluation roles, city directories, and notarized leases. Paying close attention to the particular nature of the housing stock in this working-class community and to the role of kinship in structuring domestic arrangements, Lauzon found that the proportion of shared households in Saint-Augustin in 1871 was extremely low: less than 4%, compared to the 16% that Darroch and Ornstein gave for urban Quebec, and the 25% to 35% that Bradbury calculated for various categories of working-class families in Sainte-Anne and Saint-Jacques wards.[24]

The reasons for these discrepancies are clear enough. Lauzon's research demonstrated that, at least in the Saint-Augustin village, the census takers' category of *family* often corresponded more accurately to the household than did the category *house*, which earlier studies had equated with the domestic unit. *Families*, the census takers were instructed, "may consist of one person living alone, or of any number of persons living together under one roof and having their food provided together."[25] A separate *house*, on the other hand, was "to be counted, whenever the entrance from the outside is separate, and there is no direct and constant communication in the inside."[26]

These definitions suggest that the census category *family* provides the best available approximation of the co-resident domestic group, particularly in urban settings, where a single entrance from the outside might well lead to a number of self-contained dwellings.[27] This approach has been taken in a number of recent studies of household structure in urban Quebec,[28] and is adopted in my analysis of the Saint-Hyacinthe census schedules. Short of the kind of systematic verification in other kinds of sources that characterizes Lauzon's work – a very arduous task, even for a small community – the assumption here is that the census category *family* (and not *house*) corresponds most satisfactorily to the notion of household.

Certain other problems of comparability between the 1861 census and those taken in 1871 and 1891 had to be resolved as well. The definitions of *family* and *house* cited above were those generated for the taking of the 1871 and subsequent censuses. In 1861, the enumeration had been done differently. Although the number of *families* in a *house* was usually noted, the boundaries between those *families* were not clearly indicated. In order to render the information from 1861 comparable to that from the other census schedules, an attempt was made to recreate these boundaries. Two principles were used. First, it was assumed that distinct conjugal families, particularly intact couples with or without children and widows or widowers with children, when encountered in a census *house* along with other such groupings, constituted distinct *families* in the spirit of the 1871 census instructions, and therefore distinct households for my purposes. (This assumption, incidentally, meant that the proportion of young married couples who co-resided with kin or other married or widowed individuals was probably underestimated for 1861, since any distinct conjugal family found in the same *house* had been designated as a separate household.) Second, the total number of *families* in the *house* – reported in column 34 of the 1861 census – was respected as far as possible.[29]

Once these decisions about how to infer household boundaries from the available lists were made, the census information concerning recently married couples was analyzed. Special attention was paid, first, to the presence of non-kin extras such as boarders, apprentices, and servants and, second, to the propensity of newlyweds to establish autonomous households, as opposed to relying on parents or other kin for shelter. Whether or not a young couple headed their own household was generally deduced from the position of their names on the census return; the usual assumption – that the first-named individual was the household head – was made. It was unnecessary, however, to make this assumption with the 1891 census, in which each household head was explicitly identified as such.

The fact that each couple was identified first in a marriage act and then in the manuscript census carried strong methodological advantages, particularly inasmuch as it facilitated the identification of co-resident kin. Most studies of household structure use census lists only. These lists may or may not identify household members by their relationship to the head.[30] If not, these relationships are inferred from the position of names on the census list, from common surnames, and from age differentials. Linking the census with marriage acts, however, eliminates the need for a lot of this guesswork. By providing the full names of both parents of each spouse, for example, the marriage acts allow one to verify assumptions about whether an older co-resident with a common surname was, in fact, a parent. They also provide knowledge not only of each wife's maiden name, which tended to be omitted from census lists starting in 1871, but also of the surnames of the maternal and paternal grandmothers. More distant kin, who may not have shared a surname with either the husband or the wife in the household where they were enumerated, could sometimes be identified in this way.

The basic typology applied in this analysis can be presented as follows. Newlywed couples have been classified not simply in terms of the type of household in which they lived, but also with respect to their position in that household:

1 Heads of Simple Households
   a) With extras
   b) No extras

2 Heads of Complex Households
   a) with Extras
   b) no Extras

3 Subnuclear: Inmates in households headed by kin

4 Inmates in households headed by non-kin

The distinction between the first two categories is straightforward. Simple households are those where no family member other than the husband, the wife, and their children are listed as members of the co-resident group. They are widely referred to as "nuclear family households."[31] In a complex household, as defined here, the conjugal family is augmented by at least one member of the wider kin group. Note that households containing more than one couple related to each other by kinship or marriage (Laslett's definition of a "multiple-family household") are not formally distinguished in this scheme from those that shelter unmarried or widowed kin (Laslett's "extended-family household").[32] Each of these first two household types has two principal subcategories: those in which non-kin "extras" such as boarders, servants, and employees were present; and those in which they were not.

Two further categories accommodate those couples – a small minority – who did not head their own households at the time of the first census after their marriage. Those who were living in households headed by their parents or other kin were defined as inmates of "subnuclear" households – an expression borrowed from the work of Howard Chudacoff. A fourth category was included for recently married couples who lived in households headed by non-kin, whether as guests, boarders, lodgers, servants, or other workers.[33]

This classification scheme emphasizes the distinction between couples who headed their own households (categories 1 and 2) and those who did not (categories 3 and 4). It can also be adapted to allow comparisons among couples living in simple-family (category 1), complex-family (categories 2 and 3), and other (category 4) settings. It is presented above in its simplest form. Many subcategories, such as complex families extended by the wife's kin, by widowed parents, by parents with siblings, or by other kin could have been shown. Certain conventional categories, such as "solitaries" and "no family" were of little use in a study group defined by the existence of a link from marriage act to manuscript census. By definition, at least one conjugal family was present in each household studied, unless one spouse or the other had died between the wedding and the date of the census. In the end, the few cases where this had happened were excluded from the analysis of household structures.[34]

In a subsequent phase of the analysis, the focus shifts to the census *house*, mainly so that the presence of further kin-group members on the premises, but outside the household occupied by the conjugal family in question, could be determined. Three types of *house* have been distinguished: 1) those occupied by only one *family* (household); 2) those that contained two or more *families*, but in which none of the occupants of the other dwellings could be identified as relatives of the newly married couple; 3) those that contained two or more households, at least one of which contained a relative (or relatives) of one of the newlyweds.

The point of this is not to further study household structure, using a different set of methodological assumptions. It is, rather, to use the data collected in the family-reconstitution study to provide partial answers to another set of questions. It is assumed that the presence of related individuals in distinct *families* within a single *house* reflects close residential proximity rather than co-residence. Family members who were enumerated as living in the same building, although not living with the newlyweds, were obviously very close neighbours. Residential proximity to kin has often been taken to indicate high degrees of co-operation and sociability among members of an extended family in communities experiencing the transition to industrial capitalism.[35] Although no exhaustive study of these issues was undertaken for this book, an examination of the *families* enumerated in the Saint-Hyacinthe *houses* that also contained our newlyweds – of those living in contiguous households, in other words – can shed some light on this practice. It also provides additional information on the extent to which recently married couples in Saint-Hyacinthe co-operated with their extended families in matters related to housing.

FOCUSING ON FERTILITY

This essay concludes with a discussion of the methodological apparatus I used to study fertility behaviour in Saint-Hyacinthe. The analysis is based on the 912 electronic *fiches de famille* compiled for couples in the three cohorts. Family-reconstitution techniques permitted the identification of some 2,435 children, born to 511 of these couples. The fact that no child was found for almost half of the couples relates more, as we shall see, to high levels of geographic mobility than to infertility. Figure A-1 represents the distribution across a 60-year period (1854–1914) of the births of these children.[36] The

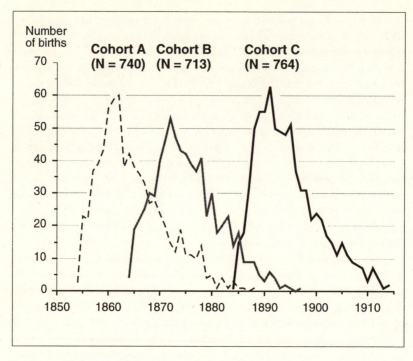

Figure A-1 Birth years: Children born to all couples in cohorts A, B, and C.
Source: Family Reconstitution Files

peaks in each of the three curves coincide with the early years of marriage and child-bearing for women in the three marriage cohorts. Declining levels after 1862, 1872, and 1891 reflect both out-migration and the reduced fertility of older women.

In an ideal world, this fertility analysis would have focused on the full reproductive lives of each of the 912 couples in the three cohorts. As shown in chapter 3, however, many of these couples never established a residence in the parish. Furthermore, of those that did, some left the town before the wife had reached the end of her child-bearing years, while others followed more complex migratory paths.[37] Due mainly to high levels of geographic mobility, then, nineteenth-century Saint-Hyacinthe is anything but an ideal world for purposes of family reconstitution.

A simple metaphor may clarify the discussion of measurement techniques in this high-mobility context. Using family reconstitution to study fertility in a single parish is a bit like early portrait photography. Should the subject move, the image will be blurred and out of focus; moreover, certain subjects may be sufficiently stubborn or shy to refuse to be photographed at all. In family reconstitution, the problem becomes one of having the "subject" – a married woman in her reproductive years – hold still long enough to have her child-bearing activity recorded over a reasonable length of time. Fertility can only be observed, in other words, to the extent that the couples selected for analysis remain within the range of the "lens" afforded by the parish-level reconstitution technique.

The difficulty with such a lens is that it is able to focus only on the geographically stable segment of the local population. Parish-level reconstitutions have often been criticized for these reasons. Gérard Bouchard, writing in 1975, posed the problem in the following terms: "Comment en effet garantir que sédentaires et migrants soumis à un environnement social, culturel, économique aussi sans doute, si différent, ont des comportements absolument identiques."[38] In the present study, this question of representativity is moot because there was no assumption (or argument) that mobile couples behaved identically to stable ones. And since the specific concern is with the impact of a particular social, cultural, and especially economic environment on demographic behaviour, it makes sense to concentrate on families who lived in that environment for sustained periods. As will soon be apparent, it also was possible to incorporate women with a range of mobility experiences into the fertility analysis.

For technical reasons, however, it was extremely important to separate out the geographically stable couples in the three cohorts from the mobile ones. To this end, the 912 couples were sorted into five categories corresponding to various types of migratory itinerary.[39] Mobility codes were assigned on the basis of a careful reading of each couple's file, with special attention given to the correspondence between parish register and census information.

Table A-1 reveals the extent to which Saint-Hyacinthe couples "held still" in the years following their weddings. Fully one-third (314) of the wives never lived in the parish as married women; because they had not lived in the town during industrial transition, it was therefore inappropriate to include them in the fertility study. Besides the small number that were excluded for other reasons, this left some 567 women who had lived in the parish for at least some part of their married lives. Of these, almost half (255) settled in the parish immediately after marriage, remaining there until the union ended (with the death of either spouse), or until they reached the end of their child-bearing years (defined for these purposes as age 45). Because the entire reproductive life of each couple had been observed, these were the most likely files to figure in any fertility analysis. However, information on shorter periods of conjugal life was available for the remaining 312 couples, of whom 168 settled in the parish after the marriage but left, definitively, before the union ended. The remaining 144 either undertook more complex (but coherent) migratory paths, or followed itineraries that could not be identified on the basis of the available information.

Table A-1
Analysis of Migratory Itineraries, by Cohort

Mobility Codes	A N %	B N %	C N %	Total N %
I Non-migrants	67 22.7	91 32.9	97 28.5	255 28.0
II Settled, but left the parish prior to end of union	50 16.9	43 15.5	75 22.1	168 18.4
III Other itineraries, including return migration	28 9.5	23 8.3	11 3.2	62 6.8
IV Itinerary unclear	29 9.8	23 8.3	30 8.8	82 9.0
V Never settled in the parish	104 35.3	88 31.8	122 35.9	314 34.4
VI Excluded for reasons unrelated to migration	17 5.8	9 3.2	5 1.5	31 3.4
TOTAL	295	277	340	912

Source: Family Reconstitution Files

The classification of *fiches de famille* by migratory itinerary constitutes a departure from Louis Henry's classic system, in which *fiches* are sorted into four main categories.[40] However, in this context, the uncritical use of Louis Henry's categories would have led to important distortions in the resulting fertility measures. In Henry's terms, all of the *fiches* in the Saint-Hyacinthe study were of type M, since the marriage act had always been the starting point for the reconstitution. As Table A-2 shows, all of the couples classified as Type I (non-migrants) would have fallen into Henry's MF category.[41] Of all (881) couples not excluded *a priori* from the fertility analysis, two-fifths were of type MF, while three-fifths were of type MO.[42] This is fine, except that it tells us, in fact, very little about whether or not a particular woman remained in Saint-Hyacinthe throughout her married life. Many couples who would have been classed as MF (on the basis of the marriage act and the burial act of whichever spouse died first) were, in fact, subject to high levels of mobility across the life cycle. The systematic comparison of parish register and census

Table A-2
Distribution of Family Reconstitution Files by Mobility Codes and Henry Codes

Mobility Codes	Henry Codes	Cohort			Total
		A	B	C	
I	MF	67	91	97	255
Non-migrants	MO	0	0	0	0
	% MF	100.0	100.0	100.0	100.0
	Total	67	91	97	255
II	MF	6	7	14	27
Settled, but left	MO	44	36	61	141
the parish prior	% MF	12.0	16.3	18.7	16.1
to end of union	Total	50	43	75	168
III	MF	10	7	4	21
Other itineraries,	MO	18	16	7	41
including return	% MF	35.7	30.4	57.1	33.9
migration	Total	28	23	11	62
IV	MF	9	9	14	32
Itinerary unclear	MO	20	14	16	50
	% MF	31.0	39.1	46.7	39.0
	Total	29	23	30	82
V	MF	1	4	6	11
Never settled in	MO	103	84	116	203
parish	% MF	1.0	4.5	4.9	3.5
	Total	104	88	122	314
TOTAL	MF	93	118	135	346
	MO	185	150	200	535
	% MF	33.5	44.0	40.3	39.3
	Total	278	268	335	881

Source: Family Reconstitution Files
Note: The 31 couples excluded from the analysis for reasons unrelated to mobility are not shown here. In Henry's terms, type MF (mariage-fermée) forms are those in which both a marriage act and a means of "closing" the observation – usually the burial of the husband or wife – have been located. Type MO (mariage-ouverte) forms are those for which there is a marriage act but no clear means of dating the end of the observed reproductive behaviour. In this sense, they remain "open."

data revealed a significant number of couples who had moved in and out of the area on which our "lens" was focused. Even though they were ultimately buried in the parish, many type-MF couples did not live out their full reproductive lives in Saint-Hyacinthe.[43] Conversely, many type-MO couples, for whom we have no confirmed *date de fin d'union*, nonetheless remained in the parish for significant portions of their married lives.

The classification of couples by migratory path was a first step toward solving the problems posed by high mobility. As already suggested, much of the fertility data is based on the behaviour of the most geographically stable couples (mobility code = I). But, mainly thanks to the availability of decennial censuses throughout the period, it was also possible to incorporate information on couples coded as types II, III, and IV, some of whom remained under observation for substantial periods of time indeed.

The methods used to generate coherent fertility measures on the basis of information for couples who experienced a variety of migratory experiences can now be described. The main strength of the family-reconstitution method is that it allows the calculation of age-specific marital fertility rates: a type of fertility statistic that is independent of the age and sex structure of the population and of nuptiality levels. Marital fertility rates are really ratios that compare the number of children born to married women in a given age category (five-year groupings are usually adopted) to the number of "woman-years" lived by women in that category.[44] In historical demography, it is preferable to use "completed families" only in the calculation of marital fertility rates.[45] But due to the high levels of mobility in nineteenth-century Saint-Hyacinthe, the number of completed families in the present study was prohibitively low.[46] It was thus necessary to relax this criterion and to examine the fertility of women in a much broader range of situations.

The basic principle of this operation was that rather than gathering information on child-bearing exclusively for women whose entire reproductive lives had been observed, fragments of those lives could be examined as well. A woman who lived in the parish between the ages of 20 and 29, for example, was included in the calculation of fertility rates for the 20 to 24 and 25 to 29 age groups. If she then left Saint-Hyacinthe for 10 years, but returned between her 40th and 45th birthdays – assuming this could be established definitively with the available documents – her child-bearing (or lack of it) in the 40 to 44 age category would also be examined.

Again, a photographic image is appropriate. A fixed video camera is able to detect behaviour as long as the subject does not move outside a certain range. But if this does occur, nothing prevents the subject from moving back into view at a later point. Similarly, the married women in our three cohorts were deemed to be under observation for various periods, which might represent their entire reproductive lives, or only certain phases – not necessarily consecutive – of those lives. These phases correspond to the age categories used in the calculation of age-specific marital fertility rates.

Once a wife's age was known and the timing and duration of her sojourn (or sojourns) in the parish established, it was a simple matter to count, first, the number of years she spent "under observation" in each age category and, second, the number of children born to her during that interval. Age-specific marital fertility rates were then calculated as the sum of all children born to all women observed in each category (say 25 to 29), divided by the total number of "woman-years" observed for that age category.

Before this could be done, however, it was necessary to set up some fairly stringent criteria for the inclusion of a particular woman's behaviour in any phase of the fertility study. The first requirement, an obvious one, was that her age had to be known. As suggested earlier in this essay, not all the age information in the database was of the same type or quality. In order to maximize the number of "woman-years" observed in each age category, therefore, I placed no restrictions on the kind of age information used. In other words, I treated cases in which a woman's birth year was estimated on the basis of a single census declaration in the same way as those in which a woman's baptism act had been located.

The second requirement was that the couple's presence in the parish during a given interval had to be established, usually on the basis of information from the census and from burial acts. In accordance with one of Louis Henry's cardinal rules, civil acts related to children were not generally used as evidence of a couple's presence at a particular date.[47] Some exceptions were made to this rule, however. Of a total of 395 periods of observation (for 386 women), I "closed" 84 – or 21% – with reference to the subsequent baptism, burial, or wedding of a child.[48] This was only done under special circumstances and in accordance with precise conventions that can be clarified using a set of fictitious examples.[49]

The first example involves a couple who marry in 1867 (and therefore belong to Cohort B), with the wife aged 23 years. Call them Joseph Petit and Marie Beauchemin. Marie gives birth to a number of children, all of them baptized at the cathedral between 1867 and 1882. The couple then disappears from the parish records. Census data confirm their presence in 1871 and 1881, and suggest their absence in 1891. In this case, I would have taken five steps:

1 Assume Marie's birthdate to be 1 January 1844, even if her exact birthday is known (a small minority of cases). She would therefore have turned 23 on 1 January 1867.[50]

2 Assume the marriage date to be 30 June 1867, even though the exact marriage date is (obviously) known.[51]

3 Close the *fiche* – that is to say, set the *date de fin d'observation* – at 1 January 1881, Marie's assumed thirty-seventh birthday, ignoring any births occurring between that date and the 1881 census, taken in April and May.

4 Conclude, on the basis of these three steps, that Marie's fertility can be observed over a total of 13.5 years: 1.5 in the 20 to 24 age group, 5 each in the 25 to 29 and 30 to 34 age groups; and 2 in the 35 to 39 age group.

5 Assign the observed live births to the appropriate age categories and move on to the next couple.

The second example involves a couple who marry in 1887 (in Cohort C); again the wife is 23 years of age. Call them Benoît Tremblay and Julie Savaria. A number of baptisms are found between 1887 and 1897 – the latter being the year the couple is last mentioned in the Saint-Hyacinthe parish register, in the burial act of an infant child. Neither Benoît nor Julie is buried in the parish (at least not prior to 1948, the last year of data collection for burials). Although they are present in 1891 according to the census of that year, there is no mention of the couple and their children in the 1901 census; this last suggests a departure after 1897 but before 1901.

Again, a five-step procedure – although a slight variant of the first – is adopted. In this case, I would take the following steps:

1 Assume that Julie's birthdate was 1 January 1864, and that, in consequence, her twenty-third birthday had fallen on 1 January 1887.

2 Assume their marriage date to have been 30 June 1887.

3 Use the 1897 infant burial to close the *fiche*, but ignore the age interval to which Julie would ordinarily have belonged at the time of that event in the calculation of marital fertility rates. Since Julie would have had her (assumed) thirty-third birthday on 1 January 1897, I would ignore whatever contribution she might have made to the fertility of the 30 to 34 age group. In other words, this means setting the *date de fin d'observation* at 1 January 1894, the date of her assumed thirtieth birthday, and taking no account of any subsequent births.

4 Conclude, on the basis of these procedures, that 6.5 "woman-years" can be observed: 1.5 in the 20 to 24 age group; and 5 in the 25 to 29 age category.

5 Assign the observed live births to the appropriate age groups and move on to the next *fiche*.

The result of all these operations was a set of decisions about which couples could be included in each stage of the fertility analysis, thinking of age-specific rates as measures of child-bearing in progressive stages of a woman's reproductive life. For inclusion in any stage of the analysis, it had to be established that the couple in question was resident in the parish and that neither party had died. In order to make these decisions, the files had to be read closely once again, this time with careful attention not only to indications of mobility but to the woman's age at each baptism, burial, or mention in a census. Ultimately, on this basis, a total of 386 women in the three cohorts were included in at least one stage of the fertility analysis. Table A-3 gives the distribution of these women by cohort and by the mobility codes assigned earlier. It shows the strong correspondence between geographic stability and the utility of a file for purposes of fertility analysis. Table A-4 gives the number of women included in each stage of the fertility analysis, and the total number of "woman-years" observed in each age category.

Although age-specific marital fertility rates were the main measures employed in chapter 5, several other methods were also adopted, each of which merits a few words of explanation. The measurement of birth spacing, for example, is a standard procedure in historical demography. Precise data for intergenesic intervals can often be derived from family reconstitution forms. Such data are particularly useful in discussions of infant mortality and its effect on fertility, of infant care in pre-industrial societies, and of contraception in societies practising birth control.[52]

In the present instance, it was extremely difficult to generate reliable measurements of birth intervals even for the 386 *fiches de famille* that were coherent enough to be included in at least one phase of the fertility analysis. For one thing, the issue of parity – or birth rank – is not always clear-cut, particularly when one is dealing with fragments of women's reproductive lives. For another, a certain number of intervals would either have had to remain invisible or be guessed at, because, even in the most complete *fiches* in this collection, some birthdates remain unknown.

Rather than pushing this aspect of the analysis, I decided to measure only the first and last birth intervals of women included in the fertility study. The final interval, a particularly interesting index of family limitation, was observed for 87 women in the three cohorts. I examined it in conjunction with the age of women at the birth of their last child, another useful measure of family limitation. Protogenesic intervals, the period between marriage and the birth of a first child, turned out to be of little help in understanding fertility in Saint-Hyacinthe. On this score, none of the relationships discovered were unexpected or dynamic.[53]

Most of the final birth intervals I was able to observe involved completed families, defined as those where the couple remained intact and under observation through the wife's forty-fifth birthday. Although there were only 102 such families in the entire family reconstitution study, it seemed worthwhile to calculate the average size of such families, for comparison with the more abstract age-specific rates discussed above. Although this calculation

Table A-3
Women and "Woman-Years" Observed in the 15-to-44 Age Group, by Cohort and Mobility Code, by Cohort

Mobility Codes		A N	B N	C N	Total N	%
I	Women	64	74	88	226	58.5
	Woman-years	835	1,151.5	1,376.5	3,363	74.6
II	Women	29	24	51	104	26.9
	Woman-years	198.5	171.5	384.5	754.5	16.7
III	Women	19	19	7	45	11.7
	Woman-years	166	155.5	36.5	358	7.9
IV	Women	2	4	5	11	2.8
	Woman-years	8.5	9.5	19	37	0.8
TOTAL						
	Women	114	121	151	386	–
	Woman-years	1,208	1,488	1,812	4,508	–

Source: Family Reconstitution Files
Note: The mobility codes employed here are defined as follows: I: non-migrants; II: settled, but left the parish prior to end of union; III: other itineraries, including return migration; IV: itinerary unclear.

Table A-4
Women and "Woman-Years" Observed, by Cohort and Age Category

Cohort		Age Category						
		15–19	20–24	25–29	30–34	35–39	40–44	(Total) 15–44
A	Women	38	72	69	59	47	43	114
	Woman-years	70	250	268	240	202	178	1,208
B	Women	40	71	75	73	70	53	121
	Woman-years	78.5	239.5	325	319.5	291.5	234	1,488
C	Women	56	111	90	83	77	55	151
	Woman-years	88.5	369	397.5	373.5	331.5	252	1,812
TOTAL								
	Women	134	254	234	215	194	151	386
	Woman-years	237	858.5	990.5	933	825	664	4,508
Average number of years observed per woman		1.8	3.4	4.2	4.3	4.3	4.4	11.7

Source: Family Reconstitution Files

had the advantage of simplicity and clarity, it also ignored all but the most geographically stable families.

It was also possible to create a synthetic index of average family size on the basis of marriage ages and marital fertility rates. The standard technique – which I adapted slightly – is to calculate the sum of all the age-specific marital fertility rates, but ignore the 15 to 19 age group, or the 15 to 19 and 20 to 24 age groups, depending upon what is known about female marriage ages. Multiplying this sum by 5 yields the Total Marital Fertility Rate (TMFR): the total number of children born to a cohort of 1,000 women – assuming all were married at a fixed age, experienced the group's age-specific fertility levels, and lived through to menopause.[54] The average number of children born to a woman in such a cohort would then be equal to one one-thousandth of the number of births thus calculated.[55]

Total marital fertility rates can provide an index of completed family size for a cohort of women in which the number of completed families is low, but where age-specific marital fertility rates are nonetheless available. They can be further refined by factoring in information about mean female marriage age and infant and child mortality rates. Rather than reporting, for example, total marital fertility rates for women marrying at age 20 in all three marriage cohorts, it seemed appropriate to calculate the rate for women married at age 22 in cohorts A and B, and at age 23 for Cohort C, thus incorporating data about changes in women's age at first marriage over the period.

While the total number of children born to the "average" woman in each cohort is a useful piece of information, I was also interested to know how many of these children survived infancy and childhood. This family-reconstitution study, like any other, is a very good source of information on infant and child mortality. It was therefore relatively easy to generate reliable figures on infant mortality (ratio of children dying in the first year of life to all live births) and child mortality (ratio of children dying between ages one and 15 years to all live births) for each cohort. By applying these quotients to the rates just described, it was possible to generate two estimates of *effective* family size: the average number of children surviving infancy per married woman; and the number surviving to age 15. The theoretical importance of measuring effective family size, as opposed to restricting one's attention to live births only, cannot be overstated, particularly as so much of the recent debate focuses on the economic interaction and exchange between parents and *adult* children.[56]

Notes

PREFACE

1 Rudin, "Revisionism and the Search for a Normal Society"; *Making History*.
2 See Granatstein, *Who Killed Canadian History?* for the English Canadian version of this argument, which can be heard from certain *québécois* nationalists as well.

INTRODUCTION

1 Historians debate the nature, causes, and pace of the socio-economic transformation that occurred in Quebec after 1850. Part of this debate has turned on the pace of industrial development in the province, which some have deemed to be inordinately slow compared, for example, to Ontario or New England. A great deal of energy has been spent explaining Quebec's industrial "lag," whether in terms of the province's natural resource endowment, the nature of its agriculture, the mentality of its bourgeoisie, or other factors. No attempt is made in this book to join this debate. Instead, Quebec's post-1850 industrialization is viewed as a crucial stage in the society's long transition from a broadly feudal, pre-industrial economic and social order to the modern, capitalist world of the twentieth century. More attention is paid, here, to the social effects of this transition, particularly on familial organization and demographic behaviour, than to its much contested causes and contours.

The best economic history of Quebec in this period is still Hamelin and Roby, *Histoire économique du Québec*. See also Armstrong, *Structure and Change*. Important Marxist views of the period are available in Ryerson, *Unequal Union* and Pentland, *Labour and Capital in Canada*. Books that focus on Quebec's industrial lag with respect to other regions of North America include Faucher, *Québec en Amérique au 19e siècle* and McCallum, *Unequal Beginnings*. A general survey that covers the main social and economic transformations of the period is Linteau, Robert and Durocher's, *Quebec: A History*. Another survey, Young and Dickinson's *Short History of Quebec*, comes closer to my own view that late nineteenth-century industrialization was an important stage in a protracted transition to industrial capitalism.

2 Rouillard, *Histoire du syndicalisme québécois*, 11–70; Burgess, "L'industrie de la chaussure à Montréal"; Bischoff, "La formation des traditions syndicales"; Harvey, *Révolution industrielle et travailleurs*; Hareven, *Family Time and Industrial Time*; Bradbury, "The Family Economy and Work"; Bradbury, "The Working-Class Family Economy"; Bradbury, *Working Families*; Vincent-Domey, *Filles et famille en milieu ouvrier*; Lauzon, *Habitat ouvrier et révolution industrielle*.

3 See, for example, Hubert Charbonneau et al., *Naissance d'une population*; Louise Dechêne, *Habitants et marchands de Montréal*; Lorraine Gadoury, *La noblesse de Nouvelle-France*; Danielle Gauvreau, *Québec: Une ville et sa population*.

4 On emigration to the United States, see, for example, Lavoie, "Les mouvements migratoires des canadiens"; Lavoie, *L'émigration des Canadiens aux Etats-Unis avant 1930*; Frenette, "La genèse d'une communauté canadienne-française"; Hareven, *Family Time and Industrial Time*; Ramirez, *On the Move*. On migration from rural Quebec toward Montreal, see Robert, "Urbanisation et population"; Gagnon, "Parenté et migration"; Bischoff, "Des Forges du Saint-Maurice aux fonderies de Montréal." The many studies dealing with migratory movements in the countryside include Maisonneuve, "Structure familiale et exode rurale"; Bouchard, "L'histoire démographique et le problème des migrations"; Bouchard, "Family Structures and Geographic Mobility at Laterrière"; Pouyez, Roy, and Bouchard, "La mobilité géographiqe en milieu rural." On the development of colonization regions in this period, more is known about the Saguenay area than any other, thanks to the work of the Institut interuniversitaire de recherches sur les populations (IREP). The project produced a synthetic treatment of the population history of the region in 1983; see Pouyez, Lavoie et al., *Les Saguenayens*. In his recent book, *Quelques arpents d'Amérique*, Gérard Bouchard draws heavily on the IREP data, using the concept of "co-integration" to describe the particular imbrication of economic and social structures with demographic behaviour

in the Saguenay. Interesting demographic work has been done on other rural regions, however. Jack Little's book on Scottish and French-Canadian settlers in the Eastern Townships, for example, contains useful information on population patterns in Winslow Township; see Little, *Crofters and Habitants*, 80–112. One can include Chad Gaffield's work here as well, since it deals with a French-Canadian colonization region that straddled the Quebec-Ontario border: the Ottawa Valley. See Gaffield, *Language, Schooling, and Cultural Conflict*, 31–61; Gaffield, "Canadian Families in Cultural Context."

5 Studies which begin to address these issues include Bradbury, *Working Families*; but see also Vincent-Domey, *Filles et familles en milieu ouvrier*. One aspect of urban demographic regimes in this period that has been examined in some detail is infant mortality. See, for example, Copp, *Anatomy of Poverty*; Gossage, "Les enfants abandonnés à Montréal au 19e siècle"; and Robert, "The City of Wealth and Death." An interesting ongoing exploration of urban demography in this period is the project led by historical geographers Sherry Olson and Patricia Thornton. They have identified three distinct fertility and infant mortality regimes in industrializing Montreal, one for each of the French-Canadian, Irish-Catholic, and British-Protestant segments of the population. See Thornton, Olson, and Quoc, "Dimensions sociales de la mortalité infantile"; Thornton, "Family Contexts of Fertility and Infant Survival."

6 A partial exception is Odette Vincent's work on Hull. See Vincent-Domey, *Filles et familles en milieu ouvrier*.

7 The full list of relevant studies would be very long indeed. But see, for example, Esther Boserup, *Population and Technological Change*; Bettina Bradbury, *Working Families*; John Caldwell, *Theory of Fertility Decline*; Christopher Clark, "The Household Economy, Market Exchange, and the Rise of Capitalism"; Jack Goody, *Production and Reproduction*; David Grigg, *Population Growth and Agrarian Change*; Michael Haines, *Fertility and Occupation*; Tamara Hareven, *Family Time and Industrial Time*; Michael Katz, *The People of Hamilton*; David Levine, *Family Formation in an Age of Nascent Capitalism*; Hans Medick, "The Proto-Industrial Family Economy"; Franklin Mendels, "The First Phase of the Industrialization Process"; Louise Tilly and Joan Scott, *Women, Work, and Family*.

8 Louise Tilly has defined the family, for purposes of historical study, as "the mediating institution between individuals and processes of large-scale structural change." This view is as useful for studying individuals and families in industrializing Quebec as in industrializing France. See Tilly, "The Family Wage Economy of a French Textile City," 383. See also Goody, *Production and Reproduction*, for an anthropologist's view of the links between economic structures and demographic regimes.

9 Much of this work has been inspired, at least in part, by the efforts and

ideas of Tamara Hareven, who has repeatedly demonstrated the tenacity of family ties in extremely turbulent social and economic contexts. See for example Hareven, *Family Time and Industrial Time.*

10 A good example is Accampo, *Industrialization, Family Life, and Class Relations.*

11 Family reconstitution techniques are described in Fleury and Henry, *Nouveau manuel de dépouillement,* and in Henry, *Techniques d'analyse en démographie historique.* See also Wrigley, "Family Reconstitution." Two recent books, drawn from large scale, collaborative projects, apply the method to much larger populations than that examined here. Bouchard uses it for the Saguenay region of Quebec in *Quelques arpents d'Amérique,* while the Cambridge Group for the Study of Population and Social Structure has – after 25 years of work – managed to use this method to synthesize 250 years of British demographic history. See Wrigley et al., *English Population History from Family Reconstitution.*

12 There are useful introductions to the work of both of these projects in Courville, ed., *Atlas historique du Québec,* 29–43; 63–80.

13 There have been very few attempts. The project headed by Sherry Olson and Pat Thornton – it focuses on a layered sample of Irish, French Canadian, and Protestant families in Montreal – is the only other one of which I am aware. (See above, note 5.) The family-reconstitution method, however, has been applied to various urban settings in Europe with great success, despite the difficulties created by mobility. See, for example, Accampo, *Industrialization, Family Life, and Class Relations;* and especially Bardet, *Rouen au XVIIe et XVIIIe siècles.* The difficulties created by geographic mobility are discussed in Bouchard, "L'histoire démographique et le problème des migrations."

14 I have included in this book a detailed description of the methodological apparatus developed for this study. It appears at the end as a technical appendix, entitled "Family Formation in Focus." This essay, designed to make the research reported here as transparent as possible, will mainly interest specialist readers. They may wish to consult it before reading chapters 3, 4, and 5.

15 In Henry's terms, *fiches de famille* are the forms on which all the information about births, marriages, and deaths pertaining to a single (conjugal) family are collected and the various demographic calculations performed. E.A. Wrigley and other English historical demographers refer to them as Family Reconstitution Forms, abbreviated as FRF. I will not use this abbreviation in this book, preferring to retain the French term *fiches de famille* or simply *fiches* where discussion of technical aspects of family reconstitution is necessary.

16 See Bouchard, "L'histoire démographique et le problème des migrations."

17 The town was over 95% Catholic throughout the second half of the nineteenth century. See Table 1-1.

18 Chapter 1 contains a description of the creation of the parish and the evolution of its borders. See Figure 1-4 for the boundaries of the two Saint-Hyacinthe parishes as drawn in the 1850s.

19 The 1854–61 and 1864–71 cohorts included all couples married at the cathedral in those years. However, the third cohort was a 75% systematic sample of the marriages celebrated between 1884 and 1891. This procedure was adopted to keep the sizes of the three cohorts approximately the same (about 300). The time periods were selected to correspond to progressive stages in the town's development. The last year of each period corresponds to a census, thereby facilitating linkage from marriage acts to these documents. The level of about 300 couples per cohort was chosen with the full knowledge that, mainly because of mobility, the number of reconstituted families would ultimately be significantly smaller.

   This marriage-cohort method was first suggested to me by Raymond Roy, Danielle Gauvreau, and other researchers during a visit to the Université du Québec à Chicoutimi in 1987. A similar, cohort-based method was used with success by Accampo in her study of Saint-Chamond. See Accampo, *Industrialization, Family Life, and Class Relations.*

20 For a fuller explanation and some figures on the prevalence of these various migratory paths, see the section entitled "Focusing on Fertility" in the appendix, especially Table A-1.

21 The only true sampling involved in this research was the 75% systematic sample taken of the 450 marriages celebrated at the cathedral between 1881 and 1891; that was done in order to keep the size of this cohort comparable to the other two. Otherwise, the quantifiable observations reported here pertain to the sedentary component within each of the three marriage cohorts, which in statistical terms are more akin to study populations than to samples. There is, therefore, no absolute need to apply tests of statistical significance to the data reported in chapters 3, 4, and 5. I have nonetheless conducted many such tests and report the results where appropriate.

CHAPTER ONE

1 See Figure 1-2, in which the ridge follows the line of Girouard Street.

2 Francoeur, "Esquisse de géographie urbaine," 23.

3 The best discussion of the geography of the Saint-Hyacinthe area and particularly its geomorphology is contained in Francoeur, "Esquisse de géographie urbaine." See also the section on Saint-Hyacinthe in Blanchard, *L'ouest du Canada français.*

4 Most of the information in the next several paragraphs is drawn from Dessureault's discussion of the early settlement history of the seigneurie of Saint-Hyacinthe. See his doctoral dissertation, "Les fondements de la hiérarchie," 22–39. For other useful accounts of the early history of Saint-Hyacinthe, see Choquette, *Histoire de la ville*; Boucher de la Bruère, "Establishment of St. Hyacinthe," in *Saint-Hyacinthe Illustré/Illustrated*; Francoeur, "Esquisse de géographie urbaine"; Voyer, *De la seigneurie à la ville*.

5 Dessureault, "Crise ou modernisation," 364. The population statistics just cited are from tables 1 and 3 of that article. Translation:

This seigneurie had some of the most fertile land in Quebec. The sandy and clay soils in the region of the Yamaska River were particularly favourable to the growing of cereals, which dominated the early nineteenth-century agrarian landscape. The quality of the land, however, was not completely uniform. For example, in La Présentation, the peasants living in the region of Les Étangs and the Salvail River had fairly moist soils with a scattering of marshes, more suitable to the exploitation of natural grasslands than to the growing of cereals. Nonetheless, the soil types of the Saint-Hyacinthe Plain, common to the five parishes of the seigneurie, should have been rather favourable to the economic expansion of the peasantry.

6 Dessureault, "Les fondements de la hierarchie," 39; Choquette, *Histoire de la ville*, 42.

7 Voyer, *De la seigneurie à la ville*, 15–17; Francoeur, "Esquisse de géographie urbaine," 24–5; Boucher de la Bruère, "Establishment of St. Hyacinthe," 3.

8 Courville, *Entre ville et campagne*.

9 See Figure 1-2 and Voyer, *De la seigneurie à la ville*, 17–20. See also the sketches by surveyor L.P. Renault-Blanchard, made in May of 1837, in Illustrations 1 and 2.

10 Rudin, "Development of a Regional Economy," 2.

11 Ibid., 2–3.

12 Ibid., 3. Desnoyers, "Histoire de Saint-Hyacinthe," manuscript at the AESH, 157. *Census of the Canadas, 1851–52*. The St. Lawrence and Atlantic was, of course, the forerunner to the Grand Trunk and was built to give Montreal merchants access to a winter port in Portland, Maine. See also Illustration 3.

13 *Census of the Canadas, 1860–61*, vol. 2, table 12; Séguin, "L'agriculture de la Mauricie."

14 Ibid.

15 *Quebec Gazette* 12:46 (3 September 1835): 511

16 *Statutes of the Province of Canada,* 13 & 14 Victoria cap. 105 (10 August 1850). The actual village covered perhaps a quarter of the 231 hectares set aside for the new municipality. See Figure 1-2.

17 *Statutes of the Province of Canada,* 16 Victoria cap. 236 (14 June 1853); 20 Victoria cap. 131 (10 June 1857).

18 Since the Yamaska bends at Saint-Hyacinthe, the orientation of streets running perpendicular to the river is roughly southeast to northwest. See Figure 1-2.

19 *Statutes of Quebec,* 51–52 Victoria cap. 83 (12 July 1888).

20 Christine Hudon explains the pressures for the creation of the new diocese as follows: "Depuis quelques années déjà, les ecclésiastiques de la région du Richelieu–Yamaska demandaient le démembrement du diocèse de Montréal, alléguant que cette mesure faciliterait les tournées pastorales, l'administration du sacrement de confirmation, la colonisation des Cantons de l'Est, de même que les relations entre les prêtres et leur évêque." Hudon, *Prêtres et fidèles,* 14. [Translation: For some years already, clergymen in the Richelieu–Yamaska region had been requesting the dismemberment of the Montreal diocese, a measure, they alleged, that would facilitate pastoral visits, the administering of the sacrament of confirmation, the colonization of the Eastern Townships, as well as relations between the priests and their bishop.]

21 Boucher de la Bruère, "Establishment of St. Hyacinthe," 3. On the 1835 courthouse, see Voyer, *De la seigneurie à la ville,* 25–31.

22 The transformation of the region's agriculture after mid-century will be addressed in chapter 2.

23 Hamelin and Roby, *Histoire économique du Québec,* 53

24 Voyer gives the village population in 1817 as 300. Rudin's estimate for 1840 is just over 1,000. These are both rough estimates, and it is not clear how either of them was generated. Voyer, *De la seigneurie à la ville,* Rudin, "The Development of a Regional Economy." Although the village was not yet incorporated in 1831, census takers in that year reported that it contained "136 houses and 914 souls." *Journals of the Legislative Assembly of Lower Canada* 1832, appendix O.o. Isidore Desnoyers gives the Catholic population of the village as 2,508 in January of 1845. Desnoyers, "Histoire de Saint-Hyacinthe," 157.

25 Rudin, for example, suggests that the arrival in Saint-Hyacinthe of the Séguin-Lalime shoe company (1883) and the Abel Hosiery Company (1881) "led to the expansion of the local population by 32%" in the 1880s. While these two factories surely did provide industrial jobs and therefore fostered a positive migratory balance, much of the population increase Rudin has observed would have resulted from the annexation of *Quartier* 5 in 1888. See Rudin, "The Development of Four Quebec Towns," 110. The only other annexation in the nineteenth century was

in 1863, when the site of the seigneurial mill (and later of the main industrial establishments) was absorbed by the city. Clearly, this did not involve any transfer of population between the municipalities. *Statutes of the Province of Canada*, 27 Victoria cap. 22 (15 October 1863).

26 AESH, *Registre des requêtes, Extrait du décrêt canonique de la paroisse de Saint-Hyacinthe*, 2 June 1832.

27 AESH, *Registre des requêtes, Décret canonique de la paroisse de Saint-Hyacinthe-le-Confesseur*, 15 October 1853. I am indebted here to the late Mgr Léo Sansoucy of the Séminaire de Saint-Hyacinthe for his explanation of the confusing details surrounding the origins of the new parish.

28 *Statutes of the Province of Canada*, 18 Victoria cap. 100, sec. 4, para. 2: "[T]he part of the parish of St. Hyacinthe the Confessor which is without the limits of the said town of St. Hyacinthe shall for the purposes of this Act be deemed to be an extra parochial place, and shall be annexed to the adjoining parish of Notre-Dame de Saint-Hyacinthe."

29 *Statutes of the Province of Canada*, 24 Victoria cap. 29. On the history of this rural municipality, see Dion, *Saint-Hyacinthe-le-Confesseur, 125 ans d'histoire*.

30 Since for religious purposes, this new *quartier* remained a part of the parish of Notre-Dame-du-Rosaire, the demographic behaviour of its residents will not receive detailed attention in this book.

31 Percentage increases were 42% in the 1870s, 32% in the 1880s, and 31% in the 1890s.

32 Rudin, "Development of a Regional Economy," 4.

33 As we have seen, this Catholic parish comprised the original four *quartiers* of the town of Saint-Hyacinthe, plus the rural municipality of Saint-Hyacinthe-le-Confesseur (see Figure 1-4).

34 Rudin, "The Development of Four Quebec Towns," 111–13.

35 The assumptions would exaggerate net in-migration to the extent that *Quartier 5* contained a greater proportion of the town's population in 1901 than it had in 1891. Although this may have been the case, the resulting distortion is unlikely to be serious. See note "f" to Table 1–2.

36 Pouyez, Lavoie et al., *Les Saguenayens*, table 6.13, 277.

37 Ibid.

38 The 1876 fire and its consequences will receive further attention in chapter 2. See also Illustration 12.

39 Pouyez, Lavoie et al., *Les Saguenayens*, table 6.18, 293.

40 Figures for 1885 are from APSHC, Parish Registers, 1885–86. On the 1885 smallpox epidemic in Montreal, see Bliss, *Plague: A Story of Smallpox*.

41 On the impact of this epidemic in the Eastern Townships, see Rioux, *La grippe espagnole à Sherbrooke*.

42 Ronald Rudin has gone so far as to suggest that current historiography exaggerates the importance of urban life in nineteenth-century Quebec.

See Rudin "Revisionism and the Search for a Normal Society." See also his *Making History,* especially chapter 5.

43 The compilers of a recent bibliography published references to almost 4,000 titles related to the history of the city. See Burgess et al., *Clés pour l'histoire de Montréal.*

44 The urban component of the Quebec population increased from 15% to 40% between 1851 and 1901. Moreover, with a population that practically quintupled in the interval between 1851 and 1901, Montreal contained some 40% of the province's urban population by the turn of the century. Hamelin and Roby, *Histoire économique du Québec,* 292. On secondary urban development in the province, see especially Rudin, "The Development of Four Quebec Towns."

45 Hamelin and Roby, *Histoire économique du Québec,* 297.

46 Ferland, "Évolution des rapports sociaux," 131–2; 131 for the citation. Translation: [These producers] found it more profitable to obtain part of their stock from Quebec City manufacturers and to pay the cost of transportation, rather than to manufacture this type of footwear in their own factories or at a competitor's in the Montreal region.

47 Ibid, 133–4.

48 Du Berger and Mathieu, eds., *Les ouvrières de la Dominion Corset,* 8.

49 See Lorimer and Gossage, "A Craftsman Remembers" for an example from the Eastern Townships.

50 Hamelin and Roby, *Histoire économique du Québec,* 292.

51 Odette Vincent, "L'industrie et le monde du travail," in Gaffield et al., eds., *Histoire de l'Outaouais,* 269.

52 Ibid.

53 Ibid., 272–5.

54 Ibid., 274–5; Vincent, *Filles et familles,* 33–4.

55 Hamelin and Roby, *Histoire économique du Québec,* 292; Hardy and Séguin, *Forêt et société,* 180–1.

56 Ibid., 183–6.

57 Hardy-Séguin, *Forêt et société,* 182–3.

58 Ibid.

59 Ibid., 182, 190–1; Hamelin and Roby, *Histoire économique du Québec,* 292.

60 Hamelin and Roby, *Histoire économique du Québec,* 271. Translation: [Cotton textile production] was the lot of a few daring individuals who feared neither English nor American competition.

61 Ibid.

62 McCullough, *L'industrie textile primaire,* 197.

63 Ibid., 197–8. These figures are for 1908.

64 Hamelin and Roby, *Histoire économique du Québec,* 292.

65 McCullough, *L'industrie textile primaire,* 198; Ferland, "Sydicalisme 'parcellaire' et syndicalisme 'collectif,'" 83–4.

66 From $2.4 million to $12.4 million. Hamelin and Roby, *Histoire économique du Québec*, 267.

67 Ibid., 272.

68 Kesteman, "Naissance et développement," 33.

69 Ibid., 33; Rudin, "The Development of Four Quebec Towns," 38.

70 Kesteman, "Naissance et développement," 34.

71 Rudin, "The Development of Four Quebec Towns," 39.

72 Ibid., 39–40.

73 Hamelin and Roby, *Histoire économique du Québec*, 273. Here again, the British American Land Company was involved. The company was now widely criticized, because it had reversed Galt's policy of promoting local manufacturing after his resignation in 1855. The public had begun to see BALCO, which owned the best mill sites and was now refusing to develop them, as the source of the city's industrial lethargy. The critics were silenced, however, when Galt's successor, R.W. Heneker, offered substantial assistance to Paton, in the form of free land and water-power rights. Rudin, "The Development of Four Quebec Towns," 40–1.

74 Rudin, "The Development of Four Quebec Towns," 41; Hamelin and Roby, *Histoire économique du Québec*, 273.

75 Kesteman, "Naissance et développement," 33; Rudin, "The Development of Four Quebec Towns," 42.

76 Hamelin and Roby, *Histoire économique du Québec*, 273; Rudin, "The Development of Four Quebec Towns," 86.

77 Kesteman, "Naissance et développement," 33.

78 Rudin, "The Development of Four Quebec Towns," 86.

79 From 223 workers in 1866 to 524 in 1871. Rudin, "The Development of Four Quebec Towns," 41.

80 Ibid., 41; Hamelin and Roby, *Histoire économique du Québec*, 292.

81 Kesteman, "Naissance et développement," 37.

82 Kesteman, "Naissance et développement," 39.

83 Kesteman, "Naissance et développement," 39; Rudin, "The Development of Four Quebec Towns," 92.

84 In fact, the asbestos deposits were discovered by construction crews working on the railway line. Rudin, "The Development of Four Quebec Towns," 97–8.

85 Kesteman, "Naissance et développement," 40; Rudin, "The Development of Four Quebec Towns," 92.

CHAPTER TWO

1 From 1,932 to 1,619. *Census of the Canadas, 1860–61*, vol. 2, table 12; *Fourth Census of Canada, 1901*, vol. 2, tables 1 and 2.

2 Saint-Hyacinthe county farmers planted 989.9 hectares in wheat in 1901, down from 3,385.7 in 1861. The average farmer in the region devoted 9.9 hectares to hay and 4.5 hectares to oats production in 1901, compared to 6.8 hectares and 3.6 hectares for the province. *Census of the Canadas, 1860–61*, vol. 2, table 12; *Fourth Census of Canada, 1901*, vol. 2, tables 1 and 2; Séguin, "L'agriculture de la Mauricie et du Québec."

3 Séguin, "L'agriculture de la Mauricie et du Québec," 544–5. See also, among many other studies that treat this transformation, Courville and Séguin, "Rural Life in Nineteenth-Century Quebec," and Hamelin and Roby, *Histoire économique du Québec*, 185–205.

4 County-level figures, again, are from the agricultural tables of the 1861 and 1901 published census. Provincial aggregates are taken from Séguin's "L'agriculture de la Mauricie et du Québec."

5 *Lovell's Business and Professional Directory*.

6 Ibid., 457.

7 Rudin, "The Development of Four Quebec Towns," 117.

8 Ibid., 119.

9 *Lovell's Business and Professional Directory*, 457–70.

10 Ibid.

11 The best discussion of public markets in Saint-Hyacinthe is found in Hébert, Dion, and Rémillard, *Le marché de Saint-Hyacinthe*. Most of the ensuing discussion is inspired by that book, especially pp. 3–34.

12 Illustration 2 shows the market as it would have looked immediately after the 1836 renovation, which increased its area by 50% – from 1,500 to 2,250 square feet.

13 The structure had a footprint covering over 5,000 square feet (more than twice the area of the previous building), a second storey in the central bay, and some 34 stalls. Hébert, Dion, and Rémillard, *Le marché de Saint-Hyacinthe*, 7–12.

14 Ibid., 8–10.

15 Ibid., 21–2; 32–3.

16 Ibid., 33. This profile is essentially borne out by the Lovell's directory for 1902, which lists 38 businesses with premises in the central market: 35 butchers; one poultry, butter and cheese dealer; one dealer in honey and canned fruit and vegetables; and one restaurant. *Lovell's Business and Professional Directory*, 452–70.

17 In 1882, the number of market days had been reduced from the traditional six to three: Tuesday, Thursday, and Saturday. Hébert, Dion, and Rémillard, *Le marché de Saint-Hyacinthe*, 33.

18 *Courrier de Saint-Hyacinthe*, 13 March 1897, reproduced in Ibid., 47.

19 The directories are *The Canada Directory for 1857–1858*, 695–8, and *Lovell's Business and Professional Directory*, 452–70. They were searched for

the following categories of shops and small commercial establishments: general stores; food dealers (including grocery stores; wine and liquor stores; butchers; bakers and confectioners; and egg, poultry, and dairy dealers); clothing stores (including tailors, merchant tailors, dressmakers, milliners, hatters, and ready-made clothing dealers); and dealers in hardware, agricultural implements, fuel, lumber, building supplies, books, newspapers, stationery, and junk or second-hand goods. Businesses offering certain services were also included in the search. These included hotels, boardinghouses, restaurants, saloons, banks, insurance agents, barbershops, and laundries. Individuals employed in the transport and communications sector – such as carters and railway agents – were also identified.

20 *The Canada Directory for 1857–1858*, 695–8; and *Lovell's Business and Professional Directory*, 452–70.

21 *The Canada Directory for 1857–1858*, 695.

22 Ibid., 697–8.

23 *The Canada Directory for 1857–1858*, 695–8; *Lovell's Business and Professional Directory*, 452–70.

24 This does not include six merchants who combined the sale of groceries with that of wines and liquors. Including these dealers with the grocery stores gives three in 1857, or one per 1,231 residents, and 36 in 1902, or one for every 256 residents.

25 *Lovell's Business and Professional Directory*, 452–70.

26 Ibid., 465–6.

27 This despite the fact that, as Bettina Bradbury has shown, working families were able to supplement their wage incomes by all kinds of activities that fell outside the formal economy. They may, in other words, have been less dependent on local shops for food, clothing, and other essentials than one might expect. See Bradbury, "Pigs, Cows, and Boarders"; *Working Families*, 152–81.

28 *Lovell's Business and Professional Directory*, 460.

29 The entries for Rouleau, Palardy, and Laporte are on pages 468, 466, and 465, respectively, of *Lovell's Business and Professional Directory*. Translation: wood merchant dealing in lumber of all kinds: boards, clapboards, panels, posts, etc. Specialty: frames and shingles.

30 *The Canada Directory for 1857–1858*, 695–8; Lovell, *Lovell's Business Directory*, 452–71. Note also that, by the time of the 1891 census, a number of local women were taking laundry into their homes. One sees this from the 14 women identified as *blanchisseuses* and the eight identified as *laveuses* in the four original *quartiers* of the town. NA, manuscript census, 1891, City of Saint-Hyacinthe, reel T-6419.

31 Ibid.

32 Ibid.

33 Rudin, *Banking en français*, 40–3 and 84–91; Lapointe, "La formation de la Banque de Saint-Hyacinthe." Georges-Casimir Dessaulles, pictured in Illustration 9, was president of this bank for much of its existence.

34 *The Canada Directory for 1857–1858*, 695–8; *Lovell's Business and Professional Directory*, 452–71.

35 MacKay, *The Canada Directory* (1851), 386–7.

36 *The Canada Directory for 1857–58*, 695.

37 At least three such enterprises were present in 1863. G.F. Barnes manufactured agricultural implements in his Cascade Street foundry. Hyacinthe Dussault, a partner in the axe factory mentioned in 1851, operated a foundry, as did Pierre Soly. See the *Grand Trunk Railway Gazetteer, Commercial Advertiser, and Business Directory* (1862–63), 461–3. On industry in the Saint-Hyacinthe region in the period up to 1861, see also Dessureault, "Industrie et société rurale."

38 The continued ability of artisans to control important parts of the work process is one of the main themes in the history of metallurgy during this period. This sector has been studied in detail from the point of view of its principal labour force, the iron moulders, by Peter Bischoff. See Bischoff, "La formation des traditions syndicales"; "Des Forges du Saint-Maurice aux fonderies de Montréal"; and "Travelling the country 'round.'" See also Laurie and Schmitz, "Manufacture and Productivity," with its discussion of the persistence of craft traditions in Philadelphia's metal industries in the 19th century.

39 NA, manuscript census, 1871, schedule 6, "Industrial Establishments," City of Saint-Hyacinthe. Six butcher's shops, which were enumerated in 1871 but not included in the census tabulations, have been recuperated for this analysis. These entries are struck out in the schedule, but the information is legible.

40 The Yamaska had been dammed above the rapids in 1822 to increase the stream flow for the seigneurial mill. The dam also reduced the risk of flooding in the alluvial plain, thereby encouraging settlement. It is depicted in Figure 1-3, slightly upstream from the bridge at Bourdages Street. The industrial character of the waterfront area on the Saint-Hyacinthe side of this bridge is plain in Illustration 6, which is a photograph of this part of the town taken in 1874. On the dam, see Joseph Roy, "Notes sur la Cité de Saint-Hyacinthe," *Courrier de Saint-Hyacinthe*, 26 December 1903.

41 Choquette, *Histoire de la ville*, 306.

42 *Almanach-directoire de Saint-Hyacinthe pour l'année 1875*, 32–3. Translation: forges, foundries, a factory making boilers and engines, machine shops, workshops for sawing and bleaching wood, etc. ... In short, everything from the most common kitchen utensil to the most powerful and specialized engine is made there.

43 Victor Côté was not mentioned in the *Canada Directory* for Saint-Hyacinthe in 1851, but was listed in 1858 as a leather merchant.

44 Louis Côté is depicted Illustration 8. See also Gossage, "Louis Côté."

45 *Lovell's Canadian Dominion Directory for 1871*, 1430. This location, well inland from the town's sources of hydraulic power, strongly suggests that the Côtés were using steam engines to run their shoemaking machinery in 1871, despite the fact that no such engine was mentioned in the industrial census.

46 No adult women were listed as employees of the Côté shoe factory at this time.

47 This includes two cases where a single proprietor operated more than one establishment, with a total labour force of 10 or more.

48 Ferland, "L'évolution des rapports sociaux," 176

49 *Almanach-directoire de Saint-Hyacinthe*, 33. Translation: an impressive factory ...; they make mostly milling machinery, notably shingle mills superior to all others. The equipment is most extensive and they can undertake any type of machinery.

50 On Saint-Hyacinthe's not inconsequential intellectual role during this period, see Bernard, "Les fonctions intellectuelles de Saint-Hyacinthe." Lussier's *Courrier*, one of six papers published in the city at the beginning of the 1870s, had a strong liberal orientation. Interestingly, the publisher was related through marriage to one of the city's leading industrialists: Victor Côté. Côté married Philomène Kérouack, the daughter of a local teacher, in February of 1860. Four years later, Lussier married Philomène's sister Marie. Family Reconstitution Files A227 and B007.

51 *Almanach-directoire de Saint-Hyacinthe*, 32. Translation: any kind of vehicle, from the most common cart to the most elegant carriage or coach.

52 Parizeau, *Les Dessaulles, Seigneurs de Saint-Hyacinthe*, 77–82.

53 Dessaulles is a good example of an individual who used seigneurial advantages to further his own industrial development agenda. The connection between seigneurial and industrial capital in nineteenth-century Quebec is explored in Shulze, "Rural Manufacture in Lower Canada." Other studies that touch on this topic include Robert, "Un seigneur entrepreneur," and Noël, "Chambly Mills, 1774–1815."

54 *Almanach-directoire de Saint-Hyacinthe*, 52. Translation: in order to provide poor women with work when none was to be found elsewhere.

55 Dumont, "Des garderies au XIXe siècle."

56 Boucher de la Bruère, "St. Hyacinthe of Today," 3.

57 Shops with five workers or less were the overwhelming majority in all sectors of production except printing, where the two concerns in town had six and 17 hands, respectively. Small shops persisted even in sectors strongly affected by industrialization, such as boot and shoemaking,

where seven shops with an average of three workers each coexisted with the Côtés' fledgling factory.

58 Rudin, "The Development of Four Quebec Towns," appendix 1, 245. My analysis of the 1901 manuscript census schedules gives a comparable estimate for that year. In the municipality of Saint-Hyacinthe, there were 1,659 individuals who declared themselves to be employed in a factory for any portion of the year. This does not, of course, include the many workers who lived in neighbouring communities, such as Notre-Dame-de-Saint-Hyacinthe and Saint-Hyacinthe-le-Confesseur, but who worked in the city's factories.

59 Choquette, *Histoire de la ville*, 302.

60 Fernande Roy and Paul-André Linteau have described the economic liberalism characteristic of French-Canadian businessmen in Montreal during this period. Roy, *Progrès, harmonie, liberté*; Linteau, *The Promoters' City*. As Rudin has shown, this ideology was just as prevalent in Saint-Hyacinthe, where local elites took on the promotion of economic development as something of a sacred mission. See Rudin, "The Development of Four Quebec Towns," and especially Rudin, "Boosting the French-Canadian Town."

61 Rudin, "The Development of Four Quebec Towns," 54; Rudin, "Boosting the French-Canadian Town."

62 Choquette, *Histoire de la ville*, 311.

63 Lapointe, "La formation de la Banque de Saint-Hyacinthe," table 2.7, 69.

64 Ibid., and Rudin, "The Development of Four Quebec Towns," 108.

65 Choquette, *Histoire de la ville*, 303.

66 It had become an important establishment employing about 100 workers by the time of the 1891 census. NA, manuscript census, 1891, City of Saint-Hyacinthe, division 2, 55–6 (sv. Silas Duclos and Paul F. Payan). See Illustration 11 for an engraving that represents the buildings occupied by the Duclos-Payan tannery in 1886.

67 The company's assets were subsequently acquired by "La Compagnie de Chaussures de Saint-Hyacinthe," a group of local investors who managed to reopen the shoe factory, but were unable to keep it afloat past the end of the decade. Choquette tilts at their managerial skills and their political orientation, characterizing these unnamed business people as "un groupe de bleus." Choquette, *Histoire de la ville*, 305–6

68 Politically, Louis Côté was one of the loudest and most influential opponents of the municipal bonusing and tax exemption policies. Rudin, "The Development of Four Quebec Towns," 107–9

69 Hamelin and Roby, *Histoire économique du Québec*, 90–1.

70 Francoeur, "Esquisse de géographie urbaine," 28–39.

71 Choquette, *Histoire de la ville*, 329–36.

72 Choquette, *Histoire de la ville*, 346.

73 Total annual output increased from $1.2 million to $2.2 million between 1881 and 1891. Note also that the percentage increase in the 1870s had been even higher, as total output rose from $0.4 million to $1.2 million. Rudin, "The Development of Four Quebec Towns," appendix 1, 245.

74 Ibid. Workers in 1891 also seem to have been better paid than in 1881. The average weekly industrial wage rose from $3.45 at the beginning of the period to $5.38 by the end.

75 Boucher de la Bruère, "St. Hyacinthe of Today," 3.

76 Rudin, "The Development of Four Quebec Towns," 110.

77 Boucher de la Bruère, "St. Hyacinthe of Today," 3.

78 In 1882, A.S. Beauchemin, shirt manufacturer, received $1,000; in 1887, E.F. Mosely received $15,000 to start up a tannery, and M.J. Aird received $2,500 for his shoe factory. See Rudin, "The Development of Four Quebec Towns," 110, 275.

79 Ibid., 110.

80 *Guide de Saint-Hyacinthe par ordre alphabétique et par ordre des rues* (1887), 6. Translation:

At least twelve important establishments provide employment to more than 1500 employees of all ages and both sexes, and at advantageous rates. How interesting it is to watch these masses of industrial workers going to, or coming from, their respective factories at certain hours of the day. One must also take into account the less substantial, yet numerous, industries which provide employment to a good number of workers.

Our magnificent and sizeable water power ... provides the energy for at least twelve factories, while steam does the rest. That is to say that more than 25 [steam] engines operate daily, and often at night in order to keep up with all the orders.

81 Boucher de la Bruère, "St. Hyacinthe of Today," 3. Illustrations 11 and 13 are reproduced from this album.

82 Rudin, "The Development of Four Quebec Towns," 112.

83 Ibid., 111.

84 *Guide de Saint-Hyacinthe, par ordre alphabétique* (1894), 4.

85 Ibid., 4. Translation: Granite Mills has undertaken some major works at the water power, and is in the process of installing turbines which will provide one thousand horsepower. Large shops are being built and the business of this important establishment, which has taken over La Compagnie Manufacturière, will triple as soon as all the construction work is completed.

Note the reference to the takeover by Granite Mills of La Compagnie Manufacturière de Saint-Hyacinthe, which until then had run the town's woollens mill. This also seems to have taken place in 1894. See Choquette, *Histoire de la ville*, 350.

86 *Guide de Saint-Hyacinthe* (1894), 4. Translation: have built a huge establishment on Cascades Street, where they hope to double, if not triple, their business.

87 Rudin, "The Development of Four Quebec Towns," 111.

88 Ibid.

89 Ibid., 112.

90 Rudin, "The Development of Four Quebec Towns," 112.

91 Ibid., 114.

92 Ibid.

93 Ibid., 115.

94 See especially Bradbury, *Working Families*.

95 With this objective in mind, the following steps were taken. Manuscript census data on profession, age, sex, and marital status were collected on an anonymous basis for the four *quartiers* that made up the City of Saint-Hyacinthe in 1861. The institutional population – those living in convents, the *séminaire*, the *Hôtel-Dieu*, etc. – was ignored, although information concerning men and women living in boarding houses and hotels was retained. A similar approach was taken to the 1891 census. In this case, the institutional population *and* the population of *Quartier* 5 (which had been annexed in 1888) were excluded. This procedure allows one to compare the occupational structure of the non-institutional population of the original Saint-Hyacinthe territory (*Quartiers* 1 through 4) in 1861 and 1891. Note that age, sex, and marital status were only recorded for those individuals who declared an occupation; the rest were simply counted. NA, manuscript census, 1861 and 1891, City of Saint-Hyacinthe.

See the section entitled "Handling Occupational Titles" in the appendix for a full discussion of the occupational categories used in this table and in the rest of the book. To summarize, three categories of manual workers have been distinguished: 1) farmers; 2) people who worked in specific, urban, manual occupations; and 3) general labourers, who are treated separately for reasons that are explained in the appendix. All non-manual workers are grouped together into a fourth category. Applying the z test for independent proportions to Table 2-2 shows that the 1861–1891 differences in the proportions of workers in all three manual categories are statistically significant. The slight difference between the proportions of people in non-manual occupations at the two dates is not.

96 The number of women declaring employment rose from 119 to 483 during this period, or from 13% to 24% of the labour force. In the same

interval, the proportion of unmarried workers rose from 36% to 42% and the proportion under 25 years of age increased from 30% to 36%.

97 This figure is calculated by adding up the three manual categories: agriculture, urban-manual trades, and labourers. The z test yields the same result as for the previous table. The observed differences between the 1861 and 1891 proportions of men in all three manual categories are statistically significant. The difference in the two proportions for the non-manual category is not.

98 See especially Burgess, "L'industrie de la chaussure à Montréal."

99 Unlike tanning and boot-and-shoe production, the relative importance of saddlery in the local economy diminished in the later 19th century. Only seven men were employed in this sector in 1891, three less than in 1861.

100 It is worth noting that five of these declared a supervisory function (*contre-maître* or *surveillant*) in this mill where, as we shall see, female labour predominated.

101 Four in shoe production; two each in agricultural implements, soft drinks, doors and sashes, and leather goods; one each in musical instruments, books, and woollens; three not specified.

102 Recent research seems to support the former interpretation. Bradbury suggests that for Montreal's working-class women of this period, the transition to married life generally meant withdrawal from the formal labour market. Bradbury, "The Working-Class Family Economy," especially p. 316. See also her *Working Families*, 169–75. This suggestion has been confirmed for the 1930s in Baillargeon, *Ménagères au temps de la crise*. There is scattered Saint-Hyacinthe evidence for the older view, according to which married women's paid work was simply hidden. One obvious, if circumstantial, point concerns the Ouvroir Ste-Geneviève. The presence of an institution that provided daycare services seems to suggest that at least some married women must have been working outside the home. Joy Parr has demonstrated the importance of married women's labour in the knit-goods industry of Paris, Ontario, during a later period. See Parr, *The Gender of Breadwinners*. There were few married women working in the local knit-goods factory during the early 1890s. But whether Penmans used similar labour force policies in Saint-Hyacinthe after the mill was acquired in 1903 is unclear.

103 The z test shows that this difference in proportions was not statistically significant.

104 Kesteman, "Naissance et développement," 35–6.

105 Parr, "Disaggregating the Sexual Division of Labour"; *The Gender of Breadwinners*.

106 See especially her book, *The Gender of Breadwinners*, which contains an extended comparison between Paris and Hanover, Ontario, where

woodworking – an industry in which most workers were men – dominated the local economy.

107 Thompson, *The Making of the English Working Class*, 581–91.

108 Parr, "Disaggregating the Sexual Division of Labour," 514.

109 Ibid., 518.

110 Rudin, "The Development of Four Quebec Towns," 110.

111 Note that the importation of knitting technology, whether from Britain or the United States, was standard in the Canadian knitwear industry. In the interwar period, all knitting technology at Penmans' Paris operation was imported, except for one machine, in about equal parts from the United States and Great Britain. See Parr, "Disaggregating the Sexual Division of Labour," 525.

112 Ibid., 526.

113 Canada, *Rapport de la Commission royale*, 1422–1500.

114 This is only about one-third of the total workforce, estimated at 300 in this period. Why the discrepancy? In the first place, occupational declarations are not necessarily discriminatory. Individuals who declared themselves to be simply "factory workers" could not be included here, although a proportion of them certainly worked at the knit-goods mill. Another reason is that some proportion of the Granite Mills employees would have lived either in *Quartier* 5 or in one of the villages located across the Yamaska River. Neither of these areas was included when the 1891 census was examined. Note that all references to census information in the ensuing sections are from NA, manuscript census, 1891, City of Saint-Hyacinthe, microfilm reel T-6419.

115 Discussions with Joy Parr about knitting technologies in the late nineteenth century have been of great help here. She has my sincere thanks. Images of workers in the Saint-Hyacinthe knit-goods mill can be found in Illustrations 16, 17, and 18.

116 Canada, *Rapport de la Commission royale*, 1459.

117 Joy Parr, personal communication, 7 July 1998. This hypothesis might help account for the large number of women who identified themselves as *courturières* when they spoke to census takers in 1891. See Table 2-4, and the discussion surrounding it.

118 Note that, for the subsequent analysis, I have translated and standardized job titles.

119 Canada, *Rapport de la Commission royale*, 1441.

120 Ibid., 1450–1.

121 Parr, "Disaggregating the Sexual Division of Labour," 512.

122 Canada, *Rapport de la Commission royale*, 1458–9.

123 Ibid., 1459.

124 Canada, *Rapport de la Commission royale*, 1458; Parr, "Disaggregating the Sexual Division of Labour," 530.

125 Parr, "Disaggregating the Sexual Division of Labour," 528–9.

126 Canada, *Rapport de la Commission royale*, 1435–6. Translation: ... the work grew so poor that we could earn nothing. By poor work I mean cloth that is full of holes, and over which we are obliged to lose a great deal of time. Official translation from Canada, *Report of the Royal Commission*, 1277.

127 Ibid., 1454. Translation: I left the mill the last time on the 20th March, because they compelled us to go over the thin parts of the stockings, and we were not able to do that work for the price given us. Official translation from Canada, *Report of the Royal Commission*, 1294.

128 The man, Samuel Logowitz, gave his occupation to the Royal Commission as "overseer in the mending and finishing rooms, and shipping department." Canada, *Report of the Royal Commission*, 1325.

129 Canada, *Rapport de la Commission royale*, 1443. Translation: because they ordered us to go over the thin parts, and we left. Official translation from Canada, *Report of the Royal Commission*, 1284.

130 Canada, *Report of the Royal Commission*, vol. 4, 1300, 1307.

131 *Rapport de la commission royale*, 1472. Maurice Boas, on hearing this embarrassing testimony, left the chamber and Helbronner insisted that his departure be recorded for posterity. His brother Féodor, the next witness, insisted that he had been called away on business. But the damage, it seems, was done. Translation:

Q. – As neither Mr Boas nor the Commissioners fully understand the work, please explain to this Commission what the difficulty really is?
A. – The difficulty was that they wanted us to go over the narrowing of the heels and toes of the stockings when there were no dropped stitches. When the stitches were dropped we could easily go over them as usual, but they wished us to go over these narrowings for the same price we earned before, [and] we refused and left the factory.
Q. – Then if I understand rightly, the work you were engaged to do and for which you were paid was to go over the dropped stitches?
A. – Yes; to go over the holes.
Q. – And the work they tried to make you do, was to go over the holes, and the thin places besides?
A. – Yes; what we call the narrowings.

Official translation from Canada, *Report of the Royal Commission*, 1398.

132 Canada, *Rapport de la Commission royale*, 1445.

133 Ibid., 1447–9.

134 The men in the mill were older and more likely to be married. The 1891 census search uncovered 22 male knitwear workers, half of whom were married; they were aged 25 years on average.

135 Canada, *Report of the Royal Commission*, 1300.

136 Ibid., 1300–1.

137 Burgess' MA research, summarized in an important 1977 article, is the most helpful in understanding the labour process of this period. See Burgess, "L'industrie de la chaussure à Montréal." Her doctoral dissertation also deals with shoemakers and other leather workers, but for an earlier period. See Burgess, "Work, Family and Community." On the structure of the Canadian shoe industry and labour organization, Jacques Ferland's work is also very useful; see his "Evolution des rapports sociaux," and "Syndicalisme 'parcellaire' et syndicalisme 'collectif.'"

138 Burgess, "L'industrie de la chaussure à Montréal."

139 Ibid., 199–200.

140 Ibid., 203.

141 Ibid., 204.

142 Ibid., 206–7.

143 See, for example, a "Machine for Forming Boot and Shoe Stiffeners" patented on 20 January 1874, Canadian Intellectual Property Office, Canadian patent number 3026. Côté's inventions are further discussed in Gossage, "Louis Côté," and in Jacques Ferland's dissertation on the Canadian leather industry. Ferland suggests that Côté patented more inventions or modifications involving shoemaking machinery than any other Canadian of his era. See Ferland, "Evolution des rapports sociaux," 176.

144 My emphasis. Canadian Intellectual Property Office, Canadian patent number 402.

145 Burgess, "L'industrie de la chaussure," 208.

146 Harvey, *Révolution industrielle et travailleurs*, 43.

147 There were 128 single boys and men (including 66 under 18 years of age), 146 married men, and 7 widowers in the shoe factories in 1891.

148 Canada, *Rapport de la Commission royale*, 1494.

149 Linteau et al., *Quebec: A History*, 185.

150 Canada, *Rapport de la Commission royale*, 1494. Unofficial translation: "I couldn't say, because I work for Papa."

151 Burgess, "L'industrie de la chaussure," 205.

152 In all, 101 shoe workers declared the occupation *cordonnier* in 1891; all but one of them were men. Another 14 boys and young men were described as *apprenti cordonnier*.

153 Burgess, "L'industrie de la chaussure," 204–5.

154 Note that of the many "leather cutters" (*tailleurs de cuir*) listed in the 1891 census, only those who specifically mentioned that they worked in a shoe factory were retained for this analysis. A good number would also have been employed in the local tanneries.

155 Canada, *Rapport de la Commission royale*, 1494. Unofficial translation:

Q. – Do they use an apprenticeship system, do they take on apprentices?
A. – They take on a great number of apprentices, but not by contract.
Q. – Do they undertake to teach the apprentices their trade completely?
A. – Not that I know of, sir.

156 Ibid., 1495. Unofficial translation: "It's because I'm a member of a labour association ... They told me so."
157 Burgess, "L'industrie de la chaussure," 205.
158 Ibid., 205.
159 Ibid., 206–7.
160 Canada, *Rapport de la Commission royale*, 1480.
161 Ferland, "Syndicalisme 'parcellaire' et syndicalisme 'collectif'," 86–7.
162 This argument has been made convincingly for England in Samuel, "The Workshop of the World." For the United States, see Laurie and Schmitz, "Manufacture and Productivity."
163 See Illustration 20, which conveys something of the industrial landscape of the town in the early years of the twentieth century.

CHAPTER THREE

1 Sections of this chapter, in a more preliminary form, were published as Gossage "Family Formation and Age at Marriage."
2 For present purposes, I accept John Hajnal's definition of heterosexual marriage as "entry into a union which is regarded as appropriate for the bearing and rearing of children in the society in question." In many societies, including our own, this would include consensual unions, or "common-law" marriages, which are extremely hard to trace in historical records. In nineteenth-century Quebec, most reproduction occurred within legally and religiously sanctioned unions, so that ignoring consensual unions, as I shall in this book, produces very little distortion. Hajnal, "European Marriage Patterns," 105. See also Laslett, "Characteristics of the Western Family"; Ankarloo, "Marriage and Family Formation"; Gillis, *For Better, For Worse*, Ward, *Courtship, Love and Marriage*.
    Incidentally, the level of non-marital fertility in Saint-Hyacinthe was very low in this period. The number of "illegitimate" children baptized at the cathedral declined from 2.2% in the 1860s to 0.7% in the 1870s and remained at approximately the latter level for the remainder of the nineteenth century. If the parish had begun "exporting" its unwanted infants by the decade of the 1870s, such an unexpected drop would be understandable. The presence in Montreal of a large foundling hospital with a wide geographic influence makes this a distinct possibility. See Gossage, "Abandoned Children in Nineteenth-Century Montreal," and "Les enfants abandonnés à Montréal au 19e siècle."

3 See the introduction and the essay on methods in the appendix for discussions of the marriage-cohorts method. Note that the three cohorts will generally be referred to as Cohort A (1854–61), Cohort B (1864–71), and Cohort C (1884–91).

4 72% in Cohort A (213/295); 82% in Cohort B (226/277); 92% in Cohort C (331/340).

5 For more details on this operation, see the section entitled "Handling Occupational Titles" in the appendix.

6 The proportion for the three cohorts combined was 24.4% (202/828). All percentages, in the text as in the table, are calculated on the basis of those cases where occupations are known and have been successfully classified. A Chi^2 test conducted on Table 3-1 shows statistically significant differences in the cohort distributions among the four broad occupational categories. Chi^2 = 27.178, d.f. = 6, p ≤ 0.05.

7 Family Reconstitution File A046.

8 See the discussion of the territorial limits of the parish in chapter 1, and especially Figure 1-4.

9 Family Reconstitution File B098. In fact, they would have married at the pro-cathedral, pictured in Illustration 21.

10 By 1891, manual workers in urban trades accounted for 62% of the male labour force in Saint-Hyacinthe, up from 51% thirty years earlier. See chapter 2, Tables 2-2 and 2-3. Note the dramatic increases in the proportion of leather workers, from 7% to 19% in the marriage cohorts and from 6% to 28% in the local male labour force.

11 General labourers are treated separately throughout this book because of the difficulty of assigning them with any confidence to either the agricultural or the urban-manual categories. See "Handling Occupational Titles" in the appendix for a fuller explanation of the logic that guided this choice.

12 Family Reconstitution File C189.

13 If we exclude farmers from the denominators on this basis, the proportion of husbands in non-manual occupations then becomes 20% in Cohort A, 33% in Cohort B, and 26% in Cohort C. Since the proportion of non-manual workers in the employed male population was steady at about 27% across this period, the conclusion is clear: non-manual occupations are slightly under-represented in the first cohort, slightly overrepresented in the second, and proportionately represented in the third. See the discussion in this chapter of the geographic origins of husbands marrying in Saint-Hyacinthe; it shows that many of the farmers in the three cohorts did, in fact, live outside the parish.

14 Family Reconstitution Files A227, B178, B090, and B255.

15 Family Reconstitution Files C268, A006, and B136.

16 Family Reconstitution Files B179, B183, and C172. In all, six teachers

(*institutrice*), one seamstress (*couturière*), one dressmaker (*modiste*), and one woman who was described as a *vagabonde* were identified by occupation in the marriage acts.

17 In a study of this kind, given the dearth of direct information on women's employment, a compromise – analyzing their marital and reproductive activity in terms of men's occupations, whether husbands' or fathers' – becomes necessary. See the discussion of this problem in the appendix.

18 The Chi² test, applied to the four broad occupational categories in Table 3-2, shows that the differences in the occupational distributions among the three cohorts are statistically significant. $Chi^2 = 22.60$, d.f. = 6, $p \leq 0.05$.

19 To be clear, marriages have been defined as endogamous when a man in a certain occupational group married a woman whose father declared an occupation that was classified the same way. Most of the endogamy identified in this way was *social*, in that it occurred within broadly defined socio-economic groups, rather than within specific occupations. But since the category "agriculture" was virtually coterminous with the occupation "farmer," and since all members of the category "labourers" made identical professional declarations, we can speak of *occupational* endogamy in these two cases.

20 Collective behaviour is defined as endogamous when more individuals choose spouses within their group than the distribution of such potential spouses in the population would have predicted. Had farmers exhibited no endogamy, 40% or less would have married the daughters of other farmers.

21 On the relationship between demography and class formation in Europe, see Tilly, "Demographic Origins of the European Proletariat."

22 Of the 893 couples in the three cohorts for whom these data are available, both parties were residents of the parish in 498 cases (56%), the wife only was a resident in 259 cases (29%), and the husband only in 21 cases (2%). In a surprisingly high number of cases – 115, or 13% – neither party was a resident of the parish of Saint-Hyacinthe. Perhaps the central location of the parish and its role as episcopal see for the diocese had something to do with this.

23 These proportions are 28% for Cohort A, 27% for Cohort B, and 31% for Cohort C. The percentages were calculated as follows: unions where the wife was from the parish and the husband was from elsewhere (79 for Cohort A, 75 for Cohort B, and 105 for Cohort C) were divided by the total number of unions where both residences were known (279 for Cohort A, 275 for Cohort B, and 339 for Cohort C).

24 This common practice had important implications for the fertility analysis reported in chapter 5. It is evaluated in the section of the appendix entitled "Focusing on Fertility."

25 More detailed, cohort-by-cohort analysis has been conducted; the results, however, are not included in this figure.

26 As already suggested, the single-parish method does not permit a parallel analysis of the parishes in which Saint-Hyacinthe men sought brides. The existence of this countervailing movement, however, is assumed and is essential to the notion of matrimonial *exchange* among parishes, counties, and regions.

27 Twenty-four dispensations for consanguinity were granted to couples in the three cohorts, most of them involving the second to fourth degrees. In the francophone parishes of the archdiocese of Montreal between 1911 and 1918, there were 56 consanguineous marriages (requiring dispensations) for every thousand unions. This level is slightly higher than that found in Saint-Hyacinthe in the period 1884–91 (53 per thousand), and much higher than the levels found in the previous two cohorts. See Fournier, "Consanguinité et sociabilité." There were also 11 dispensations granted to offset prohibitions against affine marriages in Saint-Hyacinthe; at least three of these – and perhaps more – involved widows or widowers who married siblings of their former spouses. See also Gagnon, *Mariage et famille*, in which records of this kind of dispensation support much of the analysis.

28 Family Reconstitution Files B153, C036. I have already mentioned a parallel case, where a man married his brother's widow; it involved Marcellin Dion and Octavie Harnois, who married at the cathedral on 21 May 1888 (C189). A woman might also marry her sister's widower, as in May 1887 when Malvina Duchesneau married Joseph Bourbonnière, a farmer who had previously been the husband of her sister Cédulie (C140).

29 Of a total of 35 dispensations identified for the three cohorts, 27 occurred in the period 1884–91.

30 Fournier claims that high levels of consanguineous marriages in the archdiocese of Montreal were the result of a high degree of "sociabilité" within the French-Canadian population. He also shows how the rural parts of the archdiocese had levels of consanguinity that were over three times the level for the francophone population of the city. Fournier, "Consanguinité et sociabilité."

31 Such a discovery is mentioned in only one of 10 rehabilitations identified here. Six involve unions that had been initiated in the United States some time before, and a seventh makes reference to a 19-month-old American-born child. Perhaps certain French Canadians in the 1850s, finding themselves in areas of the United States where they had no access to Catholic clergy, decided to marry in a Protestant or civil ceremony (or simply to live as husband and wife) and to wait until they returned to Quebec to formalize their unions according to Catholic rites. Two of the "rehabilitated" marriages involved the recognition (*reconnaissance*) of children born prior to the ceremony, while a third

was celebrated four days after the couple in question had buried a daughter. Such events are to be expected among couples whose Catholic weddings simply formalized existing conjugal relationships. Across the three cohorts, only four other couples either recognized children in their marriage acts or buried children prior to the ceremony. All couples in rehabilitated unions have been ignored in our discussion of marriage ages and fertility, since their marriage dates – in demographic terms – are false.

32 The proportion of remarriages in the total seems rather high. At Notre-Dame-de-Montreal, 82% to 83% of all marriages in the two cohorts 1823–26 and 1842–45 were between two single people; 10% to 11% involved a widower and a single woman, about 5% a widow and a single man, and only 3% involved a widow and a widower. See Bradbury et al., "Property and Marriage."

33 Ratios of widowers to widows in the marriage cohorts are as follows: Cohort A – 2.6:1, Cohort B – 1.8:1, Cohort C – 1.8:1.

34 See, for example, Bradbury, "Surviving as a Widow"; Gauvreau and Bourque, "'Jusqu'à ce que la mort nous sépare.'"

35 I did not find Léopoldine's burial certificate. But she had given birth to a second daughter in early November of 1868. Mother and daughter had both died by the time the next census was taken, in the spring of 1871. Family Reconstitution Files B090 and B255.

36 For a summary of the literature as it concerns Quebec, see Greer, "L'alphabétisation et son histoire." An alternative method of measuring literacy, which requires family reconstitution, is proposed in Bouchard and Larouche, "Nouvelle mesure d'alphabétisation." The data needed to calculate the rate suggested by Bouchard and Larouche – i.e., information on signatures from all the civil acts in a family-reconstitution file and not just marriage acts – were not collected for the present study.

37 The focus on previously unmarried spouses is designed to avoid the possibility of counting the same individual twice. The technique also ensures that the signatures collected are for individuals of the same generation.

38 Greer, "L'alphabétisation et son histoire," and "The Pattern of Literacy in Quebec."

39 Interesting in its own right, this analysis of social differentials in literacy also seems to provide evidence of the coherence of the occupational groupings adopted in this study. See the discussion of this point in the appendix under the heading "Handling Occupational Titles."

40 Monday and Tuesday weddings occurred in almost exactly the same proportions as in the parish of Sainte-Brigide in Montreal between 1905 and 1914 (48.2% on Mondays and 34.3% on Tuesdays). Ferretti, "Mariage et cadre de vie familiale," 248.

41 The proportion of Saturday weddings in Sainte-Brigide between 1905 and 1914, at 8%, was slightly higher. Ibid.

42 Bardet, *Rouen aux XVIIe et XVIIIe siècles*, 1:310.

43 Figures for months of less than 31 days have been adjusted to ensure comparability. Note again that Cohort-C weddings constitute a 75% systematic sample of all those occurring in the period 1884–91. The distribution in the sample should nonetheless approximate that of all weddings in the period very closely.

44 Ferretti contends that in Sainte-Brigide, "Les mariages des femmes enceintes sont les seuls pour lesquels on passe outre la prohibition du Carême et de l'Avent." [Translation: Marriages involving pregnant women were the only ones for which the Lent and Advent prohibitions were lifted.] Ferretti, "Mariage et cadre de vie familiale," 248. In Saint-Hyacinthe, other exceptions seem to have been made. About 6% of all weddings took place in March or December. Yet as my fertility analysis shows, the level of prenuptial conceptions was much lower, occurring in about 3% of all marriages. See the brief discussion of this in the appendix, note 53.

45 January and February weddings declined in importance for farmers just as they did for members of other occupational groups: from 31% in the 1860s to 22% in the 1880s. April and May weddings involving farmers increased, from 10% to 25% of the annual number during the same period.

46 See Little, *Crofters and Habitants*, 150–1, where such a pattern is identified for Winslow Township in the Upper St. Francis region of the Eastern Townships.

47 Hajnal, "European Marriage Patterns," 102.

48 Franklin Mendels first formulated the relationship between proto-industry, marriage age, and demographic growth. See Mendels, "The First Phase of the Industrialization Process." Many others have since published evidence that supports his view. See for example, Levine, *Family Formation*, and Braun, "Early Industrialization and Demographic Change." There is also evidence to support the opposing view: that proto-industry had no effect on marriage age and that the mainspring of European demographic growth in the early modern period must be sought elsewhere. See Spagnoli, "Industrialization, Proletarianization and Marriage"; Vandenbrooke, "Le cas flamand"; Gutmann, "Protoindustrialization and Marriage Ages." Wrigley and Schofield, in their monumental synthesis of English demographic history, show that a major fall in mean marriage ages indeed occurred in that country between the late seventeenth and the early nineteenth centuries. They attribute the demographic expansion of that period to this trend, although they do not see earlier marriage as a function of proto-

industry, explaining it instead in terms of increases in real wages. Wrigley and Schofield, *The Population History of England*, chapter 7.

49 Tilly and Scott, *Women, Work, and Family*, 24.

50 Recent studies in this area have built upon an understanding of the "European Marriage Pattern" first outlined by John Hajnal in 1965. For most of the modern period, Western European populations were characterized by a unique marriage pattern that featured relatively high marriage ages (above 23 years for women) and similarly high rates of permanent celibacy (10% to 20% for women). See Hajnal, "European Marriage Patterns," 108. Part of the explanation of this pattern is to be found in the linkage between economic autonomy and matrimony. Family formation was not possible until a couple had accumulated sufficient capital to set up an independent household. Later marriage in pre-industrial communities, then, indicates a relatively restricted number of economic *niches* in such communities. And earlier marriage in the nascent capitalist era suggests a multiplication of economic opportunities, even if those opportunities were in waged labour rather than in landholding or craft production. See especially Levine, *Family Formation*. The link from economic opportunities to marriage is well explained, again, by Tilly and Scott:

Marriage was, among other things, an economic arrangement, the establishment of a family economy. It required that couples have some means of supporting themselves and, eventually, their children. For peasant children this meant the availability of land; for artisans, the mastery of a skill and the acquisition of tools and perhaps a workshop. Wives must have a dowry or a means of contributing to the household. Among families with property these resources most often were passed on from generation to generation.

Tilly and Scott, *Women, Work, and Family*, 24. For similar arguments in the context of nineteenth-century Quebec, see Burgess, "Work, Family, and Community," and Gossage, "Family Formation and Age at Marriage."

51 Pouyez and Lavoie, *Les Saguenayens*, table 6.7, 261.

52 Because my readings of the manuscript census had other objectives – first, the matching of census households to marriage acts and, second, the description of the formal labour force in 1861 and 1891 – the information needed to calculate city- or parish-level age and sex ratios was not collected.

53 This measure, designed by Ansley Coale, is known as "I^m."

54 Lower nuptiality rates for Montreal women were a reflection of the unbalanced sex structure of the city, in which women – especially young, unmarried women – were overrepresented. See Cross, "The Neglected Majority."

55 I thank Marvin McInnis for giving me access to his figures for 1851. See also McInnis, "The Geographic Pattern of Fertility Decline in Canada." My own analysis of the published census data is somewhat different. I estimated the proportion of ever-married women *and* men in the 15 to 49 age category from the 1861 and 1891 census reports. This was possible for the city and county of Saint-Hyacinthe in 1861, but only for the county in 1891. County-level figures showed that female marriage ratios had increased marginally during this interval: from 53.4% in 1861 to 54.6% in 1891. The trend was replicated in the data for men: ratios increased from 52.5% to 54.9% during this same interval. In 1861, nuptiality levels were 6% to 7% lower in the town of Saint-Hyacinthe than in the surrounding region, for both men and women. This must have been due, at least in part, to the presence in the city of a number of religious institutions whose celibate personnel would have inflated the proportions of never-married persons in these age groups. Although economic factors may have been at work as well, without comparable figures for a later date these are very difficult, indeed, to evaluate. Note, finally, that men were under-represented in the 15 to 49 age group in both city and county. In 1861, femininity ratios (women per 100 men) were 109 in the county and 115 in the city. For Saint-Hyacinthe county in 1891, the figure was 111. On the influence of much stronger gender imbalances for female nuptiality in nineteenth-century Montreal, see Cross, "The Neglected Majority."

56 See the section entitled "Using Declared Ages," p. 193–6.

57 Note that there are some 59 marriage partners for whom manipulation of age declarations was unnecessary, because I already had access to precise birthdates. In all, it was possible to generate marriage ages for 512 of the 912 husbands and 533 of the 912 wives in the three cohorts. Three-fifths (59.7%) of these ages constitute what are referred to in the tables and in the text as "best values." This is to say that they are based either on known birthdates (5.6%) or on two or more census or burial declarations that match to within a range of two years (54.1%). Fuller explanations of these distinctions are given in the appendix.

58 See Gossage, "Family Formation and Age at Marriage," and "Family and Population in a Manufacturing Town," 155–80.

59 Such an analysis was nonetheless carried out for the widows and widowers in the three Saint-Hyacinthe cohorts. It showed that the average age at remarriage for Saint-Hyacinthe widowers was between 44 and 50 years; for widows, it was remarkably consistent at 45 years. But the existence of the "average" widow or widower is called into question by the high standard deviations in these distributions (generally in the order of 12 to 14 years).

60 The singulate mean is a measure of the average age at first marriage that

can be calculated on the basis of aggregate census data. Since it is based on an uncritical use of census age declarations, it can be considered a somewhat less reliable measure than the cohort means and medians used in this chapter. But there is no reason to suppose that it would systematically produce inflated values. See Hajnal, "Age at Marriage and Proportion Marrying."

61 They also married one to two years earlier than the Canadian-born men in a multi-denominational collection of parishes in mid 19th century Ontario. See Ward, *Courtship, Love, and Marriage*, appendix A-1, p. 179.

62 Historians and demographers have had a great deal of difficulty explaining the enigma of increasing marriage ages in later nineteenth-century Canada. Ellen Thomas-Gee calculates a three-year increase in the average age at first marriage for both men and women between 1851 and 1891. The average for men increased from 26 to 29, for women from 23 to 26. Thomas-Gee, "Marriage in Nineteenth-Century Canada," table 1, 315. Though the trend has stimulated a good deal of discussion, no satisfactory explanation has emerged as yet. For Quebec figures, see Henripin and Péron, "La transition démographique de la Province de Québec"; Pouyez et al., *Les Saguenayens*, table 6.10, 270. For a review of the literature concerning English Canada, see Ward, *Courtship, Love, and Marriage*, 54–5.

63 Note that the median values in virtually every category are slightly lower than the means, indicating that the latter measures have generally been influenced upward by a small number of substantially older men who were marrying for the first time. Yet the fact that the median values show the same pattern of socially differentiated age at marriage in the 1860s and 1880s demonstrates that these statistical "outliers" are not the source of the observed trend.

64 Family Reconstitution File B069.

65 Following a Malthusian logic, it would be understandable if the same kinds of forces that led to the *exode rurale* in the St. Lawrence valley also created incentives to delay marriage. That the Saint-Hyacinthe region was not exempt from these constraints in the later nineteenth century is well established. Indeed, few rural parishes in the region were able to retain their natural increase during the period; emigration to the United States, moreover, was common. On the rural exodus in a parish close to Saint-Hyacinthe, see Maisonneuve, "Structure familiale et exode rural."

66 Family Reconstitution Files C245, C289, and C253.

67 Family Reconstitution Files A077, A098, A162, and A246.

68 Family Reconstitution Files C098 and C128.

69 Family Reconstitution Files B090, C148, B065, and C110.

70 The median ages, once again, are consistently a fraction lower than the means.

71 Hajnal, "European Marriage Patterns," 108.

72 According to Ward's figures, Canadian-born women in Ontario experienced a sharper rise in marriage age during this period, starting from a lower initial level in the 1850s. Ward, *Courtship, Love, and Marriage,* appendix A-1, 179.

73 Family Reconstitution File B179.

74 Family Reconstitution File B198. The other eight are as follows: B039, B117, B138, B165, B191, B217, B227, and B276.

75 Family Reconstitution File B209.

76 Family Reconstitution File B075.

77 Family Reconstitution Files C110 and C298.

78 This was the case in mid nineteenth-century Buffalo, New York, for example. See Glasco, "Migration and Adjustment."

79 Note that these are not the same nine women for whom occupational information was provided in the marriage acts. Information on age at marriage was available for only four of those women. In the other five instances, I was able to situate the women in their parents' households prior to marriage. The occupational information in these cases, then, comes from the census. Four of the wives were from the 1860s cohort: three of these were teachers (*institutrices*) prior to their weddings and one was a seamstress (*couturière*). The remaining five all married in the 1884–91 cohort. Four were seamstresses and one worked in a tannery.

80 This may well have meant that they were all industrial outworkers, involved in either the clothing trade or, perhaps, doing finishing operations in the knit-goods industry. See above, chapter 2. The Tremblay story is reconstructed from Family Reconstitution File A077.

81 Family Reconstitution Files C019, C208, and C326.

82 Louise Tilly, studying the cotton-textile town of Roubaix, France, during the period 1872–1906, puts the relationship in these terms: "There was a tension between generational interests in families. Parents wished to keep their children in the household as wage earners, which tended to push marriage age up." Tilly, "The Family Wage Economy of a French Textile City," 386.

83 Some of the effects of parental death and disability on Montreal households in the nineteenth century are discussed in Bradbury, "The Fragmented Family." See also her *Working Families,* 182–213.

84 Laslett considers a relatively narrow age differential, with women marrying men younger than themselves fairly frequently, to be a component of the traditional Western marriage pattern, which he characterizes as "companionate." Laslett, "Characteristics of the Western Family." Bardet provides some very interesting data for Rouen. He demonstrates that bourgeois men were older in general at their first marriage than men from the popular classes, but that the women they married tended to be

younger than the women who married manual workers. The age gaps in the bourgeois group, then, tended to be wide: "Les notables choisissent des jeunesses; les ouvriers s'unissent à leurs contemporains." [Translation: Prominent men chose young girls; workers married their peers.] Bardet, *Rouen aux XVIIe et XVIIIe siècles*, 256.

85 Only those couples where both parties were marrying for the first time, where age information is available for both parties, and where the husband's occupation is known can be included.

86 This observation is based on a reading of several hundred marriage contracts written in Montreal in the 1840s. This research, conducted by the Montreal History Group, was published as Bradbury et al., "Property and Marriage."

87 See especially Burgess, "Work, Family, and Community."

CHAPTER FOUR

1 Family Reconstitution File A186.

2 Family Reconstitution File B178. This household has been described in the diary of Henriette Dessaulles, published in two French editions and one English translation. See Dessaulles, *Fadette, Journal d'Henriette Dessaulles*; Major, ed., *Journal / Henriette Dessaulles*; Dessaulles, *Hopes and Dreams*. See Adams and Gossage, "Chez Fadette," for a discussion of familial and spatial dynamics in the Dessaulles household, and particularly the tense relationship between the young diarist and her stepmother.

3 Family Reconstitution File C287.

4 The path-breaking study in this area was Laslett and Wall, eds., *Household and Family in Past Time*.

5 The most important article is Berkner, "The Stem Family and the Developmental Cycle." See also Berkner and Mendels, "Inheritance Systems, Family Structure and Demographic Patterns," and Fauve-Chamoux, "Les structures familiales au royaume des familles-souches." In Preston, Lancashire, in 1851, "most people who were not solo servants lived with their current nuclear family only." At the same time, however, "a very considerable proportion of couples probably lived in a 'stem' family at some stage in the life cycle." Anderson, *Family Structure*, 43 and n.3, 204.

6 Anderson, *Family Structure*; Modell and Hareven, "Urbanization and the Malleable Household."

7 Perhaps the most telling figure in Chudacoff's paper on Providence is the 41% of newlywed couples who lived in complex households of all kinds, compared to only 13% of the general population. Chudacoff, "Newlyweds and Family Extension," 198–9 (the citation is on p. 198). See Chudacoff, "New Branches on the Family Tree," for a similar study of Worcester, Massachusetts.

8 Chudacoff, "New Branches on the Family Tree," 203.

9 Anderson, *Family Structure*, 96. Chudacoff, "Newlyweds and Family Extension," 188–96.

10 Cohort A couples were traced to the 1861 census, Cohort B couples to the 1871 census, and Cohort C couples to the 1891 census. Because of the way the marriage cohorts were set up, the interval between marriage act and census enumeration varied from several days to over seven years. A small minority of the marriages occurred *after* the relevant census date; they were therefore eliminated from this part of the analysis.

11 Four couples – two in 1861, one in 1871, and one in 1891 – were left out of this account because they could each be clearly linked to *two* separate entries in the census. Rather than arbitrarily assigning these couples to one household or the other, these cases were simply omitted from the quantitative analysis. Furthermore, there were 12 couples in which one spouse or the other had died between the marriage and the census, and three in which the husband was declared "absent" at the time of the enumeration (see Table 4-1). These couples are included in the present profile, but omitted in the ensuing discussions of household structure and residential proximity.

12 The rates were as follows: 112 of the 295 couples in Cohort A (38%), 116 of the 277 in Cohort B (42%), and 158 of the 340 in Cohort C (46%).

13 Over 80% of the husbands linked to the census had been residents of the parish (317 of 386), compared to only 60% of all husbands in the three cohorts (519 of 912). See chapter 3, Table 3-4.

14 Family Reconstitution File A046.

15 Among the husbands in the three cohorts, 24% of all those with known occupations were farmers (202/838). See chapter 3, Table 3-1. Figures for the working male population of the town of Saint-Hyacinthe in 1861 and 1891 are discussed in chapter 2, Table 2-3. As shown in chapter 3, relative to their importance in the population of the town of Saint-Hyacinthe, farmers were overrepresented among men who married at the cathedral. Two reasons account for this: first, the predominance of farmers in the municipality of Saint-Hyacinthe-le-Confesseur; and second, the large proportion of farmers among husbands whose residences were outside the parish. Focusing, as I do in this chapter, on couples who not only married in Saint-Hyacinthe but subsequently settled in the area redresses this imbalance to some extent.

16 Whether they declared a specific trade or referred to themselves as labourers, 57% of husbands in Cohort A for whom this data is available, 49% of those in Cohort B, and 60% of those in Cohort C were manual workers of one kind or another, excluding farmers. On the male occupational structure of the town, see chapter 2, Table 2-3.

17 The following proportions of husbands traced to the census were in

non-manual occupations: 14% in 1861, 27% in 1871, and 21% in 1891.
This compares to 14%, 24%, and 21% of all husbands in Cohorts A, B,
and C, respectively, for whom this information is available. The distribution of the linked couples by civil status was also entirely comparable to
the general distribution in the three cohorts. Approximately three-
quarters (280/369) of the linked couples still intact at the time of the
first subsequent census and for which this information was available
involved two previously unmarried individuals. Thirteen percent
involved a widower and a single woman, 2% a widow and a single man,
and 9% two previously married individuals. The analogous proportions
in the three cohorts were 71% (single-single), 15% (widower-single),
3% (widow-single), and 10% (widow-widower). See chapter 3, Table 3-6.

18 The notion of a conjugal family is equivalent to Laslett's concept of a
"conjugal family unit," the identification of which is essential to the
process of household classification. In Laslett's terms, "The concept is of
the conjugal link as the structural principle, and conjugal linkage is
nearly always patent in the lists we are using. For a simple family to
appear then, it is necessary for at least two individuals connected by that
link or arising from that link to be co-resident: *conjugal family unit* (CFU)
is a preciser term employed to describe all possible groups so struc-
tured." Laslett and Wall, eds., *Household and Family in Past Time*, 29
(emphasis in the original). In the most straightforward case, a conjugal
family consists of a husband, a wife, and their children. Widowhood and
remarriage, however, can intervene to alter this reality. The death of
one spouse might truncate a conjugal family, which would then consist
of the surviving spouse and any children born to the union. Remarriages
can create stepfamilies, composed of husband, wife, their children, and
any children from former unions. Conjugal family units are necessary
building blocks for any analysis of household structure based on census
lists. Note that a detailed discussion of the composition of conjugal
families is possible mainly because of the links made in the present study
between the census lists and the parish registers.

19 The average interval between marriage and enumeration was 46 months
in Cohort A, 40 months in Cohort B, and 42 months in Cohort C.

20 Family Reconstitution File B090. Mercier was living in Notre-Dame-de-
Saint-Hyacinthe with his daughter, Éliza, and two of his late wife's relatives, Edmond and Marie-Julie Boivin, both unmarried and both in their
thirties. He had been a widower for at most three years and would
remarry shortly after the census was taken, in May of 1871.

21 Note that the 1861 census was taken in January, when those men who
engaged in logging would have been away in the bush. These cases have
been included with the "ruptured" unions in Table 4-1, though the term
may be too strong to reflect the cause of the husbands' absence.

22 The breakdown of the 54 stepfamilies is as follows. In addition to the recently married couple, seven contained the wife's children from her former union; three contained her children *and* those of the present couple; 26 contained the husband's children from a previous marriage; 16 contained his children *and* their common offspring; and two families consisted of the married couple and children from the former marriages of *both* parties, but no common children.

23 This is to say nothing of the three servants and four guests who also lived on the premises, unquestionably an inn. Family Reconstitution File A011.

24 See Gossage, "*La marâtre*," Gossage, "Tangled Webs," and Adams and Gossage, "Chez Fadette," for discussions of the familial roles and social perceptions of stepmothers in nineteenth- and twentieth-century Quebec.

25 Some readers may at this point wish to consult the section entitled "Houses, Families, and Households" in the appendix. It contains a discussion of the methodology used in the rest of this chapter, including an explanation of, first, the principles used to establish household boundaries on the basis of census lists and, second, the classification scheme used to group recently married couples by household type.

26 The 28 couples who did not head their own households are those in categories 3 and 4 of Table 4-2. See the appendix for a full discussion of the categories employed in this analysis.

27 Overall, 95% of the linked, intact couples in Cohort A, 96% of those in Cohort B, and 88% of those in Cohort C had established their own, autonomous households by the date of the first census following their wedding.

28 Table 4-2, category 3.

29 Family Reconstitution File c254.

30 There is, however, the hint of a trend. While the husband's kin provided the shelter in seven of the nine cases found in 1861 and 1871 (two cohorts together), the couple lived with the wife's family in 12 of the 15 cases located in 1891.

31 Table 4-2, category 4.

32 This figure is obtained by adding the numbers in categories 3 and 4 for Cohort C.

33 Canada, *Rapport de la Commission royale*, 1451.

34 Mean number of children already born per couple: 0.4.

35 Mean number of children already born per couple: 0.7.

36 Although the proportion increased dramatically between 1861 and 1871, caution must be used in interpreting this differential; in effect, the differences may simply reflect the ways in which the two censuses were carried out. My reading of the 1861 census, however, would tend

to *exaggerate* the number of simple households in that year, since each
distinct conjugal family encountered in a given house was treated as a
separate household. Logically, then, the figure of 59% for simple families in 1861 should be regarded as a maximum. Note also that, when
applied to the three broad groups identified in Table 4-2 under the
heading "subtotals," the Chi² test reveals that the observed relationship
between cohort and household structure is statistically significant. Chi² =
29.545, d.f. = 4, p ≤ 0.05.

37 Lalonde, "Le Village de Saint-Jean-Baptiste," table 3.4, 83; Lauzon,
Habitat ouvrier et révolution industrielle, 104. Note that Lauzon and Lalonde both studied all the households in these respective communities,
while I have concentrated on recently married couples. If newlyweds are
more likely than established couples to live with kin (as the literature
suggests), then the proportion of *all* Saint-Hyacinthe residents living in
simple-family households should be correspondingly higher.

38 The close fit between my figures and those of Lauzon and Lalonde
seems to suggest that concentrating on the first seven years of married
life does little to weight the analysis in favour of complex households. In
fact, when the Saint-Hyacinthe census for 1871 is used as a benchmark,
families formed 10 to 17 years earlier (Cohort A) lived in complex
households in exactly the same proportion (21%) as couples formed 0
to 7 years earlier (Cohort B).

39 The difficulties are explained in the section of the appendix entitled
"Houses, Families, and Households."

40 As suggested in the appendix, this finding was based on a reading of the
nineteenth-century census lists that, is now contested, especially for
urban Quebec. See Darroch and Ornstein, "Family Coresidence in
Canada," table 1, 34; Bradbury, "The Family Economy and Work";
Bradbury, "The Working-Class Family Economy," 383–7; Medjuck,
"Family and Household Composition," especially tables 1 and 5, 280,
283.

41 The identification of kinship relationships from census lists was sim-
plified by the fact that the lists had already been systematically linked to
the parish registers. The fact that 10 households – nine of them in
Cohort A – contained unidentified kin is mainly the result of a particu-
larity of the 1861 census. Enumerators were asked to note whether or
not each resident was a "member of the family." The 10 individuals who
on this basis alone were assumed to be related to the couples with whom
they shared lodgings in 1861 are categorized here. One co-resident in
1891 could not be classified as the kin of either the husband or the wife
because she shared a surname with both spouses. She was nonetheless
assumed to be a family member.

42 Côté, "La vieillesse au Québec au XIXe siècle."

43 Family Reconstitution File B073.

44 Family Reconstitution File C118.

45 Ibid.

46 Seventy-six of 343 independent households, or 22%, contained co-resident kin.

47 These results should be treated with some caution and may reflect statistical anomalies rather than real variations in group behaviour. Applying the Chi^2 test to the first set of subtotals in Table 4-3 (simple versus complex) gives Chi^2 = 3.78, d.f. = 3, p ≤ 0.05. The observed relationship, in other words, between occupational category and these broad household types is not statistically significant. On the other hand, the ensuing analysis of the relationship between occupational group and the presence or absence of non-kin extras does meet this standard of statistical significance. For this second set of subtotals in Table 4-3, Chi^2 = 9.65, d.f. = 3, p ≤ 0.05.

48 Bradbury, *Working Families*, 175.

49 Family Reconstitution File B007. See also the case of the Dessaulles family cited at the beginning of this chapter. Family Reconstitution File B178.

50 The Chi^2 test shows that differences among the three zones as to whether household structure was simple or complex were not statistically significant. Chi^2 = 0.146, d.f. = 2, p ≤ 0.05. Geographic variation as to whether or not non-kin extras were present, however, does meet this standard of statistical significance. Chi^2 = 20.28, d.f. = 2. p ≤ 0.05.

51 The total in Table 4-3 is 64 because occupational information was missing for one couple whose household contained a non-kin extra. Note also that some individuals classified as non-kin may in fact have been relatives for whom I could not detect a kin relationship to the couple in question.

52 Thirty-one percent of all (intact) couples traced to the three census schedules lived in this area (114/371).

53 Examples of "other employees" are the several young seamstresses (*couturières*) found in the household of a tailor, and the various clerks identified as co-residents in families headed by merchants and professionals.

54 Family Reconstitution File C266.

55 The meaning census takers attached to the term *house* is discussed in the section of the appendix entitled "Houses, Families, and Households."

56 As explained in the appendix, the term *family*, for census takers, corresponded to the co-resident domestic group, or household. A *house*, on the other hand, was a residential building or a fully distinct part of such a building with private access from the street.

57 The Chi^2 test shows that these differences are statistically significant. Chi^2 = 20.77, d.f. = 4, p ≤ 0.05. The figures in Table 4-5 are altered

slightly if the 28 couples who did not head their own households are omitted, as they perhaps should be in the present context. Still, across the period, about 50% (188/371) of all linked couples headed independent households in distinct houses. And the proportion increased very gradually with time: from 48% (51/107) in 1861, to 50% (56/112) in 1871, to 53% in 1891 (81/152).

58 My investigation of domestic architecture in nineteenth-century Saint-Hyacinthe was quite superficial. It was rendered especially difficult by the important fires which, in 1876 and 1903, destroyed much of the housing stock in Saint-Hyacinthe, particularly in the lower town. See, however, the several images of working-class housing which have survived from the turn of the century (reproduced as Illustrations 26 through 30). The comfortable homes of the nineteenth-century elite have survived in greater numbers and are easier to locate and study. A good example is the Dessaulles house, depicted in Illustration 25, which has been the subject of a separate study. See Adams and Gossage, "Chez Fadette." I thank Annmarie Adams for her important insights in this area and for her encouragement to think seriously about the built environment.

59 For couples in which neither spouse had previously been married and who, according to the census, were living in distinct houses, an average of 48 months had expired since the wedding, the wife was 25.1 years old, and there were 1.4 children on hand. For all such couples in multi-family houses, the corresponding figures were 40 months, 24.0 years, and 1.1 children.

60 Seventy-one percent of the couples in which one spouse or both had been widowed were living in distinct houses, as opposed to 44% of those involving two previously unmarried individuals.

61 Family Reconstitution File c181.

62 Canada, *Rapport de la Commission royale*, 1482.

63 Family Reconstitution File b158.

64 Family Reconstitution File b125.

65 Take, for example, the family of Antoine C., the Saint-Dominique farmer visited in the spring of 1887 by Léon Gérin. The 60-year-old farmer lived with his second wife Herminie, their six children, and Herminie's parents in a parish bordering on Saint-Hyacinthe. Antoine C. owned a second house, located on the farm, in which he had established his son and heir, Amédée, a young man with a wife and children. Also established on these premises, specifically, "dans une annexe de la maison habitée par la famille d'Amédée fils," was Antoine's father (Amédée's grandfather) and his second wife, aged 80 and 68 years respectively. Here is a case where a single rural house clearly lodged two households, related by kinship. If this sort of complex situation (in this

case covering four generations) were common in the rural region surrounding Saint-Hyacinthe in the late nineteenth century, it would certainly explain the apparent tendency (based, admittedly, on a tiny number of cases) for recently married farmers to share houses with kin. See Gérin, *Le type économique et social*, 114. (Emphasis added in the citation.)

66 Manuscript census, 1891; Family Reconstitution File c271.

67 Bradbury, "The Fragmented Family."

68 See, for example, Hareven, *Family Time and Industrial Time*; Hareven, "The History of the Family and the Complexity of Social Change"; Bradbury, *Working Families*; Gagnon, "Le rôle de la parenté dans l'adaptation des migrants."

CHAPTER FIVE

1 The 386 women were observed across a total of over 4,508 years of married life, referred to in demographic jargon as "woman-years." They are distributed among the three cohorts as follows: Cohort A – 114 women observed over 1,208 reproductive years; Cohort B – 121 women observed over 1,488 years; Cohort C – 151 women observed over 1,812 years. The procedures used to calculate fertility measures on the basis of the observed behaviour of these women, and particularly the controls used to deal with the thorny problem of geographic mobility, are described in the appendix in the section entitled "Focusing on Fertility." Some readers may wish to consult that discussion at this point.

2 From 196 to 163 per thousand. Henripin, *Tendances et facteurs*, 21. Note that general fertility rates do not account for variations in the structure of a population by age, sex, or marital status. They are simply ratios of births in a given year to the total population.

3 Marital fertility rates are more sensitive to variations in the structure of a population than general fertility rates. They compare annual numbers of births to the number of married women in the child-bearing years. In Quebec, this rate fell by 16% between 1861 and 1891, from 370 to 312 per thousand. Henripin emphasizes the slow pace of these reductions, compared to that in other Canadian provinces, especially Ontario. Ibid., 62–3 (table 3.1); 37 (table 2.5); and 65. Henripin nuanced his position in 1972, suggesting in a paper written with Yves Péron, that marital fertility may have been declining even before 1871. He continued, however, to emphasize the slow pace of fertility decline in Quebec, compared to English Canada. For him, family size in French Canada showed "une résistance remarquable à la diminution de la fécondité observée dans tous les pays industrialisées." [Translation: a remarkable resistance to the fertility decline observed in all industrialized countries.] See Henripin and Péron, "La transition démographique," 38–9.

4 McInnis uses "I^g," the age-standardized index of marital fertility developed by Ansley Coale at the European Fertility Project, Princeton University. For definitions, see Coale and Treadway, "A Summary of the Changing Distribution of Overall Fertility," 32–5. In Saint-Hyacinthe county, I^g fell from .965 – near the theoretical maximum of 1.0 – in 1861, to .762 – still very high by twentieth-century standards – in 1891. Other counties that experienced reductions of over 20% in I^g in this period were Brome (26%), Huntingdon (23%), La Prairie (22%), and Sherbrooke (21%). Except for La Prairie and Saint-Hyacinthe, all of these counties had substantial anglophone populations. Note that Coale and his colleagues consider an irreversible decline in marital fertility to have occurred when I^g declines by 10% from its pretransition level. For the figures, see table A-1, in McInnis, "Fertility Patterns." See also McInnis, "The Geographic Pattern of Fertility Decline," which treats similar data for the period 1891–1931.

5 The debate on this discrepancy, once framed almost exclusively in nationalist terms as *la revanche des berceaux*, has been effectively summarized recently in Bouchard and Lalou, "La surfécondité des couples québécois"; see also Fournier, "Pourquoi la revanche des berceaux?" Some of these issues are discussed, particularly for the years around World War I, in Gossage and Gauvreau, "Demography and Discourse in Transition."

6 Chad Gaffield, who has done essentially this, has shown that for French- and English-speaking families engaged in comparable economic activities in the Ottawa Valley, the logic of family formation was similar. Francophone Catholics married slightly earlier; but families in both cultu. al groups used high-fertility reproductive strategies appropriate to the agroforest economy. Gaffield, "Canadian Families in Cultural Context," 59–63; Gaffield, *Language, Schooling, and Cultural Conflict,* 46–9 and 72–4. Similarly, Jack Little, in *Crofters and Habitants,* shows that the reproductive strategies of French-Canadian and Scottish families in rural Winslow Township were not dissimilar. On the other hand, Marvin McInnis maintains that despite the great interest in economic structure, the most important fertility differentials in nineteenth-century Canada remain those between French-speaking Catholics and English-speaking Protestants. McInnis, "The Geographic Pattern of Fertility Decline"; McInnis, "Fertility Patterns."

7 For examples of this approach, see Roy, "Paramètres sociaux de la fécondité saguenayenne," and Bouchard, *Quelques arpents d'Amérique.*

8 Sherry Olson, Pat Thornton, and their team of historical geographers argue for three culturally specific demographic regimes in nineteenth-century Montreal: French-Catholic, Irish-Catholic, and British-Protestant. By examining these cultural groups individually, socio-economic

differences within each one should become apparent, provided the samples are large enough. See Thornton and Sherry Olson, "Family Contexts of Fertility and Infant Survival"; Olson, Thornton, and Quoc, "A Geography of Little Children"; Olson, Thornton, and Quoc, "Dimensions sociales de la mortalité infantile."

9 Demographic analysis tells us nothing about the means of fertility control they adopted, but we can speculate that sexual abstinence, withdrawal, and imperfect versions of the rhythm method were more widely used than such mechanical means as condoms and diaphragms. For insights into these matters, which will not be treated in detail here, see McLaren and McLaren, *The Bedroom and the State.* See also the relevant sections of Mercier and Lemieux, *Les femmes au tournant du siècle* and, for a more recent period, Gauvreau and Gossage, "Empêcher la famille."

10 I will not deal exhaustively with the international literature on the demographic transition. But much of the most important work on these questions, at least for historic Europe, has been done at Princeton University, under the direction of Ansley J. Coale. For an early statement of Coale's position, see Coale, "The Decline of Fertility in Europe." In 1975, Coale stated three preconditions for sustained fertility decline: fertility must be subject to conscious choice and consideration; reduced fertility must be perceived as advantageous; and effective techniques must be available. In his view, these conditions are likely to attain in a society characterized by a sufficient degree of "modernity." See Coale, "The Demographic Transition." For a summary of the findings of the European Fertility Project up to 1986, see Coale and Watkins, eds., *The Decline of Fertility in Europe.*

11 The classic statement of the demographic transition model states that mortality declined first, creating high rates of demographic growth in many European regions from about 1750. Growth rates remained high until falling fertility, from about 1850 (with wide variations from one area to another), stabilized populations at new, higher levels. The point, for present purposes, is that these changes coincided with the emergence of new, capitalist forms of production and exchange in European societies. In the eighteenth and nineteenth centuries, European economies were becoming more "modern," more and more types of production and exchange were coming under capitalist control, cities were growing, and families were increasingly reliant on wages for survival. At the same time, more and more European women were beginning to control their fertility. Coale has shown that the control of fertility within marriage reduced general fertility levels in most European countries by at least 50% between the 1850s and the 1960s. Only France had a substantial decline prior to 1850. But, as he writes, "by 1900 an unmistakable downturn had occurred in Scandinavia, Great Britain, Germany,

Italy, Spain, Austria, Switzerland, Holland, Belgium and Hungary, and before World War I in Bulgaria, Romania, Poland and Russia." Coale, "The Decline of Fertility in Europe," 17.

12 France, for example, began to experience a sustained fertility decline in the eighteenth century, prior to the start of its transition to industrial capitalism. England, on the other hand, was the first country to experience the Industrial Revolution; yet it lagged well behind France with respect to the fertility transition. For a good overview of European population trends, written from an economic perspective, see Grigg, *Population Growth and Agrarian Change.*

13 American economists Richard Easterlin and Michael Haines are among those who have pointed out the weaknesses in traditional views of the demographic transition. Easterlin studied fertility decline in rural areas of the United States in the second half of the nineteenth century and found that a restriction in the availability of land, rather than the impact of cities or industry, led families to restrict the number of their descendants in these areas. Conversely, Haines has studied regions of Britain and the United States where heavy industries and mining *did* develop. He noted that these forms of economic "modernization" did not promote new patterns of reproduction. For samples of Richard Easterlin's writing on fertility in the United States, see Easterlin, "Population Issues in American Economic History," and Easterlin, Alter, and Condran, "Farms and Farm Families in Old and New Areas." Haines' major published work on the topic is his book, *Fertility and Occupation.*

14 Goody, *Production and Reproduction.* On the complexity of the relationship between economic structural change and fertility decline see also, among many others, Caldwell, *Theory of Fertility Decline;* Gittins, *Fair Sex;* Graff, "Literacy, Education, and Fertility"; Lesthaeghe and Wilson, "Modes of Production, Secularization, and the Pace of Fertility Decline"; and Seccombe, "Marxism and Demography."

15 Henripin and Péron, "La transition démographique," 26. In their popular survey of Quebec history from Confederation to the Depression, Linteau, Robert, and Durocher adopt essentially this same logic, pointing out that "in all countries, industrialization and urbanization have led to a major shift in demographic behaviour," characterized by lower fertility and mortality rates. Linteau, Robert, and Durocher, *Quebec: A History,* 26.

16 Henripin, "From Acceptance of Nature to Control"; Henripin and Péron, "La transition démographique de la Province de Québec." See also Thomas-Gee, "Early Canadian Fertility Transition"; Tepperman, "Ethnic Variations in Marriage and Fertility."

17 Bradbury, "The Working-Class Family Economy," 67–8. See also her book, *Working Families,* 58–66.

18 Were this the whole picture, one would be forced to wonder why two counties lying directly between Saint-Hyacinthe and Montreal – Ver-chères and Chambly – witnessed negligible declines in marital fertility between 1891 and 1931, when the fertility transition in Saint-Hyacinthe was well underway. It seems likely that differences in the economic and social structure of these neighbouring counties were at work. McInnis, "The Geographic Pattern of Fertility Decline," 16.

19 Bouchard, *Quelques arpents d'Amérique.*

20 This is one of the central points of John Caldwell's "wealth-flows" theory of fertility decline. See Caldwell, *Theory of Fertility Decline.* Chad Gaffield has recognized the relationship between high fertility and family-based agricultural production (supplemented with waged labour in forestry) in two Ontario Townships with large French-Canadian populations. See Gaffield, "Canadian Families in Cultural Context." On the decline of the family household as a unit of production in nineteenth-century Ontario, see Cohen, *Women's Work, Markets, and Economic Development.*

21 An age-specific marital fertility rate is the number of children expected to be born each year to one thousand married women in a specified age category. A rate of 500 per thousand for women aged 25 to 29 indicates that half of the married women in the age group would be expected to give birth in a given year.

22 This is consistent with an observation made by Henripin: "La fécondité des couples n'a pas diminué également à tous les âges. En fait, elle est peut-être plus forte aujourd'hui, pour les femmes de moins de vingt ans, qu'elle l'était il y a un siècle." [Translation: Fertility did not decrease equally for all age groups. In fact, reproduction rates for women under 20 may be higher today than they were a century ago.] Henripin, *Tendances et facteurs de fécondité,* 39. In the present study, the behaviour of 134 married women under 20 years of age was observed for an average of 1.8 years. See the appendix, Table A-4.

23 To be very clear on this point, the figures presented here, and throughout this chapter, are for Catholics only. Recall from chapter 1 that they made up over 95% of the local population. See Table 1-1.

24 Here, thanks to Lorraine Gadoury, one can cite a clear exception: as in Europe, New France's nobility began to control fertility before the rest of the population. Gadoury, "Comportements démographiques et alliances de la noblesse"; Gadoury, *La noblesse de Nouvelle-France.* For a convincing interpretation of this phenomenon, see Livi-Bacci, "Social Group Forerunners of Fertility Control in Europe."

25 Compared to the 1700–50 figures, Henripin's 1851 estimates for Quebec women in the 30 to 34, 35 to 39, and 40 to 44 age categories were lower by 13.2%, 29.5%, and 34.2% respectively. These transformations were influenced both by the changing ethnic composition of the

province and by its evolving economic structure – forces which, by the 1850s, had affected Saint-Hyacinthe less than other areas.

26 Exceptions are the 15 to 19 and 25 to 29 age groups.

27 Roy, "Paramètres sociaux de la fécondité saguenayenne" (see Table 5-2).

28 In Knodel's terms, family limitation refers to "deliberate attempts to limit the number of offspring through terminating childbearing before the end of a couple's reproductive span." Knodel, "Demographic Transitions in German Villages," 367.

29 This transformation is best understood in terms of the social and economic transformations affecting the province during this period. Although this shift may also reflect new cultural norms with respect to "ideal" family size, it is important to know why such norms changed over time and whether they varied from one social group to another. John Caldwell has criticized the idea of family-size norms and ideals, especially in pretransition populations, in a chapter entitled "Toward a Restatement of Demographic Transition Theory" (*Theory of Fertility Decline*, 126). It is nonetheless very common in the literature on fertility, in Quebec as elsewhere. According to Lucie Mercier and Denise Lemieux, for example, "les familles nombreuses s'inscrivaient encore, au tournant du siècle, dans un idéal auquel souscrivait la majorité" [Translation: at the beginning of the century, large families were still part of an ideal to which the majority subscribed]. Mercier and Lemieux, *Les femmes au tournant du siècle*, 219.

30 Family Reconstitution File c295.

31 Family Reconstitution File c208.

32 The scissors metaphor was suggested to me by Hélène Laforce. She has my thanks.

33 The very notion of fertility "accidents" – youngest children born despite their mothers' attempts not to conceive – implies fertility control of the type we are suggesting for Saint-Hyacinthe. Where such accidents occur, the average final birth interval is typically extended.

34 These figures are based on a total of 83 observed final intervals: 23, 33, and 27 in Cohorts A, B, and C, respectively. As a control against births missed due to undetected migration or for other reasons, four intervals of over six years were excluded from the calculations; three of these were for Cohort-C couples.

35 This is based on 91 cases, 23 in Cohort A, 34 in Cohort B, and 34 in Cohort C. Only women who lived through age 45 in an intact union have been included.

36 In roughly the same period, age at final maternity in the Saguenay region fell by about a year, from 41.0 years for the 1840–59 marriage cohort, to 39.8 for the 1885–89 cohort. Farmers' wives consistently

continued bearing children longer than the wives of non-farmers in the Saguenay, in some cohorts by as much as two years, suggesting socio-professional differentials in fertility behaviour within the region. Roy, "Paramètres sociaux de la fécondité saguenayenne."

37 In historical demography, a "completed family" is one that meets the following two criteria. First, the couple in question must have been continuously under observation from the date of marriage until the death of one spouse. Second, that event (the death of the first spouse) must not have occurred before the wife reached the end of her child-bearing years, usually defined as 45 years of age. In this study, of the 386 couples observed through any part of the woman's reproductive years, 102 met this standard.

38 These averages are based on 20, 37, and 45 cases in the three cohorts, respectively. The 102 completed families represent 26.4% of all couples included in any phase of the fertility analysis. Only first marriages for women are included.

39 I call this synthetic measure the Average Number of Children (ANC). It is equal to the Total Marital Fertility Rate (TMFR) at a constant marriage age, divided by 1,000. See the appendix for a fuller description.

40 These estimates of the number of children born per couple are slightly higher, particularly in the first cohort, than the observed completed family size. The ratios (ANC: completed family size) are 1.12:1, 1.05:1, and 1.04:1 for the three cohorts, respectively. Since one measure is artificial and the other is based on so few observations, the point to be stressed is the close fit between the two indices and the effect of mutual corroboration.

41 Infant and child mortality figures for Saint-Hyacinthe are based on all children, with known birthdates, born to 380 of the 386 women in the fertility study. Of 1,850 such children in the three cohorts, the deaths of 498 (26.9%) prior to age one, and of 315 (17.0%) between ages one and 15 can be confirmed with reference to local burial acts. These figures must be regarded as minima, since some children who were born and baptized in the parish would have died and been buried elsewhere. Six women were excluded for a purely practical reason: this analysis was already complete when information from the 1901 census allowed these six to be included in the calculation of fertility rates. It seemed unnecessary to repeat the mortality calculations.

42 Thornton, Olson, and Quoc, examining a cohort of 4,000 infants born in Montreal in 1859, show infant mortality quotients of 293 per thousand. This figure includes illegitimate and abandoned children, for whom mortality levels were much higher than other newborns. Their figure for legitimate children born to French-speaking Catholic parents (an appropriate comparison for our purposes) is, at 276 per thousand,

almost identical to the quotient for the 1854–61 marriage cohort in Saint-Hyacinthe. Terry Copp bases his contention that "Montreal was the most dangerous city in the civilized world [sic] to be born in" on an infant mortality quotient of 268 per thousand in the period 1899–1901, a rate that presumably includes foundlings. This is appreciably *below* the level found for children born in Saint-Hyacinthe to couples married between 1884 and 1891 (286 per thousand). Thornton, Olson, and Quoc, "Dimensions sociales de la mortalité infantile," 317. Copp, *The Anatomy of Poverty*, 25–6.

43 High infant and child mortality quotients are consistent with the crude mortality rates discussed in chapter 1, which were also well above provincial levels. See Table 1-3.

44 See above, chapter 1, note 40.

45 See Gossage, "Louis Côté." These events were reconstructed from Archives de la Ville de Saint-Hyacinthe, Procès-verbaux du conseil municipal, 1884–85, and from accounts in *Le Courrier de Saint-Hyacinthe*, 1884–85. My thanks to Catherine Laforce for her help on these questions.

46 I have not done the close analysis of infant deaths and birth intervals that would illustrate these relationships in the case of Saint-Hyacinthe. But some analysis of these intervals is included in Thornton, Olson, and Quoc's discussion of infant mortality in Montreal. Thornton, Olson, and Quoc, "Dimensions sociales de la mortalité infantile."

47 We must be careful here, however, as the child might have been born prematurely,

48 Family Reconstitution File C141.

49 Family Reconstitution File C100.

50 It is possible to generate a reasonably complete set of rates for the urban-manual category, and perhaps even for certain segments within that category, since the numbers are fairly large. But the situation is less hopeful for farmers and labourers, where totals of only 228 and 206.5 woman-years (involving only 19 and 18 women respectively) have been observed across the three cohorts. As for the wives of non-manual workers, the presence of only 14 in Cohort A, with 130 years under observation, makes the calculation of a set of rates in this case problematic.

A word on the classification of couples by occupational group is appropriate here. The occupational data collected for each couple included in the fertility analysis consist of a series of declarations, rather than a single job title. Furthermore, the categories "farmer" and "labourer" were, in the present instance, defined in a restrictive way. Husbands who did not declare these occupations *exclusively* were classified elsewhere. Finally, to be considered non-manual, a husband had to declare such an occupation more frequently than a manual occupation. In the case of the present fertility study, therefore, the "urban-manual" category is a residual one, which contains individuals who at some point in their lives may have declared themselves to be *journaliers, cultivateurs,* or even *commerçants.* These matters are discussed in greater detail in the section on occupational titles in the appendix. See p. 191–2.

51 See Henripin, *Tendances et facteurs de fécondité*; Lavigne, "Réflexions féministes"; Roy, "Paramètres sociaux de la fécondité saguenayenne;" Bouchard, *Quelques arpents d'Amérique.*

52 Family Reconsitituion File C204. Amanda herself also died young, in 1909, at the age of 39.

53 This is some 30% below the observed level for 14 bourgeois women. There is certainly no evidence to support a lower estimate.

54 The rate fell to 328 per thousand, compared to 332 per thousand for the full cohort.

55 See also Table 5-6.

56 Family Reconstitution File C094.

57 Ibid.

58 Family Reconstituion Files B261 and C093.

59 One might worry, furthermore, about a systematic bias in the data. Men who made more job declarations were necessarily present at more baptisms, marriages, and burials. These same men may have been more likely to declare a range of different jobs, simply because of the greater frequency with which they were asked the occupational question.

60 There is plenty of evidence for this. As is shown in chapter 2, only one-quarter of the workers in the leather sector in Saint-Hyacinthe in 1871 worked in small shops, a figure that would be even lower if only boot and shoe workers had been considered (Table 2-1).

61 Family Reconstitution File A159.

62 Curiously, the date of enumeration is given in the census as 22 April, yet the newborn is not mentioned.

63 Family Reconstitution File C093.

64 Family Reconstitution File C087; Canada, *Rapport de la Commission royale,* 1428.

65 Some of the women married in the 1930s and subsequently interviewed by Denyse Baillargeon suggested that they restricted fertility because of doctors' warnings to avoid further pregnancies or risk death in childbirth. It is not difficult to imagine the same scenario in Saint-Hyacinthe in the 1890s. See Baillargeon, *Les ménagères au temps de la crise*; see also Gauvreau and Gossage, "'Empêcher la famille'."

66 For example, a total of only 15 final birth intervals for women in the non-manual category were observed, spread unevenly across the three cohorts.

67 Family Reconstitution File c204.

68 Family Reconstitution File c208.

69 Family Reconstitution File c268.

70 See above, Table 5-4.

71 Aggregate (3-cohort) child-mortality quotients for the three occupational groupings under discussion are: .178 (farmers); .166 (urban-manual); and .180 (non-manual).

72 Dessaulles, *Hopes and Dreams*, 338.

73 This approach is found, most notably, in the work of Jacques Henripin. See Henripin, "From Acceptance of Nature to Control"; Henripin, *Tendances et facteurs de fécondité*; Henripin and Péron, "La transition démographique."

74 See McInnis, "The Geographic Pattern of Fertility Decline." On ideologies more generally, Serge Courville and Normand Séguin contrast the "conservative agrarian" vision of Quebec society in the later nineteenth century with "a modernist current ... which was more discreet and diffuse, and created by the impact of economic transformations." Courville and Séguin, "Rural Life in 19th-Century Quebec," 23.

75 See Gossage and Gauvreau, "Demography and Discourse in Transition," for a discussion of the discourse celebrating high fertility which characterized Quebec's nationalist élites around the turn of the century.

76 Caldwell, *Theory of Fertility Decline*, 121. Caldwell has described a situation strikingly similar to that of nineteenth-century Quebec, where the transfer of economic production away from the household was well advanced but where marital fertility levels remained relatively high:

This position, whereby the traditional family retained its ancient morality and produced obedient employees for a system not based on family production and not fundamentally needing much of its morality, proved surprisingly stable. There were, of course, reasons also at the family level for maintaining the system. If the young were employed outside the family but handed over most of their earnings, then the patriarchal system could survive almost intact – but the young had to be exhorted more, for no longer were the sanctions such simple ones as denial of access to land and food. If the womenfolk would continue to live modestly and work hard to produce household domestic services, then the household could obtain these products more cheaply than they could be acquired from the outside market – but the family had to reach new heights in emphasizing the difference between the things that men were suited for and those that lay in the female sphere. High fertility helped: it emphasized the female role, it kept the mother tied to the home, and it supplied her with extra helpers. Capitalism could hardly but approve; it was able to obtain a man's labour for lower wages than would have been needed by his family to obtain all their needs directly from the market.

Caldwell, *Theory of Fertility Decline*, 212–3.

77 Canada, *Rapport de la Commission royale*, 1475–6.

78 See especially Seccombe, "Marxism and Demography," and Folbre, "Of Patriarchy Born," for fascinating "gendered" discussions of fertility during the transition to industrial capitalism.

79 Danylewycz, *Taking the Veil.* Marie Lavigne has produced the most useful feminist reading of Quebec's fertility history to date. In an influential article, she demonstrated the fact that women in this period had other options besides marrying early and raising a large brood. See Lavigne, "Réflexions féministes."

80 On these issues, see especially Nancy Folbre, "Of Patriarchy Born."

81 See Mercier and Lemieux, *Les femmes au tournant du siècle*, 222–3.

82 Hareven, "The History of the Family and the Complexity of Social Change," 118.

CONCLUSION

1 See Table 4-1.

2 As attested to by the negative mythology surrounding stepmothers, stepfamilies have persistently been characterized as sites of domestic tension and conflict. This stereotype, which dates back to classical antiquity, can be detected in fairy tales, proverbs, and other forms of European popular culture. See Noy, "Wicked Stepmothers in Roman Society"; Laslett, *The World We Have Lost*, 99–100; Darnton, "Peasants Tell Tales"; Davis, *Fiction in the Archives*, 102. Clearly, Henriette Dessaulles found her relationship with her stepmother, Fanny Leman, to be a source of frustration, bordering occasionally on anguish. She often confided these feelings to her diary; the entry for 17 September 1874, five years after her father's remarriage, is not atypical: "A miserable day! There was no school. I was unhappy and spiteful and still am. Maybe Mama is basically right, but she is sometimes so severe and her manner so harsh, it brings out all my defiance. I never talk back, the things I feel when I'm angry would be too ugly to say, besides I'm too proud to show how her harshness affects me. I wish I could live all alone in my room, at peace with God, with others and myself." Dessaulles, *Hopes and Dreams*, 18. For more on the Dessaulles family's experience, see Adams and Gossage, "Chez Fadette." On the legal grounds for conflict within Quebec stepfamilies in the nineteenth century, see Gossage, "Tangled Webs." On one twentieth-century expression of the wicked stepmother myth in Quebec, see Gossage, "*La marâtre.*"

3 The broad outlines of this research and its relationship to the Saint-Hyacinthe study were outlined in Gossage, "Les débuts du déclin de la fécondité au Québec." The project, directed by Danielle Gauvreau and myself, is entitled "Le déclin de la fécondité au Québec, 1850–1950." We have been working together since 1995 under the umbrella of the Insititut interuniversitaire de recherche sur les populations (IREP), with funding from the Social Sciences and Humanities Research Council of Canada. For the first published results of this ongoing research, see Gauvreau and Gossage, "Empêcher la famille," and Gossage and Gauvreau, "Demography and Discourse in Transition."

APPENDIX

1 Gossage, "Family and Population," appendices A, C, D, and E.
2 Code 1 was a sure link, meaning all four elements in the names of the marriage partners (two surnames, two given names) matched the names in the marriage act. Code 2 meant three nominative elements matched, and so on.
3 The sources were mainly the *Fichier Loiselle* and the other genealogical reference works listed in the bibliography, mainly local marriage *répertoires*, and *livres généalogiques* where they exist (as for the parish of La Présentation). The parish register of Notre-Dame-du-Rosaire, the manuscript census schedules, and city directories for various years between 1851 and 1915 were also consulted.
4 Henry, *Techniques d'analyse*; Wrigley, "Family Reconstitution."
5 I will omit a detailed description of the contents of the five tables, called Unions, Husbands, Wives, Kids, and Marsub (for *mariages subséquents*). This information is available in Gossage, "Family and Population," 411–16.
6 It took over two months. To place this in perspective, I spent about 13 months collecting data in the parish registers and the manuscript census.
7 See Tables 2-2, 2-3, and 2-4.
8 This is intended partly to lighten the prose, but also to reflect the changing realities of the period, especially the growth of an industrial proletariat in the strict sense. In the first place, the term "families of urban-manual workers" is much more cumbersome (if more exact) than "working-class families." In the second place, unpropertied wage labourers surely constituted a growing majority of workers in the urban-manual group as the industrial transition progressed.
9 For a fascinating slice of bourgeois life in Saint-Hyacinthe in the 1870s, see Dessaulles, *Hopes and Dreams*. On family life and domestic space in the Dessaulles household, see Adams and Gossage, "Chez Fadette."

10 See Gittins, *Fair Sex*, for an exploration of the relationship between fertility and women's work, using English evidence. Joy Parr suggests that the relationship also applied in Paris, Ontario, where many married women worked in the Penmans knitted goods factory. Parr, *The Gender of Breadwinners*, 88.

11 Marjorie Griffin Cohen's book, *Women's Work, Markets and Economic Development*, is especially good on the economic role of farm women in nineteenth-century Ontario. Women's reproductive work was the central theme in a long debate among feminists over the nature of domestic labour and the relative importance of capitalism and patriarchy in women's lives. For an update, see Seccombe, "Marxism and Demography."

12 Bonnie Smith, in *Ladies of the Leisure Class*, describes some of these functions for the French *département du Nord* in the later nineteenth century.

13 They did indicate, however, whether the bride and groom were above or below the age of majority. This information can be of help in verifying age declarations found elsewhere.

14 Note that the tests reported in the next three paragraphs were undertaken before the incorporation of age data from the 1901 census.

15 One would, of course, expect the true distribution of ages by the final digit to be roughly equal, at about 10% per digit. In other words, there should be about as many thirty-eights and fifty-eights, as forties and sixties. Interestingly, no surplus of ages ending in zero was detected in the burial acts.

16 Two of these 371 were shown to be implausible because they implied marriage ages of less than 15 years for men and less than 14 years for women. They were therefore excluded from all analyses.

17 I thank Chantal Goyette of the Université de Montréal for her help, in this matter and with the other statistical tests reported in this book.

18 I follow Gilles Lauzon in using italics to distinguish the official census definitions of the words *house* and *family* from more standard usages. See Lauzon, *Habitat ouvrier et révolution industrielle*.

19 Darroch and Ornstein, "Family Coresidence in Canada," table 1, 34. See Katz, *The People of Hamilton*; Gaffield, "Canadian Families in Cultural Context"; Gagan, *Hopeful Travellers*; Gaffield, *Language, Schooling, and Cultural Conflict*.

20 Bradbury, "The Working-Class Family Economy," 383.

21 Ibid., 385.

22 Ibid., table 5.10, 387. The citation is from p. 386.

23 Bradbury, *Working Families*, 70–8.

24 Lauzon, *Habitat ouvrier et révolution industrielle*; Lauzon, "Cohabitation et déménagements en milieu ouvrier montréalais."

25 Canada, Sessional Papers, 1871, paper 64, "Manual Containing 'The Census Act', and Instructions to Officers Employed in the Taking of the First Census of Canada, 1871," 128.

26 Ibid., 133.

27 "Au fond, pour le recenseur, c'est la porte d'entrée donnant sur la rue qui devrait faire foi de tout, pas les portes des logements. D'après cette interprétation, un immeuble d'habitation peut donc contenir plusieurs logements bien distincts. Ce serait alors *l'espace rattaché au concept de 'famille'* qui pourrait correspondre le mieux à notre définition d'un logement." [Translation: Basically, for the census taker, what should matter is the front door leading onto the street, not the doors of apartments or flats. According to this interpretation, a residential building may thus contain several distinct dwellings. It would therefore be *the space associated with the concept of "family"* that might best correspond to our definition of a dwelling.] Lauzon, *Habitat ouvrier et révolution industrielle*, 81–2 (emphasis in the original).

28 Jean-Louis Lalonde, in his study of another working-class suburb of Montreal, conducts his household analysis at the level of the *family*. See Lalonde, "Le Village de Saint-Jean-Baptiste," especially pp. 82–7 and appendix A, pp. 189–219. The same approach is taken by Odette Vincent-Domey, in *Filles et famille en milieu ouvrier*, 68–72.

29 In perhaps a dozen cases, there was no way of harmonizing my own count of families with the enumerators' count of the number of families in the house (column 34). Since it was impossible to resolve these few discrepancies without dismantling assumptions that seemed to work well for the great majority of cases, my estimates of the number of *families* in the *house* were retained, and the differences between my count and the enumerators' figures put down as "unexplained." On the particularly difficult task of detecting household boundaries in the 1861 census, see especially David Gagan, "Enumerator's Instructions." As Gagan observed, "Census enumerators in 1861 were ... under no obligation to identify complete households, and as a result the returns rarely indicate where the entries for one household end, and those of the next begin. As a result, definitions of household size and structure depend entirely on arbitrary decisions made by the researcher, based on transitions in surnames and the position of the entries for the number of families and the type of house, which most (though not all) enumerators placed at the end of an entry." Gagan, "Enumerator's Instructions," 356.

30 Of the five Canadian censuses consulted for this book (1861 through 1901), only the 1891 and 1901 schedules give this information. The 1861 census distinguishes "members of the family" from non-members. This information is too vague, however, and its reliability too uncertain to be of much help.

31 Following Laslett, then, I define a simple household as one in which the only family members present are the members of the *conjugal* family, which generally means husband, wife, and children. Laslett stipulates that simple households may nonetheless contain unrelated persons (such as guests, servants, and boarders); following David Gagan, I refer to these persons as "extras."

32 Any household, then, in which the conjugal family was augmented by one or more members of the extended family has been identified as a *complex* household. No formal differentiation exists here between those containing related *individuals* and those containing related *couples*, as in Laslett's distinction between "extended" and "multiple" families.

33 In Saint-Hyacinthe, this was rare indeed. Only 4 of 371 couples linked from marriage act to census were in such situations (see Table 4-2).

34 The typology is an amalgam of a number of systems. Laslett's grid is given in Laslett and Wall, eds., *Household and Family in Past Times*, table 1.1, 31. A useful adaptation of his classification scheme to nineteenth-century urban Quebec is reported in Bradbury, "The Working-Class Family Economy," appendix C, "Classifying Families, Households and Individuals' Relationships," 498–508. The general notion of "extras" to refer to non-kin co-residents was borrowed from David Gagan's *Hopeful Travellers*, chap. 4, "Household, Family and Individual Experience." The idea of using the rather significantly different typology developed by Chudacoff was considered and rejected, though one element – the notion of young couples living in "subnuclear" situations – has been retained. See Chudacoff, "Newlyweds and Family Extension," tables 5.7 and 5.8, 197–8.

35 By Michael Anderson, for example. Anderson argues that individuals living through Britain's nineteenth-century industrialization continued to maintain strong ties with kin, as measured by such phenomena as co-residence, house sharing, and deliberate propinquity. But he also suggests that as new ways of obtaining "psychic profit" appeared in the cities, individuals adopted a more "calculative" approach to the maintenance of kin ties, with some dropping out of kin networks almost completely. See Anderson, *Family Structure*, chap. 2 and 12.

36 Only the 2,217 children whose exact birthdates are known are included in this graph.

37 Here, one should include return migrants: couples who established their first households in the parish, moved away temporarily, and later returned to finish their reproductive careers in the community. More generally, the problems raised by geographic mobility in parish-level reconstitution studies are discussed in Bouchard, "L'histoire démographique et le problème des migrations."

38 Ibid., 32. Translation: How, in fact does one guarantee that those who

remained and those who migrated, exposed to such a different social, cultural, and, surely, economic environment, would have exactly identical behaviour.

39 A sixth category was set up for couples who had to be excluded from the fertility study for reasons unrelated to mobility. These were: a) cases where ambiguous record links remained in the files after all phases of verification were complete; and b) the handful of "rehabilitated" marriages discussed in chapter 3, couples for whom the real date of the start of the union was unknown.

40 The four types are referred to as EF, EO, MF, and MO. The first letter in these codes refers to whether or not a marriage act, marking the beginning of the union, was found. In type E dossiers it was not; in type M it was. The second letter refers to whether or not the reconstitution form was "closed" (F = fermé) with the burial act of the first spouse to die, or whether in the absence of this document it remained "open" (O = ouvert). Henry, Techniques d'analyse, 69.

41 I did not make the distinction between type MF-1, where the wife's exact birthdate is known, and type MF-2, where her approximate age (based on declarations) is used. In fact, most would be of type MF-2, since exact birthdates were known for only a handful of wives, mainly in Cohort C. For a number of couples, even in this category, no age information was available at all for the wife. Such files were, of course, useless as far as the calculation of age-specific fertility rates was concerned. See the discussion of marriage ages in chapter 3 and the more technical discussion of age information in this appendix. See also Ibid., 70.

42 In her study of the Canadian nobility in the seventeenth and eighteenth centuries, Lorraine Gadoury compiled 498 fiches de famille, 85% of which were type MF. See Gadoury, "Comportements démographiques et alliances de la noblesse."

43 Of the 346 type-MF couples, 91 were classified as migrants of one type or another (mobility codes II to V). See Table A-2.

44 In a population of 1,000 married women aged 25 to 29 who gave birth to 2,000 children while between those ages, the age-specific marital fertility rate would be 400 per thousand per year (2000/ [5 x 1000] = .400). This implies that the average married woman in this age group would have given birth to one child every 2.5 years. Overall marital fertility rates are simply similar ratios calculated for all married women of child-bearing age, usually approximated as ages 15 to 44. Hence, in a population of 10,000 married women aged 15 to 44 who gave birth to a total of 60,000 children in a given year, the overall marital fertility rate would be 200 per thousand (60,000/ [30 x 10,000] = .200), or one child per woman every five years. For the calculation of age-specific marital fertility rates from family reconstitution forms, see Henry, Techniques

d'analyse, 70–84. For a more general discussion of the rates, see Bogue, *Demographic Techniques of Fertility Analysis*, 6–9.

45 To the historical demographer, a "completed family" is a *fiche de famille* in which the wife, who married while still in her fertile period, has been observed in an intact union through the age of menopause, usually approximated as age 45. Unions in which one spouse has died before the wife reaches age 45 are not counted.

46 As was explained in chapter 5, only 102 such files have been assembled, out of a possible 881. See Table 5-5.

47 Henry points out that using subsequent baptisms, burials, and weddings of children to "close" family reconstitution forms will bias results in favour of more fertile couples. Less fertile couples are less likely to be identified in such documents, and infertile couples will not be found at all. See Henry, *Techniques d'analyse*, 67.

48 By cohort: 28 of 119 observations in Cohort A (23.5%); 18 of 124 observations in Cohort B (14.5%); and 38 of 152 observations in Cohort C (25.0%).

49 Defining the duration and timing of each married woman's presence in the parish was the most difficult problem encountered in calculating marital fertility rates under these high-mobility conditions. A more detailed explanation of my solution to this problem, which will mainly interest specialists in historical demography, is given in appendix E of Gossage, "Family and Population," 454–71.

50 This is a slight variation from Henry's method. Henry, by adding six months to all ages declared in completed years, effectively assumes that each woman was born on 30 June of her calculated birth year. See Henry, *Techniques d'analyse*, 71.

51 This is a simplification, designed to facilitate calculations, and based on the assumption that half of all weddings occurred before this calendar date and half occurred after. The real proportions in the three cohorts are quite close: 53% of all weddings occurred in the first six months of the year, while 47% occurred in the second half.

52 See van de Walle, "Infant Mortality and the European Demographic Transition"; Gadoury, "Comportements démographiques et alliances de la noblesse"; Thornton, Olson, and Quoc, "Dimensions sociales de la mortalité infantile." John Knodel distinguishes two forms of birth control: the deliberate spacing of births within marriage; and the decision to stop child-bearing once the family had reached a certain size. As discussed in chapter 5, he uses the term "family limitation" to refer to this latter practice only. See Knodel, "Demographic Transitions in German Villages," 367.

53 It was possible to observe 224 protogenesic intervals across the three cohorts, 82 of them in completed families. Seventeen observed values of

over 24 months were excluded from the analysis, because it was considered likely that an earlier birth had been missed. The mean intervals for the remaining 207 couples were consistently on the order of 12 months: 12.3 months in Cohort A (65 cases); 12.0 months in Cohort B (65 cases); and 12.5 months in Cohort C (77 cases). Women who married early had noticeably shorter protogenesic intervals, on average, than older women. Bourgeois women experienced the shortest intervals of any social group, perhaps for reasons associated with health and nutrition. Prenuptial conceptions seem to have been rare, but less so than in rural areas. About 3% of observed first births (7/207) occurred within seven months of the wedding, compared to about 1% in the entire Saguenay region over a much longer period. Statistics given by Bouchard in "Les conceptions prénuptiales comme indicateur de changement culturel."

54 Total marital fertility rates are a refinement of total fertility rates, described in Henripin and Lapierre-Adamcyk, *Eléments de démographie*, 199. Massimo Livi-Bacci uses them in his study of "Social-Group Forerunners of Fertility Control in Europe," in Coale and Watkins, eds., *The Decline of Fertility in Europe*, 182–200.

55 This is the *descendance complète* described by Henry in *Techniques d'analyse*, 94–6.

56 John Caldwell, with his wealth-flows theory, is among the most prominent proponent of this type of approach, in which children's lifetime contributions to their parents' welfare are seen as crucial to the fertility transition. Nancy Folbre also focuses on relationships between parents and their grown children, on how those relationships change during the transition to industrial capitalism, and on the implications of those changes for fertility decisions. See the discussion of these matters in chapter 5. Caldwell, *Theory of Fertility Decline*; Folbre, "Of Patriarchy Born."

Bibliography

ARCHIVAL SOURCES

Archives de la Paroisse Saint-Hyacinthe-le-Confesseur (APSHC)
Parish Registers (baptisms, marriages, and burials). 1854–1919. 20 vols.
("Registre des baptêmes, mariages, sépultures")
Parish Registers (burials only). 1920–1948.
"Répertoire des registres de la nouvelle paroisee de Saint-Hyacinthe, com-
mencé en l'année 1854." (Annual list of baptisms, marriages, and
burials, organized alphabetically)

Archives du Palais de justice, Saint-Hyacinthe (APJSH)
Parish Registers (burials). Christ-Roi. 1928–1948.
Parish Registers (burials). Notre-Dame-du-Très-Saint-Sacrement. 1946–
1948.
Parish Registers (burials). Sacré-Coeur. 1946–1948.
Parish Registers (burials). Saint-Joseph. 1922–1948.
Parish Registers. Notre-Dame-du-Saint-Rosaire. Various years between 1876
and 1948.

Archives nationales du Québec, Montréal (ANQM)
Fichier Loiselle. (Microfilmed card index covering Catholic marriages for
Quebec and parts of Ontario and New England)
Parish Registers. Saint-Hyacinthe-le-Confesseur. 1854–1875.
Parish Registers. Notre-Dame-du-Saint-Rosaire. Various years between 1777
and 1875.

National Archives of Canada (NA)
"Cité de St-Hyacinthe 1910." National Map Collection, C18055, H3/340/
   Saint-Hyacinthe/1910. (Bird's-eye view of the city in 1910)
Manuscript census. 1861, 1871, 1881, 1891, and 1901. City of Saint-
   Hyacinthe; Municipalities of Saint-Hyacinthe-le-Confesseur and Notre-
   Dame-de-Saint-Hyacinthe. Microfilm reels C-1320, C-10065, C-10066,
   C-13202, T-6419, and T-6544.
Renault-Blanchard, L.P. "Plan des limites du Village de Saint-Hyacinthe,
   telles que fixées par le Conseil de la Municipalité de Saint-Hyacinthe,
   le 11 décembre 1848." National Map Collection, H3/340/Saint-
   Hyacinthe/1849.
"Vue à vol d'oiseau de St. Hyacinthe, P.Q. 1881." National Map Collection,
   C18088, H3/340/Saint-Hyacinthe/1881.

Archives du Seminaire de Saint-Hyacinthe (ASSH)
Notes historiques sur la paroisse de Saint-Hyacinthe. 2 vols., 1853–1870
   and 1870–78. Section C, series 1, dossier 6.
Renault-Blanchard, L.P. "Saint-Hyacinthe, prise à l'est," and "Vue du ma-
   noir seigneurial et du marché." Two pencil sketches of Saint-Hyacinthe
   in 1837. Section A, series 17, dossier 18.
Various historic photographs. Section A, series 17, dossiers 5, 18, 24.6,
   24.7, and 24.8.

Archives de la Société d'histoire régionale de Saint-Hyacinthe (ASHRSH)
Collection Hélène Nichols. (Album of historical postcards.) BFG 44.
Décret canonique de la Paroisse de Saint-Hyacinthe-le-Confesseur. Section
   B, series 1, dossier 6.9.
"1881 - St-Hyacinthe bientôt reconstruite sur les cendres de 1876." General
   view of the town in 1881. Section B, series 1, dossier 12.
"Intérieur de la Penman's vers 1900." Series of four historical photographs.
   Section B, series 14, album 4.
"Plan de la cité de Saint-Hyacinthe." Map showing position of *quartiers*, with
   street grid, ca. 1900. Section B, series 1, dossier 6.1.
Various historical photographs. Section B, series 14, albums 1, 2, 3, and 4.

Archives de l'évêché de Saint-Hyacinthe (AESH)
Desnoyers, Isidore. "Histoire de Saint-Hyacinthe par l'Abbé Isidore Desnoy-
   ers." Manuscript, 1876.
Rapports pastoraux. Parishes of Saint-Hyacinthe-le-Confesseur, Notre-Dame-
   du-Saint-Rosaire, Sainte-Marie-Madeleine, Saint-Thomas-d'Aquin. 1862–
   1894.
Registre des Requêtes. Series 1, vol. 1 (1825–84) and vol. 2 (1885–1918).
   ("Registre authentique des pièces et actes qui concernent l'Erection des

Paroisses, ainsi que les bâtisses ou réparations d'Eglises, Chapelles, Sacristies, Cimétières et Presbytères, dans le Diocèse de Saint-Hyacinthe ...")
"Tableau de la population catholique, des communiants, et des écoles du Diocèse, fourni par les curés dans l'été de 1869."

Archives de la Ville de Saint-Hyacinthe
Procès-verbaux du conseil municipal, 1884–85.
Rôles de perception des taxes municipales. Various years, 1880–1900.

Canadian Intellectual Property Office (Hull)
Thirty-two patents filed by Saint-Hyacinthe industrialist Louis Côté between 1870 and 1905.

PRINTED PRIMARY AND SECONDARY SOURCES

Accampo, Elinor. *Industrialization, Family Life and Class Relations: Saint-Chamond, 1815–1914.* Berkeley: The University of California Press, 1989.

Adams, Annmarie, and Peter Gossage. "Chez Fadette: Girlhood, Family, and Public Space in Nineteenth-Century Saint-Hyacinthe. *Urban History Review / Revue d'histoire urbaine* 26, no. 2 (March 1998): 56–68.

Almanach-directoire de Saint-Hyacinthe pour l'année 1875. Saint-Hyacinthe: M.A. Kéroack, 1875.

Aminzade, Ronald. "Reinterpreting Capitalist Industrialization: A Study of Nineteenth-Century France: Proletarianization, Small-scale Industry, and Capitalist Industrialization." *Social History* 9, no. 3 (October 1984): 329–50.

Anderson, Michael. *Family Structure in Nineteenth-Century Lancashire.* Cambridge: Cambridge University Press, 1971.

– *Approaches to the History of the Western Family.* London: MacMillan, 1980.

Ankarloo, Bengt. "Marriage and Family Formation." In *Transitions: The Family and the Life Course in Historical Perspective,* edited by Tamara K. Hareven, 113–33.

Armstrong, Robert. *Structure and Change: An Economic History of Quebec.* Toronto: Gage, 1984.

Baillargeon, Denise. *Ménagères au temps de la Crise.* Montreal, Remue-ménage, 1991.

Bardet, Jean-Pierre. "La démographie des villes de la modernité (XVIe XVIIIe siècles); mythes et réalités." *ADH* (1974): 101–26

– *Rouen au XVIIe et XVIIIe siècles: les mutations d'un espace social.* 2 vols. Paris: Société d'édition d'enseignement supérieur, 1983.

Beauchamp, Pierre et al. "La reconstitution automatique des familles: un fait acquis." *Population* 32 (September 1977): 375–99.

Behrman, S.J., L. Corsa Jr., and R. Freedman, eds. *Fertility and Family Planning: A World View*. Ann Arbor: University of Michigan Press, 1969.

Berkner, Lutz. "The Stem Family and the Developmental Cycle of the Peasant Household." *American Historical Review* 77, no. 2 (April 1972): 398–418.

– "The Use and Abuse of Census Data for the Historical Analysis of Family Structure." *Journal of Interdisciplinary History* 5, no. 4 (spring 1975): 721–38.

Berkner, Lutz, and Franklin F. Mendels. "Inheritance Systems, Family Structure and Demographic Patterns in Western Europe, 1700–1900." In *Historical Studies of Changing Fertility*, edited by Charles Tilly, 209–23.

Bernard, Harry, and A.-J. Gaudreau, eds. *Annuaire-Guide de Saint-Hyacinthe pour 1927*. Saint-Hyacinthe: Imprimerie du Courrier de Saint-Hyacinthe, [1927].

Bernard, Jean-Paul. "Les fonctions intellectuelles de Saint-Hyacinthe à la veille de la Confédération." *Société canadienne de l'histoire de l'Eglise catholique, Sessions d'étude* 47 (1980): 5–17.

Bernard, Jean-Paul, Paul-André Linteau, and Jean-Claude Robert. "La structure professionnelle de Montréal en 1825." *RhAf* 30, no. 3 (December 1976): 383–415.

Bischoff, Peter. "Des Forges du Saint-Maurice aux fonderies de Montréal: mobilité géographique, solidarité communautaire et action syndicale des mouleurs, 1829–1881." *RhAf* 43, no. 1 (summer 1989): 3–29.

– "La formation des traditions syndicales chez les mouleurs de Montréal, Hamilton et Toronto, 1850–1893." *Bulletin du RCHTQ* 16, no. 1 (winter, 1990): 19–57.

– " 'Travelling the country 'round': migrations et syndicalisme chez les mouleurs de l'Ontario et du Québec, membres de l'*Iron Molders Union of America*." *Journal of the CHA* 1 (1990): 37–71.

Blanchard, Raoul. *L'ouest du Canada français: Montréal et sa région*. Montreal: Beauchemin, 1953.

Bliss, Michael. *Northern Enterprise: Five Centuries of Canadian Business*. Toronto: MS, 1987.

– *Plague: A Story of Smallpox in Montreal*. Toronto: HarperCollins, 1991.

Bogue, Donald J. *Demographic Techniques of Fertility Analysis*. Chicago: University of Chicago, 1971.

Borduas, Jean-Rodolphe. *Livre généalogique de toutes les familles qui ont habité la paroisse de La Présentation depuis sa fondation, en 1806, jusqu'à et non compris l'année 1950*. 2 vols. Saint-Hyacinthe: Société généalogique canadienne-française, 1951.

Boserup, Ester. *Population and Technological Change: A Study of Long-Term Trends*. Chicago: University of Chicago Press, 1981.

Bouchard, Gérard. "L'histoire démographique et le problème des migrations: l'exemple de Laterrière." *Hs/SH* 3, no. 15 (May 1975): 21–33.

– "Family Structures and Geographic Mobility at Laterrière, 1851–1935." *JFH* 2, no. 4 (winter 1977): 350–69.
– "Un essai d'anthropologie régionale: l'histoire sociale du Saguenay aux XIXe et XXe siècles." *AESC* 34, no. 1 (January–February 1979): 106–25.
– "L'étude des structures familiales pré-industrielles: pour un renversement des perspectives." *Revue d'histoire moderne et contemporaine* 28 (October–December 1981): 545–71.
– "L'utilisation des données socio-professionnelles en histoire: le problème de la diachronie." *Hs/SH* 16, no. 32 (November 1983): 429–42.
– "Les catégories socio-professionnelles: une nouvelle grille de classement." *L/LT* 15 (spring 1985): 145–63.
– "Les conceptions prénuptiales comme indicateur de changement culturel." Paper presented to the Institut d'histoire de l'Amérique française, Saint-Jean, 1990.
– *Quelques arpents d'Amérique. Population, économie, famille au Saguenay, 1838–1971*. Montreal: Boréal, 1996.
Bouchard, Gérard, and Michel Bergeron. "Les registres de l'état civil de Notre-Dame-de-Laterrière, 1855–1911." *Archives* 3, no. 3 (September–December 1975): 11–20.
Bouchard, Gérard, and Richard Lalou. "La surfécondité des couples québécois depuis le 17e siècle, essai de mesure et d'interprétation." *Rs* 34, no. 1 (January–April 1993): 9–44.
Bouchard, Gérard, and André LaRose. "La règlementation du contenu des actes de baptême, mariage et sépulture au Québec, des origines à nos jours." *RhAf* 30, no. 1 (June 1976): 67–84.
Bouchard, Gérard, and Jeannette Larouche. "Nouvelle mesure d'alphabétisation à l'aide de la reconstitution automatique des familles." *Hs/SH* 22, no. 43 (May 1989): 91–119.
Bouchard, Gérard, and Raymond Roy. "Les variations nominatives dans les registres paroissiaux du Saguenay." *ADH* (1982): 354–68.
Bouchard, Gérard, Raymond Roy, and Yves Otis. "Registre de population et substitutions nominatives." *Population* 40, no. 3 (May–June 1985): 473–90.
Boucher de la Bruère, Pierre. "L'industrie à Saint-Hyacinthe." *Courrier de Saint-Hyacinthe*, 3 July 1873.
Bourbeau, Robert, and Jacques Légaré. *Évolution de la mortalité au Canada et au Québec, 1831–1931. Essai de mesure par génération*. Montreal: PUM, 1982.
Bourdieu, Pierre. "Marriage Strategies as Strategies of Social Reproduction." In *Family and Society*, edited by Robert Forster and Orest Ranum; translated by Elborg Forster and Patricia Ranum, 117–44.
Bourque, Mario, France Markowski, and Raymond Roy. "Evaluation du contenu des registres de l'état civil saguenayen, 1842–1951." *Archives* 16, no. 3 (December) 1984: 16–39.

Bradbury, Bettina. "The Family Economy and Work in an Industrializing City: Montreal in the 1870s." CHA *HP* (1979): 71–96.

– "The Fragmented Family: Family Strategies in the Face of Death, Illness, and Poverty, Montreal, 1860–1885." In *Childhood and Family in Canadian History*, edited by Joy Parr, 109–28.

– "Women and Wage Labour in a Period of Transition: Montreal, 1861–1881." *Hs/SH* 17, no. 33 (May 1984): 115–31.

– "Pigs, Cows and Boarders: Non-Wage Forms of Survival among Montreal Families, 1861–1891." *L/LT* 14 (fall 1984): 9–46.

– "The Working-Class Family Economy: Montreal, 1861–1881." Ph.D. diss., Concordia University, 1984.

– "Surviving as a Widow in 19th-Century Montreal." *Urban History Review* 17, no. 3 (February 1989): 148–60.

– "Femmes et familles. In *Guide d'histoire du Québec*, edited by Jacques Rouillard, 213–228.

– "Mourir chrétiennement: La vie et la mort dans les établissements catholiques pour personnes âgées à Montréal au XIXe siècle." *RhAf* 46, no. 1 (summer 1992): 143–75.

– *Working Families: Age, Gender, and Daily Survival in Industrializing Montreal.* Toronto: MS, 1993.

Bradbury, Bettina, ed. *Canadian Family History: Selected Readings.* Toronto: Copp Clark Pitman, 1992.

Bradbury, Bettina et al. "Property and Marriage: The Law and the Practice in Early Nineteenth-Century Montreal." *Hs/SH* 26, no. 51 (May 1993): 9–39.

Braun, Rudolf. "Early Industrialization and Demographic Change in the Canton of Zürich." In *Historical Studies of Changing Fertility*, edited by Charles Tilly, 289–334.

Burgess, Joanne. "L'industrie de la chaussure à Montréal, 1840–1870: Le passage de l'artisanat à la fabrique." *RhAf* 31, no. 2 (September 1977): 187–210.

– "Work, Family and Community: Montreal Leather Craftsmen, 1790–1831." Ph.D. diss., Université du Québec à Montréal, 1986.

Burgess, Joanne et al. *Clés pour l'histoire de Montréal: Bibliographie.* Montreal: Boréal, 1992.

Caldwell, Gary. "La baisse de la fécondité au Québec à la lumière de la sociologie québécoise." *Rs* 17, no. 1 (1976): 7–22.

Caldwell, John C. *Theory of Fertility Decline.* London: Academic Press, 1982.

Canada: Atlas toponymique. Montreal: Guérin, 1980.

The Canada Directory for 1857–58. Montreal: John Lovell, 1857.

Canada. *Rapport de la Commission royale sur les relations du travail avec le capital au Canada.* Quebec, pt. 2 (Saint-Hyacinthe evidence). Ottawa: Queen's Printer, 1890, 1422–500.

Canada. *Report of the Royal Commission on the Relations of Labor and Capital.* Vol. 1, 2d report. Ottawa: Queen's Printer, 1889.

Canada. *Report of the Royal Commission on the Relations of Labor and Capital.* Vol. 4, pt. 2 (Quebec evidence) Ottawa: Queen's Printer, 1889.

Canada. *Sessional Papers,* 1871. Paper 64, "Manual Containing 'The Census Act,' and Instructions to Officers Employed in the taking of the First Census of Canada, 1871."

Canadian Illustrated News, 16 September 1876.

Census of the Canadas, 1851–52. 2 vols. Quebec: Lovell and Lamoureux, 1855.

Census of the Canadas, 1860–61. 2 vols. Quebec: S.B. Foote, 1863.

Census of Canada, 1870–71. 5 vols. Ottawa: I.B. Taylor, 1873.

Census of Canada, 1880–81. 3 vols. Ottawa: Maclean, Roger and Co., 1883–84.

Census of Canada, 1890–91. 4 vols. Ottawa: S.E. Dawson, 1893.

Charbonneau, Hubert. *Vie et mort de nos ancêtres: étude démographique.* Montreal: Presses de l'Université de Montréal, 1975.

– ed. *La population du Québec: études rétrospectives.* Montréal: Boréal Express, 1973.

Charbonneau, Hubert et al. *Naissance d'une population: Les Français établis au Canada au XVIIe siècle.* Paris: INED, 1987.

Charbonneau, Hubert, and André Larose, eds. *Du manuscrit à l'ordinateur: dépouillement des registres paroissiaux aux fins de l'exploitation automatique.* Québec: Ministère des affaires culturelles, 1980.

Chaytor, Miriam. "Household and Kinship: Ryton in the Late 16th and Early 17th Centuries." *History Workshop Journal* 10 (autumn 1980): 25–60.

Choquette, C.-P. *Histoire de la ville de Saint-Hyacinthe.* Saint-Hyacinthe: Richer et fils, 1930.

Chudacoff, Howard. "New Branches on the Family Tree: Household Structure in Early Stages of the Life Cycle in Worcester, Massachussetts, 1860–1880." In *Themes in the History of the Family,* edited by Tamara K. Hareven, 55–72.

– "Newlyweds and Family Extension: The First Stage of the Family Cycle in Providence, Rhode Island, 1864–65 and 1879–80." In *Family and Population in Nineteenth-Century America,* edited by Tamara K. Hareven and Maris Vinovskis, 179–205.

Clark, Christopher. "The Household Economy, Market Exchange, and the Rise of Capitalism in the Connecticut Valley, 1800–1860." *Journal of Social History* 13, no. 2 (winter 1979): 169–90.

Coale, Ansley J. "The Decline of Fertility in Europe from the French Revolution to World War II." In *Fertility and Family Planning: A World View,* edited by S.J. Behrman, L. Corsa Jr., and R. Freedman, 3–24.

- "The Demographic Transition." In *The Population Debate; Dimensions and Perspectives*, Papers of the World Population Conference, Bucharest, 1975, 347–55.

Coale, Ansley J., and Roy Treadway, "A Summary of the Changing Distribution of Overall Fertility, Marital Fertility, and the Proportion Married in the Provinces of Europe." In *The Decline of Fertility in Europe: The Revised Proceedings of a Conference on the Princeton European Fertility Project*, edited by Ansley J. Coale, and Susan Cotts Watkins, 31–138.

Coale, Ansley J., and Susan Cotts Watkins, eds. *The Decline of Fertility in Europe: The Revised Proceedings of a Conference on the Princeton European Fertility Project*. Princeton: Princeton University Press, 1986.

Cohen, Marjorie Griffin. *Women's Work, Markets, and Economic Development in Nineteenth-Century Ontario*. Toronto: UTP, 1988.

Collectif Clio. *L'histoire des femmes au Québec depuis quatre siècles*. 2d ed. Montreal: Le Jour, 1992.

Collins, Stephen. "British Stepfamily Relationships, 1500–1800." *JFH* 16, no. 4 (1991): 331–44.

Comité des fêtes du deuxième centenaire de Saint-Hyacinthe. *Album souvenir, Saint-Hyacinthe 1748–1948*. Saint-Hyacinthe: Imprimerie Yamaska, 1948.

Copp, Terry. *The Anatomy of Poverty: The Condition of the Working Class in Montreal, 1897–1929*. Toronto: MS, 1974.

Côté, Liette. "La vieillesse au Québec au XIXe siècle: Le cas de Saint-Hyacinthe, 1861–1891." Master's thesis, Université de Sherbrooke, 1998.

Courrier de Saint-Hyacinthe, 1884–85.

Courville, Serge. *Entre ville et campagne. L'essor du village dans les seigneuries du Bas-Canada*. Quebec: PUL, 1990.

- ed. *Atlas historique du Québec: Population et territoire*. Sainte-Foy: PUL, 1996.

Courville, Serge, and Normand Séguin. "Rural Life in Nineteenth-Century Quebec." Translated by Sinclair Robinson. Historical Booklet No. 47, CHA, Ottawa, 1989.

Courville, Serge, et al. *Paroisses et municipalités de la région de Montréal au XIXe siècle (1825–1861)*. Quebec: PUL, 1988.

Cross, Suzanne. "The Neglected Majority: The Changing Role of Women in Nineteenth-Century Montreal." *HS/SH* 6, no. 12 (November 1973): 202–23.

Danylewycz, Marta. *Taking the Veil: An Alternative to Marriage, Motherhood and Spinsterhood in Quebec, 1840–1920*. Toronto: MS, 1987.

Darnton, Robert. *The Great Cat Massacre and Other Episodes in French Cultural History*. New York: Vintage Books, 1985.

Darroch, Gordon, and Michael Ornstein. "Family Coresidence in Canada in 1871: Family Life-Cycles, Occupations and Networks of Mutual Aid," CHA *HP* (1983): 30–56.

Davis, Natalie Zemon. *Fiction in the Archives: Pardon Tales and their Tellers in Sixteenth-Century France.* Stanford: Stanford University Press, 1987.

Dechêne, Louise. "La croissance de Montréal au XVIIIe siècle." *RhAf* 27, no. 2 (September 1973): 163–80.

– *Habitants et marchands de Montréal au XVIIe siècle.* Paris: Plon, 1974.

Deschamps, Clément E. *Municipalités et paroisses dans la province de Québec.* Quebec: L. Brousseau, 1896.

Dessaulles, Henriette. *Fadette, Journal d'Henriette Dessaulles, 1874–1881.* Montreal: Hurtubise HMH, 1971.

– *Hopes and Dreams: the Diary of Henriette Desaulles, 1874–1881.* Translated by Liedewy Hawke. Toronto: Hounslow Press, 1986.

– *Journal / Henriette Dessaulles.* Critical edition by Jean-Louis Major. Montreal: PUM, 1989.

Dessureault, Christian. "Les fondements de la hiérarchie sociale au sein de la paysannerie: Le cas de Saint-Hyacinthe, 1760–1815." Ph.D. diss., Université de Montréal, 1985.

– "Crise ou modernisation. La société maskoutaine durant le premier tiers du XIXe siècle." *RhAf* 42, no. 3 (winter 1989): 359–87.

– "Industrie et société rurale: le cas de la seigneurie de Saint-Hyacinthe des origines à 1861." *Hs/SH* 28, no. 55 (May 1995): 99–136.

Deyon, Pierre. "Fécondité et limites du modèle protoindustriel." *AESC* (September–October 1984): 915–35.

Dickson, James, and Bob Russell, eds. *Family, Economy, and State: The Social Reproduction Process under Capitalism.* New York: St. Martin's Press, 1986.

Dion, Jean-Noël. *Saint-Hyacinthe-le-Confesseur: 125 ans d'histoire, 1861–1986.* Saint-Hyacinthe-le-Confesseur: Corporation municipale, 1986.

Dion, Jean-Noël et al. *Saint-Hyacinthe: des vies, des siècles, une histoire, 1757 à aujourd'hui: notices biographiques.* 2 vols. Saint-Hyacinthe: Femmes Moose de Saint-Hyacinthe, 1983.

Du Berger, Jean, and Jacques Mathieu, eds. *Les ouvrières de la Dominion Corset à Québec, 1886–1988.* Sainte-Foy: PUL, 1993.

Dumont, Micheline. "Des garderies au XIXe siècle: Les salles d'asile des Soeurs Grises à Montréal." *RhAf* 39, no. 2 (fall 1985): 233–51.

Dupaquier, Jacques. *Pour la démographie historique.* Paris: Presses Universitaires de France, 1984.

Easterlin, Richard. "Population Issues in American Economic History: A Survey and Critique." In *Recent Developments in the Study of Business and Economic History: Essays in Honour of Herman E. Kroos,* edited by R.E. Gallman, 131–58.

Easterlin, Richard, George Alter, and Gretchen Condran. "Farms and Farm Families in Old and New Areas: The Northern States in 1860." In *Family and Population in Nineteenth-Century America,* edited by Tamara K. Hareven, and Maris Vinovskis, 22–83.

1852–1952: Album historique du centenaire du diocèse de Saint-Hyacinthe. Saint-Hyacinthe: Comité de l'album historique, [1952].

Fahmy-Eid, Nadia, and Micheline Dumont, eds. *Maîtresses de maison, maîtresses d'école.* Montreal: Boréal Express, 1983.

Falardeau, Jean-Charles, Philippe Garigue, and Léon Gérin. *Léon Gérin et l'habitant de Saint-Justin.* Montreal: PUM, 1968.

Faucher, Albert. *Québec en Amérique au 19e siècle: essai sur les caractères économiques de la Laurentie.* Montreal: Fides, 1973.

Fauve-Chamoux, Antoinette. "Les structures familiales au royaume des familles-souches: Esparros." *AESC* 39, no. 3 (May–June 1984): 514–28.

Ferland, Jacques. "Evolution des rapports sociaux dans l'industrie canadienne du cuir au tournant du 20e siècle." Ph.D. diss., McGill University, 1985.

– "Syndicalisme 'parcellaire' et syndicalisme 'collectif': Une interprétation socio-technique des conflits ouvriers dans deux industries québécoises, 1880–1914." *L/LT* 19 (spring 1987): 49–88.

Ferretti, Lucia. *Entre voisins. La société paroissiale en milieu urbain. Saint-Pierre-Apôtre de Montréal, 1848–1930.* Montreal: Boréal, 1992.

– "Mariage et cadre de vie familiale dans une paroisse ouvrière montréalaise: Saint-Brigide, 1900–1914." *RhAf* 39, no. 2 (autumn 1985): 233–61.

Fifth Census of Canada, 1911. 6 vols. Ottawa: King's Printer (C.H. Parmelee), 1912–15.

Flandrin, Jean-Louis. *Families in Former Times: Kinship, Household, and Sexuality.* Translated by R. Southern. Cambridge (UK): Cambridge University Press, 1979.

Fleury, Michel, and Louis Henry. *Nouveau manuel de dépouillement et exploitation de l'état civil ancien.* Paris: INED, 1965.

Folbre, Nancy. "Of Patriarchy Born: The Political Economy of Fertility Decisions." *Feminist Studies* 9, no. 2 (summer 1983): 261–84.

Forster, Robert, and Orest Ranum, ed. *Family and Society: Selections from the Annales, économies, sociétés, civilisations.* Translated by Elborg Forster and Patricia M. Ranum. Baltimore: The Johns Hopkins University Press, 1976.

Fournier, Daniel. "Consanguinité et sociabilité dans la zone de Montréal au début du siècle." *Rs* 24:3 (September–December 1983): 307–23.

– "Pourquoi la revanche des berceaux? L'hypothèse de la sociabilité." *Rs* 30, no. 2 (May–August 1989): 171–98.

Fourth Census of Canada, 1901. 4 vols. Ottawa: Queen's Printer (S.E. Dawson), 1893.

Francoeur, Jean. "Saint-Hyacinthe: Esquisse de géographie urbaine." Master's thesis, Université de Montréal, 1953.

Frenette, Yves. "La genèse d'une communauté canadienne-française en Nouvelle-Angleterre: Lewiston, Maine, 1800–1880." *CHA HP* (1989): 75–99.

Gadoury, Lorraine. "Comportements démographiques et alliances de la noblesse de Nouvelle-France." PH.D. diss., Université de Montréal, 1988.
– "Comportements démographiques et alliances de la noblesse de Nouvelle-France." Paper presented to the CHA, Quebec, 1989.
– *La noblesse de Nouvelle-France. Familles et alliances.* Ville LaSalle: Hurtubise HMH, 1991.
Gaffield, Chad. "Canadian Families in Cultural Context: Hypotheses from the Mid-Nineteenth Century," CHA *HP* (1979): 48–69.
– *Language, Schooling and Cultural Conflict: The Origins of the French-Language Controversy in Ontario.* Kingston and Montreal: MQUP, 1987.
– "Children, Schooling, and Family Reproduction in Nineteenth-Century Ontario." *CHR* 52, 2 (June 1991): 157–91.
– et al. *Histoire de l'Outaouais.* Montreal: IQRC, 1994.
Gagan, David P. "Enumerator's Instructions for the Census of Canada 1852 and 1861." *Hs/SH* 7, no. 14 (November 1974): 353–65.
– *Hopeful Travellers: Families, Land, and Social Change in Mid-Victorian Peel County, Canada West.* Toronto: UTP, 1981.
Gagnon, France. "Le rôle de la parenté dans l'adaptation des migrants de la plaine de Montréal au milieu montréalais: 1845–1875." Master's thesis, Université du Québec à Montréal, 1986.
– "Parenté et migration: le cas des Canadiens français à Montréal entre 1845 et 1875." CHA *HP* (1988): 63–85.
Gagnon, Serge. *Plaisir d'amour et crainte de Dieu. Sexualité et confession au Bas-Canada.* Sainte-Foy: PUL, 1990.
– *Mariage et famille au temps de Papineau.* Sainte-Foy: PUL, 1993.
Gallman, R.E., ed. *Recent Developments in the Study of Business and Economic History: Essays in Honour of Herman E. Kroos.* Greenwich, Conn.: JAI Press, 1977.
Gauvreau, Danielle. "Reproduction humaine et reproduction sociale: la ville de Québec pendant le regime français." Ph.D. diss., Université de Montréal, 1986.
– "Destins de femmes, destins de mères: Images et réalités historiques de la maternité au Québec." *Rs* 32, 3 (September–December 1991): 321–46.
– *Québec: Une ville et sa population au temps de la Nouvelle-France.* Sillery: PUQ, 1991.
Gauvreau, Danielle, and Mario Bourque. "Mouvements migratoires et familles: le peuplement du Saguenay avant 1911." *RhAf* 42:4 (fall 1988): 167–92.
– "'Jusqu'à ce que la mort nous sépare': Le destin des femmes et des hommes mariés au Saguenay avant 1930." *CHR* 71, no. 4 (December 1990): 441–61.
Gauvreau, Danielle, and Peter Gossage. "Empêcher la famille: Fécondité et contraception au Québec, 1920–1960." *CHR* 78, no. 3 (fall 1997): 478–510.

– "A New Look at Quebec's Fertility Decline, 1850–1950." Paper presented to the Social Science History Association, Washington, D.C. 1997.

Gérin, Léon. *Le type économique et social des Canadiens: milieux agricoles de tradition française.* 2d ed. Montreal: Fides, 1948.

Gillis, John. "Peasant, Plebian, and Proletarian Marriage in Britain, 1600–1900." In *Proletarianization and Family History*, edited by David Levine, 129–62.

– *For Better, For Worse: British Marriages, 1600 to the Present.* New York: Oxford University Press, 1985.

Gittins, Diana. *Fair Sex: Family Size and Structure in Britain, 1900–39.* New York: St. Martin's Press, 1982.

Glasco, Laurence. "Migration and Adjustment in the Nineteenth-Century City: Occupation, Property and Household Structure of Native-Born Whites, Buffalo, New York, 1855." In *Family and Population in Nineteenth-Century America*, edited by Tamara K. Hareven and Maris Vinovskis, 154–78.

Glass, D.V., and D.E.C. Eversley, eds. *Population in History: Essays in Historical Demography.* Chicago: Aldine Publishing Company, 1965.

Glass, D.V., and Roger Revelle, eds. *Population and Social Change.* London: Edward Arnold, 1972.

Goad, Chas. E. *Insurance Plan of St. Hyacinthe, Quebec, Population 11,300; Including Providence and St. Joseph 14,000, October 1916. Revised by the Underwriters' Survey Bureau Limited, August 1922.* Toronto and Montreal: Underwriters' Survey Bureau Limited, 1922.

Goody, Jack. *Production and Reproduction: A Comparative Study of the Domestic Domain.* Cambridge (UK), and New York: Cambridge University Press, 1976.

Gossage, Peter. "Abandoned Children in Nineteenth-Century Montreal." Master's thesis, McGill University, 1984.

– "Les enfants abandonnés à Montréal au 19e siècle: La Crèche d'Youvile des Soeurs Grises, 1820–1871." *RhAf* 40, no. 4 (spring 1987): 537–59.

– "Family Formation and Age at Marriage in Saint-Hyacinthe, Quebec, 1854–1891." *Hs/SH* 24, no. 47 (May 1991): 61–84.

– "Family and Population in a Manufacturing Town: Saint-Hyacinthe, 1854–1914." Ph.D. diss., Université du Québec à Montréal, 1991.

– "Household Structure and Proximity to Kin among Saint-Hyacinthe Newlyweds, 1861–1891." Paper presented to the First Carleton Conference on the History of Marriage and the Family, Ottawa, 1992.

– "Reflections on the Writing of Family History in Canada, 1975–1993." Comité international des sciences historiques, *Bulletin d'information* 19 (Paris, 1993): 132–40.

– "Les débuts du déclin de la fécondité au Québec: réflexions théoriques et méthodologiques à partir du cas des Maskoutaines." Paper presented to the annual meeting of the CHA, Calgary, 1994.

– "*La marâtre*: Marie-Anne Houde and the Myth of the Wicked Stepmother in Quebec." *CHR* 76, no. 4 (December 1995): 563–97

– "Louis Côté." *Dictionnaire biographique du Canada* 14. Quebec: PUL, 1998), 262–3.

– "Tangled Webs: Remarriage and Family Conflict in 19th-Century Quebec." In *Historical Perspectives on the Canadian Family*, edited by Edgar-André Montigny, and Lori Chambers. Toronto: Canadian Scholars Press, 1998, 255–376

Gossage, Peter, and Danielle Gauvreau. "Demography and Discourse in Transition: Quebec Fertility at the Turn of the Twentieth Century." *The History of the Family: An International Quarterly*. In press.

Graff, Harvey. "Literacy, Education, and Fertility, Past and Present: A Critical Review." *Population and Development Review* 5, no. 1 (March 1979): 105–40.

Granatstien, J.L. *Who Killed Canadian History?* Toronto: HarperCollins, 1998.

Greer, Allan. "The Pattern of Literacy in Quebec, 1754–1899." *Hs/SH* 11, no. 22 (November 1979): 293–335.

– "L'alphabétisation et son histoire au Québec: Etat de la question." In *L'imprimé au Québec; aspects historiques, XVIIIe–XXe siècles*, edited by Yvan Lamonde, 25–51.

– *Peasant, Lord and Merchant: Rural Society in Three Quebec Parishes, 1740–1840*. Toronto: UTP, 1985.

Grigg, David. *Population Growth and Agrarian Change: An Historical Perspective*. Cambridge (UK) : Cambridge University Press, 1980.

Guide de Saint-Hyacinthe, 1915. Saint-Hyacinthe. N.p., [1915].

Guide de Saint-Hyacinthe par ordre alphabétique et par ordre des rues. Saint-Hyacinthe: Camille Lussier, 1883.

Guide de Saint-Hyacinthe par ordre alphabétique et par ordre des rues. Saint-Hyacinthe: Camille Lussier, 1885.

Guide de Saint-Hyacinthe par ordre alphabétique et par ordre des rues. Saint-Hyacinthe: Camille Lussier, 1887.

Guide de Saint-Hyacinthe, par ordre alphabétique. Saint-Hyacinthe: Camille Lussier, 1894.

Gutmann, Myron P. "Protoindustrialization and Marriage Ages in Eastern Belgium." *ADH* (1987): 143–73.

Haines, Michael. *Fertility and Occupation: Population Patterns in Industrialization*. London (UK), and New York: Academic Press, 1979.

Hajnal, John. "Age at Marriage and Proportion Marrying." *Population Studies* 7, no. 2 (November 1953): 111–36.

– "European Marriage Patterns in Perspective." In *Population in History:*

Essays in Historical Demography, edited by D.V. Glass, and D.E.C. Eversley, 101–43.

Hamelin, Jean, and Yves Roby. *Histoire économique du Québec, 1851–1896.* Montreal: Fides, 1971.

Hardy, René, and Normand Séguin. *Forêt et société en Mauricie. La formation de la région de Trois-Rivières: 1830–1930.* Montreal: Boréal Express; Ottawa: Musée national de l'homme, 1984.

Hareven, Tamara K. *Family Time and Industrial Time: The Relationship between the Family and Work in a New England Industrial Community.* Cambridge (UK): Cambridge University Press, 1982.

– "The History of the Family and the Complexity of Social Change." *American Historical Review* 96, no. 1 (February 1991): 95–124.

– ed. *Themes in the History of the Family.* Worcester, Mass.: American Antiquarian Society, 1978.

– ed. *Transitions: The Family and Life Course in Historical Perspective.* New York: Academic Press, 1978.

Hareven, Tamara K., and Maris Vinovskis, eds. *Family and Population in Nineteenth-Century America.* Princeton, N.J.: Princeton University Press, 1978.

Hareven, Tamara K., and Maris A. Vinovskis. "Patterns of Childbearing in Late Nineteenth-Century America: The Determinants of Marital Fertility in Five Massachussetts Towns in 1880." In *Family and Population in Nineteenth-Century America*, edited by Tamara K. Hareven, and Maris Vinovskis, 85–125.

Harvey, Fernand. *Révolution industrielle et travailleurs. Une enquête sur les rapports entre le capital et le travail au Québec à la fin du 19e siècle.* Montreal: Boréal Express, 1978.

Hébert, Hélène, Jean Noël Dion, and Albert Rémillard. *Le marché de Saint-Hyacinthe et quelques marchés publics du Québec.* Saint-Hyacinthe: Les éditions JML, 1989.

Henripin, Jacques. *La population canadienne au début du XVIIIe siècle: nuptialité, fécondité, mortalité.* Paris: INED, 1954.

– "From Acceptance of Nature to Control: The Demography of the French Canadians since the Seventeenth Century." *Canadian Journal of Economics and Political Science* 23, no. 1 (February 1957): 10–19. Reprinted in *French Canadian Society*, vol.1, edited by Marcel Rioux, and Yves Martin, 204–16. Also published in *Studies in Canadian Social History*, edited by Michiel Horn, and Ronald Sabourin, 74–84.

– *Tendances et facteurs de fécondité au Canada.* Ottawa: Bureau fédéral de la statistique, 1968. Also in English as *Trends and Factors of Fertility in Canada.* Ottawa: Dominion Bureau of Statistics, 1968.

Henripin, Jacques, and Evelyne Lapierre-Adamcyk. *La fin de la revanche des berceaux. Qu'en pensent les Québécoises.* Montréal: PUM, 1974.

– *Eléments de démographie: DMO 1000*. Montréal: La librairie de l'Université de Montréal, 1983.

Henripin, Jacques, and Yves Péron. "La transition démographique de la Province de Québec." In *La population du Québec: études rétrospectives*, edited by Hubert Charbonneau, 23–44. First published as "The Demographic Transition of the Province of Quebec," in *Population and Social Change*, edited by D.V Glass, and Roger Revelle, 213–31.

Henripin, Jacques et al. *Les enfants qu'on n'a plus au Québec*. Montreal: PUM, 1981.

Henry, Louis. *Techniques d'analyse en démographie historique*. Paris: INED, 1980.

Henry, Louis, and Etienne Gautier. *La population de Crulai, paroisse normande: étude historique*. Paris: INED, 1958.

Hershberg, Thomas, ed. *Philadelphia: Work, Space, Family and Group Experience in the Nineteenth-Century City: Essays Toward an Interdisciplinary History of the City*. New York: Oxford University Press, 1981.

Hopkins, H.W. *Atlas of the City and County of St. Hyacinthe, Province of Quebec. From Actual Surveys, Based upon the Cadastral Plans Deposited in the Office of Crown Lands*. N.p., Provincial Surveying and Pub. Co., 1880.

Horn, Michiel and Ronald Sabourin, eds. *Studies in Canadian Social History*. Toronto: MS, 1974.

Householder Van Horn, Susan. *Women, Work, and Fertility, 1900–1986*. New York: New York University Press, 1988.

Hudon, Christine. *Prêtres et fidèles dans le diocèse de Saint-Hyacinthe, 1820–1875*. Sillery: Septentrion, 1996.

Hughes, Everett. *French Canada in Transition*. Chicago: University of Chicago Press, 1943.

Jetté, René, comp. *Mariages de La Présentation (1806), Saint-Jude (1822), Saint-Barnabé (1840), Saint-Thomas-d'Aquin (1891), Saint-Bernard (1908), Comté de Saint-Hyacinthe*. Quebec: B. Pontbriand, 1969.

– comp. *Mariages de Notre-Dame-de-Saint-Hyacinthe (Notre-Dame-du-Rosaire), 1777–1969*. Quebec: B. Pontbriand, 1971.

Journals of the Legislative Assembly of Lower Canada. 1832, Appendix O.o. (Published census report for 1831.)

Katz, Michael B. *The People of Hamilton, Canada West: Family and Class in a Mid-Nineteenth-Century City*. Cambridge, Mass.: Harvard University Press, 1975.

Katz, Michael, Michael J. Doucet, and Mark J. Stern. *The Social Organization of Early Industrial Capitalism*. Cambridge, Mass.: Harvard University Press, 1982.

Kesteman, Jean-Pierre. "Naissance et développement d'un capitalisme régional." Preliminary draft of a chapter to be published in Jean-Pierre Kesteman and Peter Southam, *Histoire des Cantons de l'Est*, Sherbrooke, 16 June 1995.

Knodel, John. "Demographic Transitions in German Villages." In *The Decline of Fertility in Europe*, edited by Ansley J. Coale, and Susan Cotts Watkins, 337–89.

Lalonde, Jean-Louis. "Le Village de Saint-Jean-Baptiste: La formation d'un faubourg montréalais, 1861–1886." Master's thesis, Université du Québec à Montréal, 1985.

Lamonde, Yvan, ed. *L'imprimé au Québec; aspects historiques, XVIIIe–XXe siècles.* Quebec: IQRC, 1983.

Lapointe, Laurent. "La formation de la Banque de Saint-Hyacinthe et le développement économique régional (1850–1875)." Master's thesis, Université de Montréal, 1976.

LaRose, André. "Les registres paroissiaux catholiques au Québec: vue d'ensemble." *Mémoires de la Société généalogique canadienne-française* 30, no. 4 (October–December 1979): 243–62.

Laslett, Barbara. "Social Change and the Family: Los Angeles, California, 1850–1870." *American Sociological Review* 42, no. 2 (April 1977): 268–91.

Laslett, Peter. "Characteristics of the Western Family Considered over Time." In *Family Life and Illicit Love in Earlier Generations: Essays in Historical Sociology*, edited by Peter Laslett, 12–49. Cambridge (UK): Cambridge University Press, 1977.

Laslett, Peter, ed. *Family Life and Illicit Love in Earlier Generations: Essays in Historical Sociology.* Cambridge (UK): Cambridge University Press, 1977.

Laslett, Peter and Richard Wall, eds. *Household and Family in Past Time.* Cambridge (UK): Cambridge University Press, 1972.

Laurie, Bruce, and Marc Schmitz. "Manufacture and Productivity: The Making of an Industrial Base, Philadelphia, 1850–1880." In *Philadelphia: Work, Space, Family and Group Experience in the Nineteenth-Century City: Essays Toward an Interdisciplinary History of the City*, edited by Thomas Hershberg, 43–92.

Lauzon, Gilles. "Habiter un nouveau quartier ouvrier de la banlieu de Montréal; Village Saint-Augustin (Municipalité de Saint-Henri) 1855–1881." Master's thesis, Université du Québec à Montréal, 1986.

– *Habitat ouvrier et révolution industrielle: le cas du Village St-Augustin.* Montreal: RCHTQ, 1989.

– "Cohabitation et déménagements en milieu ouvrier montréalais. Essai de réinterprétation à partir du cas du village Saint-Augustin (1871–1881)." *RhAf* 46, no. 1 (summer 1992): 115–42.

Lavigne, Marie. "Réflexions féministes autour de la fertilité des Québécoises." In *Maîtresses de maison, maîtresses d'école*, edited by Nadia Fahmy-Eid, and Micheline Dumont, 319–38.

Lavoie, Yolande. *L'émigration des Canadiens aux Etats-Unis avant 1930: mesure du phénomène.* Montreal: PUM, 1972.

– "Les mouvements migratoires des Canadiens entre leur pays et les Etats-

Unis aux XIXe et XXe siècles: étude quantitative." In *La population du Québec: études rétrospectives,* edited by Hubert Charbonenau, 73–88.

Lee, Ronald Demos et al., eds. *Population Patterns in the Past.* New York: Academic Press, 1977.

Légaré, Jacques and Bertrand Desjardins. "Des registres paroissiaux aux généalogies: le rôle de l'ordinateur au Programme de recherche en démographie historique." *Archives* 16, no. 3 (December 1984): 3–15.

Lesthaeghe, Ron, and Chris Wilson. "Modes of Production, Secularization, and the Pace of Fertility Decline in Western Europe, 1870–1930." In *The Decline of Fertility in Europe,* edited by Ansley J. Coale, and Susan Cotts Watkins, 269–92.

Levine, David. *Family Formation in an Age of Nascent Capitalism.* New York: Academic Press, 1977.

– "'For Their Own Reasons': Individual Marriage Decisions and Family Life." *JFH* 7, no. 3 (fall 1982): 255–64

– ed. *Proletarianization and Family History.* Orlando: Academic Press, 1984.

Linteau, Paul-André. *The Promoters' City: Building the Industrial Town of Maisonneuve, 1883–1918.* Translated by Robert Chodos. Toronto: James Lorimer, 1985.

– *Histoire de Montréal depuis la Confédération.* Montreal: Boréal, 1992.

Linteau, Paul-André, and Jean-Claude Robert. "Montréal au 19e siècle: bilan d'une recherche." *Urban History Review* 13, no. 3 (February 1985): 207–33.

Linteau, Paul-André, Jean-Claude Robert, and René Durocher. *Quebec: A History, 1867–1929.* Translated by Robert Chodos. Toronto: James Lorimer, 1983.

Little, Jack. *Crofters and Habitants: Settler Society, Economy, and Culture in a Quebec Township, 1848–1881.* Kingston and Montreal: MQUP, 1991.

Livi-Bacci, Massimo. "Fertility and Population Growth in Spain in the 18th and 19th Centuries," In *Population and Social Change,* edited by D.V. Glass, and Roger Revelle, 173–84.

– "Social-Group Forerunners of Fertility Control in Europe." In *The Decline of Fertility in Europe,* edited by Ansley J. Coale, and Susan Cotts Watkins, 182–200.

Lorimer, Ellsworth, and Peter Gossage. "A Craftsman Remembers: Recollections of the Dominion Snath Company, Waterville, 1920–1939." *Journal of Eastern Townships Studies* 7 (fall 1995): 71–88.

Lovell's Business and Professional Directory of the Province of Quebec for 1902–03. Montreal: John Lovell and Son, 1902.

Lussier, Camille, comp. *Guide de Saint-Hyacinthe par ordre alphabétique et par ordre des rues.* Saint-Hyacinthe: Imprimerie de *La Tribune,* 1898.

– *Guide de Saint-Hyacinthe par ordre alphabétique et par ordre des rues.* Saint-Hyacinthe, Imprimerie de *La Tribune,* 1900.

– *Guide de Saint-Hyacinthe, Sorel et Saint-Jean, pour 1902*. Saint-Hyacinthe: n.p., [1902].
– *Guide de Saint-Hyacinthe pour 1904*. Saint-Hyacinthe: n.p. [1904].
– *Guide de Saint-Hyacinthe pour 1907*. Saint-Hyacinthe: n.p., [1907].
McCallum, John. *Unequal Beginnings: Agriculture and Economic Development in Quebec and Ontario until 1870*. Toronto: UTP, 1980.
McConnachie, Kathleen. "A Note on Fertility Rates among Married Women in Toronto, 1871." *Ontario History* 75, no. 1 (March 1983): 87–97.
McCullough, A.B. *L'industrie textile primaire au Canada: Histoire et patrimoine*. Ottawa: Environment Canada, 1992.
McDaniel, Susan A. "Explaining Canadian Fertility: Some Remaining Challenges." *Canadian Studies in Population* 11 (1984): 1–16.
McInnis, Marvin. "Childbearing and Land Availability: Some Evidence from Individual Household Data." In *Population Patterns in the Past*, edited by Ronald Demos Lee et al., 201–27.
– "The Geographic Pattern of Fertility Decline in Canada: 1891–1931." Paper presented to the Canadian Association of Geographers, Hamilton, 1987.
– "Fertility Patterns in Late Nineteenth-Century Ontario and Quebec." Paper presented to the Social Science History Association, Chicago, 1988.
MacKay, Robert W.S., comp. *The Canada Directory*. Montreal: John Lovell, 1851.
McLaren, Angus. "Birth Control and Abortion in Canada, 1870–1920." CHR 59, no. 3 (September 1978): 319–40.
McLaren, Angus, and Arlene Tigar McLaren. *The Bedroom and the State: The Changing Practices and Politics of Contraception and Abortion in Canada: 1880–1980*. Toronto: MS, 1986.
Magnan, Hormisdas. *Dictionnaire historique et géographique des paroisses, missions et municipalités de la province de Québec*. Arthabaska: Imprimerie d'Arthabaska, 1925.
Maisonneuve, Daniel. "Structure familiale et exode rural: le cas de Saint-Damase, 1852–1861." *Cahiers québécois de démographie* 14, no. 2 (October 1985): 231–40.
Marr, William L. "Nuptiality, Total Fertility, And Marital Fertility in Upper Canada, 1851: A Study of Land Availability, Urbanization, and Birthplace." *Canadian Studies in Population* 13, no. 1 (1986): 1–18.
Mayer, Francine M. "Histoire démographique et destin biologique de deux villages québécois." *Anthropologie et sociétés* 5:2 (1981): 17–67.
Mays, Herbert J. "'A Place to Stand': Families, Land and Permanence in Toronto Gore Township, 1820–1890." CHA HP (1980): 185–211.
Medick, Hans. "The Proto-industrial Family Economy: The Structural Function of Household and Family during the Transition from Peasant

Society to Industrial Capitalism." *Social History* 3 (October 1976): 291–315.

Medjuck, Sheva. "Family and Household Composition in the Nineteenth Century: The Case of Moncton, New Brunswick, 1851 to 1871." *The Canadian Journal of Sociology* 4, no. 3 (summer 1979): 275–86.

Mendels, Franklin. "Proto-industrialization: The First Phase of the Industrialization Process." *Journal of Economic History* 32, no. 1 (March 1972): 241–61.

– "Des industries rurales à la protoindustrialisation: historique d'un changement de perspective." *AESC* 39, no. 5 (September–October 1984): 977–96.

Mercier, Lucie, and Denise Lemieux. *Les femmes au tournant du siècle, 1880–1940: Ages de la vie, maternité et quotidien.* Quebec: IQRC, 1989.

Miner, Horace. *St. Denis: A French-Canadian Parish.* Chicago: The University of Chicago Press, 1939.

Mitchinson, Wendy, and Janice Dickin McGinnis, eds. *Essays in the History of Canadian Medicine.* Toronto: MS, 1988.

Moch, Leslie Page. "Marriage, Migration, and Urban Demographic Structure: A Case from France in the Belle Epoque." *JFH* 6, no. 1 (spring 1981): 70–88.

Modell, John, and Tamara K. Hareven. "Urbanization and the Malleable Household: An Examination of Boarding and Lodging in American Families." *Journal of Marriage and the Family* 35, no. 5 (August 1973): 467–78.

Moore, Eric G., and Brian S. Osborne. "Marital Fertility in Kingston, 1861–1881: A Study of Socio-economic Differentials." *HS/SH* 20, no. 39 (May 1987): 9–27.

Nault, François. "Structure et cycle de vie des ménages de la population rurale blanche à Saint-Barthélemy de 1840 à 1854." Master's thesis, Université de Montréal, 1983.

Noël, Françoise. "Chambly Mills, 1784–1815." *CHA HP* (1985): 102–16.

Noy, David. "Wicked Stepmothers in Roman Society and Imagination." *JFH* 16, no. 4 (1991): 345–61.

Olivier-Lacamp, Gaël, and Jacques Légaré. "Quelques caractéristiques des ménages de la ville de Québec entre 1666 et 1716." *HS/SH* 12, no. 23 (May 1979): 66–78.

Olson, Sherry, Patricia Thornton, and Quoc Thuy Thac. "A Geography of Little Children in Nineteenth-century Montreal." *Shared Spaces* 10 (September 1987). Department of Geography, McGill University.

Ouellet, Fernand. "Libéré ou exploité: le paysan québécois d'avant 1850." *HS/SH* 13, no. 26 (November 1980): 339–68.

Parizeau, Gérard. *Les Dessaulles, Seigneurs de Saint-Hyacinthe: Chronique maskoutaine du XIXe siècle.* Montreal: Fides, 1976.

Parr, Joy. "Disaggregating the Sexual Division of Labour: A Transatlantic Case Study." *Comparative Studies in Society and History* 30 (1988): 511–33.

– *The Gender of Breadwinners: Women, Men, and Change in Two Industrial Towns, 1880–1950.* Toronto: UTP, 1990.

– ed. *Childhood and Family in Canadian History.* Toronto: MS, 1982.

Pentland, H. Clare. *Labour and Capital in Canada, 1650–1860.* Toronto: James Lorimer, 1981.

Philippe, Pierre. "Analyse statistique des intervalles protogénésiques et intergénésiques à l'Isle-aux-Coudres. Etude de démographie historique." *Population* 28, no. 1 (January–February 1973): 81–93.

Plourde, Jules Antonin. *Bicentenaire de la paroisse-mère de Saint-Hyacinthe. Notre-Dame-du-Rosaire, 1777–1977.* Saint-Hyacinthe: Paroisse Notre-Dame-du-Rosaire, 1977.

Pontbriand, B., and R. Jetté, comps. *Mariages de Saint-Hyacinthe. Cathédrale (1853), Saint-Joseph (1916), Christ-Roi (1927), La Providence (1937), Saint-Sacrement (1946), Sacré-Coeur (1946), L'Assomption.* 2 vols. Quebec: B. Pontbriand, 1971.

Pontbriand, B., and René Jetté, comps. *Mariages de Saint-Simon (1833), Sainte-Rosalie (1834), Saint-Dominique (1837), Saint- Liboire (1859).* Quebec: B. Pontbriand, 1971.

Pouyez, Christian, Raymond Roy, and Gérard Bouchard. "La mobilité géographique en milieu rural: le Saguenay, 1852–1861." *HS/SH* 14, no. 27 (May 1981); 123–55.

Pouyez, Christian et al. *Les Saguenayens: Introduction à l'histoire des populations du Saguenay, XVIe–XXe siècles.* Sillery: PUQ, 1983.

Quebec Gazette. 3 September 1835.

Ramirez, Bruno. "French Canadian Immigrants in the New England Cotton Towns: A Socio-economic Profile." *L/LT* 11 (Spring 1983): 125–42.

– *On the Move: French-Canadian and Italian Migrants in the North Atlantic Economy, 1860–1914.* Toronto: MS, 1991.

Rioux, Denise. *La grippe espagnole à Sherbrooke et dans les Cantons de l'Est.* Sherbrooke: Etudes supérieures en histoire, Université de Sherbrooke, 1993.

Rioux, Marcel, and Yves Rioux, eds. *French Canadian Society.* Vol. 1. Toronto: MS, 1964.

Robert, Jean-Claude. "Un seigneur entrepreneur. Barthélémy Joliette et la fondation du village d'Industrie." *RhAf* 26, no. 3 (December 1972): 375–95.

– "Urbanisation et population. Le cas de Montréal en 1861." *RhAf* 35, no. 4 (March) 1982: 523–35.

– "The City of Wealth and Death: Urban Mortality in Montreal, 1821–1871." In *Essays in the History of Canadian Medicine,* edited by Wendy Mitchinson, and Janice Dickin McGinnis, 18–38.

Rose, Sonya O. "Proto-industry, Women's Work, and the Household Economy in the Transition to Industrial Capitalism." *JFH* 13, no. 2 (1988): 181–93.

Rouillard, Jacques. *Histoire du syndicalisme québécois des origines à nos jours.* Montreal: Boréal, 1989.

– ed. *Guide d'histoire du Québec du régime français à nos jours. Bibliographie commentée.* 2d ed. Montreal: Méridien, 1993.

Roy, Fernande. *Progrès, harmonie, liberté. Le libéralisme des milieux d'affaires francophones à Montréal au tournant du siècle.* Montreal: Boréal, 1988.

Roy, Joseph. "Notes sur la Cité de Saint-Hyacinthe." *Courrier de Saint-Hyacinthe,* 26 December 1903.

Roy, Raymond. "Paramètres sociaux de la fécondité saguenayenne au XIXe et XXe siècles." Paper presented to the CHA, Québec 1989.

Rudin, Ronald. "The Development of Four Quebec Towns, 1840–1914: A Study of Urban and Economic Growth in Quebec." Ph.D. diss., York University, 1977.

– "Saint-Hyacinthe and the Development of a Regional Economy." Discussion paper #15. Toronto: York University, Department of Geography, 1977.

– "Boosting the French Canadian Town: Municipal Government and Urban Growth in Quebec, 1850–1900." *Urban History Review / Revue d'histoire urbaine* 11, no. 1 (June 1982): 1–10.

– *Banking en français: The French Banks of Quebec, 1835–1925.* Toronto: UTP, 1985.

– "Revisionism and the Search for a Normal Society: A Critique of Recent Quebec Historical Writing." *CHR* 73, no. 1 (March 1992): 30–61.

– *Making History in Twentieth-Century Quebec.* Toronto: UTP, 1997.

Ryerson, Stanley B. *Unequal Union: Confederation and the Roots of Conflict in the Canadas, 1815–1873.* Toronto: Progress Books, 1968.

Saint-Hyacinthe Illustré. Edifices publics, religieux et industriels. Saint-Hyacinthe: La Tribune, 1909.

St. Hyacinthe Illustré/Illustrated. Montreal: George Bishop Engraving & Printing Co., 1886.

St. Hyacinthe, P.Q., Canada. Montreal: The Commercial Magazine Company, 1912.

Samuel, Raphael. "The Workshop of the World: Steam Power and Hand Technology in Mid-Victorian Britain," *History Workshop Journal* 3 (spring 1977): 6–72.

Seccombe, Wally. "Marxism and Demography: Household Forms and Fertility Regimes in the Western European Transition." In *Family, Economy, and State: The Social Reproduction Process under Capitalism,* edited by James Dickson, and Bob Russell, 23–55.

Séguin, Normand. "L'agriculture de la Mauricie et du Québec, 1850–1950." *RhAf* 35, no. 4 (March 1982): 537–55.

Shulze, David. "Rural Manufacture in Lower Canada: Understanding Seigneurial Privilege and the Transition in the Countryside." *Alternate Routes* 7 (1984): 134–67.

Sixth Census of Canada, 1921. 5 vols. Ottawa: King's Printer (F.A. Acland), 1924–25.

Smith, Bonnie G. *Ladies of the Leisure Class: The Bourgeoises of Northern France in the Nineteenth Century.* Princeton, N.J.: Princeton University Press, 1981.

Smith, Daniel Scott. "'Early' Fertility Decline in America: A Problem in Family History." *JFH* 12, no. 1–3 (1987): 73–84.

Société d'histoire régionale de Saint-Hyacinthe. *Saint-Hyacinthe, 1748–1998.* Sillery: Septentrion, 1998.

Spagnoli, Paul. "Industrialization, Proletarianization and Marriage: A Reconsideration." *JFH* 8, no. 3 (fall 1983): 230–47.

Statutes of the Province of Canada. (Various Acts between 1850 and 1863 pertaining to the municipality of Saint-Hyacinthe, its civil status and boundaries.)

Statutes of Quebec. (Further Acts concerning Saint-Hyacinthe in 1888 and 1895)

Stoddart, Jennifer. "L'histoire des femmes et la démographie." *Cahiers québécois de démographie* 13, no. 1 (April 1984): 79–85.

Tepperman, Lorne. "Ethnic Variations in Marriage and Fertility: Canada 1871." *Canadian Review of Sociology and Anthropology* 11, no. 4 (November 1974): 324–43.

Thomas-Gee, Ellen M. "Early Canadian Fertility Transition: A Component Analysis of Census Data." *Canadian Studies in Population* 6 (1979): 23–32.

– "Female Marriage Patterns in Canada: Changes and Differentials." *Journal of Comparative Family Studies* 11, no. 4 (autumn 1980): 457–73.

– "Marriage in Nineteenth-Century Canada," *Canadian Review of Sociology and Anthropology* 19, no. 3 (August 1982): 311–25.

Thompson, E.P. *The Making of the English Working Class.* Harmondsworth: Penguin Books, 1968.

Thornton, Patricia, and Sherry Olson. "Family Contexts of Fertility and Infant Survival in Nineteenth-Century Montreal." *JFH* 16, no. 4 (1991): 401–17.

Thornton, Patricia, Sherry Olson, and Quoc Thuy Thac. "Dimensions sociales de la mortalité infantile à Montréal au milieu du XIXe siècle." *ADH* (1989): 299–325.

Tilly, Charles. "Demographic Origins of the European Proletariat." In *Proletarianization and Family History,* edited by David Levine, 1–85.

Tilly, Charles, ed. *Historical Studies of Changing Fertility.* Princeton: Princeton University Press, 1978.

Tilly, Louise. "The Family Wage Economy of a French Textile City: Roubaix, 1872–1906." *JFH* 4, no. 4 (winter 1979): 381–94.

– "Women's History and Family History: Fruitful Collaboration or Missed Connection." *JFH* 12, no. 1–3 (1987): 303–15.

Tilly, Louise, and Joan Scott. *Women, Work, and Family.* New York: Holt, Rinehart, and Winston, 1978.

van de Walle, Francine. "Infant Mortality and the European Demographic Transition." In *The Decline of Fertility in Europe*, edited Ansley J. Coale, and Susan Cotts Watkins, 201–33.

Vandenbrooke, Christian. "Le cas flamand: évolution sociale et comporte- ments démographiques au 17e–19e siècles." *AESC* 39, no. 5 (September– October 1984): 915–35.

Vincent-Domey, Odette. *Filles et familles en milieu ouvrier: Hull, Québec à la fin du XIXe siècle.* Montreal: RCHTQ, 1991.

Voyer, Louise. "L'évolution urbaine et architecturale de Saint-Hyacinthe de 1794 à 1914." Master's thesis, Université Laval, 1979.

– *Saint-Hyacinthe: De la seigneurie à la ville québécoise.* Montreal: Editions Libre Expression, 1980.

Ward, Peter. *Courtship, Love, and Marriage in Nineteenth-Century English Canada.* Montreal and Kingston: MQUP, 1990.

Ward, Peter, and Patricia C. Ward. "Infant Birth Weight and Nutrition in Industrializing Montreal." *American Historical Review* 89, no. 2 (April 1984): 324–45.

Weiss, Neil A. *Elementary Statistics.* Reading, Mass.: Addison Wesley, 1989.

Withey, Lynne. "Household Structure in Urban and Rural Areas: The Case of Rhode Island, 1774–1880." *JFH* 3, no. 1 (spring 1978): 37–50.

Woods, R., and C.W. Smith. "The Decline of Marital Fertility in the Late Nineteenth Century: The Case of England and Wales." *Population Studies* 37, no. 2 (July 1983): 207–26.

Wrigley, E.A. "Family Reconstitution." In *An Introduction to English Historical Demography, From the 16th to the 19th Century*, edited by E.A. Wrigley, 96–159.

– ed. *An Introduction to English Historical Demography, From the 16th to the 19th Century.* London: Weidenfeld, and Nicolson, 1966.

– ed. *Nineteenth-Century Society: Essays in the Use of Quantitative Methods for the Study of Social Data.* Cambridge (UK): Cambridge University Press, 1972.

Wrigley, E.A., and R.S Schofield. *The Population History of England, 1541– 1871: A Reconstruction.* London: Edward Arnold; Cambridge, Mass.: Harvard University Press, 1981.

Wrigley, E.A. et al. *English Population History from Family Reconstitution, 1580– 1837.* Cambridge (UK): Cambridge University Press, 1997.

Young, Brian and John A. Dickinson. *A Short History of Quebec: A Socio- economic Perspective.* Mississauga: Copp Clark Pitman, 1988.

Index